BETWEEN ARAB AND ISRAELI

BETWEEN ARAB AND ISRAELI

By

LT.-GEN. E. L. M. BURNS

D.S.O., O.B.E., M.C.

IVAN OBOLENSKY, INC.

NEW YORK

To the memory of

DAG HAMMARSKJÖLD

COPYRIGHT © 1962 BY CLARKE, IRWIN & COMPANY, LIMITED

First Published in the U.S.A. in 1963

BY IVAN OBOLENSKY, INC.

Library of Congress Catalog Card Number: 63-12370

First Printing

Manufactured in the United States of America

Preface

THIS book is a record of my experience in the service of the United Nations in the Middle East. From August 1954 until November 1956 I was Chief of Staff of the United Nations Truce Supervision Organization, and then became commander of the United Nations Emergency Force. The story ends in the spring of 1957, when the Force took up its position along the Gaza Strip Demarcation Line and the International Frontier in the Sinai.

In general I have confined myself to reporting on those events of which I have first-hand knowledge, supplementing my experience when necessary for the continuity of the narrative, with references to the proceedings of the United Nations Security Council and General Assembly and related diplomatic negotiations which affected the Truce Organization and the Emergency Force.

Here and there I have given my interpretation of the motives and attitudes of the two sides in the conflict. In doing so, I have tried to remain impartial, just as, when I was Chief of Staff UNTSO and Commander of UNEF, it was my duty to maintain a neutral attitude towards the Arabs and Israelis alike. However, before I had been long in the Middle East, I learned that no matter how hard one tried to be objective and impartial, if one accepted the views of one side on any matter, the other side accused one of partiality. It is unlikely that this book will escape accusations of prejudice, because I have criticized the attitudes and actions of both sides. In some instances, Arabs may dislike my strictures on their behaviour, and declare that I, like most Americans and Canadians, was and am on the side of the Israelis. On the other hand, criticisms of the policy of the Israel Government will probably result in a charge of anti-Semitism. If such a charge should be laid, I would plead *Not Guilty*. Perhaps it is in order for me to say a little more on this subject.

In the Palestine drama, which is now a tragedy for its former Arab inhabitants, and may yet become a greater tragedy for the present Jewish inhabitants, where does the blame lie? Is there a villain to be condemned? Is there a crime to be expiated? In this drama the conflict is of nationalisms, Zionist and Arab. The

Zionist movement brought the Jews to the Holy Land, from which, except for numerically insignificant orthodox communities, they had been excluded for nearly two thousand years.

Anti-Semitism gives Zionism its driving force. Without anti-Semitism—the hatred and persecution of Jews in Europe in the past, and the milder modern manifestation of ' discrimination ' there and elsewhere—the Palestine problem would not have come into being. Probably few Gentile readers who have lived in a city where recent Jewish immigrants are relatively numerous have escaped exposure to the disease of anti-Semitism. Perhaps most of us have to acknow-ledge that we have had a mild case of it, or experienced some of its symptoms. But since Hitler no sensitive person can harbour anti-Semitic feelings without shame. We cannot fail to realize that hatred of any race or people debases us as human beings. If we allow ourselves to be anti-Semitic, then we are morally as guilty as the *Judenhetzers* who drove the Jews out of Europe and to Palestine.

All this having been said, it does not follow that the acts of the Government of Israel and of individual Israelis are not subject to moral judgments ; that we have not the right to say whether they were good or bad, helpful or harmful to world peace and justice between the nations.

I have found it necessary to try to expound and explain the somewhat complicated legal relationships between the parties to the General Armistice Agreements which concluded the hostilities between Israel and her four Arab neighbours in 1949. Most of the work of UNTSO lay in determining whether the parties had or had not violated some provision of the agreements, and in trying to persuade them to live up to their obligations and to settle their disputes in accordance with United Nations principles. Roughly speaking, the General Armistice Agreements constituted the inter-national law as between the parties. These agreements contained certain vague statements and compromises, essential to secure the signature of both sides, given the circumstances of 1949. It was hoped then that the difficult points would be settled in peace negotiations after a relatively short period of the armistice régime.

But the 1950's dragged on, and no peace negotiations took place. Instead there were disputes about the interpretation of the armistice agreements, and in the end they became largely inoperative because of rigid attitudes which developed. All the while, both sides violated or failed to observe the agreements, in more or less serious ways. I hope this book will give a notion of the process of disintegration or dilapidation of the armistice régime in Palestine during the period when I had responsibility in the area. It is a story both complex and depressing—as many aspects of Middle East affairs are apt to appear to the Westerner who studies them.

I cannot claim the accuracy of the historian in what I have written, although I have tried to make it as factually correct as possible. Most of it was written during 1957 and 1958, when the rôle of UNEF had become static, and the relative quiet in the area of its responsibilities which ensued left me some leisure. I reinforced my memory by the journal I kept during the whole period covered. In this diary I noted daily the principal events which occurred, including interviews with important people, the subjects dealt with, and the views expressed. The second source is the published documents of the United Nations, especially reports to and proceedings of the Security Council and the General Assembly. In writing the narrative I have had access to files of UNTSO and UNEF containing messages, letters, and reports dealing with the matters concerned. Finally, from early 1955 on, I have kept files of clippings from newspapers and periodicals relating to the events and developments in which I was involved. However, I have not generally given references for these authorities, as it seemed that the copious notes appropriate to an historical work would be out of place in the kind of book I have written.

The reader may wonder how and why I was appointed Chief of Staff of the United Nations Truce Supervision Organization. In June 1954 I was Deputy Minister of Veterans Affairs. The Honourable Hugues Lapointe, then Minister, asked me whether I would be interested in a new job. He said the Secretary-General of the United Nations had asked Canada to nominate an officer for the post of Chief of Staff UNTSO. One of the qualifications was to have held command in the field in war, and I had commanded the 5th Canadian Armoured Division and the 1st Canadian Corps during 1944 in Italy. My other qualification, I suppose, was that I had been active in the affairs of the United Nations Association in Canada since my return to Canada after the Second World War.

I had joined the Ottawa branch, and soon found myself shanghaied into the hierarchy of the organization, eventually serving as national president in 1953 and 1954. Also, in 1949 I had been an alternate member of the Canadian delegation to the General Assembly, and had spent about three months listening to interminable debates, mainly in the Fourth (Trusteeship) Committee. During this period I learned something about the attitude of Asian, Middle Eastern, and South American peoples towards the monster of the age, Imperialism ; something of the cold war as it affected relationships within the United Nations ; and so forth.

Perhaps I should explain my attitude towards the United Nations, as an ideal and as an institution. From 1915, when I had been commissioned from the Royal Military College into the Royal Canadian Engineers, until I retired as a major-general on entering the Civil Service in 1946, I had been a serving soldier. I was happy in the service, and felt I was pursuing an honourable profession, and was sustained by the philosophy that war, however regrettable many of its features, was inevitable in the then state of development of the human race ; and that peoples who refused to contemplate the possibility of war, and, indeed, to prepare for it, would be likely to be pushed off the world's stage by those who still thought of war as a means of settling differences not otherwise reconcilable.

The atom bombs on Hiroshima and Nagasaki changed all that thinking. I had seen the destruction of countless years of human effort which had been wreaked by the airmen in their blitzes, in London, in many of the smaller cities in Italy, and above all in the Ruhr. This desolation was spread by the 'conventional' high-explosive bomb. It did not need pages of laboured scientific and humanitarian explanation to convince me that there could be no quarrel between the so-called civilized nations whose settlement would be worth paying the price of the destruction that would be caused by an atom war.

So, war being something to be avoided at almost any cost, the alternative way to settle international differences had to be some supranational machinery for the purpose. The United Nations, successor to the League of Nations, was the essay of the statesmen of the world to create such machinery. Whatever the imperfections of the organization, and whatever faults might develop in its functioning, the ideal of the prevention of a war which would destroy countless million man-years of thought and labour was there, in the United Nations Charter. Every one who believed in that ideal—that common-sense alternative to mutual destruction—had a duty to do what he could to make this aspiration into a reality, however little his effort in relation to the total problem.

When I discussed my nomination as Chief of Staff UNTSO with Mr Lapointe and Mr Pearson, then Secretary of State for External Affairs, these ideas were perhaps in the background. But, in fact, the idea of working for the United Nations appeared to me as an extension of my way of life as a servant, first military, then civil, of Canada. I do not wish to give the impression that at this time, or at any time since, I have regarded myself as a person 'dedicated' to the ideal of peace, or even to the United Nations. I was taking on a job that had to be done ; the Canadian Government wanted me to do it. It seemed also that it would be a worth-while and probably exciting employment for the next year—for the appointment was only of a year's duration. I was told, of course, that during my service in this post, I would receive no directions or suggestions from the Canadian Government as to what policy I should follow, or how I should act ; and I never have received anything of the kind. Canadian politicians and diplomatic representatives have from time to time sought my views on the course of affairs in the Middle East, but no one has tried to suggest to me what views I should hold. I was to get my pay and my orders from the United Nations, and to this organization and the Secretary-General at its head, I should owe my loyalty. Writing four years later, I can say that that is how it has been.

E. L. M. B.

Acknowledgments

I GRATEFULLY acknowledge the kindness of Longmans, Green and Co., Limited, London, in granting permission to reprint in the Notes of this book copyright material from pages 561 and 563 of Oppenheim : *International Law, Vol. II* (ed. Lauterpacht).

I should also like to express my gratitude to Miss Marian Warren, my secretary during my command of UNEF, who in her spare time typed and retyped the manuscript, collated references, and in many other ways helped in the preparation of this book.

E. L. M. B.

Ottawa, April 1962

Contents

List of Abbreviations

ADL	Armistice Demarcation Line.
DL	Demarcation Line.
DZ	Demilitarized Zone.
EIMAC	Egypt-Israel Mixed Armistice Commission.
GAA	General Armistice Agreement.
IDF	Israeli Defence Forces.
MAC	Mixed Armistice Agreement.
UNEF	United Nations Emergency Force.
UNMO	United Nations Military Observer.
UNTSO	United Nations Truce Supervision Organization.
UNRWA	United Nations Relief and Works Agency.
USMC	United States Marine Corps.
USNR	United States Naval Reserve.

CHAPTER I

The Gaza Raid of February 28, 1955, and its Consequences

Maps 1 and 3

ON the night of February 28, 1955, two platoons of Israeli paratroopers crossed the Armistice Demarcation Line east of Gaza, advanced more than three kilometres into the Egyptian-controlled Strip, and attacked a military camp near the railway-station. Using small-arms, mortars, bazookas, hand-grenades, and Bangalore torpedoes, they stormed the camp and completely demolished a stone military building, four Nissen huts, and a pump-house with heavy explosive charges. They killed fourteen Egyptian or Palestinian soldiers, an adult civilian, and a little boy, and wounded sixteen soldiers and two civilians.

Some of the defending garrison fought stoutly, continuing to resist even when the camp had been entered and the buildings had been destroyed. The Israelis reported eight of their men killed and nine wounded.

Another group of Israeli soldiers entered the Strip six kilometres south of Gaza and laid an ambush on the main road from Rafah. Into this ambush careered a truck carrying a lieutenant and thirty-five soldiers, mostly Palestinians, coming up from the south to reinforce the defenders of the camp. The ambush followed a plan which the Israelis had used many times before. A wire was stretched across the road at a defile, with cans of petrol so attached that they would be pulled against the side of any vehicle which passed and set it on fire. The waiting Israelis then attacked the flaming truck with machine-gun fire and lobbed grenades into it. Only two or three of the occupants were able to get out and return the fire. Twenty-two soldiers were killed ; the officer and twelve soldiers were wounded.

Total casualties on the Egyptian side were thirty-six soldiers and two civilians killed, twenty-nine soldiers and two civilians wounded. This was the most serious clash between Egypt and Israel since the armistice had been signed, six years before.

Set against the background of the Second World War, with the wiping out of cities and the decimation of their population, the raid on. Gaza was a minor episode. But it had a decisive effect on the relations between Egypt and Israel, which had been regulated by the General Armistice Agreement terminating the hostilities of 1948. It was a crucial event in this dismal history, and set a trend which continued until Israel invaded the Sinai in October 1956. The peace which the Israelis want may be farther from their reach than it was in February 1955.

Gamal Abdel Nasser told me, when I first met him on November 15, 1954, that it was his desire that there should be no trouble on the north-eastern border of Egypt, no disturbance of the six years of quiescence of the armistice régime, no military adventures. But after the shock of February 28, 1955, as he told me and many others, he could no longer maintain such an attitude. Shortly before the raid, he said, he had visited Gaza and had told the troops that there was no danger of war ; that the Gaza Armistice Demarcation Line was not going to be a battlefront. After that many of them had been shot in their beds. Never again could he risk telling the troops they had no attack to fear ; never again could he let them believe that they could relax their vigilance. It was for this reason that he could not issue and enforce strict orders against the opening of fire on the Israeli patrols which marched along the demarcation line, a hundred metres or less from the Egyptian positions. Those positions were held by the friends and perhaps the relatives of the men who had perished in the Israeli ambush of that bloody night.

It is difficult to determine exactly what weight to give to Nasser's words. He speaks with an air of sincerity and simplicity ; there is no bluster, no menace, instead an appearance of reasonableness. Nevertheless, one remembers that he is a politician who has reached power by way of conspiracy and revolution. What really are his long-range objectives ? How would he solve the conflict between Israel and the Arabs, if he had the power to do what he wanted ? Would he be satisfied with a compromise, or does he intend to build up the Arab strength to a point where he can defeat Israel militarily and impose a peace ?

Hostile propaganda has him perpetually threatening the destruction of Israel, but in none of his speeches have I found that he has gone beyond the statement made to the *New York Times* correspondent, published as an interview on October 6, 1955 : " War is not an easy decision for anyone, especially for me. No Arab is saying now that we must destroy Israel. The Arabs are asking only that the refugees [from Palestine] receive their natural right to life and their lost property, which was promised to them by United Nations resolutions seven years ago. . . . No, we are not aggressive. The threat is from the other side." And he went on to repeat what I have written above, of how he had come to regard the armistice with Israel in another light following the Gaza raid of February 28, 1955.

Of course, in the flood of propaganda which pours constantly out of the Cairo Press and radio, there have been many threats of the direst vengeance on Israel, some of them made by persons in authority. These have been assiduously collected and published by the Israeli Government. The Israelis argue that in an authoritarian state, such as Egypt, the mass media of communication are rigidly controlled, and that what is said must therefore reflect the policy of the responsible authorities. This ignores the nature of propaganda, which is not necessarily a statement of intentions of those who control the propaganda sources, but is a mode of inducing a desired frame of mind in those who listen to it. Thus, it can properly be deduced that the Egyptian propaganda masters want the Arab population to which the broadcasts are directed to believe that Egypt is implacably hostile to Israel and proposes, at some indefinite time in the future, to go to war with the object of overwhelming the Israeli state. But it is not proof that they are actually planning to do so.

The one object which seems to emerge clearly from the study of Nasser's actions, and the Egyptian propaganda, is the uniting of the Arab states of the Middle East into one " Arab Nation," under Egypt's hegemony as the state most populous and advanced in development. As to how this was to be achieved, the pattern Nasser hoped to follow is fairly clear. He gave another interview in the autumn of 1955 to a correspondent of the London *Observer*. He was explaining why Egypt opposed the Baghdad Pact, and did not want to enter into any regional defensive agreement with the West. He said : " Nuclear weapons have changed the entire picture so that any decision to enter war would require extreme conditions beyond our calculation. As I see it, war from now on will be different. It will be fought on the internal fronts of all countries. In this area it will use nationalism as a weapon, and we—the leaders of this area—must lead nationalists and build a future on them."

The part played by Egypt in subsequent events in this area shows what he meant by " using nationalism as a weapon." He meant to influence the nationalists in all Arab countries to adopt as their programme the integration of all Arab states into the greater " Arab Nation," and if necessary to achieve this by armed revolt against the existing régimes. The nationalists would be influenced in this direction by Press and radio propaganda, persuasion by Egyptians in diplomatic positions, as well as Egyptian teachers and technicians. In the extreme case, they could be helped with money and arms. What happened in Jordan in 1955 to 1957 and what happened in Lebanon and Iraq in 1958 illustrate the technique.

It is fairly clear that Egypt could not hope to pursue such an object and simultaneously wage an all-out war against Israel. In relation to this grand plan, revenge upon Israel, and righting the wrongs of the Arabs driven from Palestine, would appear only secondary objects. If the union of the Arab states under a strong central Government could be achieved, with the oil wealth of certain of those states at the disposition of the whole, the balance of power, economic and eventually military, would turn against Israel, and the settlement of the Palestine question on terms satisfactory to the Arabs could be achieved by economic and military pressure. This possibility was by no means ignored by the Israelis.

Nevertheless, Egypt, if she aspired to the leadership of the Arabs, could not appear weak, could not seem to submit to Israeli threats and provocations. Therefore there had to be reactions to Israeli blows such as the Gaza raid. There had to be the appearance of inflexible hostility to Israel and a show of intention to obtain restitution for the refugees. The Egyptian authorities controlling the Gaza Strip could not be too severe on Palestinian Arab infiltrators ; they might even have to devise ways in which the demands of those refugees to be armed and led against the Israelis could be channelled into forms of hostile action which seemed unlikely to bring about full-scale war.

I believe that this view of Egyptian policy is consistent with the trend of the events which I shall describe in this book. Or should one say Nasser's policy ? His emergence as the leading figure of Arab nationalism in the period 1954–57 has tended to make the Western world look on him as a dictator in the Mussolini-Stalin-Hitler mould. No doubt his personal power has grown with the increase of his international stature, but I believe that in 1954 and 1955 there were definite limits to his power, that occasional impolitic courses of action may have been due to the need of keeping together the members of his Revolutionary Command Council, of avoiding schisms which could have wrecked his larger designs.

Gamal Abdel Nasser in 1954 was a successful revolutionary, who stood at the head of a group of incompletely subordinated fellow-revolutionaries. The governing junta no longer called itself the Revolutionary Command Council ; but the attitude implied by the title cannot be said to have been obsolete. Nasser must always have had in the back of his mind the possibility of being overthrown by the same sort of cabal of military officers by which he overthrew

Farouk, and eliminated Naguib. In any case, dependent as his régime is on the support of the Army, he cannot pursue or enforce policies which are unpopular with the Army.

Why did the Israelis strike the blow at Gaza which has destroyed any possibility of negotiating an early peace ? Israel was condemned for it in a resolution of the Security Council of the United Nations which stated the Israeli action to be " a violation of the cease-fire provisions of the Security Council resolution of July 15, 1948, and inconsistent with the obligations of the parties under the General Armistice Agreement between Egypt and Israel, and under the Charter." The Security Council called again upon Israel to prevent such actions, and affirmed that the maintenance of the General Armistice Agreement was threatened by any deliberate violation of it by one of the parties, and that no progress towards the return of permanent peace in Palestine could be made unless the parties complied strictly with their obligations under the GAA and the cease-fire order.

Generally, Israel justified her action as being necessary to force Egypt to respect the armistice agreement. In particular, she must be forced to respect the clauses which prohibit any acts of hostility by the armed forces of one party against the armed forces or civilians of the other party, and the clause which obliges the parties to prevent their civilians from crossing the demarcation line—' infiltrating,' as it is called.

As Egypt had refused to heed repeated condemnations and warnings by the Mixed Armistice Commission, the Israelis claimed the only way left to force her to respect her obligations was by retaliation.[1] Of course, reprisals are entirely inconsistent with the parties' obligations under the GAA, and also had been condemned by previous resolutions of the Security Council, notably in the case of the Qibya reprisal of October 14–15, 1953.

How did Israel justify the ignoring of the Security Council's decisions, the flouting of the United Nations organ which was supposed to safeguard the peace of the world ? I shall try to analyse later the state of affairs and the state of mind in Israel which led to this action, and the chain of reprisals and counter-reprisals which followed. But first it will be necessary to explain, for the benefit of the reader who is not a specialist in the Palestine question, how the Truce Supervision Organization operated as the United Nations agency to oversee the uneasy and unstable armistice between Arab and Israeli.

CHAPTER 2

The United Nations Truce Supervision Organization: Origin and Functions

Maps 1, 4, and 5

In 1954 and 1955 nobody blessed the United Nations Truce Supervision Organization in Palestine as peacemaker, possibly because it was not a peacemaking but at best a peace-keeping organization. Sometimes its members were referred to as international policemen, but they were policemen without truncheons. They were actually more like watchmen, watching on behalf of the Security Council of the United Nations for breaches of the General Armistice Agreements and the Council's cease-fire order.

There was, of course, no peace in the technical sense of international law between Israel and her Arab neighbours. There was only an armistice, and an armistice which was becoming very precarious. In October 1956 this shaky status finally collapsed; Israel invaded Egypt, and the resultant painful pacification measures have not restored the armistice régime. Israel refuses to recognize that an armistice between her and Egypt still exists, and two of the other three armistice agreements operate only uncertainly and spasmodically.

In spite of its name, the Organization did not " supervise the truce " because there was no longer a truce. It had been superseded by the armistices concluded between the parties during 1949 under the mediation of Dr Ralph Bunche of the United Nations. There was, however, a cease-fire, or perhaps one should say a cease-fire order of the Security Council, to which the United Nations Truce Supervision Organization (UNTSO) had certain responsibilities.

The above paragraphs cite several things that UNTSO was not, and several things it did not do. What it was and what it did can best be explained by giving a short history of how it came into being, and a brief and general account of how it worked—or tried to work, for in UNTSO obstruction was met at every turn, and frustration often enveloped us. There are historical causes for this.

In April 1947 the United Kingdom, which held the Mandate for Palestine from the League of Nations, and had announced that it was going to give it up, referred the dispute between Jews and Arabs in that Holy Land to the United Nations, requesting the Secretary-General to place the question of Palestine on the agenda of the next regular session of the General Assembly. The United Kingdom further requested that as soon as possible a special session should be called, to set up a committee to prepare for the discussion of the question at the regular session.

The special session was held in April and May 1947, and a Special Committee on Palestine (UNSCOP) was created. It was composed of the representatives of eleven nations,[2] and was given the task of investigating the question in Palestine and elsewhere, and presenting a report and recommendations.

UNSCOP duly presented its report and recommendations. The General Assembly considered them, and in November 1947 adopted, with the necessary two-thirds majority, the Committee's recommendations for the partition of Palestine between an Arab and a Jewish state, with an economic union. The Jerusalem area, including Bethlehem, was to be internationalized and under the direct administration of the United Nations. A United Nations Palestine Commission of five members was established to supervise the putting of this plan into effect.

The Arab states, however, refused to accept the decision of the General Assembly, and declared that they would oppose by force any attempt to impose its terms. The United Kingdom Government then stated that it could accept no responsibility for implementing the plan against the will of either party. The United States, which had supported the partition plan, also said that it was opposed to the use of force to put it into effect.

With no means of enforcing the decision of the General Assembly, the supervisory Palestine Commission could do nothing but send a small liaison and administrative group to Jerusalem to observe and report what was going on. Meanwhile the United Kingdom had announced that it would lay down its Mandate as from May 15, 1948, and would not thereafter be responsible for law and order.

But even in the interim the Mandatory Power was unable to control the situation in Palestine. Jews and Arabs alike were committing acts of terrorism and sabotage, and organizing military forces. The Security Council held many meetings between November 1947 and April 1948 trying to check the regression towards total insecurity and the threat of war, but without effect.

These being the conditions in Palestine, and there being no apparent prospect of implementing the partition plan of the General Assembly, a special session was called at the request of the United States. The General Assembly sat from April 16 to May 14, when it was decided to appoint a Mediator for Palestine. His functions were to use his good offices with the local and community authorities in Palestine to arrange for the services necessary for the safety and well-being of the population, to assure the protection of the Holy Places, and to promote a peaceful adjustment of the future situation of Palestine.

The Mediator was to co-operate with the Truce Commission for Palestine, which the Security Council established on April 23. Later Count Folke Bernadotte of Sweden was selected to fill this post.

The Truce Commission for Palestine was composed of the consuls-general in Jerusalem of Belgium, France, and the United States. The task of this Commission was to supervise the effecting of the Security Council's resolution of April 17, which had called upon all persons and organizations in Palestine to cease all violence, and all military and paramilitary activities.

When the Palestine Mandate of the United Kingdom came to an end on May 15, 1948, the Jews at once proclaimed the State of Israel within the limits of the boundaries recommended in the General Assembly partition plan. Immediate recognition was accorded by the United States, and recognition by other nations followed.

Armed forces of the neighbouring Arab League states (Egypt, Iraq, Transjordan, Syria, and Lebanon) then moved across the borders of Palestine. There was widespread fighting between Arab and Israeli forces, most intense in the Jerusalem area. After two abortive truce appeals by the Security Council, a third was accepted by both sides, commencing on June 11 and effective for four weeks.

Under the terms of the Security Council resolution, the members of the Truce Commission—i.e., Belgium, France, and the United States—were to supply sixty-three military observers as well as military and naval equipment and auxiliary technical personnel as required for the supervision of the truce. The United Nations provided professional and administrative staff, and a security force for the protection of personnel and headquarters and other installations.

The Security Council had decided that the Mediator would act in concert with the Truce Commission in supervising the truce. One of the Swedish generals was appointed the Mediator's Chief of Staff. Here was the origin of the title Chief of Staff UNTSO, which is rather anomalous at present.[3] Under an arrangement between the Mediator and the Truce Commission, the latter's authority was limited to Jerusalem. The Mediator established his headquarters on the Island of Rhodes.

The first truce was to run until July 9, 1948. Before that date the Security Council and Count Bernadotte, the Mediator, urgently appealed to both Israelis and Arabs to prolong it.   Israel agreed, but the Arabs did not, and hostilities were resumed.

On July 15, 1948, the Security Council passed another resolution, invoking Articles 39 and 40 of the Charter, which relate to threats to the peace.   It ordered the governments and authorities concerned to cease fire and to observe a truce until a peaceful settlement of the future of Palestine should be reached.   It was left to the Mediator to set the time the truce was to begin, and he arranged with the parties that it should come into effect on July 16 at Jerusalem and July 18 elsewhere.

During the ten days' interval between the truces the Israelis had gained important successes.   They occupied Lydda and Ramle, and also the lower Galilee, including Nazareth.   They failed, however, to take the Old City of Jerusalem or to drive the Arab Legion out of Latrun.

With the second truce the duties of UNTSO increased.   These had mainly to do with the attempt to prevent arms and munitions from coming into the country.   The strength of the Organization grew to about three hundred officer observers, and the other ranks and civil staff attached to the Organization were also augmented.

On September 17 Count Bernadotte and a senior observer, Colonel André Serot of France, were murdered by Jewish terrorists in Jerusalem.   The Count and his staff were in three cars coming from Government House which they had been inspecting with a view to setting up headquarters in it.   An Israeli liaison officer was with them, and no one in the convoy was armed.   When they were passing through the Katamon quarter an Israeli jeep blocked the way, and three men in Israeli uniform approached the Count's car.   The occupants thought it was for the usual checking of passes, but a sub-machine-gun was thrust through the window, and, in a long burst of fire, Count Bernadotte and Colonel Serot were shot dead.

Apologies were tendered by the Government of Israel, but the excellent Israeli intelligence system apparently was unequal to the task of finding the murderers.[4]

Dr Ralph Bunche, a senior United Nations Secretariat member, was given full authority over the Palestine mission as Acting Mediator.   The Swedish officers serving with the mission were withdrawn, including the Chief of Staff, who was succeeded by Brigadier-General W. E. Riley, U.S. Marine Corps.   Brigadier-General Riley, successively promoted to Major-General and Lieutenant-General, remained as Chief of Staff for five years.

Fighting in Palestine did not cease even with the coming into force of the second truce.   Many breaches occurred, in spite of

the efforts of the Mediator and the observers. At the end of
October the Israelis drove back from upper Galilee into Lebanon
the so-called Arab Liberation Army, which had been organized by
the Arab League and was led by Fawzi el Kaukji.

There was more serious fighting against the Egyptians in the
Negev. On October 15 the Israelis opened an offensive against
the Egyptian front which ran from Isdud to Beit Jibrin. On
October 20 they broke a gap in the defensive positions and successively captured Beersheba and Beit Hanun, cutting the Egyptians'
lines of communication which forced their withdrawal from the
line they had been holding, except for the position around Faluja,
which, though cut off, bravely held out until the end of hostilities.
Gamal Abdel Nasser was one of the officers of this garrison, whose
tenacity in defence made them the Egyptian heroes of the war.

On October 22 the cease-fire proposed by the Security Council
was accepted by both sides. A wobbly truce lasted until November
19, when an Egyptian force attempted to relieve the pressure on
Faluja by advancing from the Gaza Strip towards Nirim. On
December 22 the Israelis renewed their offensive. A diversionary
attack was made on the Egyptian positions south of Gaza, and
shortly afterwards the main attack was made on the Egyptian
forces extending from El Auja towards Beersheba. El Auja and
Bir Asluj were captured on December 27. A column was then
directed on Rafah and El Arish. Abu Aweigila was captured on
December 29, and the Israelis were close to El Arish when operations were brought to an end by the threat of British intervention
dictated by Britain's treaty with Egypt and, presumably, by her
interest in preventing any interference with the Suez Canal.

Although disregarded during these operations in the south and
the north, the Security Council's order on July 15 to the combatants to observe a truce was still in force when the armistice
agreements were concluded in 1949. Negotiations began on the
Island of Rhodes in mid-January 1949, and the General Armistice
Agreements were successively signed between Israel and Egypt,
Israel and Lebanon, Israel and Jordan, and Israel and Syria, the
last on July 20, 1949.

After the armistice agreements had been concluded the Security
Council, on August 11, 1949, passed an important resolution
concerning the status of the United Nations Truce Supervision
Organization. It relieved the Mediator of any further responsibility under previous Security Council resolutions. The UNTSO
was no longer subordinated to the Mediator, but became a sub-
sidiary organ of the United Nations with its own well-defined
functions. Its machinery for supervising the cease-fire and the

truce, established under previous Security Council resolutions, was made available for assisting the supervision of the General Armistice Agreements through the Mixed Armistice Commissions set up therein. The Chief of Staff was made responsible for reporting to the Security Council on the observance of the cease-fire order of July 15, 1948, which remained in force. The Secretary-General was requested to arrange for the continued services of as many of the personnel of the existing truce organization as were required to carry out the above duties. (A great reduction was effected in the next few years, dropping to a minimum of less than forty officer observers. There were between forty and fifty serving when I became Chief of Staff.)

Under authority of this resolution, when the cease-fire was violated the Chief of Staff was able to act quickly, without the delays and restrictions imposed by the rules of procedure adopted by the parties for the work of the Mixed Armistice Commissions. He might decide to send observers immediately to the place where an exchange of fire had started, and a cease-fire might be arranged before the observation and investigation machinery of the armistice agreement was set in motion.

This sort of action, to re-establish the cease-fire, was exceptional. Most of the work of the UN observers was the investigation of incidents involving breaches of the armistice agreements. Each armistice agreement provides that there shall be a Mixed Armistice Commission, to supervise the working of the agreement. The Commission is composed of an equal number of delegates from each party, presided over by the Chief of Staff as Chairman, or a senior observer whom he designates after consulting the parties.

The armistice agreements provide that complaints or claims made by either party are referred to the Mixed Armistice Commission. The Commission arranges for the investigation of the complaint by UN Military Observers with the participation of representatives of one or both parties. When the facts are established the Mixed Armistice Commission is supposed to meet and decide on such action " as it may deem appropriate with a view to equitable and mutually satisfactory settlement."

Unfortunately, this practical and conciliatory object of the Mixed Armistice Commission machinery was more often than not ignored by the parties. Delegates were apt to wrangle like shyster lawyers, with the object of securing a condemnation of the other party in the strongest terms for subsequent political and propaganda use. Perhaps the Mixed Armistice Commissions worked badly because they had no power to impose any sanctions for breaches of the General Armistice Agreements ; and the conciliatory spirit

which was supposed to inspire them, if it ever existed, by 1954 was
not in evidence.

The first article of each General Armistice Agreement begins
with these words : " With a view to promoting the return to
permanent peace in Palestine . . ." and later the article says :
" The establishment of an armistice between the armed forces of
the two parties is accepted as an indispensable step towards . . .
the restoration of peace in Palestine."

It will be explained later why there has been no progress towards
peace since the armistice agreements were signed.   Regrettably,
the positions of the parties in regard to peace terms now seem to
be farther apart than they were at that time.   The point I wish to
make here is that the armistice agreements were drawn up envisaging that peace would be made after not too long a period of
negotiation between the parties.   When this did not happen, and
hostility hardened as time went on, and positions became less and
less reconcilable, there was a break-down in many respects of the
armistice machinery which had been set up on the assumption that
there would be mutual goodwill and that the parties would move
in the direction of peace.

This leads us to the problems obstructing the making of peace,
or, at any rate, the beginning of peace negotiations.   The Arab
position and the Israeli position are poles apart on the principal
questions which would have to be decided before peace can be
made.

The first and most important of these questions is that of the
refugees, those Arabs who fled from Palestine in 1948, or were
driven out by the Israelis.   These unhappy people since then have
been living in camps around the perimeter of Israel, or sharing
inadequate accommodation with relatives, or living in what shelter
they are able to find, supported by the sparse rations of the United
Nations Relief and Works Agency (UNRWA).   It was said there
were about 900,000 of them in 1956, but as they and the Arab
governments who are their hosts resist the holding of any census,
or making any accurate check on the numbers of those receiving
rations, no precise figures can be given.   The Arab position in
regard to these most unfortunate people is that driving them from
their homes was an act of most flagrant injustice and inhumanity,
and that there can be no peace unless they are all given the right
to return and settle again in their ' usurped ' homeland.   They
cite the General Assembly resolution of December 11, 1948, as
supporting this stand.[5]

The Israeli position is that in 1948 the refugees fled from what is now Israel of their own accord or in response to the orders of the Arab Higher Committee to leave the way clear for the invading Arab forces to destroy or drive out the Jews. Therefore they forfeited their right to live in the country. Anyway, Israel could not possibly absorb within her borders such a great number of bitterly hostile people, and survive as a state. Although in 1949 Israel was ready to allow the return of a hundred thousand of the refugees, this offer has since been withdrawn, and now the official position is that she will allow back only a very small number of them, in cases when a family has been broken and hardship has resulted.

The next question is of boundaries. The present Arab position is that peace might be made on the basis of the boundaries specified in the partition plan for Palestine adopted by the General Assembly of the United Nations in 1947—a most complicated proposal which has become completely unreal, if it ever was real, because of the events between 1947 and now. The Israelis point out that the Arabs themselves rejected the plan when it was decided on by the United Nations, and took up arms against it—with very bad results for themselves. The Israeli position on boundaries is that they should generally follow the demarcation lines of the General Armistice Agreements, but that exchanges of territory can be made on an equitable basis to remove some of the gross inconveniences of the present arbitrarily drawn Armistice Demarcation Lines.

The third principal question to be settled in the making of peace is compensation for those Arabs who have left property in Israel, which has been taken over by the State. Here there is no great divergence, in principle ; the Israelis agree that they should pay for private property taken over. However, they say they would have to have financial assistance to do so. Mr Dulles in 1955 intimated that the interested Great Powers would provide such assistance, if peace could be attained.

The last controversial question is that of the status of Jerusalem, at present divided between the Israelis who hold the new, or western, portion, and the Jordanians who hold the Old City and eastern suburbs. The United Nations plan was that the city, and a considerable tract of surrounding country, should be internationalized, and governed under a special régime. This proposal is anathema to the Israelis, who, for historic, religious, and sentimental reasons, were and are passionately determined to have Jerusalem for their capital. Some of the Arab states still support the internationalization plan, but Jordan is against it, and wants to keep at least that part of Jerusalem which she now holds. So both parties are against internationalization, and it would be difficult in the extreme to divide the city between the two peoples so they could live in it side by side and peacefully.

Thus the obstacles to peace can be stated in terms of the widely differing views of Arabs and Israelis as to what would be equitable, or at least acceptable, peace terms. But why, the reader may wonder, cannot some compromise be reached? After all, peace has been made between peoples who had greater differences between them. That is true, but in the Palestine conflict there is a new element. That is the intervention of the United Nations " to restore international peace and security," in the words of Article 39 of the Charter. This was the first such intervention, and what happened has already been briefly described in this chapter. International peace and security was restored, to the point of concluding armistices between all the belligerents.

While the Charter gives the United Nations, through the agency of the Security Council, extensive powers, even to the use of military sanctions, to stop fighting or eliminate threats to international peace, it has almost no powers to oblige any nation to make peace. More explicitly it lacks power to impose terms of peace or a general settlement. The Security Council can recommend only; the limitations of its powers are set out in Chapter VI of the Charter.

The result is that the United Nations has obliged the Arabs and the Israelis to stop their war, but it cannot oblige them to make peace. Usually peace is made when one side has won such victories in the war that its opponent sees that it would be better to agree to the victor's terms rather than continue, and find itself in worse plight. Or both sides become so exhausted or tired of the armed conflict that they prefer compromise or a negotiated peace to continued fighting. Neither of these conditions obtained when the United Nations succeeded in stopping the fighting in Palestine. Both sides claim that they could have defeated the other and have attained their objectives but for the interference of the United Nations. Now, settlement of the contrary viewpoints by trial of force is ruled out.

Of course, there are people on both sides who propose, to the accompaniment of much fiery Arabic or Hebrew oratory, that there should be a resort to arms forthwith, with the certainty that the orator's side would be victorious. But no politician who is a member of a Government publicly advocates such a course.

A good many Arabs, when one talks to them privately, think that time is on their side, and that the questions at issue will be settled in their favour without resort to arms—or, at any rate, without an all-out war. They argue in this way : " The Arabs are forty million, and the Jews only a million and a half. It is true that, thanks to

Western aid, the Jews are technically more advanced and militarily stronger than the Arabs are now. But the Arabs will catch up with them in those respects, and, as well as the advantage in numbers, they have great advantages in resources. The Arabs do not need to be in a hurry. The Crusaders occupied this country once, but after a hundred years they were driven out. It will be the same with this Jewish state. It is completely artificial ; it cannot exist on its own resources, and the boycott will prevent it from living by trade. It is really only a colony—a colony of the West, or at least of the Jews of the West, and even with their continued support it will live only precariously. In course of time, and under Arab pressure, it will wither away and disappear—like so many other states in this theatre of age-old conflict between dynasties, peoples, and races."

This philosophical concept of how the question will be settled leaves out of account the situation and temper of the refugees, it seems to me, and the new forces in the world to-day—nationalism and communism—which will tend to create a situation where the armed conflict will be renewed and force will decide, unless a peaceful settlement can be arranged first. Or the Palestine question may be resolved as a corollary to the outcome of some greater conflict ; as, one may say, it was created following the First World War by the establishment of the National Home for the Jews, as promised in the Balfour Declaration.

Let us now examine briefly how the Israelis feel about it. They proclaim almost daily that they want peace—a peaceful settlement as soon as possible—that they are willing to sit down and negotiate with the Arabs any time, any place. But, of course, what they want is peace on their own terms, and what those terms are, and how different they are from the terms the Arabs consider just, has been set forth above.

Sometimes the Israelis have to examine the possibility that the Arabs are not likely to change their attitude, and that a negotiated peace on Israeli terms will not be possible for an indefinite period. Both Mr Ben-Gurion and General Dayan have said something like " very well, then, we will hold out as we are ; and this condition of no peace and no war may last for ten, maybe twenty, years."

In the meantime they are faced with a threat, both to their military and their economic security. The military threat is that the Arabs, numerically so much stronger, and with much greater natural resources, will build up their military strength and skill until the preponderance in military power which Israel possessed in 1956 will be lost. The first event which made this possibility patent was the deal whereby Egypt obtained large quantities of modern armaments from Czechoslovakia late in 1955.

But many Israelis think that the precarious character of their state's economy is a greater threat to its survival in its present form than the military danger from the Arabs.   No book about the Palestine question in its present aspect can be complete without giving some space to an examination of the difficult economic position of Israel.   This will find a place in the concluding chapter.

With the preceding account of how UNTSO originated, and how it operated, and the obstacles which stand in the way of a move towards peace in Palestine, it should be easier to understand the limitations on action in the events and situations with which UNTSO had to deal between the autumn of 1954 and the autumn of 1956. The incidents to be described in the following chapters were of no great importance, but they will illustrate the atmosphere of the armistice as it was in those days—the constant hostility, and the blood-letting in maraudings, reprisals, and revenges which it was the duty of UNTSO to investigate and attempt to prevent, through the machinery of the Mixed Armistice Commissions.

CHAPTER 3

An Exchange of Prisoners

Maps 1 and 2

IN the work of UNTSO we were accustomed to think in terms of four separate armistice agreements—four separate Mixed Armistice Commissions. We thought of what happened between Israel and Jordan, of what happened between Israel and Egypt, Israel and Syria, and Israel and Lebanon.[6] In 1954 and 1955 there was, in fact, little connexion between the incidents with which UNTSO had to deal on the one border and those on the others. There was no indication that there was any centrally directed Arab plan for harassing Israel by raids over the ADL. No serious attempt was made to set up a joint command of the Arab armies until 1956. There was, of course, the Arab League, and the Committee for the boycott of Israel. But these bodies were concerned with co-operation of the Arab states in putting political and economic pressure on Israel, with the object of eventually reversing the result of the 1948 war.

The breaches of the armistice between Israel and Jordan in late 1954 were incidents small in scale. Each of them involved only a very few deaths, woundings, or kidnappings—infinitesimal considered on the scale of world wars, very few even if measured on the scale of how many deaths must occur in any one event in obscure localities to make it newsworthy in the Press of the world. Yet their effect was cumulative ; small incidents between Israel and the Arab states built up stresses until the open war of October–November 1956 resulted. This narrative of small raids, retaliations, reprisals, and trans-border crimes will perhaps show how difficult it is to determine, in any situation of international tension, which country is the aggressor—a difficulty sometimes ignored in theoretical discussions of how the world's peace should be kept.

In the struggle between the Arabs and Israelis during the period covered by this book, the situation was unusually favourable for determining the facts about the actions of the parties to the conflict. UNTSO had observers on the ground, or close to it ; they had a lot of experience of the viewpoints and habits of action of both sides ; and yet the story will, I think, leave any reader unable to convince himself that one side or the other had so clearly shown itself the aggressor that it had incurred sanctions. A clear-cut situation was, of course, created by the final Israeli attack of October 1956, when the advance of their troops into the Sinai, with the announced intention of staying there until certain objects had been achieved, was indisputably an act of war, and condemned as such by the General Assembly of the United Nations.

I had arrived in Jerusalem on August 19, 1954, after a period of indoctrination and study of documents on the work of the United Nations Truce Supervision Organization in New York.

I assumed the duties of Chief of Staff at noon on September 2, 1954. At one o'clock I was to attend a farewell luncheon for General Bennike at the Eden Hotel in Jerusalem, to which we had been invited by Mr Pinchas Lavon, then Israel's Minister of Defence.

General Bennike and I arrived, with some other UNTSO officers, and discovered General Dayan, attended by Lieutenant-Colonel Shalev and Colonel Givli, staff officers for Armistice Affairs and Intelligence respectively. General Dayan briefly expressed Mr Lavon's regrets that urgent business had prevented his attending the luncheon, and taking our cocktails with us we sat ourselves at table.

As a coincidental salute or greeting on my taking over responsibility, during the previous night the Israelis had mounted an attack on the Jordanian village of Beit Liqya, lying about eighteen kilometres north-west of Jerusalem and eight kilometres north-east of the celebrated monastery of Latrun. According to first reports, the Jordanian national guards defending the village had prevented the Israelis from entering. But two ambushes had been laid for the Arab Legion supporting troops, who had moved forward to reinforce the threatened village when the attack began. An Arab Legion combat car had been blown up and set on fire ; two of its occupants had been killed, and two taken prisoner.

As soon as we had taken our seats, General Dayan observed that he did not believe in wasting too much time in preliminaries before getting down to business, and then asked me what I thought the reaction of the Jordanian authorities would be if the five Arab prisoners (including the two captured that morning) were returned without the imposition of any conditions. Would the Jordanians be similarly generous, and return the Israeli prisoner they had been holding since June 28, one Sergeant Gibli of the parachute battalion ?

My first inclination was to reject this proposition out of hand. Gibli had been taken prisoner well inside Jordanian territory in the course of an Israeli military raid, in clearest violation of the armistice agreement. For this operation Israel had been condemned by the

Mixed Armistice Commission. But the prisoners whom General Dayan proposed to exchange against Gibli had been taken in a subsequent series of raids into Jordan, which culminated in the Beit Liqya attack. Thus the proposal was morally equivalent to paying the fine levied for a first crime with the proceeds of four others.

The chain of events whose consequences General Dayan's proposition was intended to liquidate began as follows. During the night of June 28–29, 1954, an Israeli patrol raided a small detachment of the Arab Legion bivouacked near the village of Azzun, which is about seven kilometres from the nearest point on the demarcation line. I have been informed by an authoritative Israel source that this raid had been ordered in retaliation for a murder committed in Israel by some Jordanians a few days previously. The circumstances of this crime were particularly shocking, and Israel public indignation was great. An old man living on the outskirts of Ra-anana heard a noise in his garden, went out to investigate, and was shot down on his doorstep. There was no apparent reason for this act other than terrorism. Ra-anana is seven kilometres from the nearest point on the demarcation line, the well-known Arab village of Qalqilya. The strip of Israel connecting Tel Aviv to Haifa and the north is here at its narrowest—fourteen kilometres between the ADL and the sea. Ra-anana is only sixteen kilometres north of Tel Aviv. The alarm and anger excited by the crime can easily be understood.

The Israeli patrol first made contact with a two-man patrol of the Arab Legion near the demarcation line north of Qalqilya. There was an exchange of fire ; hand-grenades were thrown ; an Arab corporal was slightly wounded ; and the Israeli patrol went on towards the east, in the darkness. This was about seven o'clock.

The Arab Legion detachment at Azzun were surprised in their beds, when the Israelis opened up with their sub-machine-guns, killing two Arabs and wounding four. Then they withdrew. By then the Legionaries recovered from their surprise, opened fire, and began a pursuit.

Sergeant Gibli had been wounded in the brief action, and could not keep up with the rest of the patrol. He was taken prisoner, and it is rather surprising that his life was spared by the men whose comrades had been shot in their beds only a few minutes before.

Later, some members of the Jordanian Government wanted to treat Gibli as a criminal, and not as a prisoner of war. This was because an Arab farmer, Rafi'a Abdel Aziz Omar, was found dead on the route followed by the Israeli patrol between the demarcation line and the Arab Legion bivouac at Azzun. He had been killed by about twelve knife- or bayonet-wounds in the chest, sides, back, arms, and neck.

It would seem that a criminal case against Gibli might have stood. The Arab farmer, an unarmed civilian, had evidently been killed by the patrol of which Gibli was a member, contrary to the laws of war. Perhaps the Israeli military authorities appreciated that he stood in danger, and for that reason made strenuous—and successful—efforts to seize hostages.

In concluding the account of the Azzun incident, whatever one may think of the deliberate breach of the armistice, and the shooting down of men sleeping in their tents, one has to admit that this Israeli patrol gave proof of remarkable courage and persistence, very good morale and training. There were only five of them, from the testimony of Jordanian witnesses. After an encounter with a Jordanian patrol near the demarcation line, they pressed on, and attacked an Arab Legion camp where they must have known a more numerous enemy was stationed, and who, following the earlier clash, might be assumed to be on the alert.

The Israelis generally seemed to have an extraordinary sensitivity about having any of their men prisoners in Arab hands. In ordinary warfare one expects that a certain number of one's own men will be made prisoners of war, though in the First World War, as a general rule, it used to be considered rather disgraceful to be taken prisoner if unwounded. But when at any time during the years I was Chief of Staff UNTSO any Israelis were prisoners in enemy hands, there was great agitation in Israel about it, constant efforts through the machinery of the Mixed Armistice Commission to procure their release, and if they were held for any length of time the Israeli Army usually took military action to secure hostages to force their exchange. The most serious case of this kind will be narrated in the chapter dealing with the troubles between Syria and Israel. I often speculated as to the reason for this prisoner complex, and wondered if it was related to the personal experiences of some of the Israeli leaders who had spent terms in prison, or to the after-effect of the concentration-camp horrors in Germany, or the heritage of persecution neuroses.

It appears that Israeli soldiers taking part in hazardous missions, such as the Azzun raid, were told that they need have no fears if they were taken prisoner : the Israeli Army would see that they would be freed. We shall now see how they made good on the promise in this case.

The first Israeli operation to establish a credit in prisoners took place on the night of July 31–August 1, 1954. Some ten Israeli raiders penetrated to near Jenin, a town five kilometres within Jordanian territory which was one of the notorious ' bloody triangle ' Jenin-Nablus-Tulkarm. The raiders attacked two policemen, wounded both, and took one prisoner. On their way back to Israel territory they killed another Arab who was watching his fields, as the farmers do at that season of the year. The raiders were intercepted by a party of Jordanian national guards on the abandoned Jenin airfield, less than a kilometre from the demarcation line, but after an exchange of fire they made good their withdrawal.

The next incident took place on August 13. A routine patrol of five men of the Arab Legion was in position some two hundred metres to the east of the demarcation line, in the area of Shaikh Madh Kur, about fifteen kilometres north-west of Hebron. It was brought under fire by two larger bodies of Israeli soldiers, who had advanced into Jordanian territory. The Jordanians, after an exchange of fire, were forced to withdraw, leaving one of their men in a cave in which he had taken shelter, where the Israelis apparently made him prisoner. One of the Arab Legion patrol died of a wound sustained in this action, and another was less seriously wounded.

Next came the action at Beit Liqya, referred to briefly on page 34. This was the most serious incident which had occurred on the Israel-Jordan border for some time. An Israeli force opened fire on the village from the south, but did not press the attack with customary vigour. The defenders fought effectively under the leadership of an Arab Legion corporal. From bloodstains and other signs found during the subsequent investigation, it appears the Israelis suffered casualties. But this attack may have been a feint, intended to draw the near-by Arab Legion units into an ambush. In any case, a carload of Legionaries rushing up to the support of Beit Liqya did fall into a trap of the same kind as set in the Gaza operation which was described on page 17. Two of the Legionaries were killed, another wounded, and three taken prisoner. Another Israeli ambush failed to gain surprise ; a fire-fight ensued, resulting in casualties on both sides, and the Israelis withdrew without accomplishing anything.

The indications were that the Israelis must have used at least two companies in the operation, which being of that scope must have been sanctioned by the top military authority. There were no proceedings in the Israel-Jordan Mixed Armistice Commission, from which Israel had withdrawn some months previously, because they were dissatisfied with the Chairman's decision in the Scorpion Pass incident, when eleven Israelis were killed and two wounded when a bus was attacked by Arabs in the Negev.[7] A special report on the Beit Liqya incident was made to the Security Council.

Let us now study the balance-sheet in killed and wounded of the retaliation chain, assuming it to have been set off by the murder of the old Israeli at Ra-anana.

At Azzun four Arabs were killed and three wounded, at Jenin óne killed and one wounded, at Shaikh Madh Kur one killed and one wounded, and at Beit Liqya-Beit Sira two killed and five wounded—a total casualty list for Jordan of ten killed and nine wounded. Besides Gibli, captured and wounded at Azzun, there must have been a good many more Israeli soldiers wounded, and perhaps killed, in these operations. But the Israeli Army spokesman naturally gave no details of the casualties they had suffered, which were only evidenced by bloodstains, abandoned equipment, and tracks.

This summing-up of the results of the retaliation for one crime illustrates, in miniature, the whole defect of the Israeli policy of maintaining peace on their borders, of stopping infiltration and marauding by retaliation. The retaliation does not end the matter ; it goes on and on, as we shall see. The retaliatory actions undoubtedly gave some satisfaction to the Israeli public, or at least the newspapers, but the policy was not effective in relation to its professed aim.

The Israeli Defence Forces by this time had unbounded confidence in their ability to defeat any and all of the Arab armies if it should come to open war. Most Israeli politicians and the public seemed to hold the same opinion, and, indeed, the results of all the actions between Arab and Israeli armed forces up to and including the 1956 Sinai campaign justify this confidence. It was born of the Israeli successes in the 1948 war, and the considerable improvements in organization, equipment, and training of their forces achieved since then. The feeling of preponderant military power, not surprisingly, resulted in arrogance. The IDF authorities, with whom I usually had to deal on armistice matters, were never willing to negotiate with the other side as an equal under the armistice agreement. If there was a question involving military advantage, or even prestige, and they could not win by legalistic argument, then they simply conceded nothing, changed nothing.

Let us now return to the proposition advanced by General Dayan, that the Israelis should return the five prisoners they held, captured in the operations just described, if the Jordanians would give an assurance—a sort of gentleman's agreement to hand back Gibli in a short time. While my first inclination had been to refuse to put up such a proposal to the Jordanian authorities, after reflecting a moment I thought that, after all, I was in Palestine to try to keep things peaceful, and if the series of raids which had culminated in the Beit Liqya incident could be stopped it might be worth some compromise with strict justice. At any rate, the Jordanian authorities should be given the opportunity to decide whether they wished to accept the offer or not. General Bennike was also of this opinion.

Accordingly, the exchange was proposed to Anwar Nuseibeh, the Jordanian Minister of Defence. After brief hesitation, he decided to accept, in the interests of tranquillity. Anwar Nuseibeh was a member of one of the most important Palestinian families, a brave man who had lost a leg fighting in the 1948 war. It was a courageous decision that he took, for any Arab politician who seems to favour any accommodation with the Israelis risks a storm of abuse, if nothing worse.

We told the Israelis that the deal was accepted, and they returned their prisoners promptly through the Government House enclave. But the news leaked into the Jordanian Press, and difficulties arose over the return of Gibli, owing, it appeared, to the vengeful feelings which the whole chain of events had aroused among the Jordanians. An election campaign was in progress, and naturally this did not help.

When at last Gibli was returned to Israel, he was received with many plaudits, and was cited in an Order of the Day by General Dayan, which said : " Despite wounds, Samal Gibli continued to act with courage and daring. He demanded that his friends leave him so that they would not get hit. The conduct of Samal Gibli after he was wounded and while in captivity was exemplary."

CHAPTER 4

Jordan-Israel Troubles in late 1954

Maps 1 and 2

THE exchange of prisoners—Gibli against the Arab Legionaries—marked the beginning of a period of relative freedom from violence along the Jordan-Israel demarcation line. Nevertheless, the chain of events which began at Azzun was carried on by the private revenge of a Bedouin soldier of the Arab Legion. What he did made trouble when the Jordan-Israel Mixed Armistice Commission began sitting again in October.

The Arab Legion battalion which had been garrisoning the Beit Liqya area was made up of Bedouins. Hamad Hamid was one of the soldiers in it. His cousin had been killed in the ambush. It devolved upon Hamad, according to the Bedouin code of honour, to avenge his cousin's death. As it was the Jordan Government's policy that the Arab Legion would not break the armistice agreement by crossing the demarcation line, and hence could not enter Israeli territory to retaliate against Israeli aggressions or provocations, Hamad Hamid decided that he would retaliate personally.

The Israelis in their subsequent complaint about this incident said that their soldiers had been killed by an Arab Legion " unit " ; Hamad Hamid in his confession claimed that he had been alone, and I was assured by a high Arab Legion authority that it was believed he told the truth. The UNTSO never had evidence to prove whether he was alone or whether he had one or more companions with him.

Early in the morning of September 10, 1954, Hamad Hamid made his way to a hill just on the demarcation line, near Bir Ma'in, about five kilometres north-west of Beit Liqya. The Israelis had an observation post there, which apparently they manned only during daylight hours. Hamad lay in wait, and when, about nine o'clock, two Israeli soldiers approached, he killed both of them with rifle and hand-grenade. By the time the Israeli officer in charge of the sector got to the post and discovered the bodies of his men, Hamad had got away. Then he went to his commander and confessed what he had done.

He was tried by court-martial for having crossed into Israel in contravention of orders. While awaiting sentence, he escaped from the guard-room, probably with the connivance of sympathetic guards. He promptly went back to Bir Ma'in, to resume his private war with the Israelis, and tried, again single-handed, to ambush a truck carrying seven Israeli soldiers. This time, however, the Israelis were on the alert, and after a brief action Hamad Hamid was killed. His body was brought to Jerusalem, and his identity was established before a UN observer, but the Jordanian authorities disclaimed all knowledge of him, and he was buried in Israel.

When the Israelis again began attending the MAC after the departure of their *bête noire*, Commander Hutchison, there were nearly 1500 unsettled complaints on the agenda, most of which had accumulated during the period when the Israelis had been out of the MAC, from December 1953 to October 1954. As very few of these cases were of any importance, I proposed that they should be wiped off the slate, so that the MAC could begin afresh, and operate effectively. But the Bir Ma'in case blocked this ; the Israelis insisted on its being dealt with, although they were willing to drop all others. The Jordanians said that if Bir Ma'in were discussed, they had a number of cases that they would insist on discussing. Soon, as no agreement could be reached, the MAC began to operate again with a year's backlog of cases.

The cases individually were of little moment, as I have said, but the effect of having so many unsettled was to discourage subtly the members of the MAC and the observers, and tend to make them feel that it was not of much consequence whether a complaint was or was not investigated and dealt with by the MAC. It gave the feeling that the machinery of the MAC was clogged, and grinding to a standstill—which, in effect, it was.

In very serious cases, where there had been persons killed or wounded, or where firing across the lines had taken place and might be resumed, there was an emergency procedure. Such cases, on the decision of the Chairman, could take precedence over all others, and be dealt with quickly. So, when both sides wanted to make the machinery work, it could. Nevertheless, the deadening effect of the large amount of ' unsettled business ' was there. By August 1955 the number of unsettled complaints on the Jordan-Israel MAC docket stood at 2150.

The story of the Ein Hashofet sheep, whose restoration to their rightful owners was called by the observers " Operation Bo-Peep," may seem a rather trivial one to include in this narrative of bloody borders and clashing nationalisms. But it illustrates a conflict in the realm of Israel's defence and foreign policies.

First of all, it is to be noted that the sheep were a specially bred and selected flock, the pride of the *kibbutz* Ein Hashofet.[8] Their shepherd said, in his evidence, that they were a locally improved breed, and that there were none like them in all Israel.   The common sheep in the country are the fat-tailed breed, seen all over the Middle East.   These frugal herbivores are able to subsist, if not to thrive, on the scanty pasture available during the long rainless periods.   But the 480 sheep of the Ein Hashofet flock not only had this characteristic, but gave four times as much milk as the common variety.   They were all marked with ear-tags, or tattooing.

On September 27 the sheep passed from Israeli into Jordanian custody—to state the fact in terms which could be accepted by both sides.   But of course each side had its own version of how they came to cross the demarcation line.   The Israeli account, furnished by Abe, the shepherd of the prize flock, was that he had been superintending the grazing of his charges about seven o'clock in the morning of September 27, some 350 metres from the demarcation line.   He had previously seen suspicious movements in a weed-filled wadi, and was collecting his woolly charges to get them farther into Israel, when three Arabs suddenly appeared from the weedy area.   When they shouted in Arabic, Abe began to run, and when they started firing at him he continued running, somewhat faster.   He said : " I had the idea while I was running that they had dropped to their knees to fire.   I may have gotten this impression when I looked behind."   When he was about a hundred metres away, he was slightly wounded.   (When the observers saw this wound, some ten days later, it was seen to be on his left arm, midway between the elbow and the shoulder, and only a small scab, about half a centimetre in diameter, remained.   In fact, it looked rather like a vaccination mark.)

Then, according to Abe's story, the Arabs rounded up the sheep and herded them back across the demarcation line and in the direction of Zububa village.   One of Abe's colleagues, herding another flock about a kilometre away, noticed the dispersion of the Ein Hashofet sheep, and then heard shots.   He saw the Arabs getting the flock together, and herding them towards the south.   He fired his rifle at the marauders, but didn't hit any of them, perhaps because he prudently fired at a rather long range.

The Jordanian version was that the flock, unattended, had crossed the demarcation line, and begun eating the pasturage, or gleaning in the stubble of the Arab cultivation.   Indignant at this depletion of Jordan's resources, some of the villagers had taken the sheep into custody.

The private opinion of the observer who investigated the case,

Captain De Barr, an officer of considerable experience and, through this and his pre-army legal training, well able to weigh the testimony of witnesses, was that Abe had probably exhibited the same failing as the best known of shepherdesses, and just shut his eyes for a minute or two. And during his brief lapse, the sheep, or some of them, had seen the greenness of the more distant pastures and had strayed across the demarcation line.

The colonists of Ein Hashofet by origin are American or Canadian Jews. Abe, the shepherd, was a Canadian, and a graduate of the University of Toronto—perhaps in philosophy ? Anyway, I found out later that he was a classmate of a friend of mine, who saw him in Israel. Abe professed to be vastly contented to be a member in a *kibbutz*, as it was altogether a better way of life than the hurly-burly of economic competition in Toronto.

After the customary haggling between the delegates of the two sides, and runnings to and fro by UN observers, the flock was handed back twelve days after its infiltration. There was more wrangling, of course : thirty-nine inferior Jordanian sheep were included in the 462 produced. Also, the Israelis claimed, fifty-five of their prize sheep were still missing, including a particularly fine and valuable ram. The stragglers, or most of them, were turned over later. Last of all came the prize ram. The Israelis complained that he seemed to be very tired.

On a Sunday afternoon, six days after the sheep had strayed, I received an urgent summons to see Mr Moshe Sharett, then Prime Minister and holding also the portfolio of Minister of Foreign Affairs.[9] Mr Sharett said he wanted to speak to me about the Ein Hashofet sheep. Probably I would think it strange that the Prime Minister of the country should call me in to confer on such a relatively trivial affair, but a question of principle was involved. There were some people of great influence in the Government and elsewhere (by implication in the military forces) who advocated that Israelis should always retaliate by force against acts of Arab violence, or breaches of the armistice. He, himself, supported by the majority in the present Government, believed in following the procedures laid down in the GAA through the MAC, and, where appropriate, using the UNTSO.

If the sheep question could be settled satisfactorily through the MAC and UNTSO machinery, this would support his policy, which would then stand a better chance of being adhered to in more important incidents. But if I couldn't succeed in getting the sheep back, the advocates of retorting to violence by greater violence would have another argument, and in more serious situations which could arise in the future it would be more difficult to maintain the policy of settlement of disputes by discussion in the MACs rather than by retaliation and intimidation.

This was the first and only time which Mr Sharett spoke to me of the two trends in Israel's defence and foreign policy. However, many others who were of his view, mainly people in the foreign affairs ministry, propounded the same thesis. Unfortunately, their urgings that I should do what I could to support the efforts of the " negotiation " party as opposed to the " retaliation " party were usually coupled with the suggestion that I should see that the Israel viewpoint in respect of incidents under deliberation by the Mixed Armistice Commission should be upheld by the Chairman. In other words, it was represented that it was up to me to see that the " pacific " party would have a diplomatic success, so that they could hold their own against the adherents to the " activist " or militarist theory.

Unhappily, during the two years from September 1954 to September 1956, the pacifists fought a losing battle, and the militarists more and more imposed their point of view and policies. The turning-point was when Mr Ben-Gurion came back to active politics, as Minister of Defence, late in February 1955. Mr Ben-Gurion was generally considered to be the proponent of the " activist " line in Israel's military and foreign policy, while Mr Sharett was believed to favour a quiet line, non-aggressive and conciliatory attitudes which could lead towards peace, and which would find favour with the Western Powers on whose support Israel so greatly depended.

In the summer of 1955 there was a general election. Mr Ben-Gurion headed the ensuing Coalition Government, in which Mr Sharett became Foreign Minister. But it was an open secret that the conflict between the two men's views on foreign policy remained, and in 1956 Mr Sharett resigned.

Compared to Mr Ben-Gurion, Mr Sharett as a leader lacked glamour, dynamism, crowd-appeal. Is it a general rule that even in a democracy an advocate of peace appeals less to the people than the leader who does not shrink from the idea of war to attain national aims ? Perhaps in every race the image of the leader is that of the hero who heads the nation in war, even though heroes have sometimes led their peoples to disaster.

About this time, when the acute troubles on the Jordan-Israel border began to die down, tension started to build up on the marches between Israel and Egypt—that is, the semi-arid prairie surrounding the Gaza Strip.[10] But there was still to come a tragic incident of sudden death on the Jordan-Israel demarcation line near Battir, of more blood spilled uselessly.   Compared to later events which will be chronicled in this book, four dead, two wounded, and one captive is a small casualty list, but it was shocking at the time.   Ironically, the Jordanians who suffered these losses had technically violated the armistice agreement, and were condemned for it by the Mixed Armistice Commission.   No technical violation stood against the Israelis, and they were not condemned.

The place where it happened, some six kilometres south-west of Jerusalem, is a fitting scene for a tragedy.   Steep barren hills with the characteristic limestone stratification of Judea descend to a deep gloomy wadi, or ravine, which carries off the drainage from the southern part of New Jerusalem, and through which the Tel Aviv-Jerusalem railway runs.

The cause of the incident was a quarrel in a family of refugees, who had formerly lived in El Maliha, a village two kilometres north-west of where the clash took place, on the Israeli side of the demarcation line.   Omran the son, about sixteen years old, wanted money for a pair of shoes, and to get married.   His father refused him, and after violent language the boy left the house, saying that he was going away, and the father would get into trouble.

Early the next morning a patrol of six Arab Legionaries, com-manded by a corporal, was sent off to bring the boy back.   He was making for Israeli territory and, descending into the valley, had passed the spring called Ain Yalu, and nearly reached the road in the valley, close to the railway, when the patrol caught up with him.   After tying his hands with a *keffiya* (head-kerchief) they continued along the road to the south-west.   This is where the patrol leader made the mistake fatal to him and three of his men, for the road lay within Israeli territory.   The only survivor did not know why they had gone along the road instead of returning the way they had come.

On the Israeli side, an inspector of the border police gave the following evidence.   A patrol under his command had started out from Aminadav, a settlement about three kilometres farther west. They had seen the Jordanian patrol coming down from the spring, and crossing the demarcation line.   He ordered his men to take up a position behind a stone wall, on the slope about twenty metres higher than the road.   Then he had called, in Arabic, on the Jordanian patrol to halt and hold up their hands.   Instead of doing so, they opened fire.   So he ordered his men to fire.

The Jordanians had been caught in the open, the only cover being a few large boulders, behind which they vainly tried to take shelter.   In a few minutes the patrol was wiped out—the corporal and three of the men killed, one wounded in the leg and taken prisoner, while another soldier, also wounded, managed to escape on the rocky hillside. The boy Omran was also slightly wounded. The wounded prisoner, in his statement to the observers, said that he had been the leading man of the patrol, that he had heard no warning shout, and that the Israelis had opened fire first. On the other hand, Omran said he thought he had heard a shout from the Israeli side that sounded like " Waqquf ! " (Stop). He also said that he had told the corporal that the road was in Israeli territory, but the corporal had said it didn't matter.

When the incident was discussed in the Mixed Armistice Commission, the Israeli resolution, which stated that the Jordanians had violated the article of the armistice agreement which forbade crossing the demarcation line, was adopted. Technically and legally this was correct, and as it was impossible, owing to the conflicting evidence of the two sides, to determine which of them had opened fire first, the Chairman, Lieutenant-Colonel Charles Brewster, U.S.A., had no option but to vote for the Israeli resolution.

The senior Jordanian delegate was then Dr Hazem Nuseibeh, a younger brother of Anwar Nuseibeh, the Minister of Defence. He was very indignant at this decision, unjust and heartless in his opinion. There was a good deal of adverse comment in the Press, and, as usual, Brewster was charged with bias in favour of Israel and there was talk of demanding his replacement. I saw Anwar Nuseibeh, who, though naturally aggrieved at the outcome of the MAC meeting, eventually accepted my assurances that Brewster was as impartial as anyone could be.

Unfortunately, both sides were only too ready to charge partiality or prejudice against the senior personnel of the UNTSO when an adverse decision was given, especially when the case was one in which much blood had been spilled, and emotions were aroused. Allowances have to be made for such emotions, otherwise it would be intolerable for officers to have their honour impugned by assertions in the Press that they had made decisions to curry favour with one side or another in order to " hold on to their jobs." Chairmen of MACs in particular have often been attacked like this and, in the cases that come within my knowledge, always unjustly. The officer observers of the UNTSO are instructed to observe impartially, to think and act always as an officer of the United Nations, as an international servant. I know of none who has not lived up to those principles to the best of his abilities. Although doubtless many mistakes have been made, they were honest mistakes, natural enough in military officers, most of whom have little legal training or experience.   And the cases they had to try often would require a Solomon to resolve.

The period of quiet on the Jordan-Israel borders after the Beit Liqya raid which lasted for nearly a year and a half was only relatively so ; there were still incidents and lives were lost on both sides.   The statistics which follow, taken from the records of the Mixed Armistice Commissions, compare the casualties suffered by both sides on the Jordan border with those on the Egyptian border, and also the casualties on the Jordan border for 1955 with those for the first nine months of 1956.

CASUALTIES JORDAN-ISRAEL COMPARED WITH CASUALTIES EGYPT-ISRAEL, YEAR 1955

Jordan-Israel Front		Egypt-Israel Front
Israelis killed	8	Israelis killed 47
Israelis wounded	30	Israelis wounded 118
Jordanians killed	18	Egyptians and Arabs killed 216
Jordanians wounded	7	Egyptians and Arabs wounded 188

CASUALTIES JORDAN-ISRAEL FOR 1955 COMPARED WITH THOSE FOR JANUARY–SEPTEMBER INCLUSIVE, 1956

	1955	Jan.–Sept. 1956
Israelis killed	8	19
Israelis wounded	30	33
Jordanians killed	18	78 *
Jordanians wounded	7	39

* Most of the 78 were Jordanian soldiers or police killed in the Israeli retaliatory raids at Rahwa September 11, Gharandal September 13, and Husan September 25.

The Israelis attributed this calm to the severe lessons they had given the Jordanians in the retaliatory raids at Qibya, Nahhalin, and other places.   They claimed that Jordan had found that it did not pay to allow infiltration, with its accompaniment of terror and sabotage within Israel. There may have been something in this contention. However, the determined effort to suppress infiltration stemmed from Glubb Pasha and the British officers who served under him.[11] Glubb has explained the reasons for this policy. It was because Jordan alone could not face war with Israel, and the experience of 1948 had shown that no effective action in her support could be expected from the other Arab states. If marauding and reprisals went on unchecked, the eventual result would be war—as the chain of events on the Egypt-Israel front was to demonstrate during the next two years.

It is also certain that the British Government constantly pressed the Jordan Government to suppress marauding into Israel, because it did not wish again to become involved in operations in Palestine, through Britain's commitments under the Anglo-Jordanian treaty. General Glubb and most of the others in high posts in the Arab Legion were after all British, and their desire to apply the non-infiltration policy in Jordan's interest would be reinforced by the fact that it was also in the United Kingdom's interest.

The United Kingdom's treaty of alliance with the Hashemite Kingdom of Jordan was in effect from 1948 until it was abrogated in 1957, by mutual consent. Under its terms, if either party became involved in war, in spite of efforts to settle the dispute by peaceful means in accordance with the Charter of the United Nations, the other party would immediately come to his aid as a measure of collective defence.

The treaty did not prejudice the rights or obligations of either of the parties, under the Charter of the United Nations. This, in practice, meant that, as war under the Charter is allowed only in self-defence (Article 51), the Anglo-Jordanian alliance would come into operation only if either party were *attacked*. It is a very difficult matter, in the circumstances in which wars tend to break out nowadays, to determine who is the attacker—the aggressor. An intending aggressor always takes care to confuse the issue, so as to escape the censure of world opinion, and possibly more serious consequences.

For very many reasons Britain would not wish to become engaged in a war against Israel, although in October 1956 she did warn her that if she invaded Jordan it would mean war. In 1954 and 1955 the possibility of the treaty's coming into operation happily appeared remote, and it was in Britain's interest to keep it so. The only danger seemed to be that if the retaliatory raids were pressed, Jordan might be provoked into counter-retaliation, and a situation might arise in which the Israelis could make a case before the world that they were the victims of aggression, and in ' self-defence ' would have to resort to hostilities on a larger scale, which would result in the occupation of territory held by Jordan on the West Bank, in Palestine. And there were many Israelis, not only in the extreme Herut Party, who thought that it would be an excellent thing to expand Israel's narrow borders, and remove some of the strategic disadvantages which the close of the fighting in 1948 had left her, improve her communications, and round out her territory.

The repression of infiltration is by no means an easy thing for a Jordanian government to accomplish. The Arab Palestinians who populate the border villages, being filled with hatred of the Israelis, and desirous of revenge for the defeat of 1948, tend to regard anyone as a hero who crosses the demarcation line at great risk, and inflicts hurt on the enemy. So they are inclined to hide and protect the infiltrators—or marauders, as they should more properly be called.

Evidence of the attitude of the Jordan Government in this matter is contained in a letter written by Sir Patrick Coghill to the London *Times* on October 13, 1956. He was head of the Criminal Investigation Department of the Jordan Police for some years before his dismissal on March 1, 1956, along with Glubb Pasha and other senior British officers. He wrote, in part :

> What may not be generally appreciated is the nature of the difficulties with which the Jordan Government has to contend along the frontier. Thanks to the way in which the Armistice Line was drawn, more than 100 Jordanian villages are cut off from their lands. . . . A line so drawn could but invite illegal crossings. . . . All such infiltrators naturally have the tacit sympathy of the rest of the population, which is a severe handicap to the police and other frontier guards in their efforts at prevention. To help them the Jordan Government gave special powers to the civil district commissioners under the defence regulations to deal summarily with infiltrators, many of whom were caught, and received long prison sentences or periods of forced residence in areas remote from the frontier.
>
> Of these infiltrators, some crossed the line to . . . see their relations or smuggle a few pounds of tea or rice, commodities which command a premium in Israel. There were also the smugglers of sheep and cattle . . . a traffic which the Jordan Government did its best to stop.
>
> One more form of infiltration caused the Jordan Government the deepest concern. This was the existence in Damascus of groups financed by Egypt, Saudi-Arabia, or the ex-Mufti, whose rôle was to enlist and train men to carry out sabotage in Israel. Luckily these groups achieved little or no success, partly thanks to the vigilance of the Jordanian authorities and partly because most of the funds so lavishly supplied stuck to the palms of the organizers in Damascus. . . .

B.A.I.—4

Admittedly there were examples of trigger-happy frontier guards. But, given the unceasing tension and the constant provocation of the Israeli forces and armed *kibbutzim*, in fact the Jordanians should be congratulated for their restraint.

Sir Patrick went on to contrast the Israeli record of retaliations with the Jordanian effort to keep the peace.

With the elimination of Glubb Pasha and British senior officers from command, discipline deteriorated, and incidents multiplied, as the statistics quoted above show. At this point a few remarks on the influence which Glubb Pasha exercised and his personality may be appropriate.

Briefly, it can be said that while he held the loyalty of the Arab Legion he was the ultimate source of power in Jordan. The Army is, of course, the final arbiter of politics in Egypt and Syria as well as in Jordan. So Glubb was the power behind the throne in Jordan, and not so far behind as to be hidden. His power was patent, and attested particularly by the way in which he was made the target of attack by nationalists and Communists who wanted to upset the existing régime. But although he was powerful, he was a most loyal servant of the Hashemite sovereigns, and had no personal ambition. His attitude comes out clearly in the articles he wrote for the newspapers immediately following his dismissal, and in his book *A Soldier with the Arabs*. The following, taken from a foreword he wrote for a book by an officer who had served under him, is illustrative :

> King Hussein had himself been touched by the emotional enthusiasm of nationalism. Youth all over the world is filled by ideals for which it longs to fight. . . . I told the King that I was his servant, and not that of the British Government, and that if he wished it, I would resign. But it is difficult for a man past middle age to enjoy the full confidence of a young man of twenty. He had other advisers nearer his own age.
>
> And so the end of my service came in a manner which I regretted. The same result could have been achieved so easily without disturbance or friction. . . .

I first met Glubb Pasha on October 7, 1954, in Amman. The business that came up on that occasion was the return of the Ein Hashofet sheep, and the negotiation of a local commanders' agreement for Jerusalem. I had formed my impression of him from a few fragmentary journalists' articles and photographs, and I expected to see rather a romantic if not swashbuckling type, big and blond and bold.

Instead I was surprised to find a mild, placid man, rather under middle height, his hair thick and grey, and his aspect generally benevolent. He seemed more the administrative type of British officer than the leader of desert patrols. Perhaps this impression was formed from the paraphernalia of his office—the battery of telephones and intercommunication sets on his desk, the trays of files, and the frequent interruptions to our conversations when he spoke in Arabic to some subordinate or colleague.

For the position he occupied, and the power he exercised, his office was certainly not impressive : it was hardly more than twelve feet square, two walls almost covered with maps. On one wall were hung enlarged photographs of King Hussein, his grandfather King Abdullah, and his great-grandfather the Sharif Hussein of Mecca, who was the titular head of the Arab revolt during the First World War.

The window looked out on a narrow, noisy traffic-filled Amman street, descending steeply from the heights surrounding the town. The Arab Legion's general headquarters was at this time in a very cramped and unsuitable building, surrounded by a barbed-wire fence, parked land rovers and other military vehicles, and numerous Arab Legion sentries.

I found it easy to talk to General Glubb. We were both sappers, and had been commissioned within a few months of each other in 1915 (he in the Royal Engineers and I in the Royal Canadian Engineers). He had also been at Chatham about the same time that I was, in 1920, at the School of Military Engineering, following courses giving the technical instruction which the officers commissioned during the war had missed. I had many friends in the Royal Engineers, some of whom he knew, and this broke the ice.

In our first meeting he was cautious, as was natural until he could get to know my approach to the duties of my appointment. When I had come, the view had been expressed in some organs of the Arab Press that as I was replacing General Bennike, who was considered to be pro-Arab and who had been removed through Jewish influence with the United Nations, obviously I, the replacement, could be trusted to favour the Israelis. This notion was strengthened because I had been nominated by Mr L. B. Pearson, the Canadian Secretary of State for External Affairs, who, because of his attitude when leading the Canadian delegation to the United Nations in 1948, at the time the Palestine question was being dealt with, and the State of Israel was being established, was thought to be pro-Israeli. It is hardly necessary to say that I never received any instructions or suggestions from Mr Pearson other than that my task was one which required complete impartiality, and that my duty on taking up the appointment was to the Secretary-General of the United Nations. Mr Hammarskjöld, of course, repeated the adjuration to impartiality, and reminded me of the necessity of behaving always as an international receiving no instructions from any other source than the United Nations, and even avoiding being influenced by the representatives of any particular nation, including my own.

After I had done business with General Glubb for a while, I think he grew to trust me, and gave me confidential information and explanations of difficulties in the way of some of the measures for keeping the border quiet which, we agreed, would be desirable in principle.

When one visited him, one was served the traditional ceremonial coffee made in the Bedouin style (*qahwa saada*) very strong, flavoured with cardamom, a few sips in the little cups, and served by his personal coffee-man, a fierce-looking Bedouin corporal in the uniform of the Desert Patrol, complete with crossed bandoliers and dagger.

As he talked he " fiddled " (to use the expression he himself used in his book *The Arab Legion*) with a *masbaha*, a sort of rosary usually made of amber beads, an aid to Moslem prayer. For this reason, at first I thought he had become a Moslem, but this was not so. Glubb, who did not smoke, had picked up this common habit of the Moslems in the Middle East, just for something to do with his hands when talking. The Americans call these rosaries " worry beads " ! But Glubb never seemed worried.

The abrupt dismissal of Glubb and the senior British officers with the Legion came as a shock to me, as to so many others. One felt that the principal element of stability in the kingdom of Jordan had disappeared. However, as Glubb himself has written since, his departure, and the passing of control of the Legion into Arab hands, was inevitable. He had foreseen that, and, indeed, had offered his resignation to the King, which had not been accepted. The final results of the change of command, and the passing of the Glubb régime at the time it did, have yet to reveal themselves.

I never had a very close relationship with him ; I estimate our meetings averaged less than one a month. Though dismissed with discourtesy, and without recognition of his great services to Jordan and its Hashemite rulers, he went with the respect and admiration of all impartial observers—certainly with mine.

Not long after I took over the duties of Chief of Staff UNTSO, I learned that the Israeli Defence Forces and the Government looked on the United Nations Truce Supervision Organization with a jealous eye, sometimes with imperfectly concealed hostility. It was not until I had been in Palestine for some time that I understood why this was so.

It was early in October 1954 that I first met obstruction to the kind of work which I thought the UNMOs were intended to do. Jerusalem then was still in a state of some tension in the area bordering the no-man's-land, which varied in width from six hundred to a few metres, and extended from the neutral zone surrounding the headquarters of UNTSO, the former Government House on the El Mukabbir hill, for some five kilometres northward.

In the first days of July 1954 there had been a dangerous outbreak of firing between the Israeli-held and the Jordanian-held parts of the Holy City. Beginning with a few rifle-shots, it had increased in volume, with machine-guns and three-inch mortars joining in. No one could determine who had fired the first shot. This went on for three days, sometimes dying down, or being stopped through the efforts of my predecessor, General Bennike, to achieve a cease-fire, and then flaring up again. Eventually an effective cease-fire was established, but not before nine people had been killed and fifty-five wounded, nearly all of them civilians.[12]

I recall that when I arrived in Jerusalem, during the latter half of August, nearly every night a shot or two could be heard from my room in the King David Hotel, facing the Old City wall, across no-man's-land. Complaints were submitted, first by one side, then by the other, but it was never possible to find out who had done the firing.

Commander Hutchison, USNR, then Chairman of the Jordan-Israel MAC, had been sending observers to patrol the sensitive areas, such as the Musrara, Mamillah Road, and Abu Tor quarters. This was partly in the hope that if shooting or stone-throwing did occur, an observer might be on the spot and able to place the blame. Presumably the party whose fault had been detected would take proper disciplinary measures to prevent recurrence. He also hoped that the presence of the UNMOs in their white jeeps would reassure the inhabitants of the front-line areas, who were mostly recent immigrants.

In October the random shots were still to be heard. There had been no serious casualties, but any shot might begin a chain reaction leading to a fire-fight on the scale of that in early July. It was decided to increase the patrolling, and we thought that if observers occupied a number of fixed posts which overlooked the areas where most of the incidents started, perhaps the shooting could be cut down. So half a dozen observation posts were selected, on both sides of the demarcation line, and we began to man them.

Very soon the Israelis began to object. The stated grounds were that the functions of the UNMOs were limited to carrying out such investigations as the Mixed Armistice Commissions directed. The only status they had in the country was given by the General Armistice Agreements. As the Mixed Armistice Commission had not ordered them to investigate anything, they had no business in these danger areas in Jerusalem.

The position of the United Nations, however, was that the UNTSO had more functions than those stipulated in the GAAs. By its resolution of August 11, 1949, the Security Council directed that the UNTSO should continue to exercise supervision over the cease-fire which the Council had ordered in its resolution of July 15, 1948, and which was to remain valid even if the parties to the General Armistice Agreements should seek to abrogate them.

To supervise the cease-fire meant to watch what was going on, not only whether one or both sides were firing, but also whether either side was moving troops, or doing anything else which pointed to possible aggression. Obviously, the Security Council must have intended that the observers would be free to move anywhere in the territory controlled by the two sides in order to see these things, and report them. The Truce Supervision Organization and its observers, in Palestine as in other places where the Security Council has established similar organizations, constitutes the Council's information-gathering organ. Clearly, unless the Council has positive and accurate information of the situation, it cannot issue appropriate orders, under the authority of Article 40 of the Charter, to remove the threat to the peace.

Apart from the general principle, the right of UNMOs to move freely in Jerusalem was supported by one of the provisions of the General Armistice Agreement. This relates to the so-called defensive zones in which the numbers and kinds of troops and armaments allowed are specifically set forth in articles or annexes. The object is to keep the main forces of the two sides sufficiently separated, and to reassure both that they could not be suddenly attacked in force. Jerusalem is in one of these defensive zones.

I maintained that our observers had the right to go anywhere in pursuance of their duties in observation of the cease-fire, and was supported in this stand by UN headquarters. But, in fact, our observers were stopped by Israeli police and military when they tried to enter the sensitive areas near the no-man's-land. It would, of course, have merely invited humiliation for the observers if I had ordered them to push ahead until they were stopped by physical force. The Israelis actually placed sentries, day and night, on the entries to these sensitive areas for a while. Meanwhile I had conferences with Israeli Army representatives to try, by negotiation, to get the UNTSO's right to observe acknowledged, and the restrictions withdrawn. Eventually we arrived at a sort of agreement, which established our right to visit any areas where I thought there was a danger of breach of the cease-fire, provided the Israeli authorities were notified beforehand, so that they could send one of their officers to accompany the observer if they desired. This negotiation took several weeks, and during this period the tension in the Jerusalem area fortunately lessened.

This was the first of several controversies I had with the Israel authorities, arising out of proposals to place the observers of the UNTSO in localities where there had frequently been trouble, so that they would be able to determine who was starting incidents, and by their presence exercise some deterrent and reassuring effect. We proposed later to place observers around the perimeter of the Gaza Strip, and on the shores of the Sea of Galilee, and in each case the Israelis resisted the idea at first, usually giving a reluctant and conditioned consent in the end.

I found it difficult to understand these refusals to allow observers to watch over danger areas. I used to argue that surely the innocent party, which never started the trouble, would be happy to have its blamelessness proclaimed to the world by unbiased witnesses. Conversely, only the party with some aggressive intentions to conceal could object to the presence of neutral observers. These arguments did not have any noticeable effect. The Israelis reiterated their contention that the UNMOs should only observe when they were asked to do so by the MAC. That really meant that the Israelis would have a veto on any observer's activity within Israel.

I gradually became convinced that the real reasons for wishing to restrict the movements of UN observers were not those which were publicly voiced. For one thing, both sides feared that the observers, who could pass freely from the Israeli side to the Arab side, would obtain military information concerning troop dispositions and fortifications, armament, and so forth, and tell the other side about it. Of course, observers were under strict orders not to give military information to one side or the other, and I think that these instructions were nearly always obeyed. I do not claim that there were never cases of information getting from one side to another. Nevertheless, it still remained true that if both sides had been adhering strictly in fact and intention to the armistice agreement, particularly to the restriction in the defensive zones, there would have been practically no intelligence of importance in which the observers could have trafficked. But military intelligence staffs are hyper-suspicious, and it is their ambition to close every possible crevice through which information can leak to the enemy.

Another reason occasionally advanced against allowing free movement of UN observers was that it was an infringement of national sovereignty. The Israelis were particularly vociferous about their sovereignty, which occasionally reminded one of men who are always protesting their virility. Perhaps they had some cause to be anxious about sovereignty, especially in the Jerusalem area. The 1947 resolution for the partition of Palestine into Jewish and Arab states had made Jerusalem and a surrounding enclave an international territory under a special régime. It might have been dangerous to Israeli contentions, at some future period, to acquiesce in UN observers' having too much authority in the Jerusalem area.

Again, it seemed to me that the Israeli leaders, who mostly had begun their active careers by fighting against the British Mandatory Power, in one way or another, had transferred some of their dislike of the authority of the Mandate to the rather exiguous authority of the United Nations. It was sometimes said by extremists that they hadn't got rid of the British to have another parcel of foreigners come into the Land of Israel, and tell them what they could or could not do. The result, at any rate, seemed often to be that the Israelis looked on the UN as an organization to be kept in the dark, and even deceived, as an enemy may be deceived. The result was that one felt hostility against the UNTSO always latent, and that co-operation from the Israelis only came when it suited their propaganda purposes.

The Arabs had, more or less, the same attitudes. Many of those with whom we had to deal had anti-colonial complexes. This was natural enough. Having recently escaped from being dominated by British or French military officers and officials, they were very quick to resent fancied slights to their new independent status by the Westerners who made up the observer corps. They were also suspicious that we sympathized with the Jews rather than the Arabs, as the Jews were more Western in their outlook, and Israeli propaganda was so influential in most Western countries. From time to time the Arabs limited the observers' rights of movement. This was particularly so in the Gaza Strip and the adjacent territory in the Sinai, when the tension built up there in 1955, and the Egyptians had troops and fortifications to conceal.

With such an attitude by both the contestants one would have thought that the umpires would have been pretty unhappy. But, in fact, most of the observers liked the work and life, and tended to renew their engagement after their first term expired. This may be explained by the fact that generally the pay and allowances were better than in most military jobs, rank for rank, and the work not too hard or too continuous—on the whole interesting, and occasionally exciting.   Added to which, Palestine and the Middle East are fascinating places to live in for anyone with a taste for history or archaeology, or religion, or just sunshine.   The Arab and Israeli attitude was more a hostility towards the Organization than towards the individuals who composed it.   Probably, at the head, I felt it more than any of the observers under my control, except perhaps the chairmen of the Mixed Armistice Commissions, who from time to time incurred the displeasure of one side or the other, because of an allegedly unfair decision.   Generally, the observers were able to meet the Israeli and Arab delegates to the MACs on friendly, and sometimes cordial, terms.   I myself was always treated politely, and generally very kindly, and remember much genuine friendliness from individuals on both sides of the demarcation line.

CHAPTER 5

The Israeli Policy of Retaliation

On February 8, 1955, I made a speech to the Rotary Club at Haifa. Its main theme was that retaliation failed to prevent the Arab marauding, and if continued could lead only to war. At that time I felt that the Israel Government was turning away from the retaliation policy. The Gaza raid, twenty days later, showed how mistaken I was. Perhaps the pacific policy had been replaced by the activist in the early months of 1955. At that time Mr Ben-Gurion rejoined the Israeli Cabinet as Minister of Defence. Mr Sharett was Prime Minister, but people soon got the feeling that Mr Ben-Gurion was the policy-maker.

When I presented the arguments against retaliation to the Rotary Club, I was only elaborating on the decisions which the Security Council had rendered on the Israeli retaliatory attacks on Qibya in October 1953 and Nahhalin in March 1954. It is not difficult to tell a group or a government that a certain course of action is wrong. It is much more difficult to determine what they can do instead. It will help the reader to understand the connexion between the successive events which I shall record in the following pages if we examine the apparent reasons for the Israelis' decision to follow a retaliation policy.

The Israeli theory of the necessity for retaliation, so far as I have been able to understand it, is this : The " infiltrator," in nearly every case, was paid by some Arab " higher-up " to go into Israel and steal, or attack the inhabitants. The " poor farmer returning to his former property to pick a few oranges " type of infiltration had ceased a long time before. It was the responsibility of the governments party to the General Armistice Agreements to prevent anyone from the territory under their control from crossing the Armistice Demarcation Lines. If an Arab government failed to do that, the Israelis argued, it was more than just inefficiency and negligence ; it meant that the government concerned condoned and secretly favoured such action against Israel.

It should be understood that these arguments and the resulting attitude were developed long before August 1955, when the Egyptians began to send *fedayeen* into Israel, and publicize their exploits.

The Israelis claimed that it was easy for the Arab governments to find out who was marauding into Israel. The raiders boasted of their deeds in the village coffee-shops. The Oriental habit of gossip allows any reasonably efficient secret-police organization to find out who has committed or been concerned in any serious crime of a political sort. The Arab states all had a numerous and fairly effective secret police. Therefore, if the Arab governments did not find out and punish marauders into Israel, it was because they did not wish to do so, not because they could not. Hence it was necessary to make the Arab governments realize that if they allowed infiltration to go on they would suffer unpleasant consequences.

The Israelis had a very efficient espionage organization. The Arab villagers were poor, often holding grudges against their neighbours ; many of them had relations in Israel. It was easy for them to cross the line in either direction. So the Israelis could enlist agents to keep them informed of what was going on in the border villages of Jordan, and in the Gaza Strip. On several occasions Israeli representatives on the Mixed Armistice Commissions gave the UNTSO the names of persons alleged to have raided into Israel. UNTSO passed these names to the Arab authorities, but, as I recall it, the responses always followed the pattern that the man was unknown, or in prison, or somewhere else where he could not have been implicated.

The evidence which the Israelis obtained through espionage could not, of course, be used in the proceedings of the Mixed Armistice Commissions or the Security Council. They would not risk compromising their espionage system. So, in this dilemma, they used to insist, in the MAC deliberations on infiltration cases, on the responsibility of the Arab governments. The Arab representatives would deny all knowledge of the acts, and, while admitting that the GAA bound them to maintain the regulations forbidding civilians to pass through the lines, which had existed during the 1948–49 hostilities, they pointed out that if raiders were determined to get through it was practically impossible to stop all of them.

In this discussion about infiltration the expressions " Arab governments " or " Arab representatives " refer to the Jordanians and Egyptians. While there was infiltration across the Israel-Lebanese demarcation line it never became really serious, and was usually cleared up without difficulty in informal meetings of the MAC members. There was practically no infiltration across the Israel-Syrian ADL, the troubles there being of another kind.

The Israelis, I believe, were right in their contention that the Arab governments could stop infiltration if they wanted to. It is proven by the fact that from September 1954 until March 1956 there was no serious trouble on this score between Israelis and the Jordanian authorities. This was while Glubb Pasha remained as Jordanian Chief of Staff, and a power in the country. He has set forth in detail the problem as it was then seen, and the measures taken to deal with it, in Chapter 20 of his book *A Soldier with the Arabs*.

But Glubb was ousted, and a major point in the agitation against him was that " he held the Arabs back." His book tells us that the agitators fulminated because the Arab Legion was concentrated in rearward areas to resist an Israeli attack, and not lined up on the borders. This was, of course, perfectly sound from a military viewpoint, but unfortunately vulnerable to political attacks. It also seems quite likely that the policy of repressing marauding, and putting the trouble-makers in jail, which was naturally unpopular among the Palestinians, may have been looked on as another way of " holding the Arabs back "—in the interests of Israel, of course. It meant to the Palestinians a suspension of hostilities against Israel, a state of affairs which would lead towards a peace leaving Israel in possession of the lands from which she had forcibly expelled the Arabs. A policy of severely repressing infiltration could thus be politically dangerous to any Arab government. We shall examine later the application of this fact in the complex of Egypt-Israel conflicts.

While the Israelis may have been convinced that the marauding into their country was organized and paid for by some non-governmental Arab agency or other, and that the Arab governments could stop it if they wanted to, they were far from being able to prove it before the Security Council. If the Security Council had found Egypt and Jordan guilty of culpable negligence in not stopping infiltration, as they were obligated to do by the General Armistice Agreements, and even if there was evidence adduced pointing to their secretly promoting infiltration, what sanctions could the Council have imposed on the Arab governments? If the Three Powers (the United States, Great Britain, and France) [13] had agreed to put forward a resolution providing sanctions against the guilty governments if they allowed infiltration to continue, the U.S.S.R. would doubtless have welcomed the chance to veto it, taking the rôle of the Arabs' champion. They had done something almost exactly similar in vetoing the resolution put forward in March 1954, intended to oblige the Egyptians to permit Israeli traffic through the Suez Canal.

Apart from the probability of a Russian veto, would the Three Powers have been justified in setting in motion the ponderous and uncertain machinery of Security Council sanctions to eliminate the alleged danger to peace? Economic sanctions would have led to grave complications for the Western Powers, as the results of the Suez interventions prove.

For the Israelis, however, the situation was not one to be dealt with as an exercise in international law and diplomacy. The facts were that settlers on the border and other citizens were being killed by Arab marauders. Beginning in the year 1955, UNTSO collected and tabulated a record of casualties suffered by all parties to the General Armistice Agreements. This was given in summary and partial form in the previous chapter. But before 1955 no statistics of this kind were systematically kept by UNTSO or any other independent body. The Israelis claimed, in justification of their invasion of the Sinai in October 1956, that 1237 Israelis had been killed or wounded by Arab marauders since the armistice had been signed.[14] This figure is shocking, but it was not the actual deaths which outraged the Israelis. During the ten years of Israel's statehood, 1720 people were killed and 11,300 seriously injured in road accidents, without arousing more than the sort of verbal condemnation that road tolls do in other countries.[15]

I believe that there was another factor operating in the Israeli reaction to the Arab marauding. That was the essential insecurity of Israel. The Israelis remembered that their state had had its birth in armed conflict. Recognition by other nations and membership in the United Nations were all very well, but it had really been the Jews in Palestine, hoping, enduring, and fighting, who had created the State of Israel. But that state, in its forcible creation, had aroused the implacable hostility of the surrounding Arabs, and as the years passed, the hostility did not lessen. The refugees, ousted from their homeland, and encamped miserably around its borders, were always there as remembrancers. The recurrent raidings were a stinging reminder that the Arabs did not accept the Armistice Demarcation Lines as a basis for a peace settlement, that for them the issues were still unresolved. The war was only suspended, to be resumed later when the Arab states should be militarily stronger and more united. Israelis could only be secure if they could make peace (on Israeli terms) with their Arab neighbours, and those neighbours would not make such a peace. So every incident in which Israelis suffered death or injury from the emissaries of the sullen and hatred-filled Arabs on every side of them reawakened the sense of insecurity in the heart of the average Israeli.

The Israelis always vehemently insisted that a government must protect its citizens. With no effective protection against Arab marauding being given by the United Nations, or to be expected from that quarter, the Israelis felt that taking reprisals was the only means of protection left to them.

The subject of reprisals is one of the most difficult covered by the so-called laws of war. (Oppenheim has some observations very pertinent to the use of reprisals by the Israelis against the Arabs.)[16] Generally speaking, the efficacy of reprisals depends on the power of the party taking them to do more harm to his opponent than the opponent can do to him in return. For example, although in the early days of the Second World War the Allies objected to certain treatment of prisoners of war by the Germans, they decided not to take reprisals since they held far fewer prisoners of war than the Germans did.

We can examine the Israeli reprisal policy from the viewpoints of morality, of efficacy, and of expediency. From the viewpoint of morality, if one agrees that the evidence captured in 1956 proved that Egypt was always behind the marauding from the Gaza Strip, one cannot condemn the Israelis for taking reprisals against it. The Arabs from Egyptian-controlled territory were breaking one of the clauses in the General Armistice Agreement, causing death and destruction, and so if protests could not induce the Arab governments to stop it they must be made to do so by reprisals.

It may occur to some readers, familiar with the history of Palestine before 1948, that the Israelis learned from the British to practise reprisals. As every one knows, the British forces had conducted punitive operations against rebellious Arab villages in Palestine, and for many years before that on the north-west frontier of India and elsewhere. This is doubtless the main source of the Israeli military technique ; but the position of Israel vis-à-vis its Arab neighbours and that of the British Empire vis-à-vis the Mahsuds and Afridis was very different. To *punish,* one must have such power that the culprit cannot return the punishment. The Israelis were trying to punish Arab states that were potentially, though not actually, more powerful than themselves. The Arabs were greater in numbers, had more natural resources, and needed only cohesion and organization, arms, and training to become more powerful militarily. The Israelis were not in the position of the British Empire versus isolated Arab villages, or barbarous tribesmen, but sometimes they behaved and talked as if they were. And, in the end, the British themselves found that reprisals would only keep lawless villages and tribes quiescent for a time. No problem was or could be finally settled by them.

There is a further point, one which the Israelis would probably call " legalistic." In launching reprisals by its armed forces, the Israeli Government was itself breaking the General Armistice

Agreements, and in a way that was extremely glaring. The General Armistice Agreements allow no exception to the clause that forbids hostile acts against the other party. There was no provision that reprisals were justifiable in any circumstances. So, when Israeli troops blow up a police-post, killing and wounding many of the garrison, and the Arabs complained of it to the Security Council, the Council had to condemn the Israelis' action. On the other hand, when the Israelis tried to justify their retaliatory action, they could not prove that the Arab governments had ordered the marauders to perpetrate the outrages in Israel.

I have tried to set out the reasons by which the Israelis justified their reprisal policy, in spite of the Security Council's frequent condemnations. But I shall now quote a much more authoritative exposition of the matter, by General Dayan. Some time in late August 1955 he made a speech to Army officers.

" The aim of battles fought in peacetime is to ensure peace," General Dayan is reported to have said, and he went on that Israel did not seek these battles, but they were necessary to impress on the neighbouring countries that it " did not pay " to allow marauding into Israel. There was no means to prevent the blowing up of water pipes, or the murder of a family in its sleep. " But we can set a high price for our blood." [17] The price must be so high that the Arab governments across the border will feel obliged to take unpopular measures and punish marauders.

So far, General Dayan has given the theory of reprisals as I have set it out above ; but then he went on to give some additional reasons why it was a good policy for Israel in the present circumstances. He said that clashes with Israeli forces had important repercussions among the Arab states, for the outcome of any battle was interpreted as a measure of the country's strength. " If the Egyptians did not declare war after the Gaza clash, or the Jordanians after Nahhalin, it is an indication that they and the other Arab countries were unable to defeat Israel." An act of retaliation by Israel could serve as an encouragement to an Arab government to consider the possiblity of accepting the existence of Israel rather than to lose face continuously by opposing it.

The *Post* further quoted General Dayan as saying that retaliatory actions were punitive actions, not revenge. They were also a warning that if the government concerned did not itself impose discipline on its citizens and prevent their transgressions in Israel, Israeli forces would play havoc across the border.

This statement received much publicity in the Israeli Press, excited expressions of approval, and aroused no protests of which

I am aware. It must also be assumed that if a statement of this character is made by the Chief of Staff of the defence forces of a country, it is made with the knowledge and approval of the Minister to whom he is responsible. In this case the Minister of Defence was Mr Ben-Gurion, who was also Prime Minister designate, then engaged in the formation of a government following the elections of July 1955. No disapproval of General Dayan's address was registered by Mr Ben-Gurion, and it is therefore fair to assume that the statement of retaliatory theory and policy corresponded to the ideas and policy of Mr Ben-Gurion at that time, for, in addition, it was well known that General Dayan was personally devoted to Mr Ben-Gurion, and that between them there was a degree of mutual confidence and identity of outlook far beyond the usual relationship of a Chief of Staff, or head of the armed forces, and his Minister.

Here we see that something has been added to simple reprisal for enforcing adherence to the provisions of the GAA. Dayan calculates that the Arabs, seeing themselves helpless to counter the drastic Israeli military retaliations, would be forced to realize that they must make peace with Israel.

If General Dayan and other Israeli political and military leaders really believed that such a result would come about, they gravely miscalculated, as the history of the next two years shows. The chain of events led, through provocations, reprisals, and attempted counter-reprisals, straight to the acts of war in October 1956. The wrongness of the policy was not that it sought to make the Arabs stop sending marauders into Israel, but that it was a slightly indirect method of using military power to force the Arab states (primarily Egypt) to accept the Israeli terms of peace. That is to say, it was an attempt to settle an international dispute by military force, in complete disregard of Israel's engagements as a member of the United Nations.

But Mr Ben-Gurion could doubtless see quite clearly, in late 1954, during his meditations in the Negev wilderness, that the Arab states were not prepared to make peace unless the right of the refugees to return to Israel was first acknowledged ; and this he ruled out as impossible—as inconsistent with the continued existence of the State of Israel. Did he therefore adopt a policy of trying to force the Egyptians to make peace ? That is something which I must leave to the judgment of the reader. However, I think it will be shown, in the chapters which follow, that all the successful military reprisals failed to check the marauding—in fact, led to worse attacks. And the military success of the Sinai campaign failed to win peace, and has left the situation in the Middle East as dangerous to Israel, and to world peace as it was before.   In other words, whether morally justified or not, the Israeli policy, for which Mr Ben-Gurion must bear the responsibility, was ineffective, and therefore a bad policy.

What other policy would have been possible ?   Could Israel have submitted to the endless goading of the Arab marauders ?   For one thing, retaliation on a lesser scale, and not so patently set-piece military operations, would probably have satisfied the desire of the Israeli public for revenge, and would not have resulted in a worsening of the general situation.   There were a few cases of such private revenges being taken for marauders' crimes which had caused great indignation in the Israeli public.   But, of course, such a policy, while it might not have worsened the general situation and the security of Israel, would not have improved it.   It is hardly profitable, at this time, to try to puzzle out what policy Israel should have decided upon and followed in 1955.   We can only consider what was the outcome of the policies she did adopt.

General Dayan attained celebrity even before the Sinai campaign, and journalists have written a great deal about his career and personality.   There is not any significant fact that I can add.   But it is important for the purposes of this book to indicate the kind of man he is—or the kind of man I think he is—and the influence his personality had on the conflicts between Israel and her neighbours in the period covered by this book.

General Dayan was born in Israel, in the *kibbutz* of Deganiya. I am told he was the first male child to be born in the settlement. When he was a boy his parents moved to the *moshav* of Nahalal in the Emek (Valley of Esdraelon).[18]   When he was about fourteen, he began his career of fighting Arabs, as a member of the defence organization of the settlement.   When he was about twenty-two, he came under the influence of Orde Wingate, then a captain on the British Intelligence staff.   Wingate became a great partisan of the Jews, and began to teach them that attack is the best defence.   If they wanted the Arabs who had been harassing the Jewish settlements to let them alone, they had to teach them that attacks would bring unpleasant reprisals.   So Wingate began training young Jewish settlement guards in night attacks.   According to Leonard Mosley's *Gideon Goes to War*, a popular biography of Wingate, Dayan was one of his first and most apt pupils, and became his principal assistant in this kind of operation.   But Christopher Sykes' later and fuller biography, *Orde Wingate*, only mentions Dayan as having been a member of the special night squads.

B.A.I.—5

The influence of this early conditioning on the thought of Dayan, and no doubt of very many other young Israelis who made up the solid core of " Hagana," the secret Jewish defence organization under the Mandate, certainly shows distinctly in the policies they advocate and the tactics they practise.   Incidentally, the Israeli Army is modelled more on the British Army than any other, which is natural, as many of the senior officers of the Israeli Army served during the Second World War with the British, and learned the British Army organization, administration, and tactics.   But the Israeli infantry is probably more intensively trained, in commando style.   The British Army's spit and polish is conspicuously absent, although on ceremonial occasions the Israelis can put on a smart parade.

Dayan is personally very brave, being famous for having led his troops from in front when a battalion commander during the 1948 war against the Arabs.   Even when Chief of Staff he went along with the troops during the retaliatory raid on the Sharafa police-post, in August 1956, and, according to newspaper accounts, was disciplined by Mr Ben-Gurion for taking unnecessary risks.

With such a man at its head, offensive spirit was rife in the Israeli Army.   The emphasis was on maintaining moral ascendancy over the Arab enemy.   Every act of violence had to be repaid—with heavy interest.   The result, it must be admitted, was that the Israeli Defence Forces were a very fine fighting organization, but one which was always looking for trouble, from the viewpoint of the UNTSO.

One practice which gave rise to many incidents was patrolling parallel to the demarcation line, at a few metres distance from it. The patrols, of the Army or the border police (a paramilitary organization), would proceed along their side of the demarcation line.   Every week or so, or in times of tension every day or so, some nervous or exasperated Arab would fire a shot at them ; the Israelis would return the fire ; and a fire-fight usually developed that went on for hours, might result in casualties, and usually required the intervention of UNTSO to stop—by calling on both sides for a cease-fire at some stipulated time.

I could never see the necessity for this business of patrolling right along the demarcation line.   It is not too unkind to call it trailing the coat, especially if there were tension in the area due to preceding incidents.   I frequently asked the Israeli authorities, especially Dayan, to carry out their patrols farther away from the demarcation line.   The answer was that the Army had to protect the farmers who might be working their land right up to the DL.   I suggested that even from the viewpoint of tactics it would be better to cover the farmers by fire from points in the rear.   The answer was that if the Arabs once thought they could make the Israeli forces stay away from the DL they would get bolder and become more aggressive. The Israelis also made the point that they were quite within their rights, under the GAA, to move their troops anywhere they wanted, right up to the DL, and the Arabs were breaking the agreement when they fired on them. This was true, but I used to argue in turn that it was not always advisable to insist on one's rights to the limit. In delicate international situations, hostilities are usually brought on by a show of force close to the frontier ; and nations who do not want trouble keep their troops out of situations which cause apprehension to their neighbours, or provoke those neighbours to begin hostile actions.

Besides sending routine patrols along the demarcation line, the Israelis from time to time carried out military exercises with forces a company or more in strength, advancing towards the demarcation line. On more than one occasion the Arab Legion thought an attack was being mounted upon them, and opened fire, which was, of course, returned, with casualties to both sides. When I protested against the practice of conducting manœuvres in such explosive areas, I was told : " Where its [Israel's] sovereignty over territory is beyond dispute or cavil it is the best judge as to what measures are necessary within its own lines to train its forces for the fullest and most adequate defence of the country." [19] In other words, the Israeli Army was going to do exactly what it liked, and it was of no importance that the Jordanians and UNTSO thought such actions unnecessarily provoked incidents.

I have mentioned General Dayan's close relationship with Mr Ben-Gurion. It was perfectly clear, when one saw the two men together in conferences, that Ben-Gurion was the boss, and that Dayan was happy to have it so. But one wondered whether in their private conclaves Dayan's aggressiveness may not have turned Ben-Gurion, who is not exactly a dove of peace himself, towards more violent and warlike solutions. At any rate, one can surmise that Dayan's influence with him, which was bound to be considerable, was usually exercised in the direction of solution by force.

Mr Ben-Gurion after November 1955 was Minister of Defence as well as Prime Minister, and occasionally acted as Minister of Foreign Affairs in the absence of Mr Sharett or, later, of Mrs Meir. Sometimes, it appeared, he used to constitute himself a majority of the Cabinet, and take important decisions in the sphere of defence on his own responsibility.

It should be said that the officers of the Israeli Army do not take a direct part in politics, as the officers of the armies of its Arab neighbours do. They sometimes mention that they belong to this of that political party, and the parties appear to angle for the Army's support in questions of foreign policy and defence. To date there has been no sign that the Israeli officer corps departs from the British or American practice of holding themselves aloof from political activity. Israeli politicians from time to time claim, and I think justly, that the military are strictly subject to civilian control, as in Anglo-Saxon democracies.

The Israeli Defence Forces are constantly mentioned as one of the great educative and integrating forces in the country, to unify the immigrants of diverse origins in the nation. Every able-bodied young man and most young women must serve in the Defence Forces for two years. This period of service might nominally be reduced if the conscripts agreed to settle in a border village. This was only national service in another guise, as all border villages in sensitive zones were organized in military fashion for defence. It would be difficult to say whether the young men and women living in these villages were farmers serving part-time as soldiers, or soldiers serving part-time as farmers.

It is not unreasonable to deduce that a society whose young elements have passed their most formative years in an atmosphere in which the military virtues and especially aggressiveness are given the highest values, and where the Arab is always the enemy, to be made to submit to Israel's demands by ruthless force, will grow increasingly militaristic and less inclined to the solving by negotiation of external problems. The *sabra*, or the Israeli who has come to the country as a young child, shut in as he is on all his borders by hostility, and precluded from travel abroad by lack of money, does not know much of the world beyond the bounds of Israel and does not at all care about its opinion.[20] And so, born of the successes of the campaigns of 1948 and 1956, there is a certain arrogance, an inability to see that Israel should yield anything for peace, an inability to compromise. Such an attitude in what will soon be the majority of the population does not promise a peaceful solution of Israel's problems, or a peaceful future for the Middle East.

CHAPTER 6

The Gaza Strip: April–August 1955

Map 3

THIS book began with a description of a reprisal raid in the Gaza Strip ; the narrative will end with the United Nations Emergency Force established there ; and the name of Gaza, more frequently than any other, will appear throughout. The ancient city was a focus of strife.

The Gaza Strip is the remnant of the Palestinian territory in the south-west allotted to the Arabs under the 1947 partition plan, which the Egyptian Army still occupied at the end of hostilities in December 1948. It runs from north-east to south-west, one boundary being the Mediterranean Sea and the other being a line drawn at three kilometres' distance from the main El Arish-Gaza-Jaffa road. This road, incidentally, follows generally the route of the Darb El Sultan—the Road of the Kings—along which, since recorded history began, armies from Egypt have trudged north towards Syria, and invading armies from West Asia have marched south, according to the ancient cycles of power.

The Strip is about forty kilometres long, and averages eight and a quarter kilometres in width ; thus it contains about 330 square kilometres. Only two-thirds of this area is more or less arable ; the rest is sand-dunes spreading inland from the coast for varying distances. There are about 310,000 Arabs resident in the Strip, 210,000 of them refugees from the southern parts of Palestine now occupied by Israel. Thus there are 1500 persons to the square kilometre of arable soil—about 3900 to the square mile. There is water enough from deep wells for usual domestic needs, and some irrigation. The available fertile soil is intensively cultivated, with crops of wheat, barley, and millet ; tomatoes, onions, and okra ; oranges, plums, grapes, and melons. But, of course, it is impossible for the food thus produced to feed more than a fraction of the population. The 210,000 refugees are fed by the United Nations Relief and Works Agency. The standard ration provides 1600 calories a day, mostly carbohydrates. By Western standards 1600 calories is a reducing diet. The cost of maintaining the refugees is about $27.00 *per capita* per annum.

They live in little huts of mud and concrete blocks, corrugated-iron roofs, regimented row after row. Fairly adequate medical service is provided, probably better than they enjoyed before they were expelled from their native villages. It is especially good in the maternity and child-care clinics, with the result that the infant death-rate is low. Children swarm everywhere. There are primary schools for nearly all of them—little girls in cotton dresses with fine black and white stripes, little boys in khaki shirts and shorts. There are secondary schools for a good proportion of the adolescents ; and a great number of youths can always be seen, around examination times, strolling along the roads memorizing their lessons : where else could they concentrate to study ? And what will all these youths and girls do when they have finished their secondary school training ? There is no employment for them in the Strip, and very few can leave it to work elsewhere.

Besides the 210,000 refugees there are about 30,000 inhabitants who can earn a living from farming or the small trades and merchandising of the area ; the balance of the 310,000, not refugees by UNRWA definition, are poverty-stricken, and are supported by a dole from the Egyptian Government. One does not see people starving or dying of disease in the streets ; nevertheless the Gaza Strip resembles a vast concentration camp, shut off by the sea, the border between Palestine and the Sinai near Rafah, which the Egyptians will not permit them to cross, and the Armistice Demarcation Line which they cross in peril of being shot by Israelis or imprisoned by the Egyptians. They can look to the east and see wide fields, once Arab land, cultivated extensively by a few Israelis, with a chain of *kibbutzim* guarding the heights or the areas beyond. It is not surprising that they look with hatred on those who have dispossessed them.

The Security Council, on March 28, towards the conclusion of its hearings on the February 28 Gaza raid, passed a resolution which noted that in my report on the incident and the causes of tension between Egypt and Israel on the demarcation line around the Gaza Strip, I had suggested certain measures which should help to preserve security and observance of the GAA. The Council called upon the governments of Egypt and Israel to co-operate with me in putting such proposals into effect, in order to reduce infiltration and the consequent disturbances to a minimum.

These proposals had first been advanced in the report I made on November 11, 1954, on the situation round the Gaza Strip. For some weeks prior to that report there had been a good deal in the Israeli Press to the effect that the infiltration and resultant crimes were getting worse, and that if they continued Israel could not remain passive. In other words the Press threatened retaliation if infiltration were not stopped. My report listed Israeli and Egyptian complaints for several months previous, and the decisions in the MAC. The facts did not indicate that the frequency and severity of the incidents really amounted to a critical situation. However, on the advice of officers of UNTSO who had considerable experience in the area, I suggested that the parties should agree on the following measures :

(a) Joint patrols along sensitive portions of the demarcation line ;
(b) A local commanders' agreement ;
(c) A barbed-wire obstacle along certain portions of the demarcation line ;
(d) Outposts and patrols to be manned by regular Egyptian and Israeli troops only.

The purpose of the first of these measures was obvious. If Egyptians and Israelis were patrolling together along the ADL the patrols would not be fired on from either side, nor would mines be placed in their tracks. Both kinds of incidents had been occurring, and were usually pretty serious. The joint patrols would have the secondary effect of showing that both sides were resolved to prevent crossing of the ADL by unauthorized persons—infiltration. Joint patrolling had, in fact, been practised for a while in the early years of the armistice. Later, the Egyptians had withdrawn. I was told by Lieutenant-Colonel Gohar, Director of Palestine Affairs in the Egyptian Ministry of War, that this was mainly because the Israelis had made propaganda use of the arrangement, in particular had circulated photographs of the joint patrols showing Israelis and Egyptians together, and implying that they would soon be on the road to peace negotiations.[21]

Local commanders' agreements had been in operation between Israel and Jordan at one time, but had lapsed when Israel withdrew from the MAC in late 1953. In the autumn of 1954 I had been trying to get a local commanders' agreement for the Jerusalem area. It was signed, after a lot of wrangling over what seemed trifling issues, in April 1955. The idea behind the agreements was that they would permit unimportant incidents of infiltration, exchange of prisoners who had committed no crime except the technical offence of infiltration, exchange of cattle that had been impounded, and so forth, to be handled by the local commanders of each side meeting together, instead of invoking the rather ponderous and time-consuming MAC procedure. Both sides, Jordan and Israel, were in favour of this type of arrangement, but their ideas of its purpose and operation were somewhat different.

Glubb Pasha saw the arrangement working on the level of the local police inspectors. The prevention of infiltration to which the Jordan Government was committed was for him essentially a police function. It happened, sometimes, that the police officer on the Jordan side and the police officer on the Israeli side had been colleagues under the British Mandate. In the Jenin area this had been so, and troubles in this area had been settled very quickly when the arrangement had been in force.

General Dayan, on the other hand, wanted an arrangement under which commanders of fairly high rank—for example, brigade commanders—should deal with one another. At the end of the hostilities between Israel and Jordan, General Dayan, then a lieutenant-colonel, had been in command in the Jerusalem area. He had established good relations with Lieutenant-Colonel Abdullah El Tell, who commanded the Arab Legion there. The two got along quite well, and the circumstances remained impressed on Dayan's mind. It seemed that he felt that if fairly senior Israeli and Arab officers could only get together and talk, without the presence and interference of the United Nations representatives, they would usually manage to agree. The only trouble with this idea was that the Arabs, one and all, wanted none of it.

The idea of a local commanders' agreement appealed to me as a practical means of settling minor incidents, without the legal, formalistic procedure of the MAC, where, as I have said, the representatives of the two sides wrangled with each other, apparently more with the intention of scoring points in the propaganda war than of taking measures to prevent recurrence of disturbances. I thought that if it could work between Jordan and Israel, then it could also work between Egypt and Israel.

The suggestion to erect a barbed-wire obstacle is obvious, if one assumes that both sides really want to stop infiltration. Of course, such a fence by itself would be of no use. Unless it were patrolled and watched constantly, it would quickly be removed by the local inhabitants, among whom there is seemingly an inexhaustible demand for barbed wire and iron stakes.

The last provision, that all outposts and patrols on both sides should be manned by regular troops, was put in because the reserves, militia, national guard, or whatever they happened to be called, were in the nature of things less disciplined than regular troops. So they could not be relied upon to observe strictly the orders against firing across the ADL, which both sides said were in force. Further, these non-regular troops were usually resident in the vicinity and often bore grudges against the other side, perhaps because of casualties in a recent incident. They were hence more likely to take a shot at the hated enemy, if they saw a good chance of doing so without being detected by a superior officer.

I had been discussing these proposals with both sides since the previous November, but had made little progress. The Israelis didn't like the joint-patrol idea ; the Egyptians didn't like a fence along the ADL. Both gave a lukewarm assent to the proposals to negotiate a local commanders' agreement, and to have only regular troops in the front lines.

Besides the incidents which happened from time to time on the Gaza border, two other affairs exacerbated Egypt-Israel relations between November 1954 and February 1955. One was the attempt to pass the *Bat Galim*, a vessel under the Israel flag, through the Suez Canal in defiance of the Egyptian blockade. The other was the trial of a number of Jews in Egypt for espionage and sabotage, and the subsequent execution of some of them.

The *Bat Galim* incident resulted in lengthy MAC proceedings. The Egyptians complained that the crew of the ship had fired on an Egyptian fishing-boat and killed the crew, while waiting to enter the Canal near Suez. The Egyptians, by this quick manœuvre, diverted attention from the issue the Israelis wanted to raise—*i.e.*, the prevention of the Israeli ship from using the Canal, contrary to a decision of the Security Council of September 1, 1951, which called upon Egypt to terminate restrictions on the passage of international commercial shipping and goods through the Suez Canal wherever bound. After a legalistic argument in the MAC lasting several weeks, Egypt dropped her complaint, and the crew of the ship was repatriated. The Israelis were also offered the cargo—in lorries at the demarcation line at Kilo 95, which they did not accept. The Egyptians, however, maintained their refusal to let the ship through. The Israelis could take it to Israel *via* the Red Sea and the Cape of Good Hope, but not through the Suez Canal. The Egyptians later propounded a legal argument justifying their prohibiting ships carrying the Israeli flag from passing the Canal. It was that, in spite of the armistice, a state of war still subsisted between Egypt and Israel, and that the Convention of Istanbul which controlled the status of the Suez Canal gave Egypt the right to take measures to prevent damage to the Canal or shipping in it. Presumably the rest of the argument was that if Israeli ships were allowed through the Canal, they might, in pursuit of strategic or political aims, blow up or sink a ship in the Canal thus blocking it. But the real reason, of course, was that the embargo on Israeli shipping through the Canal was a supplement to the general economic blockade of Israel by the neighbouring Arab states, whose other parts were the boycott of Israeli goods, blacklisting of shipping calling at Israeli ports, and of firms which maintained important commercial or industrial relations with Israel. Egypt could not give up this blockade without losing face among the other Arab states which she aspired to lead. It meant giving up a weapon, or means of pressure, for achieving the Arab aims in the continuing cold war with Israel.

The subject had come up in the Security Council again in March 1954 following a complaint of Israel that Egypt had put restrictions on the passage through the Canal of ships trading with Israel, and had interfered with ships going to Eilat, in the Gulf of Aqaba. New Zealand had put forward a resolution which recalled the earlier one of September 1, 1951, and called upon Egypt to comply with it. The resolution was vetoed by the U.S.S.R., Mr Vyshinski stating, with patent cynicism, that as the previous resolution had not been complied with, it was of no use passing another in the same sense. The U.S.S.R. had voted for the previous resolution, and, of course, his veto was imposed as a favour to the Arabs, to establish the U.S.S.R. as their friend and protector of their interests.

The Israelis were very frustrated as a result of the *Bat Galim* fiasco. The whole issue of Egypt's blocking Israeli shipping in the Canal was brought out into the open again. The timing of this attempt got the Israelis little sympathy from the Three Powers (U.S., U.K., France), as it coincided with attempts to get Egypt to join a Middle East defence pact, which probably would have been unsuccessful anyway, but certainly were not helped by Israel's renewed activity.

The spy trial was a simpler matter, but provoked more emotion in Israel. A number of Jews resident in Egypt were accused of espionage and sabotage activities and, among other crimes, of perpetrating a bomb outrage in a cinema. After the trial, which was followed closely in the Israeli Press, a number of the defendants were found guilty. About this point, Mr Sharett, who had been in communication with Prime Minister Nasser through an intermediary, was led to believe that Nasser promised that the death penalty would not be imposed on any of those found guilty. Nevertheless, some of them were executed. The reaction in Israel was bitter. Nasser afterwards let it be known that he had been reluctant to confirm the death sentences, knowing the probable effect in Israel, but that he could not avoid doing so. A short time before some agents of the Moslem Brotherhood had been convicted of similar acts and had been executed. It would have been politically disastrous for Nasser to seem to be more lenient towards Jewish than towards Moslem terrorists.

Rumours were current that the activities of these Jews had been authorized by the head of the Israeli intelligence service. It was said that a dangerous division in the Israeli Cabinet arose because of the affair, and that Mr Ben-Gurion had to be brought in to take the place of Mr Pinchas Lavon as Minister of Defence.

When I returned from New York after the Security Council meetings on the Gaza raid incident, I found that the situation on the Gaza border was bad, and I reported to the Council about it. Since the February 28 raid there had been firings across the ADL, both Israeli and Egyptian, nearly every day, numerous crossings by parties of armed men, and seven minings of Israeli command cars patrolling along the ADL. In several of the incidents when Israeli patrols had been fired on, they used armoured vehicles and the fire of medium mortars to extricate them. The incidents thus tended to increase in seriousness.

I said, in this report, that I thought most of the incidents were a consequence of the tension in the garrison of the Strip and of its population following the raid. The Israeli detachments which had been mined or fired upon were patrolling immediately next to the demarcation line, and were extremely vulnerable. Egyptian or Arab soldiers, or civilians with arms, might have fired in revenge, or because they really feared that the Israelis were advancing to attack. Unless Egypt repressed the firing and mining firmly, and the Israelis also stopped patrolling in an unnecessarily provocative manner, the situation would get worse. I had appealed to both parties in this sense on April 7, and followed it up by seeing General Dayan on the 11th, and Major-General Ahmed Salem, who was commanding the troops in the Strip from a headquarters in El Arish, on the 14th. I pressed them to start negotiations regarding the measures which I had recommended in my report of March 17, and which had been endorsed by the Security Council. I also urged them in the meantime to issue such orders as would put a stop to the incidents.

The Egyptians had requested that UNMOs be placed in positions on the Egyptian side of the ADL, so that they would be able to see who was really starting the incidents. This seemed to me an indication that the Egyptians at the top did not want trouble ; but the difficulty seemed to be that the Egyptians lower in the military scale, or the Palestinians who now were holding part of the line, did not respect those wishes, and, as I have said, would take a shot at an Israeli if they thought they could get away with it.

The sequence of events following the Gaza raid showed that the Israelis were sadly mistaken if they believed that the Egyptians and Palestinians would be cowed by it into repressing against infiltration. On the contrary, the result had been the mining of Israeli patrol vehicles. There had been very few instances of this kind of hostile act before. If the Israelis thought that the programme that seemed to have succeeded with the Jordanians would be equally successful with the Egyptians, they ignored essential differences in the two cases. Britain had been able to cause Jordan to control infiltration, because British subsidies sustained the Arab Legion and the country ; and there were British officers in charge to see that proclaimed policies were actually carried out. But with the Egyptians, there was no tutelary power to hold them back. It is true that British troops were still in the Canal Zone, but they exercised no control over the Egyptian Army elsewhere, and diplomatic advice alone was ineffective.

The Israelis had given a stinging slap in the face to the Egyptian Army, still sore from its defeats in 1948 ; and the men who were Egypt's Government, the Revolutionary Command Council, were all Army or Air Force officers. They could not allow this insult to pass without any counteraction, still less take unpopular measures to comply with Israeli demands. Prime Minister Nasser, and the cooler heads among his colleagues, knew that the Egyptian Army was not really ready to challenge the Israelis in open warfare. But the prestige of the Egyptian Government, and the emotions of the men comprising it, were peculiarly bound up with the prestige of the Egyptian Army. While they could think of no safe plan of action which would enable their army to win successes which would offset those of the Israelis, they were not going to submit tamely to doing what the Israelis wanted. Especially, they wanted to avoid even the appearance of being coerced into peace negotiations.

About mid-April the Israelis put forward proposals for a conference at a " high level " between themselves and the Egyptians, to discuss the means of improving security in the Gaza Strip area. Mr Walter Eytan, of the Ministry of Foreign Affairs, would be Israel's representative, if the Egyptians would appoint some one of equivalent status.[22] At the time this idea struck me as a good one. I assumed that the subjects discussed would generally be those covered in my recommendations to the Security Council. I had seen enough of the wranglings between Lieutenant-Colonel Shalev on the Israeli side and Lieutenant-Colonel Gohar on the Egyptian side to make me feel that little, if any, progress would be made in a conference to which they were the principal delegates. The suggestion for a high-level conference was therefore passed to the Secretary-General, Mr Hammarskjöld, who left it

to me whether it should be pursued or not, but would back me up
if I decided in favour of it.   The Israelis asked the United States
to support the idea and Mr Henry Byroade, the U.S. Ambassador
in Cairo, then talked to Dr Mahmoud Fawzi, the Foreign Minister,
about it.   Dr Fawzi did not appear enthusiastic, but left the door
open.   However, he and Prime Minister Nasser were going off to
the Afro-Asian Congress at Bandung.   Their absence for about a
month delayed decision in this, as in other matters relating to the
situation around the Strip.

The Egyptians wanted to know what the agenda of the high-level
meeting would be.   Mr Eytan produced a very vague formula.
The Egyptians were apparently confirmed in their suspicion that
the Israelis wanted to get them at the same table, and then
gradually turn the conversations into discussion of terms for a
general peace.   The Israelis, by the way, had a fixed idea that if
they could get the Egyptians, or any of the Arabs, to " sit down
with them " they could win them to a complaisant—that is to say,
peacemaking—attitude.   I do not know what grounds the Israelis
had for this confidence in their own charm and persuasiveness at
the conference table.

I met the Egyptian suspicions in acute form when I began to
talk the high-level idea over with Lieutenant-Colonel Gohar.   He
did not see why negotiation by anyone at a higher level than
himself was needed.   The subjects I had proposed should be
discussed were such that only a person who was thoroughly familiar
with Palestine and armistice affairs would know the background.
He would have to be the chief adviser at the senior delegate's
elbow, in any case.   So why put up a major-general or high
Foreign Office official as a stooge ?

In the end, Gohar's point of view prevailed, and there was no
high-level conference.   Some of the Egyptian papers represented
the episode as the skilful avoidance by the Egyptians of a determined
attempt to trap them into peace negotiations.   Gohar, a year or
so later, remarked to me that " The man in the café, in Egypt,
from reading the newspapers, could have thought in the summer of
1955 that we were engaged in negotiating peace at Kilo 95.   But
fortunately the man in the café in Egypt does not believe what he
reads in the newspapers."   This is a comforting reflection, as
regards the intelligence of the Egyptian public, but perhaps it also
explains some of the difficulties that attended the negotiations.

My attempts to get the parties to sit down together and agree
to something to remedy the conditions which were causing frequent
incidents on the border dragged on.   The fact is, neither side was
anxious for such negotiations.   The Israelis did not want them,

unless they could have them on the high level that might be represented as leading in the direction of a peace on their terms —otherwise they would prefer to continue to apply retaliations and the threat of force. The Egyptians did not care for some of the proposals, and wanted to avoid compromising themselves with the Israelis, in the eyes of the other Arab states. But neither party wished to seem to flout the Security Council recommendation, which both had agreed to—that is, to co-operate with me in finding practical measures to decrease the tension along the demarcation line.

On May 30 a most serious incident occurred. It began by an Israeli jeep's being fired on from an Egyptian post near Kilo 95. The Israelis returned fire to extricate it, and then small-arms and mortar fire extended along quite a length of the border. The casualties were fairly severe : one soldier killed and four wounded on the Egyptian side, one soldier and one civilian killed and four soldiers and four civilians wounded on the Israeli side. The border defensive *kibbutzim* of Ein Hashelosha, Kissufim, and Nirim had been mortared. It happened that on this occasion some UNMOs had been in a position to see who had begun the shooting, and they were sure it was the Egyptians.

I met the U.S. Ambassador, Mr Lawson, the British Ambassador, Sir John Nicholls, and the French Ambassador, M. Pierre Gilbert, at an official party for U Nu, the Burmese Prime Minister, who was visiting Israel. I tried to impress on them the danger which could arise from the Egyptian lack of control over their troops in the Gaza area. The three countries which they represented in Israel might find themselves under the necessity of implementing their pledges under the Three Power Declaration.[23]

All the parties to the armistice agreements had well learned the lesson that a Security Council decision or condemnation by itself was of little practical importance. To get them to do anything which could make for more peaceful conditions—or to refrain from upsetting them—there had to be diplomatic pressure, or at least persuasion, in addition to the arguments and pleas of the UN heads at New York, and myself in the theatre. The British, as I have said, could do a good deal to control the Jordanians ; the Israelis had to listen to, if not to do, what the American State Department said ; and in Cairo and Damascus all three embassies had more or less influence. This, it is to be remembered, was in early 1955, before the Czech arms deal had been made by Nasser, and a fundamental change in the diplomatic balance of power had been effected.

On the 31st Mr Eytan asked me to see him at the Ministry of

Foreign Affairs, where he told me that Israel was taking a most serious view of the May 30 incident. He read out a statement Mr Sharett had recently made to a *Newsweek* reporter, to the effect that Egypt had forfeited her right to control the Gaza Strip, through her failure to implement the armistice agreement. Mr Eytan suggested that I should fly to Egypt, and impress the danger of the present situation on Prime Minister Nasser. Although Eytan conveyed this proposition politely, and his manner was personally friendly, as usual, it constituted to my mind a definite threat that Israel would use armed force if the incidents on the Gaza border were not stopped.

I flew to Cairo, picking up the Chairman of the Egypt-Israel Mixed Armistice Commission, Chef de Bataillon François Giacco-maggi, together with the senior Egyptian delegate in Gaza. Giacco-maggi told me that he was sure the Egyptian officers on the ground in Gaza were sending inaccurate reports to their H.Q. in Cairo, and that consequently Prime Minister Nasser was being misinformed on what was happening on the Gaza border.

It turned out that this was so. I had an hour and a quarter's interview with Prime Minister Nasser and Dr Fawzi, and found that the Prime Minister had a factually incorrect report of how the incident of May 30 had started. I told what my observers had seen and reported, and I think convinced Nasser that he had been getting falsified reports. He knew from his own military experience how reports of events in combat are distorted as they pass up the echelon of command—even when the officers originally reporting are not trying to conceal anything.

I also told the Prime Minister of the dangerous mood the Israelis seemed to be in. I said the numerous incidents of mining and opening fire by troops on the Egyptian side did not conform with what he had told me of Egypt's desire to keep things peaceful in the Gaza area at my first interview with him the previous November. I suggested several practical measures to get better control : the removal of unreliable elements among the locally recruited troops and civil population ; the marking of the demarcation line with barrels, so it could be seen from a distance ; having more officers on duty in the outposts ; more co-operation with the UNMOs.

In reply the Prime Minister said that the trouble was the tension in Gaza since the February 28 raid. He could no longer rely on the good intentions of the Israelis ; the troops had to look to their own protection. He finally said that it was his experience that if hostile troops were close enough together to see each other there would always be incidents of firing. It was inherent in the soldier's psychology. He proposed that each side should withdraw its posts and patrols one kilometre from the demarcation line. He was ready to put this measure into effect. But he could not issue drastic orders imposing a strictly passive attitude on the troops in the Gaza Strip. Such orders to men who had been shocked by the Gaza raid would destroy their morale.

I was unable to obtain any further verbal commitment from him, though he was very pleasant throughout. But, in fact, things took a better turn from this time on—for the next three months. Some firmer orders to the local Egyptian command must have been issued. There were no serious incidents, and we began arranging for the discussions of the measures I had proposed to reduce tension. Egypt finally decided that she would send no one to the talks on a higher level other than Lieutenant-Colonel Gohar. The Israeli representative was Mr Yosef Tekoah, the Director of Armistice Affairs in the Ministry of Foreign Affairs.

It would be tedious to describe the course of the meetings which went on sporadically over the next two months. There were long wrangles over the agenda. Egypt insisted on the joint-patrol proposals being discussed first. Apparently it was calculated that as the Israelis objected to this proposal, they would reject it, and thus give Egypt an excuse for rejecting the proposal for an obstacle along the ADL. It gradually became apparent to me that the fence idea was resisted by Egypt because of its effect on the refugees. A fence along the ADL would seem to make it more of a permanent boundary, and not merely the line on the ground separating the combatants when they ceased fire. Clauses in the GAAs gave it precisely this status, and said it was without prejudice to territorial claims either side might advance in the eventual peace negotiations, which alone could fix permanent boundaries. The refugees in the Strip would consider that if Egypt acquiesced in the erection of a fence it would amount to accepting the ADL as a final boundary, and hence to abandoning their cause. And, of course, other Arab states might feel the same.

A lot of time was taken up discussing the local commanders' agreement, or, as its title became after successive amendments by Gohar, the "Arrangements for Security on the Gaza Demarcation Line." One of the most controversial points was whether there should or should not be a direct telephone-line between the Egyptian commander and the Israeli local commander. The Egyptian side fought this, and the Israelis equally pressed it.

The Israelis seemed to be anxious to include in the agreement provisions which would allow the local commanders of the two sides to meet, without the presence of anyone from the United Nations Organization. This effort to arrange "direct negotiations," even in less important matters, seemed to have become a policy the Israelis pursued with a great deal of pertinacity. The Egyptians, and the Jordanians too, resisted it, and always wanted to have an UNMO present, even at the local meetings of quite junior officers. My position, at first, was that it would usually be better for the two parties to settle minor differences between themselves, without the intervention of the UNMO as a kind of umpire. Later, after I had had some experience of the apparent determination of the Israelis to eliminate the UNTSO from the negotiation machinery, I took the attitude that if the Arab side wanted UNMOs present at any kind of meetings, then we were ready to meet their wishes, and said that I failed to understand why the Israelis were so anxious to get UNTSO out of the way.

The Egyptian objection to having a direct telephone-line between their local commander and the Israeli was also difficult for me to understand. The most important function of the local commanders would be to arrange cease-fires, if shooting was going on anywhere along the demarcation line. For this they obviously needed to be able to communicate with each other by the quickest means. The only reasons I could get Gohar to give me, privately, were that they were afraid that if a line existed the Israelis would use it to extract information in their devilishly clever way. Some simple Egyptian sergeant would be seduced into gossiping by some honey-voiced Israeli girl soldier, for example.

This did not seem a sufficient reason to me. Usually, in the Middle East, the more or less plausible reason given publicly for doing or not doing anything in the field of armistice relations tended to be different from the real reason.

We ploughed away at our agenda during the hot summer days in the little corrugated-iron meeting hut at Kilo 95. This was where the ADL intersected one of the roads which led to Gaza from Jerusalem, at the ninety-fifth kilo from the capital. The MAC had formed the habit of meeting there, especially for emergency meetings, although El Auja was specified as the regular MAC meeting-place. However, somewhere on the border of the Gaza Strip was more convenient for both parties, and for the UNMOs. The first MAC meetings were in a tent, and later the Egyptians erected a small corrugated-iron shelter, which was destroyed by the Israelis when they occupied the Strip in 1956.

Sometimes we seemed to be making progress towards an agreement both sides would accept. But on the whole the experience was very frustrating to hopes that the parties would, if the atmosphere could be calmed for a while, work out practical measures to minimize infiltration and other incidents, and prevent outbreaks of

B.A.I.—6

hostilities, small-arms fire, and mortaring, and even crossing of the line by armed forces, which, though relatively unimportant up to then, could easily develop into something much more serious.

During this period my work included business in regard to the other three armistice agreements. Although these fronts were relatively quiet, and the serious threat was between Israel and Egypt, yet there were points at issue which required me to go periodically to Damascus, Amman, and Beirut. This interfered at times with the negotiations about the Gaza Strip security.

Israel had been having an election campaign during most of this period ; the elections actually took place on July 20, and the result was that, as usually happened under the system of proportional representation in force in the country, no party had a clear majority. Mapai, of which Mr Ben-Gurion was the leader, had the most seats in the new Knesset, and would have to be the dominant partner in the coalition that would eventually be formed. It was also understood that Mr Ben-Gurion would be Prime Minister in the new Cabinet. Meanwhile, as was the custom, the previous Cabinet, headed by Mr Sharett, who would have a place in the new Cabinet anyway, carried on. The negotiations in forming the new Government were protracted, difficult, and complex, and the Government was finally constituted only in November, delay having been caused by Mr Ben-Gurion's illness.

During the political campaign, naturally a good many promises were made by the embattled politicians. Two of those made by Mr Ben-Gurion have a particular bearing on the course of relations between Israel and the Arab states. At Beersheba, on July 9, he was quoted as promising to " bring water and youth from the north to the Negev." The water he meant, of course, was primarily the water from the Jordan, an undertaking which had aroused vigorous Arab opposition. He also promised to assure the freedom of passage from Eilat to Asia and Africa. Egypt was preventing navigation to the Eilat port by the fortifications she had erected at Ras Nasrani, overlooking the Tiran Strait, at the entrance to the Gulf of Aqaba. Mr Sharett on the same day was even more explicit. He was reported as warning that Israel would assure by force the freedom of the sea approach to Eilat " should our enemies fail to respond to our efforts through international channels and peaceful negotiations to lift their blockade."

After the election Mr Ben-Gurion reaffirmed this policy, to open the port of Eilat. Negotiations would first be attempted with the Egyptians ; if these were unsuccessful, force would be used. " We can do it by air, by land, or by sea," he told the *New York*

Times' correspondent on April 25, 1956. Mr Ben-Gurion cannot, in this instance, be accused of failing to keep his election promises. However, there can be no doubt that the language used by himself and his Foreign Minister on this particular issue was noted by the Egyptians, and that it helped to confirm their suspicion that the Israelis were trying to pressure them into negotiations in which they might have to face far wider issues than the stabilization of conditions around the Gaza Strip.

The dragging negotiations were brought to an abrupt end by an incident which occurred on August 22, near the Kilo 95 hut. The pattern was about the same as the incident of May 30. An Israeli patrol was allegedly fired upon, they fired back, there were casualties on both sides, and finally the Israelis drove into the position in their armoured personnel carriers, killing and wounding some of the small Egyptian garrison.

I had arranged to go to Cairo on August 23, in an endeavour to settle some of the points in the Gaza negotiations on which we seemed to have reached a deadlock. I had a discussion with Mr Khairat Said, at that time Under-Secretary for Foreign Affairs, but made no progress. I then asked to see Prime Minister Nasser. That evening I saw Mr Byroade, the U.S. Ambassador, and brought him up to date on the negotiations. He told me that the latest incident had been taken badly by the Egyptians, and deplored Israeli activism. He also told me that the Russians were offering Egypt arms and many economic advantages and the Prime Minister was under much political pressure to accept the Russian offers.

I saw Prime Minister Nasser the next day, about ten o'clock. He was pleasant, and apparently frank, as usual. He said, however, that they had decided to suspend the talks because of the incident of August 22. This time I had no evidence of UNMOs as to who had fired first. I had no evidence against the Egyptian contention that the incident had been provoked by the Israelis. However, I argued that the Israelis had broken off negotiations after certain incidents in which they had suffered severe casualties, yet had renewed them again, and I hoped that his decision was not final. He then asked why the proposals for joint patrols, a barbed-wire obstacle, and his suggestion of a neutral zone between the parties had not been taken up. I said we had touched on them briefly, but it had been impossible to deal with them thoroughly, owing to procedural wrangling, in which his representative had done his share. He said that Egypt would consider proposals which I might advance for these or other practical measures, but could not talk further on a local commanders' agreement.

I returned to Gaza, and reported to the Secretary-General about the break-down in the negotiations on the Gaza DL Security Arrangement (local commanders' agreement). He began *démarches* to get the talks going again, but before these could have any effect a renewed wave of violence began. We heard for the first time the expression *fedayeen* applied to the Palestinian agents sent into Israel to carry out attacks on the population and destroy property.[24]

CHAPTER 7

Egypt-Israel Tension grows: August–November 1955

Maps 1, 3, and 4

ISRAEL propaganda has made the Arabic word *fedayeen* synonymous with marauders, cutthroats, murderers. It used to have an honourable connotation. The Arabs gave it the ancient meaning of a person ready to give his life for his companions, a participant in forlorn hopes ; their English-language newspapers and broadcasts usually translated the term as " commandos." What the Egyptian motives for organizing them were is not easy to determine exactly, as, perhaps naturally, they admit little if any connexion between the decisions of responsible Egyptian authorities and the acts of the *fedayeen*. So much of what follows has to be speculation. The Israelis loudly proclaimed the responsibility of Prime Minister Nasser and his colleagues, and thereby justified their reprisals, including, finally, the invasion of the Sinai and the Gaza Strip.

The Revolutionary Command Council—that is, the Egyptian Government—were in a dilemma when the humiliation of the Gaza raid was succeeded by other incidents, represented to them as Israeli aggressions and provocations. They knew the Egyptian Army and Air Force were incapable of defeating the Israeli Defence Forces in open war, yet they could not submit to the injuries and insults with no reply whatever. The Government depended on the support of the Army, and if the Army's prestige suffered too much, and its internal discontent mounted, nobody knew what might happen. In this situation, the expedient of a sort of guerrilla warfare of revenge was attractive.

The members of the Revolutionary Command Council remembered the success of terrorist tactics against the British in the Canal Zone—a war of sabotage, explosions, shots from ambush, and the other accompaniments of the revolt of peoples against alien ' imperialist ' governments. But what the Egyptian leaders did not take into account was that while world opinion is generally tolerant of any excesses in the methods used against a ' foreign oppressor ' by so-called patriots, the same view would not be taken of a secret attack by rifle, machine-gun, grenade, and dynamite against the civil population of a neighbouring state.

In the early summer of 1955 the boasting of certain men in the Gaza Strip indicated that a guerrilla of this kind against the Israelis might be in preparation. They declared that they had got the British out of the Canal Zone by these methods, and now they were going to apply them against the Israelis.

One might think, to read the panegyrics in the Egyptian Press, that the *fedayeen* were Egyptian heroes, " self-sacrificers " who had volunteered to fight the battles of the Palestinian refugees for them. Although there were some reports that Egyptians accompanied the raids, I have not been able to obtain any evidence that any of the *fedayeen* captured or killed by the Israelis, and there have been a good many of them, have been other than Palestinian refugees. The Egyptians contented themselves with organizing the raids, training the men, sometimes rewarding those who were fortunate enough to return.

At times, it seems to have been the Israeli propaganda line to refer to the marauders as " Egyptians." However, the following extract from an article in the *Jerusalem Post* of February 9, 1956, apparently making use of information from the Israeli intelligence service, shows that the Israelis knew the true state of affairs. It referred to " the growing embitterment of the refugees at the increasing number of Egyptian-trained and commissioned *fedayeen* killed or detained by the Israeli security forces while the Egyptians themselves sit back and suffer no casualties."

For some years the Palestinian refugees had been demanding to be given arms, and be organized into an army to recover their lost homeland. How seriously they meant these demands is problematical. The Egyptians' response appears to have been at first limited to making encouraging noises, but eventually they did organize some units, and called them the Palestine Army. Some of these, mainly officered by Egyptians, from time to time formed part of the garrison of the Strip, and doubtless started many of the incidents. But others were trained for intelligence work within Israel. They knew the country, or some part of it, intimately, for it had been their home. Hence they could penetrate as scouts, or spies, and bring back information. UNTSO had pretty definite information that there was a sort of intelligence course run by the Egyptians for these people. The passing-out test was to go into Israeli territory, and observe traffic on certain roads, noting down vehicles that passed, and so forth. Several of these embryo agents were captured by the Israelis with their lists, and the evidence came to UNTSO with the complaint.

The first of an organized series of attacks on persons, vehicles, and buildings within Israel happened during the night of August

25–26. A man in a jeep was killed near Yad Mordechai, the nearest *kibbutz* to the north of the Gaza Strip, and there was also an attack on an Israeli outpost near Kissufim. When I was at the Israeli Foreign Office the next day, on other business, Mr Sharett called me in and asked me to warn the Egyptians that Israel would react if the incidents continued.

When I had seen Prime Minister Nasser in June, the Israeli Press had published stories to the effect that I had warned the Egyptians that Israel would no longer tolerate the hostile acts which had been almost continuous since the Gaza raid. The Egyptian Press had, of course, reacted with hostility to the expression " warning," and it had greatly reduced the effectiveness of any advice or suggestions I could offer. So I replied to Mr Sharett on this occasion, as I did later to other Israeli authorities who made similar requests, that I could not be put in the position of conveying threats by one party to the other. I said, however, that I would appeal to the Egyptians to control their troops, and I did so, also asking them to agree to the posting of UNMOs at various points along the ADL, a measure which they themselves had previously requested, but which had been discontinued during the quiet period.

There was no improvement in the situation following this intervention. On August 28, 1955, there was an outbreak of firing near Ali el Muntar, south-east of Gaza, which became quite intense. It was only stopped on my appeal to General Dayan, through Mr Tekoah, of the Ministry of Foreign Affairs, and Commandant Giaccomaggi's appeal to Brigadier Aghroudy, the commander of the Egyptian troops within the Strip, whose headquarters was at Rafah.

On the same date UNTSO obtained very significant evidence about the organization of the raids. Two of our observers were investigating an incident in which a party of infiltrators had been ambushed by Israeli soldiers near Majdal Askelon. They found an Arab who had been wounded, and had hidden in the scrub. Captain Gerhard Svedlund, who was able to speak Arabic fluently, interrogated the man on the spot, and found out he had been released from jail to accompany the party on the raid into Israel. He gave other testimony which substantiated the Israeli contentions that many raids into Israel were organized by the Egyptians. The Israelis had obtained this information by interrogation of prisoners they had captured, but they would never let an UNMO be present at the interrogations. They doubtless obtained other information through espionage. So it happened that until this occasion UNTSO had never had before it direct and positive evidence to prove the Israeli allegations.

The Israelis complained to the Security Council on August 29, 30, and 31 of Egyptian attacks, listing a number of other incidents besides the above, of mining of Israeli vehicles, night ambushes of Israeli military and civil vehicles, blowing up of various water-pipes and a radio tower, and other attacks on civilians and incursions a short distance across the ADL by Egyptian troops near Gaza. The most serious of these incidents was the wounding of a family of five persons by small-arms fire near Rehovot, forty-three kilometres from the ADL. One of these persons later died. Then four unarmed workmen in an orange-grove not far from Rishon le-Zion, forty-seven kilometres from the border, and only about fifteen kilometres from Tel Aviv, were slaughtered by sub-machine-gun fire.

According to the information UNTSO collected, eleven military and civilian Israelis were killed, and nine wounded. I said in my report : " The number and nature of these acts of sabotage perpetrated well within Israeli territory suggest that they are the work of organized and well-trained groups. Investigations so far completed by United Nations military observers tend to support this view. The sudden resumption of this type of incident after they had practically ceased for three months is significant."

I had Commandant Giaccomaggi, Chairman of EIMAC, write to Colonel Gohar, to the Governor of Gaza, and to Brigadier Aghroudy on August 28, citing cases of this type of incident investigated by UNMOs and advising them that if there were any more such incidents there would be Israeli reactions which might lead to the gravest situation. This advice was evidently too late, and the incidents continued. It was a feature of this and later *fedayeen* campaigns that once the *fedayeen* had been sent off on their terrorist mission, it was not possible for the Egyptian authorities to call them back, or order them to stop their attacks. The *fedayeen* had no radio receivers, nor any other means of communication. So, until they returned to their base, after the two, three, or four days' and nights' operations for which they were rationed and equipped, they continued to carry out their original orders.

When I realized the extent and character of this campaign I was deeply shocked. The incident in the orange-grove was particularly repellent. I felt that what the Egyptians were doing in sending these men, whom they dignified with the name of *fedayeen*, or commandos, into another country with the mission to attack men, women, and children indiscriminately was a war crime. It was essentially of the same character, though less in degree, as the offences for which the Nazi leaders had been tried in Nürnberg, to cite the most recent example.

While some of the *fedayeen* may have been mere hired cutthroats, it is probably true that the majority were Palestinian Arabs who had a burning sense of the injustice that they had suffered at the hands of the Israelis. Even so, their actions were certain to alienate opinion throughout the world. In fact, after this, the crimes of the *fedayeen* became the principal theme of Israeli propaganda, and a most effective one. The blame, of course, attaches to the Egyptian higher-ups who authorized the campaign.

Here we come to a difficulty in placing responsibility, not only in this connexion, but as to other acts or omissions affecting the observance of the General Armistice Agreement. This difficulty is due to the uncertainty as to how the Egyptian governmental system really functions. I have said that it is erroneous to picture Gamal Abdel Nasser as a dictator who controls everything, or at any rate everything relating to military and foreign affairs. Other important members of the Revolutionary Command Council have a finger in the pie, and may not always stir it in the way Nasser would prefer. Furthermore, the Egyptian governmental machinery, according to my observation, is by no means so positive in its operation as we are accustomed to expect in Western democracies. Every kind of government has to practise decentralization to a greater or lesser degree. Some of the actions which caused the most trouble between Egypt and Israel may have been due to initiatives taken by hotheads or irresponsibles in the lower echelons of the Army. Or juniors may have exceeded their instructions, even if acting generally in accordance with governmental policy.

It was never possible to prove that the orders for the *fedayeen*, or any other marauders, to enter Israel and commit terroristic acts came from Cairo. When challenged on this point privately by myself or the Secretary-General, the most that would be admitted was that the raiding could be stopped by the authorities, not that it had been initiated by them. Of course, there is no doubt as to the ultimate responsibility of a government for the actions of its agents. But there was a certain doubt about the effectiveness of the Egyptian Government's control.

The situation was getting worse, and Israeli retaliation seemed more and more probable. On August 30 I appealed to both parties to order their troops along the ADL in the Gaza Strip area and before the El Auja demilitarized zone to observe a strict cease-fire, and to issue and enforce the most positive orders to prevent anyone's crossing the demarcation line and attacking persons in the other's territory, laying mines, or committing other acts of sabotage. The Egyptian authorities accepted—subject to Israel's committing no aggressions after the period of the cease-fire.

The Israelis invited me " to obtain the assurance of the Egyptian Government that it accepts responsibility for these acts, and that it is ready to give guarantees for immediate, complete and definitive cessation of all further hostile acts in strictest compliance with its obligations under the Armistice Agreement."

I replied to the Israelis that the Egyptians had, in accepting my cease-fire proposal, agreed to stop all hostile acts. I thought it unreasonable for Israel to insist, as a condition for accepting a cease-fire, that Egypt should acknowledge responsibility for previous incidents. I again urged the Israelis to accept the cease-fire without further conditions. But, about an hour after I had sent this last message, I was told by the Israeli Foreign Office that two more civilians had been killed in an incident that night; and they had doubts on other grounds whether the Egyptians would really respect the cease-fire. I could get no more favourable reply in subsequent attempts. Presumably, by this time, the decision to retaliate had been taken.

The next day I heard that six United Nations Military Observers were being detained in Beersheba by the Israeli military authorities. I protested to the Foreign Office, and, after some delay, towards evening the observers were allowed to proceed towards Jerusalem or Gaza, but escorted by Israeli officers. This obviously indicated that some military action was in preparation, and the Israelis did not want our observers to see anything of it.

During the night of August 31–September 1 the Israeli retaliatory raid on Khan Yunis took place. A light armoured Israeli unit, in half-tracked scout cars, advanced through about six kilometres of the Egyptian-occupied territory to the police-station at Khan Yunis. They opened covering fire on the loopholes and windows of the fortified post with machine-guns and mortars, and then forced an entry into the ground floor and blew up most of the building with heavy explosive charges, burying a good number of the garrison in the ruins. A hospital under construction next door was also partly destroyed by explosives. The attacking Israeli party had passed through the village of Bani Suheila, and to keep the inhabitants from interfering with them had machine-gunned right and left, but without inflicting more than one or two wounds. The Egyptian defensive position near Abasan, an adjacent village, was also attacked by fire, to cover the main attack.

The Egyptians reported casualties of thirty-six killed and thirteen wounded—soldiers, policemen, and civilians. UNTSO had difficulty in establishing the exact number of casualties, and the observers did not see many of the dead, but the above figures seem approximately correct.

The Israelis claimed, in the newspaper reports of the attack, that Khan Yunis police-station had been chosen as a target because the *fedayeen* campaign had been directed from it. No evidence was produced to substantiate this, but by attacking this building (and other police-posts both in the Sinai and Jordan later on) the Israelis ensured that nearly all the casualties would fall on the police or military, and they would thus avoid the very hostile reaction of world opinion which had followed their retaliation on Qibya in 1953, when many women and children had been killed and wounded. It must also be allowed that the Israeli Armoured Corps unit had carried out the attack with skill and daring. Conversely, the inertness of the defence reflected little credit on the Egyptian military forces in the Strip.

After reporting to the Secretary-General on the incident, and receiving his instructions, I again appealed to both parties for a cease-fire, and this was accepted on September 4. I then reported to the Security Council, saying that it had been impossible to get agreement between the parties on any of the measures proposed in my report made after the Gaza raid. I gave my view that the clashes between Egyptian outposts and Israeli patrols could be avoided only if there was a physical barrier along the ADL, and the outposts and patrols of both sides were kept at least 500 metres behind it.

The Security Council met on September 8 and passed a resolution sponsored by the United Kingdom, France, and the United States. It noted the acceptance of a cease-fire, called on both parties forthwith to take all steps necessary to bring about order and tranquillity in the area, and in particular to desist from further acts of violence ; endorsed my view that the armed forces of the parties should be effectively separated ; called on both parties to have representatives meet with me and co-operate fully to these ends, and declared that freedom of movement must be afforded to UNMOs in the area. It will be noted that there was no condemnation of Israel, as there had been in the resolution following the Gaza raid. This was no doubt due to the aversion which the *fedayeen* campaign had excited, and possibly also to the feeling that the Egyptians were as much to blame as the Israelis, if not more, for the break-down of the negotiations which had been conducted in accordance with the Council's 28th of March resolution.

I have mentioned the Czech sale of arms to Egypt. (See page 32.) I have been told that Prime Minister Nasser decided to accept this offer immediately after the Khan Yunis raid. The Gaza reprisal had been followed by a period during which the Israeli forces flaunted their patrols along the demarcation line, as

if to challenge the garrison of the Strip to interfere with them.
Then had come the further bitter pill of Khan Yunis. It was
reported that Major-General Abd El Hakim Amr, Minister of
War and Commander-in-Chief of the Egyptian forces, wanted to
launch a counter-offensive when the news of the Khan Yunis raid
came in. Following the Gaza raid, the Egyptian forces had been
strengthened in the El Arish-Rafah-Abu Aweigila area, though
they were not as strong as they later became. However, Nasser
refused to sanction the move until more definite information had
been received, and when it was learned that the Israelis had withdrawn, and that the operation had been just a raid, the idea of a
counter-offensive was abandoned. But the sting remained, and
further pressures were to follow.

As I have remarked several times, the prestige of Nasser and the
Revolutionary Command Council was bound up with the prestige
of the Egyptian Army. Something had to be done to restore the
Army's self-esteem. Nasser cannot have forgotten how the revolution which placed him in power had begun. During the 1948
campaign, he and other officers in the Faluja pocket had felt
frustrated and indeed betrayed by the current régime in Cairo.
They blamed their defeats at the Israelis' hands on the defects of
their munitions and armament, while realizing that these were
symptoms of graver weaknesses in the Egyptian Government and
nation, that could only be cured by revolution. Nasser could not
have wanted history—or, at any rate, revolution—to repeat itself.

The principal focus of the conflict between Israel and Egypt now
changed to the El Auja demilitarized zone, an area which had been
given a special status in the GAA between Egypt and Israel. This
was due to its strategic importance, being a junction of roads
from the Sinai and the road from Beersheba. It lay across the
second principal route for the invasion of Palestine from Egypt
(or *vice versa*), the first being, of course, that which ran through
El Arish and the Gaza Strip. It was from this general area that the
decisive attack by the Israeli forces on the Egyptian forces had been
launched in December 1948, and that another was to erupt again in
October–November 1956. If, indeed, the zone had remained
demilitarized—that is to say, if it could not have been traversed
or occupied by the armed forces of either side—it would have been
almost impossible for either to have carried out an offensive
successfully, the balance of forces being as they were.

The area covered by the zone is desert, although there are several
wells, at El Auja itself and at Bir Ain. El Auja was the site of a
customs and border control post erected in the days of the Turkish

régime, to control traffic from Egypt to Palestine. The original inhabitants of the zone were some 3500 nomadic Bedouin of the Azazme tribe. They were expelled by the Israelis in 1950. The Egyptian complaint against this action was the subject of long-drawn-out proceedings in the Mixed Armistice Commission, and eventually reached the Security Council. Finally, Israel was called upon to allow the Azazme to return to their former grazing-grounds. The Israelis, at this point, in November 1954, while refusing to allow all the Azazme back, said they were willing to consider the admission of a small number. I invited the parties to discuss the question, but other more immediate conflicts prevented any such discussions taking place.

Before this, Israel had taken another step to get possession of this strategic area, and nullify its demilitarization. On September 28, 1953, according to evidence before the Mixed Armistice Commission, the Israelis, under protection of elements of their armed forces, which killed a number of the Bedouin and their cattle, established in the zone a settlement afterwards called Ketsiot. The Israeli argument then, and later, was that there was no prohibition in the GAA of civil activity in the demilitarized zone, including farming, and that the settlement was a pioneering farming venture, experimental perhaps, but designed as an element of the plan for the opening up of the Negev for settlement and agriculture. They claimed that the demilitarized zone was part of Israel territory, and that the only restrictions were those relating to its demilitarization. The Egyptians contended that the settlement was a military organization, and not an innocent agricultural collective.

This contention was confirmed when on October 6, 1954, one of the *kibbutz* members drove a water-truck across the International Frontier, and gave himself up to the Egyptian post at Abu Aweigila. He was later questioned in the presence of an UNMO, and said he was a private in a certain company of a certain battalion of the Israel Army. He also said all the inhabitants of the *kibbutz* were soldiers in this unit, and consisted of one captain, four NCOs, sixty-five men soldiers, and fifteen women soldiers. They had the usual armament of an infantry company—rifles, sub-machine-guns, light machine-guns, mortars, and anti-tank weapons. The Israeli carried identification papers proving he was a member of the Army, and his story sounded truthful. Some days later, UNMOs visited the *kibbutz*, but, of course, found no arms, nor any evidence of military organization, though they remarked that the inhabitants (whose numbers corresponded to the deserter's statement) were all young and unmarried, and that the amount of farming being carried on did not seem to account for the size of the settlement. The

Mixed Armistice Commission, in a meeting on September 30, 1954, found that the settlement was organized as a unit of the Israel Armed Forces, in breach of the article of the GAA relating to the demilitarized zone, and called on the Chief of Staff to see that this article was implemented. This decision was appealed by the Israeli representatives. The appeal then had to be decided by the Special Committee provided under the Egypt-Israel GAA. But there was a long waiting-list of appeals, and it was impossible to get the parties to meet and clear them off. So, pending decision of the appeal, the *kibbutz* stayed where it was.

Owing to newness in the job, and preoccupations in other quarters, I did not understand the character of the settlement, and the importance of the deserter's evidence in particular, until later, in the autumn of 1955, when the troubles in the demilitarized zone became acute. I did visit Ketsiot in 1954, and noticed the youth of the inhabitants, and the lack of farming activity. The place was defended by barbed-wire obstacles and some slit trenches, but so were all the collective settlements which were near Israel's borders, and those of Ketsiot did not seem stronger than would be necessary to keep out casual Arab marauders.

Having little farming to do, the young *kibbutzniks* used to wander round the demilitarized zone, sometimes with the excuse that they were looking for archaeological specimens. In the early summer of 1955 there were several clashes with the " checkposts " which the Egyptians had set up at the frontier, in the vicinity of the roads to Rafah, to Abu Aweigila, and to El Quseima. The *kibbutzniks* also interfered with the Egyptian delegate to the MAC, and on one occasion took his jeep away, in spite of the protests of an UNMO who was present. This was really the beginning of the trouble in the demilitarized zone, to which the limelight now shifted from Gaza.

After the cease-fire was established, following the Khan Yunis reprisal, I had been principally occupied trying to get the parties to agree to the measures for separation of their armed forces which I had suggested in my report. This time I followed the plan of seeing first one side and then the other, to try to get them to accept the proposals. After my experience of July and August, I did not think that Lieutenant-Colonel Gohar and Mr Tekoah, or any other representatives of the two sides, were likely to reach any useful conclusions when sitting at the same table.

Earlier in the year, the EIMAC had decided that the International Frontier between Egypt and Palestine, which formed the western boundary of the demilitarized zone, should be clearly marked, by re-establishing the position of the original survey. Neither side would then cross it by accident, and there would be no excuse for opening fire at people in their own territory, in the belief that they had crossed the boundary. This was a reasonable idea, but, as usual, a block developed. The dispute was about who was to mark the International Frontier, and how. Having agreed to a procedure for joint marking of the frontier, the Egyptians suddenly withdrew their consent. This change of mind seems to have been due to Lieutenant-Colonel Gohar's idea that if the demilitarized zone were marked only on the side of its triangle that was constituted by the International Frontier, and not all around, it would be a tacit admission that the demilitarized zone was part of Israel.

It had been found, in the course of survey work by the UNMOs, that two of the Egyptian checkposts were a few metres across the frontier, and so inside the demilitarized zone. The Chairman of EIMAC requested Lieutenant-Colonel Gohar on August 15 to have these withdrawn, and he promised to do so, but no action was taken. After the Egyptian refusal to proceed jointly, the Israelis decided to erect markers themselves, although UNTSO discouraged this action. They put up a number of pillars, but, on September 13, an UNMO found that the greater part of these had been overturned, apparently by some heavy vehicle. The Israeli reaction to the opening which Egyptian imprudence had given them was not long in coming.

During the early hours of September 21 about two companies of Israeli infantry entered the demilitarized zone, occupied the buildings used as headquarters by the MAC, and seized the Egyptian personnel, who by agreement were attached to the Commission, wounding two of them. These were released to the Egyptians shortly afterwards. I promptly made a strong protest to the Israeli Ministry of Foreign Affairs, demanding immediate withdrawal of the troops. Mr Arthur Lourie, Assistant Director-General of the Ministry, to whom I spoke, said the Israeli action had been taken because the Egyptians had not withdrawn their checkposts, and had interfered with the marking of the frontier. He said the Israelis would withdraw when the Egyptians had taken their checkposts out of the zone.

The next week or so was occupied in negotiating with both sides on the terms of the withdrawal, which was finally carried out on October 2. I had agreed, during the discussions, to the Israelis' stationing a number of civil police in the zone, for the protection of the *kibbutz* Ketsiot. At that time I still was not aware of its essentially military character. This caused further trouble. I had made the mistake of not fully informing the Egyptians of the condition which I had agreed to mainly as a means of getting the two Israeli infantry companies out. I regarded the civil police as justifiable if a settlement was to be allowed in the zone ; and the Security Council had failed to deal with the Egyptian complaint that it was really a military organization. A few police seemed a lesser evil than two infantry companies.

As soon as the Egyptians learned about the police, they complained that they were really a military force and their presence in the demilitarized zone was contrary to the GAA provisions for its demilitarization. The Israelis in turn complained that the Egyptian checkposts were really defensive positions, which were not allowed in the area to the west of the demilitarized zone. Neither of these complaints could be settled in the MAC owing to a long list of incidents which had happened round the Gaza Strip, for which emergency meetings had been arranged. The rules of procedure of the Mixed Armistice Commissions were such that when either party wanted to block discussion of a particular incident or condition, it was easy for them to do so. Neither the MAC Chairman nor the Chief of Staff UNTSO had any power to change the rules of procedure.

The Egyptians, offended because of the concession about the police, refused to allow the surveying of the International Frontier, and also refused to allow inspection of their checkposts. It was necessary to determine whether these were restricted in numbers and armament to the size which the President of the Security Council had pronounced would be consistent with their alleged purpose—*i.e.*, to prevent casual crossings of the line by smugglers or infiltrators. The Egyptians threatened to fire at anybody, including UNMOs, who might be in the vicinity of their posts, and once or twice actually did fire, though without inflicting casualties. I reported all the above circumstances to the Secretary-General on October 20. He called me to New York for consultation. The General Assembly of the United Nations was in session, and Mr Hammarskjöld thought that something could be done to straighten out the El Auja impasse by negotiation with Dr Mahmoud Fawzi and the Israeli representatives. Fawzi had promised that the Egyptians would do nothing to aggravate the situation during my absence, and I obtained a similar assurance from the Israeli Government through Mr Lourie.

I got to New York on October 26, to receive the news that the Egyptians had raided one of the posts manned by the " civil police " near Bir Ain, and had captured two prisoners. Interrogation of these prisoners revealed that they were not really policemen, but soldiers who had been given a different outfit of uniform. The Israelis played this trick of camouflaging soldiers as civil police on other occasions, but at the time I had agreed to " civil police " being posted in the El Auja demilitarized zone, although I had been over a year in Palestine. I was still sufficiently naïve to believe that statements of senior officials of the Ministry of Foreign Affairs could be relied upon to represent the intentions of the real directors of Israel's foreign and defence policies.

The Egyptian attack at Bir Ain was a breach of Dr Fawzi's promise that nothing would be done to upset the situation during my absence. It was another proof of the lamentable fact that in the Israel-Arab conflict, the fair and reasonable promises of the diplomats can be set aside by the action of some irresponsible or irreconcilable person within the echelons of the military command.

I had by this time reached the conclusion that the trouble in the demilitarized zone would go on as long as the Israelis maintained Ketsiot, or any such settlement there, because if they had a settlement it would have to have protection of some sort. This would be a military foothold in the demilitarized zone, and the conflicts between the Egyptians and the crypto-military Israelis would go on. When I presented this view to the Secretary-General he said he would ask the representatives of the Three Powers whether it would be possible to get the Security Council to rule on the exclusion of the *kibbutz* from the zone. Meanwhile I was to see Dr Fawzi.

I did so the next day. Dr Fawzi's idea was that the situation in the El Auja zone as it then existed should be stabilized. While in principle Egypt would not consent to the presence of either the *kibbutz* or the civil police, she would not raise the question. On the other hand, Egypt expected not to be pressed about her dispositions in the area between the International Frontier and the line El Quseima-Abu Aweigila, in which, under the GAA, no defensive positions were allowed.

On October 28, 1955, it was reported that the Israelis had raided the Egyptian police-post at El Kuntilla. This was in retaliation for the Bir Ain raid. Five Egyptians had been killed and thirty captured. The Egyptians captured in this raid, and the two Israelis captured at Bir Ain, remained prisoners until the general exchange following the Israeli withdrawal from the Sinai in January 1957.

Reports were received from U.S. sources that the Egyptians were moving troops with the intention of attacking the Israelis in the zone. Colonel R. Hommel, USMC, my principal military assistant, who was acting as Chief of Staff during my absence, signalled on October 31 that in the El Auja zone " tension is such that it only seems a question of which party will attack first."

Preliminary discussions with the representatives of the Three

B.A.I.—7

Powers at the United Nations had shown that they were not ready to take any forceful action to remedy the dangerous state of affairs. In a meeting on October 31, Mr Cabot Lodge for the United States, Sir Pierson Dixon for the United Kingdom, and M. Alphand for France would go no further than agreeing to present the plan, later known as the " Secretary-General's Three Points " to their governments. This three-point plan was that (i) UNTSO should mark the International Frontier along the extent of the El Auja demilitarized zone ; (ii) Egypt should withdraw all the posts which she had established encroaching in the demilitarized zone ; (iii) Israel should withdraw all troops, and any civilian police exceeding the number that had been in the zone before October 26, the date of the Bir Ain raid. The raid had, of course, given the Israelis an excellent excuse to reoccupy the zone. I stressed to the representatives of the Three Powers that strong diplomatic pressure would be needed to get the parties to agree to the three-point plan.

On November 3, after a very brief visit to my home in Ottawa, I started back to Jerusalem. When in Montreal, waiting for the plane, I received word that the Israelis had attacked positions which the Egyptians had recently established in the zone, near El Sabha. After a telephone consultation with Mr Cordier, it was decided I should continue to Jerusalem, and that the Secretary-General would call on the parties to withdraw and accept the three-point proposal.

In London the next day I was asked to meet Mr Anthony Nutting, Minister of State for Foreign Affairs, with his Middle East experts. He and his advisers thought nothing could be achieved by having a meeting of the Security Council at that time, as the United States would be reluctant to take any strong action in regard to Israel, while the Soviet could be expected to block any measures distasteful to Egypt. My diary notes that we discussed the possibility of introducing United Nations troops between the armed forces of the parties. I said I thought it would take extraordinary pressure to get the Israelis out of the El Auja zone, and that I did not think it would be possible to get UN troops in without a prior military intervention by the Great Powers. This turns out to have been a good prediction. The conclusion was that nothing more than the proposals of the Secretary-General could be advanced at that time.

The next day I was surprised by an invitation by Sir Anthony Eden to have lunch with him at 10 Downing Street. Only he and his wife were present besides myself. We discussed the same points that had been covered with Mr Nutting on the previous day, and reached the same conclusion, or lack of conclusion— that is, no strong and simple solution to the Middle East problem as it then stood was to be found. Sir Anthony spoke of Mr Sharett's talk to Mr Molotov at Geneva, in which he had endeavoured to persuade the Russians to reverse their policy on arming Egypt, but without effect.

Prime Minister Nasser's acceptance of the Czechoslovak offer to supply Egypt with arms was a decisive event in the development of the Middle East crisis. This deal was announced about the end of September 1955. In Israel a great diplomatic turmoil ensued, and it involved the Three Powers. The arms to be supplied would be sufficient to give Egypt a considerable technical superiority in tanks, artillery, and fighter and bomber aircraft. Their acquisition of Ilyushin jet bombers was particularly alarming to the Israelis, as these aircraft could bomb their cities from a height at which Israel's Meteor jet fighters could not reach them. And the Meteors would be outclassed as fighters by the MIG 15s the Egyptian Air Force was to receive. The rearmament was discussed in terms of how soon the Egyptian forces, with their superior technical equipment, would be able to launch a war of annihilation against Israel.

To those who queried me on this point, I answered that I believed it would take the Egyptian forces a considerable time, after they had received their equipment, to master its operation, and still longer to develop tactical efficiency with it, including the command and staff techniques required to make proper use of the technical superiority. In terms of time, I guessed that it was not likely that the Egyptian forces would be ready for an offensive against the Israelis for at least two years. The relative ineffectiveness of the Egyptian forces, in spite of their modern equipment, in the fighting of October–November 1956 bore this guess out, although one must remember that in that contest the Egyptian forces had first been dispersed by the threat of the Anglo-French attack, and then more or less pinned down by the Western Allies' air action. It was by no means a straight Egyptian-Israeli contest. But even allowing for that, there was little to show that the Egyptian forces had really become much more effective because of the equipment they had received.

What the Egyptian Army needed more than modern arms was better morale, better discipline, better training. The defects in these respects were plain to be seen whenever one met any Egyptian troops, even the small posts near the borders, and when one considered their performance in face of the Israeli reprisals. This really meant that their officer corps needed improvement—more energy, better training, more devotion, harder work at their profession, and more care in the training and welfare of their troops. (*Note*. Napoleon is quoted as saying, " There are no bad troops ;

only bad officers.'')   Such improvement of an officer corps is not
to be effected overnight ; and many of the ablest of the younger
Egyptian officers were taking more interest in a career in politics,
or in lucrative business careers which the Revolution of 1952 had
opened to the military.

The real significance of the Czech arms deal was political.   In
the first place, to the dismay of the Western Powers, and particularly
the U.S.A., Russia established her influence in the Middle East,
from which she had been hitherto practically excluded.   Premier
Nasser became a great hero throughout the Arab countries.
Egyptian propaganda made a great victory out of this acquisition
of arms.   The victory had been won over the imperialist supporters
of Israel who had denied arms to the Arabs.   The presumption was
that the Arab armies, now they had modern arms, would shortly
be able to challenge and defeat the Israelis, and recover Palestine
for its former inhabitants.   Previous Arab defeats were ascribed
to super Israeli armament, supplied to them by the West.   This
explanation naturally was agreeable to Arab self-esteem.

The increase of Nasser's stature and influence through the Czech
arms deal greatly strengthened the pro-Egyptian elements in Jordan,
and contributed much to the movement that caused her rejection
of the invitation to join the Baghdad Pact, the dismissal of Glubb
Pasha, and the abrogation of the Anglo-Jordanian treaty.   The
Arab Legion and the Egyptian Army were placed under one
command in the autumn of 1956, as will be related in due course.
Nasser's stock in Syria also went up, and the trend began which was
to culminate in 1958 with the union of Egypt and Syria in the
United Arab Republic.   All these developments were dangerous
for Israel, and of course inimical to the efforts of the Three Powers
in maintaining stability in the Middle East.

On the other hand, Nasser's sudden increase in prestige probably
made him overconfident and caused the bad timing and the unnecessarily provocative manner of nationalizing the Suez Canal,
which nearly brought him to disaster.   His prestige certainly
went to the head of many of his supporters and subordinates in
Egypt.   One of the evidences of this was that one Egyptian military
attaché after another, in countries in Europe as well as the Middle
East, got caught in intrigues of various sorts against the interests
of the host government, and was declared *persona non grata*.

Israel's reaction to the news that Egypt was to have this up-to-
date Russian equipment was that the Three Powers, if they could
not stop the Russian equipment's getting to Egypt, should at least
supply Israel with equipment equivalent in quality and quantity,
to enable the arms balance to be maintained.   The United States

EGYPT-ISRAEL TENSION GROWS: 1955   101

and Great Britain rejected this proposal with the argument that
to begin a sort of arms race, or contest with the U.S.S.R. and
satellites arming the Arabs and the West arming Israel, could only
worsen the existing dangers.   Naturally, the Three Powers wanted
to maintain a position as arbiters of the Middle East's problems,
and not become outright partisans of Israel.

No Israeli ever so much as suggested that it was the tough Ben-
Gurion-Dayan policy that had practically forced Nasser to accept
the Russo-Czech arms proposals.   What other enemy threatened
Egypt ?   Nor was this theme given much publicity in the Western
nations, nearly all of whose publicity media accept the Israeli
version of events in the Middle East.   Of course, the diplomats
and internationally-minded politicians understood what motivated
Nasser, and, although this doubtless played a part in the U.S. and
Great Britain's refusal to give Israel the arms she wanted, there was
no public airing of the issue.   Mr Alfred Lilienthal sets out the
case quite clearly in Chapter 8 of his book *There Goes the Middle
East*.

When I got back to Jerusalem on November 6, I found there
had been no significant developments since the Israeli attack on the
Egyptian position within the demilitarized zone near El Sabha.
The Egyptian papers on November 4 had published statements
that Egyptian forces had recaptured El Sabha, and killed 200
Israelis.   An Egyptian colonel, who said he led the counter-attack,
told the *News Chronicle* correspondent an elaborate story of the
" victory."   He said his troops had lost twenty-two killed and
twenty-seven wounded, but that the Israelis had lost between
150 and 200 dead.   " Eight five-ton Israeli lorries were soon bearing
away their dead."

The Israelis derided this as a complete fabrication.   As far as
UNMOs could learn, there was no evidence of Israeli casualties
beyond the seven or so admitted in their *communiqué*.   While the
height of El Sabha, which is on the Egyptian side of the International
Frontier, had apparently been occupied by the Israelis during the
action against the Egyptian positions within the demilitarized zone
they had later withdrawn, and the Egyptian counter-attack, if it
could be described as such, reoccupied the undefended hill.   The
Egyptians did not go back to the positions they had had within the
demilitarized zone.   I visited these a few days later.   Apparently
about a company of Egyptian infantry had been strung out along
a line nearly a kilometre long, on a rise several hundred metres
within the demilitarized zone.   There were slit trenches and wire
obstacles ; but the siting of the defences said very little for Egyptian

tactical training, as there was no depth, nor defence against an attack coming from the right flank, as the Israeli night assault did.

The heads of the " sister Arab states " sent congratulatory telegrams to the head of the Egyptian state. It was reported that Said El Mufti, then Jordanian Prime Minister, had sardonically added that he was sure the Egyptian Army would win many similar victories in future.

The next week or so was mainly occupied in trying to gain acceptance of the Secretary-General's Three Points to restore the situation in the El Auja demilitarized zone. A tentative arrangement for me to see Prime Minister Nasser had been made, but before I went to Cairo, I was called in to see Prime Minister Ben-Gurion on November 9. This was my first meeting with him, although he had been Minister of Defence since the previous February, and I had on several occasions suggested that I should like to meet him. He explained at this time that he had not thought it proper to meet me before he had become Prime Minister. It was only a few days before this that he had completed the long-drawn-out negotiations with the several Israeli political parties and formed his Coalition Government, in which Mr Sharett was Minister of Foreign Affairs.

So once again he was in office, presiding over Israel's military and foreign policy. Even during his self-imposed exile in the Negev, when he had been living in the desert settlement of Sde Boker, practising the avocation of a shepherd, it had seemed that the centre of power was in that remote spot. After his return to the Government rumours began to spread that as a result of his meditations in the wilderness, he had developed new ideas of the direction Israel policy should take—that he had in mind adventurous and potentially dangerous lines of action.

I find it difficult to imagine what Israel would be like without Mr Ben-Gurion. He was the leader in the act that created the State of Israel, and since 1948 his has been the voice that has chiefly directed and expounded its development and course.

This does not mean that in any sense he is a dictator. Indeed no ; Israel is a very democratic country, and politicians lambaste each other, Mr Ben-Gurion with the rest, with blistering invective and mordant wit. Press and public join in. This is one circumstance which makes an enforced habitation in Israel tolerable. There is seldom a dull moment. But in all the wrangling free-for-all, Mr Ben-Gurion sits on top ; often attacked, he maintains his lofty station, and there seems no one likely to dislodge him, if he keeps his health.

So there is no doubt at all that he was the person responsible for Israel's policies during the period of which this book treats. If I criticize those policies, by implication I criticize him. But that is not to derogate his personal character and qualities. He must be recognized as a great man, one of the very few great men now living. By his own will and acts he has affected the course of world events—made history, in short.

When one acclaims a man as great, that does not mean that he is not capable of making mistakes ; and they may be mistakes on the scale of his greatness. It is possible to be too brave, too determined, too inflexible in pursuing what one regards as the good.

All his adult life Mr Ben-Gurion has been inspired by a burning determination to achieve the creation of the State of Israel, and to gather into it all the Jews in the world—the ingathering of the exiles, to use a phrase constantly on his lips. This is the supreme object with him, and it would seem as if he assesses all propositions, acts, and situations in relation to that purpose. If they further it, they are good ; if they hamper it, they are bad.

Perhaps that is too absolute. No one should say that Mr Ben-Gurion is incapable of unbiased moral judgment where the welfare and future of the State of Israel are concerned. But his frequent refusals to compromise or yield during the events described in this book seemed to be based on a conviction that right and justice were always on the side of Israel.

It does not seem that Mr Ben-Gurion practises the Judaic religion, in any of its varieties from orthodox to reform. Yet he is devoted to the Bible, refers to it constantly, and sees its record of the promises made by Jehovah to the Children of Israel, *circa* 1250 B.C., as the justification for the reoccupation of Palestine in the twentieth century. His study of other religions is often noted—evidence that he does not find a satisfactory philosophy and rule of life in the Bible alone. But one cannot presume to determine how he really thinks and what he believes about these matters. One can only record his actions and his words, and try to understand them as best one can.

Mr Ben-Gurion was very pleasant to me throughout this talk. It began with a friendly greeting he wanted conveyed to Mr Lester Pearson, who was to be in Cairo within the next few days, coupled with an invitation to visit Israel, which was not then included in his travel plan.

The Prime Minister then gave an outline of Israel's policy towards Egypt. He repeated what he had said in the Knesset a few days before, on his Government's taking office. It was that

Israel wanted peace with Egypt, but if Egypt would not make peace, Israel expected as a minimum a strict adherence to the GAA. He, Ben-Gurion, was ready to meet Nasser at any time to discuss peace, or an improvement in relations between the two countries.

My part of the conversation was to point out that the habit of both parties to excuse breaches of the terms of the GAA by quoting previous breaches by the other side could only lead to the complete break-down of the agreement—as, in fact, it did, a year later. In particular I deplored the Israeli attack on the Egyptians in the El Auja demilitarized zone, even though they had no right to be there. Mr Ben-Gurion said that when the United Nations proved unable to get the Egyptians to vacate, he had to authorize military measures to drive them out, and that he had only done what any head of a state would have done anywhere, if foreign military forces encroached on that state's territory. The flaw in this argument lay in the fact that there was a special status, internationally recognized, for the El Auja demilitarized zone, which admittedly the Egyptians had been violating, but because the Israelis had previously violated it also.

I also remarked, apropos of his readiness to meet Nasser to discuss peace, that it seemed to me that what stood between Israel and the Arab states and prevented peace was the Arab refugees who had been displaced from Palestine during the 1948 war. He replied to this by giving the stereotyped Israeli answer : that the refugees had left Palestine of their own accord, or, rather, on the orders of the Arab Higher Committee and in accordance with its war plan against the new-born State of Israel. The return of nearly a million bitterly hostile aliens could not possibly be accepted by Israel, as it would amount to self-destruction. But limited numbers might be admitted, to allow for the reunion of separated families, if there were a general peace settlement, and Israel would help in settling the Arab refugees elsewhere. It seemed to me that no real progress towards peace would be possible while the Israeli refugee policy remained as stated. However, it was not my business to negotiate peace, but only to try to see that Israel and the surrounding Arab states observed the provisions of the armistice agreements they had concluded. If these were broken, the cease-fire ordered by the Security Council was a sort of second line of defence of peaceful conditions.

I went to Egypt the next day to see Mr Pearson. I also had a meeting with Dr Fawzi on November 11, 1955, to discuss whether Egypt would agree to the Three Points. As most of the questions were military, he left these for a talk I was to have with Major-General Abd El Hakim Amr the next day. But he did take pains to make the point with me that Egypt objected to receiving concerted representations by the Three Powers. He said Egypt was always ready to listen to disinterested advice, but did not appreciate anything that savoured of pressure, and furthermore did not recognize that the Three Powers had any special authority to tender advice in relation to the area. I pointed out the terms of the Three Power Statement of May 25, 1950, and that the Three Powers, as permanent members of the Security Council, had a special responsibility for the maintenance of peace. Of course, the real meaning of Dr Fawzi's observations, which were intended to be conveyed to the Secretary-General, was that with the changed state of affairs following the acceptance of arms from Czechoslovakia Egypt could have the U.S.S.R.'s support in resisting any course of action prescribed by the Three Powers which was distasteful to her. Particularly she would reject courses of action which seemed to favour Israel at the expense of the Arabs, or, I suppose, even those which could detract from the prestige of Egypt as the would-be leader of the Arab states.

I saw General Amr the next day, and we had a talk that was useful in clarifying the Egyptian position, if not productive in respect of acceptance of the Secretary-General's Three Points. General Amr and his advisers remained convinced that the Israeli " civil police " were really troops, and would not agree to the Three Points while the " civil police " remained in the demilitarized zone.

He was frank about his strategical and tactical problem. If the Gaza Strip was to be defended, which the Egyptians considered as an essential obligation, the main body of the force to counter an Israeli attack on the Strip would have to be in the area El Arish-Rafah, with some extension southward. But a force so disposed was open to a thrust from the Israeli offensive forces which must be assumed to be in the area of Beersheba and to the south-west, operating through the El Auja zone, which Israel now effectively controlled. To guard against such a thrust, the Egyptians had to have forward, or outpost, positions in the area between the El Auja demilitarized zone and the line El Quseima-Abu Aweigila. In other words, Egypt could not comply with Article VIII, paragraph 3, which prohibited her from having defensive positions in this area, while Israel did not comply with Article VII which prohibited her from having offensive forces west of Beersheba.[25] From the military point of view I could not but agree with General Amr.

The grouping of the Egyptian forces dictated by the necessity to defend the Gaza Strip, combined with the terrain and communications of the Sinai, made their position inherently weak strategically. The Israelis naturally took advantage of this weakness in October 1956.

In the late afternoon I saw Prime Minister Nasser, and he confirmed the stand which General Amr had taken. He reiterated that Egypt wanted peace. Orders to the forward troops not to fire were in effect ; and there would be no retaliations by Egypt for the recent events in the demilitarized zone and El Kuntilla.

I repeated to him Mr Ben-Gurion's offer to meet him, and outlined what he had stated to be Israel's policy, but he made no comment. It is a curious fact that during the period from about midsummer 1955 to midsummer 1956 there were, to my knowledge, four or five people who saw Nasser and then saw Ben-Gurion, or saw them in the reverse order, all endeavouring to discover whether common grounds for the beginning of peace negotiations could be found. Both leaders were apparently very ready to give audiences and even encouragement to these amateur heralds of peace, whose well-intentioned efforts were unfortunately uniformly and completely unproductive.

The negotiations on the Three Points went on for nearly a month. The Egyptians repeated they could not accept Israeli police in the demilitarized zone. The Israelis kept bringing up the question of Egyptian defensive positions in the " quadrangle." The Egyptians said they could not vacate these positions while the Israelis had offensive forces in the Western Front. The Israelis said they had no forces other than defensive in this area, but would not agree to letting UNMOs visit the area to confirm it, to convince the Egyptians. Both sides wanted to avoid being in the position of rejecting the Secretary-General's Three Points, and tried to put the blame on the other. It was a most frustrating business ; and the situation remained full of danger, as from time to time there were incidents of firing along the Gaza DL in the familiar patterns, and there had been a number of *fedayeen* maraudings into Israel from Jordan. General Glubb told me the raids had been discovered to have been promoted by the Egyptian military attaché. When I complained to General Amr, he disclaimed knowledge of any such activity. The Israelis were aroused and threatening statements were published in the papers. Mr Ben-Gurion, through the Minister of Foreign Affairs, pressed me to obtain a public statement by the Egyptian Prime Minister that he would order a " complete cease-fire, to include all *fedayeen* activities."

The tense and frustrating situation was ended—or suspended— by the Israeli attack on the Syrians on the shore of Lake Tiberias, on December 11. This, for a time, took attention away from the Egypt-Israel situation.

CHAPTER 8

Syria-Israel 1955

Map 5

FROM the raid on Gaza until nearly the end of 1955, I had been mainly occupied by the clashes and increasing tension between Egypt and Israel, as described in the last two chapters. During the same period there had been a relative calm between Israel and Jordan. Between Lebanon and Israel there were very few difficulties. With Syria, however, there was always the possibility of the underlying hostility erupting into armed conflict.

On December 11, 1955, which was a Sunday, I was urgently summoned by Mr Ben-Gurion to his office. It was unusual for the Israeli Government to do business with UNTSO on a Sunday, unless there was an emergency. Mr Ben-Gurion said he was sorry to interfere with my day of rest, but he was very anxious to learn the outcome of my discussions in Cairo, where I had been on the three preceding days, trying to get the Egyptians to agree to the Secretary-General's Three Points for liquidating the El Auja impasse, and also trying to get a promise from General Amr and Prime Minister Nasser to impose effective controls to stop firing at the Israeli patrols along the Gaza ADL.

I explained to the Israeli Premier the Egyptians' stand regarding the Three Points, and also told him that Premier Nasser had disclaimed any responsibility for the *fedayeen* who were coming out of Jordan. I said I had hopes that the ambassadors of the U.S.A. and Great Britain in Cairo (Mr Henry Byroade and Sir Humphrey Trevelyan) would be able to persuade the Egyptians to accept the proposals. (They eventually did.) Mr Ben-Gurion asked when I expected to get a firm answer from the Egyptians, and I said I hoped there would be one by the 15th—in four days. Mr Ben-Gurion said he would wait, but was vaguely threatening about what might happen if in the meantime " blood was spilt."

I wrote in my diary that night that " maybe Israel is preparing something." Syria had not been mentioned in the conversation, but it was against Syria that Israel was preparing a reprisal, and not against Egypt. I finished my conversation with Mr Ben-Gurion before five o'clock. About ten o'clock the same night, several companies of Israeli troops crossed the demarcation lines at the northern end of Lake Tiberias, and attacked Syrian military posts at Buteiha Farm and Koursi, some eight kilometres to the south.[26] Some troops forded the Jordan River ; some crossed by boats ; another small force, including armoured vehicles, advanced north-ward from the Israeli settlement of Ein Gev, on the east shore of the lake. The attack was covered by mortar and heavy machine-gun fire, and was skilfully and boldly executed.

The statement issued by the Israeli Ministry of Foreign Affairs the same night said that the attack was made because, on the 10th, Syrian positions had opened fire on an Israeli police boat protecting fishermen on the east side of the lake. No one with any knowledge of military affairs would believe that such an elaborate, co-ordinated attack had not been planned well before, and probably rehearsed. Certainly it was not improvised in a few hours. When he was talking to me Mr Ben-Gurion must have been well aware that the attack was mounted, and what the zero hour was. There was time to stop it after I had left his office. Presumably the reply I had brought, the answers I was able to give him about the Egyptian attitude, were not satisfactory. I feel that he must have had in mind the possibility of calling off the attack if the Egyptians had not seemed obdurate. I cannot explain his unusual step in calling me to his office on a Sunday afternoon, with very little warning, on any other assumption. The connexion between Egypt's attitude and the attack on Syria will appear later.

What were the real causes for this heavy raid, which caused the Syrian casualties—three officers and thirty-eight other ranks killed, seven policemen and eight civilians (including three women) killed ; nine wounded and thirty-two missing ? The reasons given by the Ministry of Foreign Affairs' statement were only an excuse, and not a very good one. To know the real reasons, we shall have to go back a space into the dismal history of the armistice to under-stand how the Syrian-Israeli tensions built up.

A year and three days before, on December 8, 1954, a party of five armed Israeli soldiers had been captured by Syrian troops, some kilometres within Syrian territory. The Israelis had blundered into the more numerous Syrians in circumstances which made resistance impossible. At first there was no clue as to what they had been doing. But soon one of the Israelis told his captors, under interrogation, that their task had been to pick up a device for tapping a Syrian telephone-line, which had been placed there some time before. All this came out at the proceedings of the MAC, or in course of the UNTSO investigation.

On January 12, 1955, in the early part of the night, one of the

Israeli soldiers committed suicide by hanging himself in the prison. The Syrians immediately reported it to the MAC, and an observer was shown the body, the cell, and other evidence. There were no signs of physical ill-treatment on the body. However, the unfortunate young man had left messages the purport of which was " I am not a traitor." It seems very likely that the Syrians had used the common technique of telling him his comrades had been shot as spies, and that he could only save his life by giving information, and he had then broken down.

There was a great uproar in the Israeli Press against the barbarity of the Syrians, kidnapping and torture being alleged. No Israeli newspaper, of course, pointed out the plain fact that whatever officer had ordered the patrol to enter Syrian territory (and due to the nature of the mission it was probably ordered at a fairly high level) had done so in deliberate breach of the armistice agreement, and was morally responsible for whatever had happened to the soldiers sent on the mission.

The MAC met on January 12, and found Israel had committed a breach of the GAA. There was a rider to the resolution, calling upon the Syrian authorities to treat the captured Israelis in the same way as prisoners of war were supposed to be treated under the Geneva Convention of 1949. A second resolution proposed by Israel and voted for by the Chairman of the MAC " called upon " the Syrian authorities to release the prisoners through the MAC.

It is important to note that the Syrians were not obliged, by the terms of the GAA, to release any Israelis captured within their territory. The Israeli practice was to imprison civilian infiltrators for lengthy terms. A soldier violating the ADL, and captured in the territory of the other party, had no status as a prisoner of war. However, I had discussed the question of these prisoners with my advisers and the Chairman of the MAC, and I had decided that there would certainly be trouble between Israel and Syria if the prisoners were held. This followed the experience with the prisoner Gibli—described in Chapter 3. Perhaps it was wrong policy to try to save the Israelis from the consequences of their illegal act for fear that they would commit further aggressions. However, that is the decision I took at the time, in the hope of avoiding more trouble. During 1955 I visited Damascus a number of times trying to get the Syrian Army authorities to let their prisoners go.

Generally I discussed this question with General Shawkat Shuquair, who was then Syrian Chief of Staff. He was a Druse, and came originally from Lebanon. I found him a pleasant and able man, sitting uneasily in his chair, presiding over the turbulent and faction-ridden Syrian Army, with its recent history of military cabals and coups. His policy as regards Israel was to avoid incidents and situations which might involve Syria in active hostilities, for he realized his Army's weakness in the face of the Israelis' superior armament, training, and organization. I got on very well with him, and was sorry when he was displaced as Chief of Staff early in 1956, and retired to obscurity in the Lebanon.

However, I was quite unsuccessful in securing the release of the prisoners. Shuquair never refused, but always said that political difficulties prevented his meeting my request. There was said to be an influential element in the Army, backed up by certain politicians, which was very averse to letting the Israelis go. I have no doubt this was so. Shuquair always hoped to be able to overcome the opposition, at a favourable time, but the time never came. He was able to prevent the men from being tried as spies, or for some other offence under military law, which course some of the Syrians favoured, and which certainly would have caused serious reactions in Israel.

Towards midsummer 1955 the Syrians found another reason for not releasing their prisoners. They alleged that there were a number of Syrians in Israeli prisons, some of them concealed there since the hostilities of 1948, after which all prisoners in the hands of both parties were supposed to have been exchanged.

There was a good deal that was quite mysterious about the Syrian insistence that the Israelis were holding certain persons, whom they named, that could not be explained by a mere desire to delay the return of the Israeli prisoners, and so annoy Israel— a dangerous pastime, it proved, when dealing with men of the peremptory character of Mr Ben-Gurion and General Dayan. I put the mystery to the intervention of the Deuxième Bureau, the intelligence branch of the Syrian Army. The power of the officers in this branch of the staff in all Arab armies is very considerable, perhaps especially so in Syria, as the career of Lieutenant-Colonel Abd El Hamid Serraj illustrates. In Israel the branch possesses much influence also. We found periodically that one side or the other would exhibit an extreme curiosity about some person the other side was supposed to be holding as a prisoner, a curiosity that did not seem to be warranted by the nominal grounds for their inquiry. In such cases we usually guessed that the inquirers suspected that the person they were asking about had been subverted by the other side for espionage or some other intelligence service. Perhaps the Syrian Deuxième Bureau were using this negotiation to obtain information about a number of former Syrians who reportedly had disappeared, but whom they still had on their files as potential spies for Israel.

The whole negotiation was very unsatisfactory from my viewpoint. In any case I could devote only a small part of my time to it, events and dangers on the Egypt-Israel border being so much more insistent.

Israel's plan to divert the waters of the upper Jordan contained a serious possibility of overt conflict. However, in the event, it did not come into the open and require me to act in regard to it, in my capacity of Chief of Staff UNTSO. The scheme involved the building of a canal to tap the Jordan River waters just below Jisr Banat Yakub (the Bridge of Jacob's Daughters) in the Israel-Syrian demilitarized zone. When the Israelis began this work, in 1953, they explained it as a relatively small diversion which was to provide the water-power for an electricity generating station on the shore of Lake Tiberias. Investigation showed the section of the canal to be much greater than would be needed for the alleged purpose, and later the Israelis admitted to the engineers working with Mr Eric Johnston that it was also intended to divert a considerable volume of water to a reservoir at Beit Netufa, whence it would be piped, partly through tunnels, to the Sharon plain and eventually to the Negev.

The Israelis had commenced cutting the canal in the demilitarized zone in September 1953, and it caused great Syrian excitement, some shooting, and the possibility of a serious conflict. My predecessor, General Bennike, ordered the Israelis to stop the work. His principal reason for this decision was that the canal would alter the balance of the military situation in the DZ.

During 1955 I caused a group of officers to re-study the military problem, and their conclusions, with which I agreed, were opposed to General Bennike's. The study was made in case the question should be reopened, and I should have to give a decision on it. Although the evaluation of the military effect of the canal upon which General Bennike based his decision might be contested, in my opinion it was absolutely right to halt the Israeli project. It was in effect a unilateral diversion of the waters of a river to which Syria and Jordan also had rights. Also, General Bennike had pointed out that the diversion could have adverse effects on the rights of Arab landholders. His decision was backed up by the Security Council—and still more important by the U.S. Government. The Israel Government had at first refused to obey General Bennike's order, but the U.S.A., after warning, issued an order that economic assistance to Israel would stop, which quickly brought a change of attitude. This economic sanction of the U.S. Government, in fact, continued to operate throughout 1955 and 1956 to prevent the Israelis from taking matters into their own hands again, and completing the canal diversion. If the Syrians had attempted to prevent it by force of arms (in doing which they would have put themselves in the wrong) the Israelis were confident that they could easily settle the question by force, and doubtless they could have.

The problem was politically very delicate. Mr Ben-Gurion in a key speech before the election in June 1955 had promised, if entrusted with the government after the election, to bring the waters of the Jordan to the fields of the Negev. No doubt on general principles he wished to keep his election promises, but furthermore the development of the Negev was and is particularly dear to his heart. He could not, he thought, publicly state that he would not go ahead with the Jisr Banat Yakub diversion unless agreement with the Arab states for the division of the Jordan waters could be reached. This difficulty persisted through the negotiations which Mr Hammarskjöld conducted in the spring of 1956, as will be related in another chapter.

In 1955 President Eisenhower assigned Mr Eric Johnston to the task of getting agreement between the several Arab states and Israel on the development of the use of the Jordan waters. Mr Johnston made several visits to the Middle East in the course of these negotiations, which in my judgment he conducted with great skill. He came very close to success at one point. The engineers and lawyers of both sides agreed that the division of the waters he worked out after many consultations with both parties was a fair and reasonable one. There was no doubt that the project, if put into execution, would greatly benefit the countries concerned. Probably Jordan stood to gain the most, as a considerable area of the lower reaches of the river in Jordan territory could have been irrigated and hence opened to settlement by the Palestine refugees idle in their camps. Two hundred thousand refugees, it was said, could be so settled.

In the negotiation, Mr Johnston told me, the Egyptians had played a useful and constructive rôle. They were not immediately interested then, as their territory of course did not touch the Jordan, but anyway they acted as moderators in persuading the Syrians and Jordanians to accept, or be reasonable about, Mr Johnston's proposals. This attitude was perhaps not purely disinterested, as at the time Premier Nasser was hopeful of getting large-scale U.S. assistance in building the new Aswan Dam on the Nile, and it had presumably been hinted that if the negotiations about the Jordan turned out well, it would be a factor favourable to American participation in this great scheme for the Nile.

This sketchy history illustrates well the complexity of the Middle

East problem, and the Palestine problem within it. It is like a large ball of string. Several loose ends protrude, but when one begins to draw out any particular little bit of string, one finds it is inextricably tangled up with the other pieces in the ball. It constitutes a Gordian knot, and so far no Alexander bold enough to cut it has come along.

The Johnston negotiation, seemingly close to success, was stalled by the obduracy of the Syrian politicians. They simply would not agree to anything that would benefit Israel, even if the Arab states would thereby achieve greater benefits. Later, Abdullah Yafi, then Prime Minister of Lebanon, put it to Mr Hammarskjöld : " Suppose some one occupies your house illegally, and you cannot evict him. Then he comes and invites you to help him arrange the water supply to that house. Would you do it ? "

In December 1954 the Syrian Government laid before me a number of complaints as to the observance of the GAA in the demilitarized zones, particularly the central DZ. After studying these complaints, I made a report on them to the Security Council, dated January 6, 1955. They were, generally speaking, aspects of the dispute between Israel and Syria as to the interpretation of Part V of the GAA which related to the status of the demilitarized zone. (See Map 5.) The Security Council, by resolution of May 18, 1951, had made certain rulings in this matter.

Briefly, and stripped so far as possible of technicalities, the question at issue may be put thus. The Israelis claimed sovereignty over the territory covered by the DZ, subject only to the specific restrictions against military forces therein, and related matters covered in Part V of the GAA. They then proceeded, as opportunity offered, to encroach on the specific restrictions, and so eventually to free themselves, on various pretexts, from all of them. It was essentially the same process as they adopted in the El Auja demilitarized zone.

The Security Council's May 1951 rulings had followed an outbreak of fighting in the zone, which began with the resistance of Arab landholders to Israeli workmen who were beginning excavations on their lands in connexion with the plan for the drainage of the Huleh marshes. The Syrians supported the Arabs. There were various acts of violence, in flagrant breach of the armistice agreement, by both sides. The Israelis at one point bombed El Hamma village from the air, and at another time Syrian irregular troops entered the zone at the hill of El Mutilla, just north of where the Jordan flows into Lake Tiberias. During these disturbances the Israelis evacuated the Arab inhabitants of

B.A.I.—8

Baqqara and other Arab villages in the zone, and sent them to Sha'ab, near Acre, following this up by razing their houses to the ground with bulldozers.

The Security Council called upon the governments of Israel and Syria to abide by the decisions of the MAC or its Chairman in regard to all complaints, and not to refuse to attend meetings of the MAC or comply with the request of its Chairman. The complaints referred to in this 1951 ruling were subject to no exceptions, and hence were meant to include complaints relating to the conditions or incidents in the DZ. The Security Council recognized that it was within the competence of the Chairman to act in regards to certain matters, while it fell to the MAC to deal with others. The Israelis claimed that *all* matters relating to the demilitarized zone on which a decision should be required were for the Chairman alone to deal with, or to negotiate with them. The Syrians claimed that the MAC was competent to deal with certain questions, if not all.

The deadlock was complete, and, in spite of the exhortation of the Security Council, remained complete. No regular meetings of the Mixed Armistice Commission had been held since June 20, 1951. Occasional emergency meetings were held, as in the case of the five captured Israeli soldiers, but, in general, the Chairman and observers of the MAC were reduced to investigating incidents, and negotiating informally, sometimes usefully, usually unproductively. The Mixed Armistice Commission machinery no longer operated as between Israel and Syria.

The Israelis in fact exercised almost complete control over the major portion of the demilitarized zone through their frontier police in the area. This was directly contrary to Article V of the GAA and the " authoritative interpretation " of it (by Dr Bunche) which formed part of the proceedings of the committee negotiating the armistice between the two countries, and had been agreed to by both sides.

The frontier police in Israel are more than an ordinary police-force, concerned with the enforcement of the internal laws of the state. They are a paramilitary force. In most parts, they are the first line of defence, so to speak, of the long and vulnerable Israel borders. They have pistols and rifles, which is normal armament for police in the Middle East, but they also have machine-guns and mortars, which they frequently deploy and use. They are all trained soldiers. Hence their introduction into the demilitarized zone was essentially a violation of the demilitarization principle, although not perhaps one easy to demonstrate with legal precision.

We shall now see how the Israelis used their police power to deal with the Arab villagers in the zone. At the time of my January 1955 report there were about 350 Arabs living in Baqqara village, or, rather, amid its ruins, for the original buildings had been bulldozed to the ground by the Israelis when the villagers had been evicted during the course of the 1951 fighting. In fact, the Arabs living there were the survivors of the two villages, Baqqara and Ghranname, and possibly some other places. There were two *mukhtars* who spoke for them, Jabr Ali of Baqqara and Osman Hamid of Ghranname. The Security Council resolution of May 18, 1951, provided that "Arab civilians who have been removed from the demilitarized zone by the Government of Israel should be permitted to return forthwith to their homes," and that "the Mixed Armistice Commission should supervise their return and rehabilitation in a manner to be determined by the Commission."

When I first visited them in December 1954, their rehabilitation had not progressed very far. They were living in miserable conditions, in tents and indifferent mud huts, with no school or medical facilities. They could not circulate beyond the limits of their village without getting a pass from the Israeli police each time, and, of course, were not allowed to cross into Syria, where they would have liked to trade.

They were cultivating lands of which some were their own, and some of which belonged to other Arabs—about 5000 *dunams* (1250 acres). They raised crops of wheat, barley, tobacco, and citrus fruits, but they could sell only to the Israelis, who paid them a very low price. In the year 1954, until late in December, they were not given a chance to sell at all. Since 1951 no Chairman of the MAC had been able to get satisfactory co-operation from the Israeli authorities in the matter. On the other hand, the Israelis had made attempts, in consultation with the Chairman, to organize a school, medical services, and a store, but the Arabs always found some reason for not accepting the proposals. They were not very reasonable people, I thought ; but then the treatment they had received was not calculated to promote sweetness and light.

The *mukhtars* took me to their tent, where with the notables of the village we sat on mattresses and drank sweet tea and coffee. Then they exposed their grievances. An Israeli policeman interpreted. They finally said they despaired of achieving a proper life where they were, and they wanted to be allowed to leave, to go to Syria, where they could "live like Arabs."

This, in fact, meant that they would become refugees ; but they did not realize that they would not be entitled to aid by UNRWA, whose terms of reference allowed support only of those former residents of Palestine who had been forced to leave their homes. 1 told the *mukhtars* that they were better off where they were, and should stay. Their conditions, though bad, were definitely better than those of the refugees, a number of whose camps I had seen. I had also learned that the Government of Syria was not prepared to receive them, and would prevent their crossing the Jordan. The *mukhtars* threatened to go, nevertheless, and let the Syrians shoot them down, if they would.

I then went to Damascus and discussed the case with the Syrian authorities. They confirmed that they would not permit the Baqqara-Ghranname villagers to enter Syria, and said it was up to me to oblige the Israelis to treat these people decently, and live up to their obligations. The next day we saw the representatives of the villagers at Jisr Banat Yakub, and Colonel Kottrash, the senior Syrian delegate to the MAC, spoke to them, confirming the Syrian stand. I said I would try to get the Israeli Government to meet their most pressing needs, and also report their condition and complaints to the Security Council. They agreed, rather grudgingly, to await the results of my efforts.

I then wrote to General Dayan asking that (*a*) the villagers should be allowed to sell their 1954 crop and buy their needs with the proceeds, (*b*) that arrangements should be made for grinding their grain so they could have proper flour to make their bread, (*c*) that they be allowed freedom of movement within the zone, subject to carrying identification papers, (*d*) that later arrangements should be made for schools, medical care, and the rebuilding of their houses, and (*e*) that UNRWA should supply them with their immediate necessities, mainly groceries.

In a short while I had a reply from General Dayan agreeing to everything, except the request that UNRWA should give the villagers supplies. He made the point, which was fair enough, that they would have a good deal of money when they sold their crops, for which they would get a good price, and for UNRWA to give them free issues would be treating them like paupers, which they were not. A good deal of the success of this appeal was due to the intervention of Mr Walter Eytan, Director-General of the Ministry of Foreign Affairs, with whom I discussed the affair. He saw clearly that Israel was not living up to her obligations in respect to these people, and, I think, made the military authorities see the point.

I saw the villagers again on December 29, and they had received a good sum of money for their crops, with more to come, their grain was being ground, and though they were not at all happy their most serious complaints were remedied.

This relatively satisfactory state of affairs did not last very long.

In the course of the next year there were disputes between the Arab villagers and the adjoining Israeli settlements, in which the Arabs naturally got the worst of it. Then the Israeli police from time to time entered their village and arrested some of the men. It was not possible to get the Israeli authorities to give any particulars of the charges or evidence against those detained. The most serious incident arose out of the killing of one of the villagers. It seems that he had been informing for the Israelis, and paid for it with his life. Several other villagers were held as prisoners for a long time after this, without specific charges against them.

The villagers' freedom of movement was still very restricted ; they had to do most of their purchasing at Tiberias, where, according to their complaint, " there was nothing to be had except bananas," and could not go to Nazareth, where there was a large Arab population, and the sort of goods they wanted could be bought.

One lighter episode concerned the wife of Jabr Ali, the *mukhtar*, a tall, rather good-looking man of at least seventy years of age. Some of the villagers, including Jabr's wife, had crossed into Syria at the time of the 1951 uprooting of Baqqara. The Israelis would not allow any of them to come back. He made a number of pathetic requests that his wife be allowed to rejoin him : she was nearly of his age, and it seemed sad that they should be separated in the few years that remained to them on earth.

I wrote to General Dayan urging that this case be treated in a compassionate way, and after a while he kindly agreed to make an exception. Lieutenant-Colonel J. P. Castonguay, Chairman of the MAC, witnessed the reunion at the Jisr Banat Yakub. The old lady was in a state of great emotion, and kissed the hand of her lord, as the village custom was. Jabr, however, seemed less than pleased. " Where are the cows ? " he roared. It seems that his spouse had taken the family cattle with her when she escaped, and Jabr's joy at having her back was considerably mitigated by the non-return of the beasts.

Near the start of the negotiations with which I was concerned, the Israelis made the villagers an offer to exchange their lands for others beyond Nazareth, in a predominantly Arab part of Galilee. This would have removed them from the strategically sensitive demilitarized zone, where they were an embarrassment, as the Israelis admitted in moments of frankness. The villagers, however, refused the exchange, fearing they would receive inferior land. Their life went on uncomfortably. Finally, in 1956, when every one's attention was centred on the Sinai and the Suez Canal, the Baqqara and Ghranname villagers got what they had been demanding. They were allowed to cross into Syria, and the Israelis had the demilitarized zone to themselves. By Lieutenant-General Riley's estimate, there had been about 2000 Arabs in the zone before 1951.

As a reason for the attack on the Syrian positions near the shore of Lake Tiberias, the Israeli Foreign Ministry had cited the firing by Syrians on Israeli fishing-boats and their police escort on December 10, 1955. They also alleged that during 1955 there were " at least twenty-five incidents on the lake following the opening of fire by Syrian outposts on Israel fishermen and police launches causing loss of life and property." In fact, the Israelis had submitted twenty-two complaints to the MAC, but in none of them did they ask for an emergency meeting, or state there had been any Israeli killed or wounded. In most of the complaints the fire was alleged to have been at police boats, not fishing-boats. These police boats followed the practice of cruising close to the shore, whether escorting Israeli fishing-boats or not. The Syrians considered this provocative. It was the same policy on Lake Tiberias that the Israeli mechanized patrols followed along the ADL bordering the Gaza Strip.

Actually, arrangements had been made with the Syrians through the Chairman of the MAC to try to prevent firing at Israeli fishing-boats during the current fishing season, which ran from about mid-November to mid-April. The Syrian delegate had passed on the word to the Syrian outposts, and no firing at Israeli fishing-boats had taken place since the beginning of the fishing season. The incident on December 10, which was alleged to have provoked the Israeli retaliation on the night of December 11–12, occurred when an Israeli police boat or boats approached the shore near Buteiha Farm. Both sides claimed the other fired first.

All the circumstances point to the probability that the police boat was sent on December 10 deliberately to provoke an incident which should serve as excuse for launching the attack, which had, as I have said, obviously been prepared long before the 10th. While the incidents of firing at fishermen may have been a contributing cause, more important causes were the failure to return the prisoners —in which the Syrians were within their legal rights, although they acted in an imprudent and aggravating manner. Then, there was the more significant circumstance that Syria and Egypt had recently concluded a Mutual Defence Pact, which provided for the placing of the forces of the two nations under a single command, and other measures of co-operation.

The comment in a *Jerusalem Post* editorial of December 14, 1955, is illuminating :

> Most certainly an element in the comparatively early raid was the fact that the Syrian and Egyptian fronts are now considered an indivisible unit by the Israeli security authorities. Since the signing of the military pact between these two countries, and the establishment of joint airfields in Syrian territory, Egypt must be considered as operating out of Syria as well as through the Gaza Strip and Sinai.

Thus it would seem that part of the reason for the Tiberias action was to convey to the Syrians that they would do well not to link themselves too closely to Egypt, which did not have the power to defend Syrian territory.

On January 19, 1956, the Security Council passed a resolution condemning Israel for the attack, in terms described by the French delegate, M. Hervé Alphand, as " the strongest ever passed by the Council on the subject." It expressed the Council's grave concern at the failure of the Israel Government to comply with its obligations, and called on Israel to do so in future, " in default of which the Council will have to consider what further measures under the Charter are required to maintain or restore the peace."

This last clause was generally considered to be a threat that sanctions of some sort would be employed against Israel if she carried out further attacks of this sort. The grounds for her successive reprisals had become palpably inadequate. The Security Council had passed its resolution unanimously, although the U.S.S.R. and Yugoslavia would have preferred one in even stronger terms. I felt that the Security Council should have taken more positive action to restrain the aggressive Israeli policy, which seemed to me to constitute the greatest danger to peace at that time.

Instead, however, I was instructed to pursue certain suggestions for the avoidance of similar incidents, which I had appended to my report. I had put these forward reluctantly, in view of the lack of success in negotiating agreements between Egypt and Israel, and Israel and Jordan. The proposals were that there should be a gentleman's agreement that Israel would keep her police boats two hundred metres away from the shore in the sensitive area ; that prisoners should be exchanged ; and that the MAC should be set in operation again, through acceptance of the clause providing for the interpretation of disputed sections in the GAA by the MAC itself. None of these suggestions was accepted by the parties, except the exchange of prisoners, which after further tedious negotiations took place on March 29, 1956, when, at the Jisr Banat

Yakub, four Israeli soldiers and one civilian were handed over against thirty-five Syrian soldiers and six civilians.

It was reported that there was a good deal of dissatisfaction in the Israeli Cabinet following the Tiberias operation. Mr Ben-Gurion, who at that time was acting as Foreign Minister, as well as Premier and Minister of Defence, had, it seems, taken the decision to allow the attack without consulting his colleagues. It was soon perceived that the disproportion between the scale of the operation and the alleged cause put Israel in a worse light than usual. This was particularly unfortunate, from the Israeli viewpoint, since Mr Sharett, the Foreign Minister, was engaged in negotiations in the United States for the supply of armaments to balance those the Egyptians had acquired from the Czechoslovaks. The incident put a quick end to these negotiations, whatever hope there might have previously been of their success. A current witticism in Israel was that the biggest explosion of the Tiberias attack was that which went off under Mr Sharett. It was later reported that Mr Ben-Gurion had agreed that in future no operation of such importance would be authorized without the Cabinet's being consulted.

UNTSO had very few difficulties in connexion with the General Armistice Agreement between Israel and Lebanon. In fact, the Israel-Lebanon MAC worked as it had been intended all MACs should. It met at periodic intervals, and seldom had serious complaints to deal with. Those that were presented related mostly to grazing of cattle on the wrong side of the ADL. The ADL was the pre-war frontier between Palestine and Lebanon, and so was generally accepted by the inhabitants, and was not a galling innovation like the ADLs around the Gaza Strip and the West Bank in Jordan. There were, from time to time, incidents between the inhabitants on the two sides of the line—local feuds and clashes, having nothing to do with the interests of the two states. The activities of smugglers occasionally caused minor trouble. But the MAC met and, for the most part, without formal procedure or resolutions decided to take whatever action was necessary to discipline the offenders, or prevent future trouble of the same kind.

During my tenure as Chief of Staff UNTSO there were only two serious difficulties between Israel and Lebanon. The first arose when three Israeli youths, all about twenty-two years old, were apprehended on April 12, 1955, some ten kilometres inside Lebanese territory, and were taken to Beirut and imprisoned. They explained that they were just going for a hike up Mount

Hermon, although they admitted knowing well it was in Syrian territory.

Unfortunately for this explanation, they had equipped themselves with sub-machine-guns, grenades, maps, bully beef, and other military impedimenta which would be considered unusual for a picnic in most countries. They had done their military service. Naturally, the Lebanese looked on their jaunt with considerable disfavour, and at first treated them as military personnel carrying out an intelligence mission in Lebanese territory.

However, it was by no means uncommon for adventurous Israeli boys, and girls too, to undertake these expeditions into Arab territory, to prove their daring and endurance. It was foolhardy, of course, and unfortunately there were several cases where the adventurers paid for it with their lives. But a good many must have ventured, and lived to tell the tale. The Israeli Government had laws against clandestinely crossing the border, but presumably these only came into operation when some one got caught on the other side, as in this case.

As soon as their capture became known, there was a great hullabaloo in the Israeli Press, as usual. This was intensified because of the concurrent affair of the four Israeli soldiers imprisoned in Syria. Indeed, the Syrians put considerable pressure on the Lebanese to hand these three hikers over to them, on the grounds that they had been heading for Mount Hermon, in Syria. But the Lebanese fortunately did not do so.

The Israel Ministry of Foreign Affairs began to press me to procure the ' hikers' ' release, on the grounds that their crossing into Lebanese territory was merely a foolish prank. I could not help thinking of how the Israeli Army would have dealt with three young Arabs, similarly equipped, whom they might have caught in Israel. However, I still believed, at that time, that it would be a good thing to avoid the irritation caused by the holding of prisoners by one side or the other, so early in May I had a talk with Colonel Salem, the Lebanese Chief of Staff. He said that public opinion in Lebanon was pretty excited about the case, the young men having been represented as spies. Nevertheless, in a month or thereabouts, when the excitement had died down, the Lebanese authorities would bring them before a military court, and give them a relatively light sentence for infiltration, after which they could be released fairly soon.

This promise was not good enough for the Israelis, who proceeded to secure bargaining points for themselves. They seized a large number of sheep, and some shepherds, alleged to have been grazing on the wrong side of the DL, though it is by no means certain that they were. When the Lebanese representative at the MAC applied for their release, according to the usual understanding, it was made clear to him that the flocks would be returned only when the hikers were freed. This arbitrary action naturally stiffened the Lebanese attitude in turn, and for a month or so the smooth working of the Israel-Lebanon MAC was interrupted. Eventually, through the tactful negotiation of Colonel Communal, of the French Army, Chairman of the MAC, and the sensible attitude of General Fuad Shehab, commanding the Lebanese Army, an agreement was reached, and on August 3 the hikers were returned, and the cattle also.

Lebanon has a smaller army than the other three " armistice states," even relative to its population. While it possesses a quantity of military armament, its main function is in the sphere of internal security. The policy of the Lebanese is, while maintaining solidarity with the other Arab states in regard to its attitude towards Israel, to avoid anything which might exacerbate the situation. The length to which they would go to appease Israeli aggressiveness is shown by the incident just related.

The other trouble arose later in 1955, when there was a resumption of *fedayeen* activity in Israel. This time the marauders came not from the Gaza Strip, but from the other Arab states. There were one or two bad incidents in the Galilee region, when Israelis were killed or wounded, and it was proved that the attackers came from Lebanese territory. The Lebanese authorities were alarmed at this, and took energetic action. They soon found out that the attackers had been recruited from the refugee camps, and that an assistant Egyptian military attaché had organized the business. He was got rid of, with an energetic though private protest to Egypt. Furthermore, all refugees and people other than old-established residents were cleared from a zone ten kilometres deep on the Lebanese side of the border. These measures proved effective, and the raiding into Israel ceased.

These two were the only serious incidents between Israel and Lebanon during the years 1955 and 1956. If only the other borders had been as quiet !

CHAPTER 9

Israel-Jordan 1955–56

IN my diary for December 31, 1955, I find an entry : " The year ends with uncertainty as to what is ahead. I feel that unless a positive move is made towards a peace settlement there will be great danger of hostilities on a larger scale. These may begin with the Jisr Banat Yakub canal project—or may be precipitated by a small action near Gaza, or El Auja."

I do not suggest that this observation shows great prophetic powers. There must have been many others, familiar with the problems of the Middle East, who were saying the same thing to themselves. The endeavours of the Security Council and its agent, the UNTSO, to maintain peaceful conditions in accordance with the armistice agreements seemed to be becoming less and less effective. The tension was building up, not diminishing, and the safeguards against hostilities and provisions for negotiation of complaints between the parties were being rendered inoperative one after another, as has been described in the previous chapters.

Was there any positive move towards a peace settlement? Were the Great Powers doing anything to solve the problem? The United Nations has no authority under its Charter to enforce a settlement of any dispute ; it can only recommend. But the Great Powers, permanent members of the Security Council, had means of putting pressure on the parties to agree to a peace treaty. The trouble, they found, was to discover any terms of peace which stood any chance of being accepted by both sides.

During the latter half of 1955, kites had been flown to test reactions to various solutions of the principal problems preventing peace between Israel and her Arab neighbours. On August 26, 1955, Mr Dulles had discussed the subject in an address to the Council on Foreign Relations, in New York. In this very important statement Mr Dulles made it clear that he spoke with the authority of the President of the United States.

He enumerated the problems which were unresolved when the armistices were signed in 1949, and which, in his view, prevented peace between the Arabs and the Israelis.

> The first is the tragic plight of the 900,000 refugees who formerly lived in the territory that is now occupied by Israel.
> The second is the pall of fear that hangs over the Arab and Israel people alike. The Arab countries fear that Israel will seek by violent

means to expand at their expense. The Israelis fear that the Arabs will gradually marshal superior forces to be used to drive them into the sea, and they suffer from the economic measures now taken against them.

Mr Dulles went on to say that the 900,000 refugees should be resettled, or " to such an extent as may be feasible " repatriated. Israel should compensate the refugees, but would need financial aid to do so. President Eisenhower was ready to recommend that the U.S.A. should make a substantial contribution to an international loan for this purpose, and also contribute to the cost of water development and irrigation projects which would help Arab refugee resettlement, if the refugee and related problems were solved. The President would also recommend that the U.S.A. subscribe to a treaty for the prevention of the alteration of the Arab-Israel boundaries by force. However, there must be prior agreement on what these boundaries should be. Mr Dulles pointed out that ". . . the existing lines separating Israel and the Arab states were fixed by the Armistice Agreements of 1949. They are not designed to be permanent frontiers in every respect."

Mr Dulles' proposals, which seemed to constitute a cautious and moderate approach to a negotiated peace, as well as a most generous offer to contribute money and assistance towards making peace possible, received little favourable response from any quarter.

On August 29 Mr Ben-Gurion gave an interview to the London *Times*' Jerusalem correspondent, in which, answering the question whether if it were proposed as a means to peace, Israel would agree to modification of the present borders with the Arab states, he said, " We can agree to no changes whatever in the present frontiers. We would be prepared to consider minor frontier corrections by mutual agreement, but as the result, not as the condition, of peace. There can only be peace with Israel as it exists geographically to-day."

He set out his terms for peace—namely, genuine fulfilment of the conditions laid down by the armistice agreement, and cessation of all such hostile activities as the economic boycott—after which there should be a non-aggression pact between Israel and the Arabs, and peace, with active co-operation economically and culturally. He also said : " It is my view that a security pact between us and the United States would have the effect of convincing the present Arab governments that they cannot isolate us, and would create conditions in which some progress towards peaceable relations would be possible."

It will be recalled that on August 29, 1955, the first *fedayeen* campaign was in full swing. (See Chapter 7.) It is not surprising that Mr Dulles' proposals did not receive replies in the spirit in which they were conceived.

On October 18 Mr Sharett, speaking in the Knesset as Foreign Minister, replied more specifically to Mr Dulles' suggestions. His statement, while more diplomatically phrased, was no more favourable than Mr Ben-Gurion's earlier impromptu rejection. Mr Sharett said : " The main solution advocated by Mr Dulles was resettlement of the refugees in the neighbouring countries. On the basis of Israel's standing pledge to pay compensation for abandoned lands, Mr Dulles announced his Government's readiness to participate in a loan which would enable Israel to carry out its undertaking." Mr Sharett went on to indicate that Israel would not pay any compensation until the Arab boycott and blockade were lifted, and that the property left in Arab lands by those who had emigrated into Israel would also have to be taken into consideration.[27]

Mr Sharett further said that Mr Dulles' remarks about the borders between the Arab states and Israel " might well be interpreted as aiming at the contraction of Israel's territories in order to satisfy the expansive ambitions of the Arabs, particularly in the Negev, including Eilat. We asserted in unequivocal terms that Israel was determined to preserve its territorial integrity from Dan to Eilat and that no unilateral concessions on its part were even conceivable."

The Dulles proposals elicited no better response from the Arab side. A Jerusalem daily newspaper, Al Difaa, published a reaction which can be taken as generally typical of Arab opinion. It said that the Dulles statement was a patent shift from UN decisions (on boundaries and the refugees), and a new imperialist attempt to secure acceptance of Israel's existence. In Egypt the Government newspaper El Goumhouria said that the Dulles plan was Republican propaganda for the forthcoming presidential election, and that " not a single Arab government would agree to discuss the proposals which are designed to serve no purpose other than the consolidation of Israel."

There was no public reaction by the Egyptian Government to the Dulles proposals. They were made, it will be recalled, before Premier Nasser had made the fateful decision to accept the Czech arms deal, while he perhaps still had hopes of getting arms and economic assistance from the United States. It was therefore prudent to say nothing against them. On the other hand, they could scarcely be welcomed, as no Arab leader, least of all Nasser, could seem to be moving towards peace with Israel, and the Dulles proposals were certainly for a peace by compromise. And the first fedayeen campaign had been launched, designed as a reaction against the humiliation of the Gaza raid of February 28 and what the Egyptians were convinced was an attempt by the Israelis to force them to negotiate peace.

Later, early in November, Premier Nasser gave an indication of the position of Egypt in regard to a settlement with Israel, in an interview with the correspondent of the London *Observer*. He said that the UN resolutions, including the 1947 partition plan, were still the basis of the Arab terms for settlement. The Arab leaders had not so far discussed among themselves any other peace terms, and the question of the return of territory to the Arabs was most important because it would also help solve the refugee problem. The correspondent went on to say that he understood on good authority that the plan proposed by Count Bernadotte just before his assassination in 1948 offered a better basis for settlement than the 1947 partition, in Egypt's opinion. The principal feature of Bernadotte's plan was that the Arabs would be given a considerable section of the Negev, awarded to the Jews under the 1947 partition, in exchange for territory in Western Galilee allotted to the Arabs.

The Israelis inferred that Egypt's peace terms included the cession of territory in the Negev by Israel, and their hackles rose. They interpreted the speech which Sir Anthony Eden made at the Guildhall on November 9, 1955, in the light of this idea. After discussing the change in the Middle East situation brought about by the Czech arms deal, and the increasing tension on the Egypt-Israel boundary, he said in effect that the United Kingdom supported the Dulles proposals, and that the Arabs and Israelis, instead of insisting respectively on the boundaries of the suggested 1947 partition and the demarcation lines of the armistices, should come to a compromise.

A few days later Mr Ben-Gurion, in reply to a question in the Knesset, set out Israel's position towards Sir Anthony's proposals. His statement began :

> I have read the statement made by the British Prime Minister on November 9 with the close attention it deserves, and regret that its main contents are a complete contradiction of its objective. His proposal to truncate the territory of Israel for the benefit of its neighbours has no legal, moral, or logical basis, and cannot be considered. Instead of fostering better relations and bringing peace nearer, it is likely to intensify the Arab States' aggression and to lessen the likelihood of peace in the Middle East.

Other portions of his statement are revealing of his inflexible determination to yield nothing, and the reasons by which he justified his inflexibility. He said :

> History does not begin with the United Nations General Assembly's resolution of November 29, 1947. The Jewish people will always remember—and remember in gratitude and esteem—that thirty years before . . . the British Government, under the leadership of Lloyd

George and Balfour, and with active co-operation of the President of the United States, Woodrow Wilson, acknowledged the historical link between the Jewish people and the Land of Israel. . . . This link was in existence throughout the generations, and we live in our land as of right and not as of sufferance. A State of Israel was in existence in this country in a period when human history knew nothing of the existence of America or Britain. And Jerusalem was the capital of Israel when the World was unaware of the existence of London, Moscow, or Paris.

Another statement he made is frequently echoed, with variations, as the explanation of why Israel will not now consider implementing the UN resolutions. " The invasion of the Arab States [in 1948]," he said, " has made all the UN resolutions on Palestine null and void. They cannot be brought back to life any more than can the thousands of Jewish defenders who gave their lives for the salvation of their people and the renewal of its freedom."

This statement, with its great emotional appeal, ignores the fact that the UN resolutions calling for the repatriation of the refugees were passed in August 1948, and renewed yearly thereafter, after the Arab invasions were history. The Arab states, of course, proclaimed the object of their invasions was to go to the help of the Arabs in Palestine, threatened by the superior military force of the Jews there. It would seem that Arabs outside Palestine should have as much right to come to the assistance of Arabs in Palestine as Jews outside Palestine to come to the assistance of Jews within.

So much for the efforts of the political leaders of the United States and Great Britain to suggest a basis for peace negotiations in the latter part of 1955. In the last month of that same year a new source of instability in the Middle East appeared, which was to grow in seriousness through 1956. This was the movement in Jordan to eliminate British influence especially in the Arab Legion, and to bring the country into the Egyptian orbit.

General Glubb has described the chain of events which led to his dismissal, and the eventual abrogation of the Anglo-Jordanian treaty in his book *A Soldier with the Arabs*, chapters 21 to 26. It will therefore be necessary to refer to only a few of the salient happenings which affected the situation as between Israel and Jordan, or the work of the Truce Supervision Organization.

The riots in Jerusalem and other centres throughout Jordan from November 17–20 began mildly enough. The first demonstrations were, as usual, schoolchildren, led and inspired by their teachers, who were generally violently nationalist in political orientation, and a good many of them probably Communist.

The demonstration was against Jordan participation in the Baghdad Pact. On the 17th, a Saturday, in the late afternoon, I was on the Arab side of Jerusalem and found some of the streets were blocked. A crowd of small boys tried to stop my car, and threw some mud at it. This, incidentally, was the only occasion during my service with UNTSO that anything approaching violence was offered or threatened towards me, and it could hardly have been more trivial. On the same day a UNTSO jeep had its windows smashed, and the car of a well-known French doctor was burned.

The next day things were quieter, but we heard that there had been very serious riots in the refugee camp at Jericho (the largest in the country) and that the rioters had sacked the widely famed farm establishment of Musa el Alami, near by, which existed for training refugee boys in agriculture, and had also destroyed many of the camp administration buildings. Similar rioting and destruction took place in other places. On Monday the crowd in Jerusalem attacked the Italian Consulate, sacking it. They were later dispersed by the police, with difficulty. On Tuesday the 20th everything seemed quiet, but shortly after noon a mob formed and pulled down the flag of the American Consulate from the flagpole in the garden near the Mandelbaum Gate. They then had gone to the French Consulate, apparently their primary objective, and attempted to break in, but were repulsed through the courageous stand of M. de Beauvais, the French Vice-Consul, who held them off with a sub-machine-gun until the police took control.

During all these disturbances the most alarming feature was that the Jordanian Government had seemingly abdicated its responsibility to maintain law and order. Neither the police nor the Arab Legion received any orders or instructions as to what to do, though subsequent experience showed that they could easily handle the rioting and the mobs with a minimum of force.

The rioting created a problem for UNTSO. The attacks were concentrated on Europeans, whether the nations to which they belonged were connected with the Baghdad Pact or not. With the trifling exceptions I have noted, no violence was attempted against any UNTSO personnel this time. But many families of the military observers, UN Secretariat, and Field Service members were living on the Jordan side of Jerusalem, where accommodation and servants were easier to get than in Israel. Most of them were in houses or apartments in and around the suburb of Sheikh Jarrah, where many foreign consulates were also. It was therefore necessary to make plans for their security and their evacuation, if necessary, in case of further riots. These plans were actually put into effect in October 1956, when the Israelis invaded Egypt and the French and British intervened in Port Said.

Why had the rioting been set off by the possibility that Jordan would join the Baghdad Pact? This alliance, concluded between Iraq and Turkey in February 1955 and joined by Great Britain in April, Pakistan in September, and Iran in October, with the general support and approval of the United States, was for the purpose of defence of these Middle Easterners and Asians against possible Russian aggression, and Communist subversion, which they all had reason to fear, because of their geographical position. The Russians naturally deployed every resource of diplomacy, propaganda, and subversion to destroy the Pact, or at least to prevent other Middle Eastern states from joining it. In this purpose they found a most effective ally in Egypt. It is generally considered that Egypt fought the Pact because it might have brought the Arab states together in a defensive grouping with the West. Egypt had rejected the idea of a Middle East Defence Organization, on these lines, and did not want to see an alternative organization with Iraq as its leading Arab member. So the Egyptian propaganda machine loudly denounced the Baghdad Pact as a scheme for the perpetuation of Western domination—'imperialism'—and even more boldly asserted that it was a deep plot to entangle the Arab states in the Western web, and then oblige them to make peace with Israel, finally betraying the cause of the refugees. This propaganda had an enormous emotional appeal to the refugees and Palestinians in Jordan.

Saudi Arabia also disliked the Pact, because it increased the stature of Iraq, and still more disliked the idea that Jordan might join it, which would bring together the two countries ruled by the Hashemites, hereditary enemies of the Saudi dynasty.

The Israelis also objected strenuously to the Pact, because they were excluded from it, and because they had useful trading relations with Turkey, whose friendship they cultivated assiduously. Turkey had accepted the implicitly anti-Israel features of the Pact, and might be expected to be further alienated from Israel. Furthermore, Iraq and other Arab states which might join would receive arms which they had not pledged they would not use against Israel. Iraqi spokesmen had more than suggested that the Pact would apply in case of aggression from any quarter, including Israel. Of course, Iraq had no frontier with Israel, but Iraqi troops had participated in the 1948 war against her, holding a sector in the north of West Bank Jordan. The Iraqi troops had withdrawn at the time the armistices were signed, but Iraq had never negotiated an armistice with Israel. The Israelis were apprehensive that the

Iraqis might again send troops into Jordan, and, indeed, this became a real issue in the summer of 1956.

How had the possibility of Jordan's joining the Baghdad Pact arisen in December 1955? The question had been raised during the visit of a Turkish diplomatic and military mission in November. King Hussein and the Jordan Government were anxious to obtain more arms and financial support for the Arab Legion, and approached the United Kingdom to this end. It was suggested to them that they might get what they wanted, and at the same time convert the existing Anglo-Jordanian treaty into the multi-lateral Baghdad Pact, as Iraq had converted its treaty with the United Kingdom. Early in December Sir Gerald Templer, the Chief of the General Staff of the British Army, was sent to Amman to negotiate with the Jordanian Government in regard to these matters. The Egyptian and Communist propaganda machines went to work with great effect, backed up by Saudi money, which was lavishly spent to induce political and popular opposition. So, in Jerusalem particularly, there was collaboration between the opponents of the Pact, the activities of the Egyptian and Saudi consuls-general in this being carried on quite openly, and those of the Communists covertly.

It was effective too ; the Government of Said El Mufti resigned after a couple of days of the disorders, following the defection of three of the Palestinian ministers. A short-lived government was formed with Haza el Majali as Prime Minister, who announced that his policy was for Jordan to join the Pact. But the popular opposition was too strong ; several of his ministers resigned, and on December 19 he gave up the attempt to govern. Another government was formed under the elderly Ibrahim Hashim, a former Prime Minister and then Speaker of the Senate. His was to be a caretaker government until elections could be held, in the following April.

It was only a few weeks before more rioting broke out. This time the agitation was in regard to the alleged illegal dissolution of the Parliament—a curious constitutional point to cause rioting by a Jordanian mob, mainly of schoolchildren. But of course it was merely a pretext, for the inspirers of the previous riots, having prevented Jordan's adhesion to the Baghdad Pact by their propaganda and subversion, were eager to follow up their success. The eventual object was to eliminate the British control of the country and subordinate Jordan, one way or another, to the Egyptian policies—or, as the propagandists put it, to " liberate " Jordan.

However, the rioters did not have things their own way this time. Shortly after the rioting had begun the police and the Arab Legion received firm orders to repress it. There was stone-throwing at the American Consulate, and the flag was again pulled down. The Marine Corps guard under the Vice-Consul, Mr Slater Blakiston, however, prevented the rioters from getting into the premises. The Arab Legion post near by did nothing to control the rioters. But by the next day the situation was under control. The police and the military kept the crowds moving, and in the evening a complete curfew was imposed. It was kept in effect for some days' time until the excitement had died down, the population being allowed out of doors for brief periods each day to buy food. Many of the known agitators were arrested, and others fled the country.

For a considerable time thereafter affairs in Jordan did not concern me in particular, busy as I was in trying to deal with the Egypt-Israel situation around the Gaza Strip and in the El Auja demilitarized zone, until, on March 2, the news of General Glubb's dismissal by King Hussein took everybody by surprise. It was indeed an unpleasant shock. Not only did one feel great sympathy for this good man and faithful servant of the Jordanian monarchy who had been so summarily deprived of his post and ejected from the country, but one feared for the stability of the régime, and the relatively peaceful conditions that had lasted for over a year along the Jordan-Israel demarcation line. These fears were before long to be justified.

General Glubb has himself described the events and pressures which led up to his dismissal in a remarkably detached way. The leading part in the secret movement in the Arab Legion to unseat him was taken by Ali Abu Nuwar, at that time personal aide-de-camp to King Hussein, over whom he had established a considerable influence. I first met Lieutenant-Colonel Abu Nuwar, as he then was, on March 13, 1956. In the rapid spate of promotions which followed the ejection of General Glubb and practically all the British officers who had held commands or senior staff appointments in the Legion, Lieutenant-Colonel Abu Nuwar had obtained the command of the Southern Brigade Group of the Arab Legion, with headquarters a little to the north of Jerusalem. On this day Major Ishaq, the senior Jordanian delegate to the Jordan-Israel MAC, said the brigade commander would like to see me in regard to certain important matters, so I went along to his headquarters.

At this time it had not become generally known that Ali Abu Nuwar had been the principal member of the Jordanian " Free Officers " Group who had prevailed on King Hussein to dismiss General Glubb. Certainly I was unaware of it myself. I was introduced to a young lieutenant-colonel, good-looking, and giving an impression of considerable vigour and intelligence. He spoke very good English. His most remarkable feature was his eyes, bright, rather prominent, but patently insincere. He began to lay down, in a somewhat arbitrary way, certain action he wanted me to take in regard to Mount Scopus. I did not much appreciate being spoken to in this way by a lieutenant-colonel, Jordanian or any other ; however, I had learned by this time that it was a grave error to lose one's temper or show annoyance in dealing with the Arabs, so I explained that I understood his dissatisfaction with the Mount Scopus situation (which I shall deal with in more detail in a later chapter) and how it must preoccupy any Jordanian officer charged with the defence of the area. However, the situation had developed and hardened over the course of years, since the original agreement in regard to the area had been made in July 1948, and there was not much, I had found, that I could do to improve it. In any case, complaints and requests in regard to this should properly come to me through the Mixed Armistice Commission, or the Jordanian Government, with whom I had been dealing on Mount Scopus matters.

The new brigade commander also said he wanted an end put to overflights by Israeli aircraft, and thought that Israel had been introducing troops into Jerusalem beyond the numbers allowed in the General Armistice Agreement. I finally said I would see what could be done about the overflights—not much, I feared, as the Israelis always denied they had flown over Jordan territory, and we very seldom had UNMOs in position to see them. Anyway, the horizontal co-ordinate position of an aircraft flying at any height is difficult to establish without special instruments. As for the alleged illegal concentration of troops in Jerusalem, we would look into it. (There proved to be none.)

So ended my first meeting with the man who was soon to become commander of the Arab Legion. I next saw him on March 29 at Amman. I was paying a visit to the Minister of Foreign Affairs, Fakhri Khalidi, and also to Major-General Radi Enab, who had been named as commander in succession to Glubb. Radi Enab was a middle-aged officer, senior in rank in the Legion, but he had spent most of his service in the police section. He was reputed not to know much of military affairs. By this time it had become known that Ali Abu Nuwar had been the principal mover in engineering Glubb's dismissal, and really controlled the Legion. It was generally assumed that Radi Enab was a mere figurehead, keeping Glubb's seat warm until Abu Nuwar should think the time ripe to occupy it himself. At the time of this visit Abu Nuwar stood in an undefined relation to the Chief of Staff. Lieutenant-Colonel Sadiq Shera'a seemed to be the principal General Staff

Officer, and Abu Nuwar hovered in the background. Shortly after this he assumed the title of Director-General of the General Staff, a new conception in staff appointments, but within a month or so he had Radi Enab quietly removed, and became the Chief of Staff of the Legion (really its commander) with the rank of Major-General.

At this meeting he showed me an order to the troops on the borders that no aggressive action was to be taken against the Israelis, and, in short, that the policy which had been followed in this respect during Glubb's régime would be continued. I had expressed concern at some recent incidents which seemed to show that the bonds of discipline in this respect had been relaxed, and pointed out that unless control was maintained there was bound to be trouble with the Israelis. This order was intended to reassure me, and, I suppose, the British and other diplomatic representatives who would also have been concerned at any deterioration of the border situations. The terms of the order were all right, but it did not prevent incidents, which in their cumulative effect brought ferocious retaliations from the Israelis, and a situation which in the latter half of the year created a great danger of more extensive hostilities, and even seizure of Jordanian territory, until Egypt suddenly became the Israeli target, in the latter half of October.

Whether Ali Abu Nuwar and his officers knew who was raiding into Israel, with shootings and sabotage, I cannot say. Of course they denied direct knowledge, and professed to be trying to find the offenders and proceed against them in accordance with the previous practice, but I could place little confidence in Abu Nuwar's assurances. General Glubb has stated in his book that most of the raids into Israel that started out from Jordan territory were organized and paid for by the Moslem Brotherhood and other irresponsible and vindictive elements in Damascus—and later by the Egyptian military attaché at Amman and his associates. The Israelis took the position that they held the Jordanian authorities responsible for preventing infiltration and marauding, as, indeed, they had a right to do under the provisions of the GAA. They also, when it suited their current propaganda position, asserted that Egypt was behind some of the *fedayeen* incursions from Jordan. They must have credited the Egyptian military attaché with some responsibility for it, for they wreaked vengeance on him, in a way that will be described later.

During the first two months of 1956, however, relations between Egypt and Israel were the principal cause of anxiety, and most of my time was taken up with them, when the after effects of the

Lake Tiberias crisis had died down. I have described (see page 98) the so-called three-point plan for restoring the situation in El Auja, occupied by the Israelis in flagrant contravention of Article VIII of the GAA. On pages 102–106 I have given an outline of the negotiations I had undertaken, during the latter part of November and early December, to try to get Israel and Egypt to accept this plan. This frustrating business went on during most of the first half of 1956, with pauses. It was part of the object of Mr Hammarskjöld's mission to the Middle East during April and May to clear up the El Auja situation. But neither I nor Mr Hammarskjöld, with his much greater authority and all his diplomatic skill, was able to restore the situation to that prescribed in the armistice agreement.

Neither side refused outright to accept the Security Council's recommendation. They manœuvred by imposing conditions for acceptance. " We will accept the proposals," the formula ran, " but only if the other side will stop violating another part of the GAA." Looking back, it seems to me that probably the basic reason for the non-acceptance of the three-point plan by Israel was that the commander of the Israeli Defence Forces—that is to say, General Dayan—naturally appreciated the great advantage it would be to hold the El Auja demilitarized zone, without the possibility of effective control of it by UNTSO, as the jumping-off point for the columns that would be used for the invasion of the Sinai, should the occasion for hostilities arise. Having seized control of the zone, they must have used all their influence to avoid any agreement which would deprive them of this military asset. The thinking of the Ministry of Foreign Affairs may have been that a compromise agreement would be politic, but if that really was their view, it did not affect the final issue.

On January 3, 1956, I received a letter from Mr Walter Eytan, Director-General of the Israel Ministry of Foreign Affairs, saying that Israel accepted the three-point proposals. This was a surprise, and I asked for an assurance that the acceptance was unconditional, which I received. Perhaps the sudden change from the previous prevarications may have been due to a feeling that Israel should now show a more conciliatory attitude, in view of the bad impression created in Great Britain, the United States, and even in France by the Tiberias raid. The Israel Foreign Office may also have calculated that the Egyptians would never accept the proposals ; hence Israel could score a point in doing so, and would risk nothing.

Mr Hammarskjöld decided to visit the Middle East on his way back from a tour to the Far East, and arrived in Cairo on January

21, 1956. He persuaded Dr Fawzi to accept the three-point proposal (having, as he thought, already received Israel's acceptance). He then came to Jerusalem and had an interview with Mr Ben-Gurion on January 24, 1956. He told me Mr Ben-Gurion had been very insistent in asking why Prime Minister Nasser didn't order a complete and positive cease-fire. In the preceding weeks there had been sporadic clashes along the Gaza DL between Egyptian outposts and Israeli patrols, and some other incidents.

After the Secretary-General had left I took up with the Israel Foreign Office the implementation of the proposals they had accepted. A long delay ensued, in spite of my repeated requests for action, until finally, on February 21, I received a letter from Mr Eytan refusing to implement the three-point proposals unless additional conditions were included. This was despite his previous assurance that acceptance was unconditional. Subsequent meetings with Mr Sharett confirmed this stand, which was maintained in spite of a message of protest sent by Mr Hammarskjöld.

On the face of it, acceptance of the three-point proposals, unconditionally, and the subsequent refusal to implement them was a breach of faith by Israel. I do not believe, however, that it was intentional on the part of the Ministry of Foreign Affairs. Two explanations are possible : the first, that the matter had not been clearly explained to Mr Ben-Gurion before the acceptance was given ; the second, that he did understand the implications of unconditional acceptance at the time, but later changed his mind, and gave orders that a way out of the obligation was to be found. In his reply to Mr Hammarskjöld's protest Mr Sharett found another argument, which had not been put forward previously, to the effect that since the ' acceptance ' of the proposals the Egyptians had brought up additional forces with some of their new armament to the Gaza-Rafah-El Arish area.

The tension along the Gaza demarcation line did not abate, and one never knew when it might result in an incident causing serious casualties, which would set off hostilities on a large scale. Demand and counter-demand followed the pattern I have previously described. The Israelis kept demanding that Premier Nasser should issue a positive cease-fire order ; the Premier's stand was that he would issue no orders to his troops " tying their hands " in the light of what had happened at Gaza in February 1955, and elsewhere since then. He in turn repeated his previous suggestion that each side should withdraw troops 500 metres from the DL, but this proposal, which I considered a useful one, was flatly refused by Mr Ben-Gurion. And so it went on.

CHAPTER 10

Clashes, Egypt-Israel, and Secretary-General's Mission

Maps 3 and 4

I HAVE mentioned that in my conversation at the British Foreign Office, in early November 1955, they had asked me if I thought it would be practicable to interpose troops, under the aegis of the United Nations, to make a sort of buffer zone between the Israelis and Egyptians in the sensitive areas, and so prevent serious clashes which would lead to war. I had said at the time that I thought that extreme pressure would be needed to make either party accept the entry of foreign troops into territory under their control. As this idea of interposition of an armed force kept cropping up, and was, in fact, used as an excuse for the Anglo-French intervention along the Suez Canal in November, it will be of some interest to discuss it briefly from the viewpoint of early 1956. If the United Nations Emergency Force eventually came into existence to fulfil just this function, and has done so successfully since 1957, why was the experiment not tried during 1956, before war broke out?

Mr Selwyn Lloyd asked me about this again on March 13, 1956, during a short visit he paid to Israel, and later Mr Hammarskjöld asked me for my views as to what military dispositions and arrangements would be needed to give effect to the proposal. A general study of the military factors was accordingly made.

The essence of the problem was to prevent the relatively small incidents along the Gaza Strip or the International Frontier from building up and developing into full-scale hostilities. If each side could be assured that no invasion of its territory by the other would be possible without immediate intervention by the Three Powers, there would be a sense of security which would enable the lesser problems of firing at patrols and infiltration to be dealt with. These incidents were primarily due to the insecurity which the forces of both sides felt. It often seemed that the Israelis were following a deliberately provocative policy in their patrolling, with the object either of overawing the Egyptians or of provoking full-scale hostilities which they were confident of turning to their advantage. But if invasion of the Sinai should be made impossible to them, there would be no point in following such an aggressive policy.

Invasion, to be successful from either direction, would have to pass through either the El Auja demilitarized zone, or the area of Rafah, or both. (In 1956 the decisive Israeli advances used both routes.) Therefore, if a " United Nations Force " (which would presumably be made up of troops from the Three Powers) occupied an area round Rafah and also the El Auja demilitarized zone, no invasion could take place without the aggressor's committing hostile acts against the troops of the nations concerned, and incurring the full weight of sanctions. I concluded that if a force of about the size of a Brigade Group (British Organization) or a Regimental Combat Team (U.S.A. Organization) consisting of all arms, with sufficient air support at call, should be placed with its main elements in Rafah, and the equivalent of a battalion with supporting arms in El Auja, it would be adequate.

This military speculation was interesting, but I never thought that there was a possiblity of putting it into effect. The U.S.A. would have had to put the most extreme pressure on the Isrealis to get them to accept such a proposal. Even the pressure put on them to make them evacuate the Sinai and the Gaza Strip, in March 1957, was not enough to make them accept UNEF troops on the territory they controlled. They definitely rejected the recommendations of the General Assembly which included the stationing of UNEF troops in the El Auja demilitarized zone in particular.

On the other hand, the Egyptians disliked the idea of having foreign troops on their territory nearly as much as the Israelis did, and were in process of getting rid of the last of the British garrison in the Canal Zone. They would certainly have resisted having British and French troops in the areas mentioned, and if they objected Russia would have vetoed any proposals to the end put forward in the Security Council. The Security Council, if all the permanent members had been in agreement, would have the power to station such a force in the area, to prevent a breach of the peace, but, in the case we are considering, there could have been no such agreement.

Early in February 1956 Sir Anthony Eden went to Washington to consult with President Eisenhower, among other subjects, about the Middle East situation and the danger of war there. It was reported that they would discuss the possibility of developing definite plans for intervention in the case of aggression, as provided under the terms of the 1950 Three Power Declaration. If they did, nothing concrete came of the discussions. The *communiqué* issued at the end of the talks merely expressed the wish that the parties would settle their differences peaceably, and stated, rather vaguely, that both the U.S.A. and the U.K. were determined to intervene against any aggressor in the Middle East. The *communiqué* also mentioned that any necessary enlargement of the UNTSO, and improvement of its capabilities, would be favourably considered.

The Israeli reaction to this suggestion is probably fairly given in an editorial in the *Jerusalem Post* of February 3, 1956. Editorials and articles by the military and diplomatic correspondents in this paper, if not actually dictated or inspired by the officials of the Foreign and Defence ministries, never showed significant variation from the official position on the subject.

About the suggestion to enlarge the Truce Supervision Organization, the *Post* editorial said :

> This is interpreted as a planned large increase in the number of UN Observers, their permanent encampment on the borders, their being armed to put down skirmishers, and the creation of a de-militarized zone of one kilometre on each side of the border. This amounts to the creation of a UN Force ; if that is indeed the suggestion, it is both unrealistic and unacceptable. Israel is peopling its desert and has settlements along the borders. The attempt to proclaim a kilometre of territory as a neutralized zone means disarming these settlers, and perhaps subjecting them to the same kind of searches and checks as in the last days of the Mandate, and it would once more render them defenceless. It is not a proposal that can be accepted by a sovereign state.

On March 6 there was an important debate in the Knesset, on a non-confidence motion by the leader of the Herut Party, Mr Menahem Begin, asking for an immediate preventive war.[28] Mr Ben-Gurion was reported as saying (newspaper's translation from the Hebrew) :

> If war breaks out, we will meet it with armed strength, and bring about their downfall. But we do not lust for battle. . . . If the war is not prevented, the responsibility will rest with the United States, which could have prevented it. If it breaks out, the moral responsibility will rest on the U.S.S.R., which sent arms to the Egyptian dictator, who declared that he was preparing to fight against us. We believed that we had a moral and a political right to ask for American arms, and still think so. If these arms are not given to us within the coming days, America will be shouldering a very heavy responsibility indeed. But we will not start a war.

Mr Begin, after mentioning the increased danger to Israel from the Jordan side, following General Glubb's dismissal, and stating that Israel would be able to face this threat with equanimity if the Government had only taken his advice some months back to take the offensive towards the south, went on to say, " To-day, even to-day, we must carry out a carefully planned military initiative in pursuance of the sacred right of self-defence, in order to break the bonds that are threatening to strangle us."

Mr Begin interprets the right of self-defence in a very different way to what most people would. The " sacred right of self-defence " apparently includes the right to attack anyone whom Israel suspects of harbouring hostile intentions. However, Mr Ben-Gurion, who differed from Mr Begin on this occasion, maintained very obstinately, in the discussions with Mr Hammarskjöld a few weeks later, that the right of self-defence included the right of reprisal, which Israel had been practising, and which had been condemned so many times by the Security Council. And perhaps, by the latter part of October, he had been convinced by Mr Begin's arguments.

On March 12, 1956, the Israelis complained to the Egypt-Israel Mixed Armistice Commission that there were Egyptian troop concentrations, including armour and other offensive arms, in the Gaza and El Arish areas, which was contrary to Article VII of the GAA. Under this article the Egyptians were allowed only a strictly limited force, of defensive character, in the area east of a line El Arish-Abu Aweigila-El Quseima. (See Note 25 for fuller details.) They were probably violating this article, as they had been refusing the observers of the EIMAC permission to go into the area east of this line, to investigate another and prior Israeli complaint that they had defensive positions in the area, contrary to Article VIII 3. But according to the best information we were able to obtain at the time there had been no increase in the Egyptian forces in the area since January, when Israel had accepted the three-point proposals, except for a limited amount of armour.

But the Israelis by the same Article VII were only allowed to have similar " defensive " forces in the area between the demarcation line and a line running roughly south from Faluja, passing a little to the west of Beersheba. The Egyptians had submitted numerous complaints that the Israelis were violating this provision. The Israelis refused investigation also. There was a deadlock again.

On March 14, 1956, Israel submitted a protest to the Security Council, alleging a sharp deterioration of the situation in the Gaza Strip and a menacing build-up of Egyptian forces along the frontier. They listed 180 incidents of aggression against Israel in the three months between December 5 and March 9. These were firings at Israel patrols and posts, infiltrations, and some minings. A Security Council meeting was not asked for. Of course, the Egyptians could have produced a similar list of complaints of Israeli aggressions.

There was no doubt that the situation was getting worse, and that neither side would accept the proposals for separating the combatants introduced at various times by me, and endorsed by the Security Council. Consultations between the U.K. and the U.S.A. finally resulted in the calling of a meeting of the Security Council. At this time the Jisr Banat Yakub diversion problem was also causing a good deal of worry. The retaliatory raid on Lake Tiberias had, of course, wrecked whatever prospect there may have been of getting Syrian agreement to the Johnston plan. Israeli authorities were uttering dark threats about resuming the digging operations in a month or so, and of what they would do if the Syrians attempted to interfere. Not only the United Nations, but the diplomats of the Three Powers were concerned.

The Security Council met on April 4, and passed a resolution requesting the Secretary-General to visit the Middle East and report on the situation, especially the degree to which the parties were complying with the General Armistice Agreements and the resolutions of the Security Council which had followed the Gaza, Khan Yunis, and Tiberias incidents. But before he could reach the area the situation along the Gaza demarcation line developed in a most alarming way.

On April 4 there had been an incident of firing on the Gaza ADL between the Israeli and Egyptian forces, which had resulted in three Israelis' being killed. It had become all too frequent that initial rifle-shots had been followed by extensive machine-gunning and the fire of mortars and artillery. On the 5th another exchange was set off, which went on most of the day, the appeals of the Chairman of EIMAC, Lieutenant-Colonel R. Bayard, U.S.A., for a cease-fire taking effect only at about 6.40 P.M. In the exchanges the Egyptians had fired some mortar-shells at Israeli settlements, causing a few casualties. Thereupon, in retaliation, an Israeli major ordered fire by 120-mm. mortars on Gaza. A heavy fire was poured in, centred on the middle of the town, full of civilians about their ordinary business. Fifty-six Arabs were killed and 103 wounded, men, women, and children.

The unjustifiable savagery of this retaliation shocked the Israeli authorities, I believe. It seems to have been due to the bad judgment, to use the mildest possible phrase, of a local commander. But the Israeli Army tried to offer the excuse that their mortars were firing at military objectives. Unfortunately for this contention, the UN observers were able to investigate the occurrence before the mortar-shells had ceased falling, and the location of the hits was promptly plotted. It showed the " mean point of impact " right in the middle of the town, in the principal square, while the Egyptian mortars were upwards of two kilometres away, somewhere near Ali Muntar. Later, the Israelis averred that there was some undefined kind of headquarters in Gaza which had been their target, but we found no evidence that there was such a headquarters. The well-known Police H.Q. in the " Taggart Fort," also cited by the Israelis as a justifiable target, was about 1500 metres distant from the Israelis' point of aim. However, argument on this point was soon stopped, for in a few days the *fedayeen* were sent into Israel as a reprisal, and the Israeli authorities and Press concentrated on the various crimes they perpetrated, conveniently forgetting to mention anything about the dead and wounded Arab civilians in Gaza.

On the following morning, April 6, there was a resumption of mortar-fire south-east of Gaza. This Lieutenant-Colonel Bayard managed to get stopped. I had sent messages to the governments of both Israel and Egypt on the previous day, backing up the Chairman's efforts with the representatives of both sides for a cease-fire, and on this day, also, I urged Mr Tekoah to ask Mr Ben-Gurion to issue an order that no Israeli patrols should approach closer than 500 metres to the demarcation line. Greatly to my surprise, Mr Tekoah informed me, about half an hour later, that Mr Ben-Gurion agreed to this request, as a special gesture in view of the Secretary-General's forthcoming visit, and subject to Mr Hammarskjöld's obtaining a promise from Premier Nasser to give a binding order to his troops not to fire on Israelis in Israeli territory.

Mr Tekoah told me that Israel had received reports that Egypt would send *fedayeen* into Israel from all Arab states, as a retaliation for the bombardment of Gaza. I sent messages to the Lebanese, Syrian, and Jordanian authorities to be on the alert to stop any such attempts, and I also sent a message to Egypt, referring to the rumours of *fedayeen* action, and hoping they would assure me that these were without foundation. I got no reply from Egypt, but the other countries answered the next day, saying they would prevent infiltration.

By about ten o'clock on the night of April 7 messages began to come in, reporting attacks during the day on vehicles on the Beersheba-Tel Aviv road. By 1 A.M. seven attacks had been reported, including grenade-throwings and demolitions. It was clear that the *fedayeen* operation had begun on a large scale.

On the following day, April 8, I sent a message to Premier Nasser, calling on him to withdraw the *fedayeen*. In Jerusalem I requested a meeting with Mr Ben-Gurion, but this could not be arranged at first, as the Cabinet was in session. So I sent a message, urging that Israel refrain from reprisals. About 4 P.M. I saw Mr Ben-Gurion and Mr Sharett. After some discussion Mr Ben-Gurion agreed to undertake no reprisals until noon on Tuesday the 10th ; and I agreed to ask Premier Nasser for an undertaking that Egypt would fully observe the provisions of Article II 2 of the GAA, which prohibited the parties from all hostile action against military or civilians of the other side. Mr Ben-Gurion had used his favourite term of a " complete cease-fire " ; the terms of the armistice agreement article were, however, more precise and comprehensive. This message was sent an hour or so later.

It had been intended that I should meet the Secretary-General at Rome for consultations before he began his mission, but in view of the critical situation he agreed that I should stay at my post in Jerusalem. I reported the above discussion to him, and also informed the consuls-general of the Three Powers in Jerusalem of what was happening, so that they could tell their governments, which might be expected to use their influence in both Cairo and Tel Aviv to check the rapid worsening of the situation. Next day the Secretary-General sent messages for transmission to the heads of both governments backing up my request for their undertaking to observe the no-hostilities article of the armistice agreement.

On the 10th the Secretary-General arrived at Lydda, on his way to Cairo, where he had decided to begin his negotiations. His first efforts were concentrated on getting Egypt and Israel to agree to observe a cease-fire. After an interview with Premier Nasser on the 11th, he secured this agreement from Egypt, although no commitment was made regarding the time of the withdrawal of the *fedayeen*. I pointed out privately to the Secretary-General that, however much the Egyptian authorities might wish to do so, they could not give any assurance about what the *fedayeen* might do before they returned to their bases, since the gangs, once launched, could not be reached by any orders.

By the next day the *fedayeen* attacks had ceased. Nearly a dozen Israelis had been killed, and more injured. A particularly repulsive act of one of the *fedayeen* gangs had been to attack a group of schoolchildren in an institution not far from Ramle, when they were at their prayers, killing and wounding many of them. The Israeli police and defence forces, taking energetic counter-measures, had succeeded in killing nine and capturing four of the invaders. The Cairo Press hailed the *fedayeen's* return in extravagant terms : *El Goumhouria* said, in a long article full of denunciation of Israel and the ' imperialists ' who supported her, " The heroes are back from the battlefield . . . . They have come back after they taught Israel a lesson she will never forget. They gave her a warning about her inevitable end as a result of her folly and the folly of the imperialists." *Al Akhbar* said, in less flamboyant style, " Egyptians and all the Arabs feel they are deeply indebted to those heroes who courageously and with no regard for life attacked the enemy in his own house. . . . War is not part of our programme, but we want to teach those who want war how expensive to them war is. . . . The commandos have done their duty and punished Israel for her attack on the innocent civilians.''

For the next month Mr Hammarskjöld devoted himself with the most untiring energy to the mission with which the Security Council had entrusted him. He flew from Cairo to Jerusalem, from there to Amman and Damascus and Beirut, then retraced his itinerary. At each capital he had exhaustive discussions with the heads of state, and the foreign ministers ; sometimes the military heads took part. I accompanied him throughout, with some of my advisers, to provide information on details and technicalities, and from time to time to discuss detailed programmes involving the UNTSO. But the great burden of this negotiation was undertaken by Mr Hammarskjöld himself. Throughout this gruelling pro-gramme his stamina was astonishing ; he never seemed weary, nor did his perceptions flag. His name had become synonymous with diplomatic skill, and he deployed his great resources throughout the four weeks of his mission. At the beginning of it he found a situation in which all-out war seemed possible within hours ; at the end, though he had not accomplished all that he had hoped for, he had secured engagements from all the countries which, had they been kept, would have ensured stability under the general frame-work of the armistice agreements.

A narrative of diplomatic negotiations for the purpose of pre-venting war does not make very exciting reading ; it is dull indeed compared with histories of assaults, treasons, stratagems, and spoils. Therefore the following account of the important negotiations carried out by the Secretary-General, as required by the Security Council's resolution, has been kept brief. Those who desire to study Mr Hammarskjöld's proceedings and the results obtained in more detail may refer to his report to the Security Council, dated May 9, 1956.

Looking back, one can see that by the spring of 1956 the currents which were bearing the antagonists in the Middle East towards the whirlpool of war were too strong to be stemmed just by diplomatic interventions, or changed by simple mediation by third parties, including the United Nations and its agent the Secretary-General. If the Three Powers had remained firmly determined to enforce their declaration, peace could have been maintained—but in a few months, Nasser's nationalization of the Suez Canal would put an end to that, making enemies of two of the Three Powers that had undertaken to keep the peace.

The Secretary-General's purpose was to get the Arab states and Israel to comply fully with the armistice agreements. The persistent breach of many of their important provisions by the several parties to the GAAs had grown up by degrees, as the result of many incidents, some of which have been described in these pages : distrust between the two sides was profound.

Each side excused its own contraventions by claiming previous contravention of some provision by the other side. But, Mr Hammarskjöld pointed out, if one infringement was used to justify another, then logically a single breach could lead to the break-down of every provision of the agreements. Mr Hammarskjöld's logic was accepted, but there was no firm promise of reform.

The Secretary-General stressed particularly the importance of the so-called cease-fire clause in all of the General Armistice Agreements, which read :

> No element of the land, sea, or air military or paramilitary forces of either party, including non-regular forces, shall commit any war-like or hostile act against the military or paramilitary forces of the other party, or against civilians in territory under the control of that party ; or shall advance beyond or pass over for any purpose whatsoever the Armistice Demarcation Line. . . .

He made it his main effort to get the parties to agree that no breach of *another* article would justify a party in opening fire, crossing the ADL or doing other things prohibited by the cease-fire clause ; the right of self-defence would operate only if the other side fired first or committed some other act prohibited under the same clause.

But Mr Ben-Gurion claimed that the right of self-defence could be construed as permitting Israel to retaliate when the other side failed to prevent crossings of the borders resulting in the commission of crimes within Israel. Syria tried to assert that her troops could open fire in self-defence if Israel insisted on diverting the Jordan River.

Eventually, by dint of great persuasiveness, moral force, and persistence, Mr Hammarskjöld got the agreement of all parties to the principle that the provisions of the cease-fire article must always be observed, unless the opposing party broke them first. But subsequent events showed that the parties were not really convinced or converted, and privately maintained their reservations.

The Secretary-General also obtained verbal assent to the principle that the observers of UNTSO should be free to move anywhere, and might be stationed in sensitive areas—*e.g.*, the Gaza ADL and Lake Tiberias—to facilitate compliance with the GAAs—or at least to place the blame for any breaches where it properly belonged. Despite these promises, thereafter there were still the usual difficulties in arranging for the presence of UN observers where it was most needed.

One argument which Mr Ben-Gurion brought out repeatedly and with great emphasis to justify Israel's failure to honour certain provisions of the General Armistice Agreements was that Egypt was contravening the provisions of Article I of the agreement, which ran, in part, as follows :

> No aggressive action by the armed forces—land, sea, or air—of either party shall be undertaken, planned, or threatened against the people or the armed forces of the other. . . .
> The right of each party to its security and freedom from fear of attack by the armed forces of the other shall be fully respected.

He claimed that Egypt, by alleging that a state of war existed between Israel and itself, and thereby justifying the closing of the Suez Canal to Israel's shipping, was in breach of this article. Also, Egyptian propaganda in Press, radio, and speeches of government personalities was constantly threatening attack upon Israel— another breach.

Complaints of the breach of this article could not be dealt with by the Mixed Armistice Commissions, the questions being too diffuse and legally complicated. Mr Hammarskjöld said that it was a defect of the machinery for ensuring compliance with the GAA that there was nothing appropriate to handle conflicts of this kind, unless the parties wished to bring them to the Security Council.

Mr Hammarskjöld reported to the Security Council that he had been assured by the governments of Egypt and Jordan that they would enforce vigorous measures to prevent all crossings of the demarcation line. The obligation to do this, imposed by another article of the GAA, was not so explicit as the duty to prevent hostile actions by the armed forces. However, as has been shown in the earlier chapters, it was maraudings by persons who could not be proved to be military, or even ' irregulars,' which had inspired the retaliations by Israel.

The Secretary-General also brought it to the Security Council's attention that in the El Auja militarized zone neither Israel nor Egypt had put into effect the three measures he had proposed on November 3, 1955. (See page 98.) Both sides could also be presumed to be violating the article of the GAA which allowed only a strictly limited number of troops in the defensive zones of the Western Front. (See page 105 and Note 25.) They would not permit UNMOs to visit the areas in question to determine whether complaints by the other side were justified or not. The two parties had taken the position that they were not willing to comply with this article except under certain conditions.

Mr Ben-Gurion had refused to comply while Egypt, in his opinion, was violating Article I and did not allow Israel shipping to pass through the Suez Canal or use the port of Eilat. The Egyptians took the stand that they would not relax their restrictions on Israel shipping while Israel absolutely refused to make any concession towards meeting the UN General Assembly resolution providing for return of the Arab refugees to their former homes. Furthermore, Egypt and Syria wanted assurances from the Israelis that they would not proceed with the diversion of the Jordan waters without agreement of the Arab states. This assurance Mr Ben-Gurion refused to give.

During the negotiations proposals for local arrangements " to protect the cease-fire "—for example, withdrawal of armed men from a zone on either side of the Gaza ADL, the erection of an obstacle along it, and the various measures proposed for avoiding incidents on Lake Tiberias (see page 119)—were discussed. In the end it was left for me, as Chief of Staff UNTSO, to continue detailed negotiations for putting them into effect. But in spite of the parties' promises of " favourable consideration " it proved impossible to get any of these measures actually implemented during the period between the Secretary-General's departure, about the end of April 1956, and the outbreak of general hostilities in October.

In the talks the representatives of Jordan, Syria, and Lebanon had shown much concern regarding the possibility of Israel's recommencing work on the Jordan River diversion scheme. Such action on Israel's part would " put the situation along the demarcation line under an undue strain," Mr Hammarskjöld noted, in a characteristically deflationary sentence. His recommendation was that the parties should abide by the Security Council's and Chief of Staff's decisions on this matter, but that in any case Israel's digging in this area would confer no right on the other party to violate the cease-fire article.

Also discussed during the negotiations was the sensitive question of Mount Scopus. Mr Ben-Gurion declaimed with considerable heat that the Jordanians were denying Israel the rights given to them by Article VIII of the GAA. But this article, in fact, only called for the creation of a special committee to try to arrange for traffic on certain vital roads, the resumption of the working of the railway to Jerusalem, also water supply and electricity services disrupted by the 1948 hostilities, and also to get the " cultural and humanitarian institutions " on Mount Scopus in operation again.

The special committee had met during the year 1949, and had settled the question of the railroad into Jerusalem. The questions of the water-supply from Latrun, electricity to the Old City, and the roads to Bethlehem and from Jerusalem to Tel Aviv had been settled by each party's making its own arrangements on its own side of the demarcation line. The special committee had not met since 1950, although in November of that year, there was a resolution of the Security Council calling for it to do so.

Israel now demanded that the committee should meet to arrange for the free access to Mount Scopus and the Holy Places, which they desired so much. Jordan's position was that it was impossible in the existing circumstances to find practical means of solving these and other remaining questions. It was basically a matter of security, which will be explained later in the context of certain difficulties which arose concerning Mount Scopus. The Government of Jordan favoured maintaining the existing status of Mount Scopus until changes in the general situation removed these security problems. That was as much as to say, until there should be peace.

Mr Hammarskjöld, in concluding his report to the Security Council, said that he had obtained agreement to a cease-fire, and from that the parties could advance to a state of full compliance with the armistice agreements. Such full compliance was a stage which had to be reached before progress could be made on the main issues, which had been outside his mandate.

The final passages of the report included the following : " What has been done may open the door to new fruitful developments. The initiative is now in the hands of the Governments party to the Armistice Agreements. . . . If we have previously experienced chain reactions leading to a continuous deterioration of the situation, we may now have the possibility of starting a chain of reactions in the opposite direction."

Unfortunately, the change in the direction of the " chain reaction " which Mr Hammarskjöld hoped for did not take place. The patterns of reaction had become too set, and in the wrong direction ; the tide of violence was flowing, and flowing towards the coasts of war.

CHAPTER II

The Armistice disintegrating: May–October 1956

Maps 2 and 3

EVEN while Mr Hammarskjöld was still in the area on his mission, incidents in breach of the cease-fire occurred. On April 29 the secretary of Nahal Oz (the border *kibbutz* nearest to Gaza), hearing that Arabs from the Strip were harvesting the *kibbutz's* crops, got on a horse and imprudently dashed up to the demarcation line. He was armed with a pistol, but had nobody with him. The subsequent MAC investigation found that there had been a dispute, and that he had been shot by an Arab policeman. Rothberg, the secretary, had been on his own side of the DL, but the policeman, with the help of another Arab, had dragged him across. This was a trick that was played very often, to make it appear that the victim had infiltrated, and that the killing had been in self-defence.

On the same day an Israeli vehicle was blown up on a mine near Nir Yitshaq, a settlement somewhat farther to the south. These events did not augur well for the effectiveness of the cease-fire just promised by Egypt. However, the first incident was fortuitous, and the second may have been caused by a mine which had been planted in an earlier foray. The Israelis complained violently, but did not denounce the cease-fire.

When I returned from Rome, where I had been helping in the preparation of the Secretary-General's final report, I began trying to get the UNMOs into position on both sides of the ADL around the Gaza Strip, a measure accepted by both parties. Immediately there were difficulties. The Israelis had stipulated that the agreement should be ratified in the MAC. The purpose of this stipulation was presumably to avoid admitting that UNTSO, independently of decisions by the MACs, could have authority to "observe the cease-fire" as ordered by the Security Council in its August 11, 1949 resolution and at other times.

As both sides had agreed to the idea of posting observers anyway, it might have seemed that endorsement by the MAC was a simple formality. But a difficulty arose as to where the MAC was to meet. The Egyptians would not attend unless regular meetings were held

in El Auja, as stipulated in the GAA article about the MAC ;
and the Israelis refused to consent to this, asking for meetings at
Kilo 95 or anywhere else along the ADL. This deadlock went on
for some time, but eventually a compromise was reached, and the
observers were placed in position.

It was arranged that I should go to New York for the meeting
of the Security Council which would consider the Secretary-
General's report. The resolution, adopted on June 4, declared
that the parties should speedily carry out the measures already
agreed upon with the Secretary-General and should co-operate with
him and the Chief of Staff UNTSO in putting into effect the further
practical proposals mentioned in the resolution of April 4, 1956 ;
also that UN observers must have full freedom of movement along
the Armistice Demarcation Lines, in the demilitarized zones and
defensive areas ; requested the Chief of Staff UNTSO to carry out
his observation of the cease-fire pursuant to the Security Council
resolution of August 11, 1949, and report whenever any action in
violation of the cease-fire was so serious as to require action by the
Security Council. The Council requested the Secretary-General to
continue his good offices, with a view to full implementation of the
Council's resolution of April 4, 1956, and full compliance with the
armistice agreements. It will be noted that, in the main, this
resolution only repeated previous Security Council decisions and
recommendations.

During the Security Council's discussion of the resolution based
on the report of the Secretary-General a minor tempest arose over
the wording of the preamble. As originally drafted, it spoke of
the hope that there would be a peaceful settlement of the Palestine
question on a " mutually acceptable basis." This phrase, which
would seem almost pleonastic, was attacked by Mr Ahmed Shukeiry,
then acting as the delegate of Syria. He professed to see in it an
attempt to force the Arab states into peace negotiations, with the
condition that Israel must find the eventual terms acceptable.
This would mean that Israel could veto terms embodying the
General Assembly resolution on the partition of Palestine, and the
various resolutions providing for the repatriation of and restitution
to the refugees. Syria was supported in this stand by Iran, and also
the U.S.S.R., whose representative appeared to be unembarrassed
by the facts that the words used were almost identically those in
the Soviet official statement on the Middle East published over
Moscow Radio on April 17, which followed, in this particular, the
communiqué put out after the visit to England of Messrs Bulganin
and Khrushchev earlier in the year, during which the possibilities
of a Middle East settlement had been discussed between the Russian

visitors and the British Prime Minister and his colleagues. Eventually the phrase was deleted, and the resolution was passed.

After a few days' leave in Ottawa I returned to Jerusalem *via* London, where I had a short interview with Mr Anthony Nutting (then Minister of State) and the Foreign Office experts on the Middle East, Mr Shuckburgh and Mr Rose. I spoke of the dangers of undisciplined actions by the Jordanians. Mr Nutting intimated that Britain had to tread warily in dealing with Jordan at that time, and hoped that I should be able to control any tendency to trigger-happiness.

The suggestion that I should be able to induce the parties to the armistice agreements to behave peacefully and in all respects as the Security Council and the General Assembly would wish was flattering. However, I had never had any illusions as to what the parties would be willing to do *pour mes beaux yeux*. I regarded myself as the agent of the United Nations, and felt it my duty to point out, when necessary, to the parties when their actions were in breach of the armistice agreements which they had signed, or the resolutions of the Security Council. They should have considered the Security Council's decisions binding, if they had sincerely accepted the provisions of Articles 25 and 40 of the UN Charter. But, instead, the parties always found all sorts of reasons for not doing what the Security Council said they should, or what they themselves had promised in signing the GAAs, and they nearly always excused their own lapses by citing some previous breach of the same or another order or agreement by the adverse party.

Now, if some one in the position of a diplomatic agent cannot persuade those he is negotiating with to act in accordance with their obligations under agreements they have made, or decisions given by a body in authority, what can be done? If the parties slight the obligation, they can be persuaded to honour it either by promise of some benefit if they do, or by the threat of the imposition of some penalty if they do not. Obviously, neither I nor the United Nations had " a carrot or a stick." The Great Powers, on the other hand, had carrots (the provision of arms, economic assistance, and various subsidies) and they had sticks : either the withholding of the assistance, or even other economic sanctions, and in the last resort they would be able legitimately to use military force under the UN Charter, if the Security Council so decided, to prevent breaches of peace and security.

While I always did my best to persuade the parties to peaceful courses, in accordance with the UN principles, it was a great help and comfort to know, as I did through contacts with the diplomatic representatives of the Three Powers, that the great nations were using their diplomacy to the same end as the UN ; and it had unusually prevented the situation from getting entirely out of hand. But in 1956, the fourth Power, the U.S.S.R., entered the picture, and not a great deal could be done, it was soon found, if Russia did not want it done. She could veto Security Council resolutions, if the Arabs did not like them, as she did the Suez Canal resolution of March 1954. Also she could, and did, supply the Arab states with arms and give them economic assistance, if the Western Powers refused to do so.

One result was that the Israelis claimed that the dice were always loaded against them in the Security Council, and that they could not get a favourable decision no matter how just their complaint. This argument could not be disproved, and it detracted to that extent from the authority of the Security Council. Therefore it absolved the collective Israeli conscience (assuming that there was such a thing) in case of condemnation by the Security Council. The ' judge ' was bound to find against Israel, whatever happened, therefore Israel could disregard his verdicts, and feel righteous about it.

The control which had been exercised by the Three Powers began to be loosened as soon as the Czech arms deal was consummated. When the last of the British garrison evacuated the Suez Canal Zone in June 1956, Britain lost, along with general pacificatory influence in the area, the ability to intervene quickly to prevent general hostilities.

Although the Secretary-General and I, on different occasions, had been given assurances by Major-General Ali Abu Nuwar and other Jordanian authorities that strict orders to check infiltration over the ADL were in force, nevertheless incidents continued to occur between Jordan and Israel. The following is a partial list. On May 15 an Israeli motor-cyclist was wounded in an ambush on the Hadera-Afule main road. An Israeli policeman on duty in the Jewish section of the Mount Scopus neutralized zone had been wounded by fire from a near-by Jordanian position on May 23. On June 5 two Israelis were wounded during an exchange of fire which followed the uprooting of trees on the Jordanian side of the demarcation line by an Israeli tractor. On June 24 two Israeli policemen were killed ; one Israeli settler and one Jordanian national guard were wounded in an exchange of fire. I considered this a particularly serious incident, because both sides had broken their commitment to observe an unconditional cease-fire.

The incident of June 24 had, like the others mentioned, been discussed in the Mixed Armistice Commission. Both sides had submitted complaints. Because the Jordanian complaint had been submitted first, it was discussed first in the emergency meeting of the Commission. The Chairman of the Commission voted for the Jordanian complaint, whereupon the Israeli delegation walked out of the meeting, and refused to discuss their complaint in turn, although they had reason to believe that the resolution they had prepared would have also been voted for by the Chairman. The Israelis on this and on many other occasions decried what they described as the practice of the Mixed Armistice Commissions and the UNTSO in "equalizing blame for incidents." It did often happen that the MACs adopted, by the Chairman's vote, two resolutions relating to the same incident, each side condemning the other for a breach of the GAA. There was nothing else the Chairman could do, legally. To fire across, or to cross, the ADL was a breach of the GAA, even if the other side had fired first, or crossed first. And there was hardly ever evidence as to who had fired first, or started the trouble. However, the Israelis always maintained that they never started trouble, and therefore it was unreasonable to blame them for technical breaches of the GAA in the same way that the aggressive Arabs were to be blamed.

On June 28, accompanied by M. Henri Vigier, my senior political adviser, I had an interview with Mr Ben-Gurion and Mrs Meir, who had recently succeeded Mr Sharett as Foreign Minister. There was a good deal of speculation in the Press in Israel and elsewhere at the time as to the reasons for Mr Sharett's leaving the Foreign Office. The general impression was that it was due to irreconcilable differences of opinion between him and Mr Ben-Gurion as to foreign policy—that Mr Sharett feared the consequences of the ' active ' policy which Mr Ben-Gurion had determined to follow. Denials were issued by various high quarters, but it continued to be believed. Mrs Meir was considered to be likely to reflect Mr Ben-Gurion's policy and ideas very faithfully. She was a dedicated Zionist, a person who seemed selflessly devoted to the cause she served. Although I had several rather acrimonious arguments with her, it was impossible not to respect her, even to like her, although one very much disliked the policies she was defending. One could say that she believed honestly in what she advocated, in the complete justice of the Israeli position. But, conversely, she seemed to me to suffer from a complete inability to see that there was anything to be said for the Arab case.

On this occasion Mr Ben-Gurion did practically all the talking for the Israeli side. He began by complaining of the number of incidents (some of which I have listed above) and said that it was evident that Jordan was not keeping her agreement about an unconditional cease-fire and to prevent crossing of the ADL for nefarious purposes. He said the Government of Israel could not stand by and see its people murdered. If the United Nations and the United Kingdom, which still had influence in Jordan, could not stop these aggressions, Israel would herself take steps.

This obviously indicated that he meant that there would be reprisals, and taking reprisals had been expressly excluded in Mr Hammarskjöld's negotiation of the cease-fire agreement. I drew this to his attention, but Mr Ben-Gurion said that he did not agree with the Secretary-General's contention that self-defence did not include the right to retaliate.

He then went on to discuss the situation about Article VIII of the GAA with Jordan. (See Chapter 10, page 146.) He claimed that the Jordanians were violating that article. Israel had a " right " to free access to Mount Scopus and free functioning of the university and hospital there. He claimed that as the article arefered to " agreement in principle," the Jordanians were violating an agreement. He remarked, " Why should not Israelis—as many s wrant to—go to Mount Scopus at any time ? " I answered that there was a provision in the GAA against crossing the ADL, of which he was well aware. He replied to the effect that if the Jordanians did not comply with Article VIII, then the article about the ADL did not exist for Israel.

This was an alarming statement. In fact, Mr Ben-Gurion's demeanour throughout the interview had made me very uneasy. The reader will recall the interview I had had with him on the eve of the Tiberias attack. (See Chapter 8, pages 107 and 108.) I felt that he was in a dangerous mood. He insisted on Israel's rights under Article VIII, in regard to Mount Scopus, Latrun, and the Holy Places in the Old City, and that Jordan was breaking her agreement under the article. This, together with the doctrine which he had been enunciating—i.e., that the breaking of any one article by the other party to the armistice agreements released Israel from the obligation to comply with any other article which she found not currently in her interest—all combined to give me the impression that he was building up a case against Jordan which would justify him, when he found the opportunity ripe, in seizing certain vitally important points such as Latrun and a corridor to Mount Scopus. Once such operations should start, it was even possible that the Israelis would try to seize the whole of the West Bank. However, it did not seem likely that such a drastic solution (though advocated by Mr Begin and his party and a few other extremists) would be within the intentions of the responsible rulers of Israel. The principal reason for doubting that such an offensive would be undertaken was that there were nearly a million Arabs living in the West Bank portion of Jordan, including refugees from the Israel-controlled territories, and Israel could not count that any substantial portion of these would again flee the country. She could not absorb them, and their expulsion by force would be likely to rouse such a storm of condemnation that it would be out of the question. But this objection would not necessarily apply if the territorial targets were limited to the relatively small, but strategically very important, areas I have mentioned.

I told Mr Ben-Gurion that I did not agree to his interpretation of Israel's " rights " under Article VIII, and that neither did Mr Hammarskjöld nor any legal opinion I had received. This apparently made little impression, but I had not expected it would. I also told him that I would shortly be going to Amman, and I would again urge the Jordanian authorities to respect their obligation to repress crime resulting from crossings of the ADL.

At the same meeting we discussed one of the measures recommended in the Secretary-General's report of May 9. This was the marking of the armistice line round the Gaza Strip by UNTSO. Mr Ben-Gurion said Israel had never agreed to it. This was certainly contrary to our recollection of the transaction ; and Israel had had the text of the report containing the recommendation for three weeks before the Security Council passed it, without their drawing attention to the section which stated that both parties had agreed to this measure. The Israeli position now was that the Egyptians should mark the line, as this would impress on the Gaza Strip residents that they intended to enforce the provisions against crossing the demarcation line. Mr Ben-Gurion also refused to consider having regular meetings of the MAC in El Auja as provided by the GAA.

There had been a complaint by the Syrians that two villages in the demilitarized zone, Hagovrim and Susita, had been fortified. The first place was near Jisr Banat Yakub, the latter near the southern end of Lake Tiberias. UNMO investigations had shown that, while the Susita defences were unimportant, Hagovrim was strongly fortified, and resembled a company defensive position, with barbed-wire obstacles, fire trenches, and dugouts. I had accordingly ruled that the defences of Hagovrim were inadmissible under the terms of the GAA, and should be dismantled. The question was brought up at this meeting, without result, and later discussed by me with Mrs Meir on more than one occasion. After the Israelis found they could not get me to change my opinion, they simply did nothing about reducing the place's defences.

The June 28 interview was reported in detail to the Secretary-General.

On July 2 I went to Amman and saw Major-General Ali Abu Nuwar. I told him of my interview with Mr Ben-Gurion, and let him know how dangerous I considered the Israeli frame of mind to be. I said that I thought that unless there was more evidence of effective Jordanian control of border-crossing, and maraudings, there was great danger of the Israelis' carrying out retaliatory actions. If the Jordanians retaliated in turn, it was quite likely, I thought, that the Israelis would use the excuse to try to seize a corridor to Mount Scopus, and perhaps Latrun. Therefore it was most important that strong measures be taken by the Jordanian authorities to make effective the orders against firing and crossing the border of which he had several times informed me.

General Abu Nuwar appeared to take this advice very well. He admitted there had been slackness in fire discipline after the Glubb dismissal, but said this was being tightened up, and that he had personally punished a man who had disobeyed orders. As to the possibilty of an important conflict developing out of the kind of incidents we had been having, followed by Israeli retaliation, he said, in a bellicose way (to which his subsequent actions fortunately did not correspond), that he was convinced that the Palestine question would only be settled by force of arms, and that he would welcome the day when war broke out, as it inevitably would. He said the Arab states would not attack, but if Jordan were attacked the others would come to her assistance, and the war would go on until the Palestine question was settled.

I had lunch with Mr Duke, the British Ambassador at Amman, and told him of my *démarche*. During lunch a call came from the palace that King Hussein wanted to see me. I had an interview with His Majesty almost immediately. He said that Abu Nuwar had told him about our interview, but he wanted to hear himself what the situation was. I repeated what I had said to the Chief of Staff. His Majesty listened attentively, and appeared to take what I had to say much in the same way as Abu Nuwar had, but without any of the fire-eating talk about what would happen if Israel committed any warlike acts. He repeated Abu Nuwar's assurances that the situation would be controlled on the Jordanian side, and that they would co-operate with UNTSO.

I had prepared what I was going to say at my interview with Abu Nuwar carefully. However, I had not thought it appropriate to put the substance in the form of an aide-mémoire. I had no doubt of the meaning I intended or that my words conveyed that meaning.

On the 3rd I went to Cairo, and after some discussion with Colonel Gohar about the refusal of the Israelis to allow marking of the ADL around the Strip or to hold MAC meetings in El Auja, I saw Dr Fawzi, the Minister of Foreign Affairs. In the course of this interview I told him of my interview with Mr Ben-Gurion and the subsequent interviews with General Ali Abu Nuwar and King Hussein.

I said I hoped that the influence of Egypt in Amman would be used to promote a policy of control and moderation. He gave me to understand that Egypt would favour such a policy.

The next day I was shown messages at the British Embassy which indicated that King Hussein had called in the diplomatic representatives of the Three Powers, and also Egypt, Syria, and Lebanon, and had told them that I had said Israel was preparing to attack Mount Scopus and other places in the near future. I at once gave the Ambassador, Sir Humphrey Trevelyan, a correction to be sent to the British diplomatic missions and the Foreign Office.

I went back to Jerusalem on the same day. On July 6 I heard of troop movements of the Arab Legion towards the West Bank. The story of the " war danger " had become public also, apparently reaching the Press in Beirut as a result of the indiscretion of one or other of the Arab diplomatic representatives. I sent an urgent message to Ali Abu Nuwar saying that there appeared to be a mistaken interpretation of what I had told him and King Hussein. Future developments depended on the control Jordan exercised on the demarcation line. Later he asked me to see him the next day.

On July 6 I also saw Mrs Meir about various matters. Concerning the Jordanian " war scare," she assured me that there was no concentration of Israeli troops in the Jerusalem sector. I saw Ali Abu Nuwar in Amman the following day. The interview was difficult, as he insisted that I had warned him of imminent Israeli action. I said that the essence of my warning had been that developments would be conditional on whether there was quiet on the Jordanian demarcation line or not, and that if they wanted to avoid these possible adverse developments, they should control the people on their border, particularly their troops. We eventually got Mr Duke to come in and give his version of what I had told him on the 2nd. This generally supported my contentions and the argument was not carried further. General Abu Nuwar agreed to withdraw the troops he had sent to reinforce the West Bank if inspection by UNMOs confirmed the Israeli Foreign Minister's assurance that there had been no Israeli reinforcement of the sector. This report had come to the Jordanian staff from agents, or observers who watched the traffic into Jerusalem up the main road from the Wadi el Bab. False alarms of this character were constantly being raised, and usually could be quickly disproved by the UNMOs driving about unobtrusively and looking for extra military transport, men in uniform, and so forth. In this case, as in nearly all others, there was no foundation for the reports of additional Israeli troops in Jerusalem. When this information was passed to the Jordanian military authorities, their reinforcements were withdrawn, and UNMOs visited their area in turn to confirm that all had reverted to normal. So ended this episode.

On the whole, although it left a feeling of distrust between Ali Abu Nuwar and myself, I was not unhappy that the publicity had occurred. Attention had been drawn to the danger of the Mount Scopus dispute, and Mr Ben-Gurion's insistence on the right to retaliate. The developments on the Jordanian border were bad enough in the next three months, but they might have been worse if it had not been for this early warning.

The particular importance attached by both sides to Mount Scopus requires some explanation. The Israelis affected to consider they had an incontestable right to the area, because the ground and buildings of the Hebrew University belonged to them. The creation of this university had been a most important step in the development of the new Zionist state. The Mount itself had religious associations, as it was from there that the observations of the moon determining the date of various Jewish religious observances were supposed to be made. Following the construction of the University, the Hadassah hospital was built on Mount Scopus with funds collected by that organization in the United States and Canada. It was a fine, modern hospital plant, and another sign of progress in the Jewish Homeland. Arabs as well as Jews were treated there, and its facilities were of great benefit to the community.

On July 7, 1948, both sides agreed, with UN participation, to insulate an area around the university and hospital buildings, and also around the Augusta Victoria Hospital on the Mount of Olives, making a sort of dumb-bell-shaped neutral territory. This agreement was said to have been due to Mr Truman's personal intervention. At the time, it must have seemed like a sound idea to prevent the destruction of cultural facilities which had been useful to both the Arab and Jewish communities. Unfortunately the agreement, drawn up by soldiers and officials who were anything but skilled diplomatic draughtsmen, had clauses in it whose meaning was very doubtful. The neutralized areas were supposed to be under the control of the Chief of Staff UNTSO, and the civil policemen who were to guard the property in the area were supposed to obey his orders. In the course of the six years that had elapsed since the signing of the agreement up until when I took over as Chief of Staff UNTSO, there had been a gradual erosion of the observance of the terms of the agreement. It will be of little interest to recapitulate the arguments between the sides. The principal point at issue, when I came, was that the Jordanians were sure that the Israelis had improved the fortifications around the buildings, and had brought in considerable additional munitions and warlike stores. They wanted me to conduct a thorough inspection of the premises, to determine that no such violations of the agreement had occurred—or to correct them, if they had. The Israelis after a while agreed to my inspection, but they did not produce the keys to the doors of several rooms in the hospital, which might have contained munitions or arms. It was pretty certain that they had smuggled a good deal of stuff in, from one or two attempts that were detected—such as the notorious barrel episode during General Riley's tenure as Chief of Staff UNTSO, described in Commander Hutchison's book *Violent Truce*, Chapter 3. The Jordanians had also intercepted parties carrying in munitions by the back way.

The significance of all this was that Mount Scopus absolutely dominated the roads into Jerusalem from the east (the Jordan) and the north (Ramallah and Nablus). Jerusalem was the nexus of all important roads connecting the larger towns in the Arab-held Palestine. If the Israelis could connect up with the sort of fortress held by the detachment of Israeli police (who were probably regular soldiers) they would dominate and could eventually compel the surrender of Jerusalem, and probably cause the collapse of Jordanian control of the area west of the Jordan River.

Such is the tactical importance of Mount Scopus, in my opinion. Therefore the seizure or occupation of it by Israel would be a disaster for Jordan, and it is perfectly understandable that they were very concerned about Israeli encroachments. Needless to say, the Israelis, particularly the soldiers, are equally aware of its military importance. The 'cultural' value of this area to Israel is not significant now (May 1958) since newer and bigger university premises have been opened west of the New City, and a new Hadassah hospital is progressing towards completion beyond Ain Karim, to the west. But the seizure of Mount Scopus, if the politically favourable moment arrived, would be equivalent to guaranteeing their eventual control of the whole of Jerusalem—a scarcely concealed objective of the State.

One of the factors which made for instability and danger at this time was that it was not certain whether Great Britain, after the cavalier dismissal of General Glubb and the senior British officers of the Legion, and the other developments contrary to her wishes, would still consider herself bound by the Anglo-Jordanian treaty. It seemed almost certain that the treaty would be denounced sooner or later. It also seemed likely that there might be a break-up of the Kingdom of Jordan, following which there would be a scramble for pieces of the territory among the neighbouring Arab states—Syria, Iraq, Saudi Arabia, and possibly Egypt. Israel probably thought it advisable to stake her claim, or at any rate have justificatory arguments ready to back up her claim, to a piece of the Jordanian pie.

Mr Hammarskjöld paid another visit to the area on July 19. Between the date of my interview with Mr Ben-Gurion and this visit, there was no cessation of the incidents between Israel and Jordan. Israel complained of twenty-four crossings or firings across the demarcation line, while Jordan complained of twenty-six of the same sort. (Complaints of aircraft flying across the demarcation line are not included.) There were three bad incidents of attacks on Israelis on roads well within Israel, in which three Israelis had been killed and two wounded. In response to UN and diplomatic pressure to do something to stop these marauders, on July 13 a military spokesman issued a statement in Amman, to the effect that "recent infiltrations into Israel were merely individual cases which are contrary to Jordan's policy and commitments under the GAA. Orders have been issued to Jordan forces to open fire on any infiltrator."

On the night of July 14–15 a considerable body of Israeli troops (about 100) had penetrated four kilometres within Jordan territory near Gharandal police-station, in the Wadi Araba. The force withdrew without any hostile action, but the crossing of so many troops was in itself a serious breach of the GAA. The significance of this happening appeared when Gharandal police-station was attacked and destroyed a couple of months later, as a reprisal for an infiltrator's crime in the Negev.

The Secretary-General returned to Jerusalem on July 19, and had two two-and-a-half-hour talks with Mr Ben-Gurion, at which I was not present. The following day there was a meeting with Mr Ben-Gurion and Mrs Meir, supported by Mr Tekoah, while I and M. Vigier accompanied the Secretary-General. The Israelis, some time before, had stopped our observers from moving in the demilitarized zone in El Auja. This removed another of the safeguards against the outbreak of hostilities in that area. I had received no satisfaction from the Israeli authorities in my protests about this. Mr Hammarskjöld also was unable to get Mr Ben-Gurion to withdraw the restrictions, telling me later that if in ten days there was no favourable response by Israel, the matter would have to be referred to the Security Council.

The Jordanian infiltration attacks were then discussed. Mr Ben-Gurion said he would withhold retaliation until the Secretary-General would admit that he could in no way control Jordan. Mount Scopus also was touched upon. Mr Ben-Gurion maintained his theory of Israel's " rights " there, but in much milder tone than he had used to me in the interview of June 28.

On the 21st the Secretary-General had an interview in Amman with Awni Abdel Hadi, Minister of Foreign Affairs, and Ibrahim Hashim, the Permanent Secretary, and General Abu Nuwar. They repeated the assurances that the Arab Legion and Jordanian police were taking energetic measures against infiltration.

I accompanied the Secretary-General to Cairo, where he had an interview with Dr Fawzi, but, I understood, made no progress beyond the points of agreement registered in his May 9, 1956 report. Mr Hammarskjöld intended to return to the area in October, hoping the climate would be more propitious then. He instructed me that in the meantime I was to press General Abu Nuwar to take effective action to detect and punish those responsible for incidents within Israeli territory, and at the same time I was to try to restrain the Israelis from retaliating.

Mr Hammarskjöld had hardly left the area before a number of serious incidents showed how little reliance could be placed on the pledges of the parties to observe an unconditional cease-fire. These centred about a locality called Sheikh Abd el Aziz, on the Jordan side, six kilometres north-west of Jerusalem and about 1750 metres north of the main Jerusalem–Tel Aviv highway. It was on a high spur of some 800 metres' elevation and dominated a lower spur on the Israeli side of the demarcation line, where terracing work was being carried out by the Israeli settlers of Mevaseret Yerusha-layim, lately arrived from North Africa. Sheikh Abd el Aziz also looked down on a long stretch of the Jerusalem-Tel Aviv highway, the vital link between the Israeli Jerusalem salient and the rest of Israel. On July 14, 15, and 16 there were complaints from both sides about firing across the line. Then a pause, and again on July 22 complaints from both sides of fire by the other. As usual, it was impossible to determine which had been the first to begin the shooting.   The Chairman of HJKIMAC proposed that UN observers should take post near the area, so that they could determine the responsibility for opening fire, if there were further incidents.   The Israeli delegate said he would submit the proposal to higher authority.   The Jordanians were willing to agree to posting observers on their side if the Israelis would do the same.

The next day, the 24th, Chairman and MAC were occupied with a bad incident on Mount Scopus, where Arab Legion soldiers had occupied a house in a disputed area.   Israelis had begun firing at them, and they had returned the fire.   Eventually the UN observer in charge of the Mount Scopus area for me, Major Marcel Breault of Canada, succeeded in getting both sides to stop the firing.   He then went out, with Major George Flint, also an observer from the Canadian Army, and Lieutenant Daoud, one of the Jordanian delegation to the MAC, to get the Arab Legion soldiers out of the house.[29]   He followed a path which he had previously used, but by mischance one of the party kicked a trip-wire, and an anti-personnel mine severely wounded all three officers.   Fortunately, through good medical care in the Hadassah hospital on the Israeli side of Jerusalem, the Canadian officers' lives were saved, and they were able to return to duty after a month or so, though with some continuing disability.   Lieutenant Daoud also made a good recovery.   The whole incident was due to the occupation of the house by the Arab Legion, contrary to instructions I had given.   The minefield was one several years old, subsequent investigation showed, put there by the Israelis.   It was not their fault the party had blundered into a trip-wire ; the minefield's existence was known to the party, and, in fact, relying on previous safe passage by the path, they had refused an offer of the Israelis to guide them.

On July 25 the trouble near Sheikh Abd el Aziz flared up again.   Both sides complained of shooting in the area, and the Jordanians requested an investigation.   When the investigating team reached a village called Beit Surik, some one and a half kilometres north of Sheikh Abd el Aziz, they stopped their jeeps to look at casualties from the village which had been fired on by mortars.   Some persons among the crowd of Beit Surik villagers ran amok and attacked the party with sub-machine-guns, severely wounding Lieutenant-Colonel E. H. Thalin, of the Swedish Army, and Captain Barghouti, the Jordanian delegate.   The commander of the Arab Legion in the village quickly brought the situation under control, and I was told the attackers had been arrested and would be tried ; but I never heard whether they were punished.   The unfortunate Lieutenant-Colonel Thalin, who had come out to the mission only shortly before, was shot through the spine, and paralysed in the lower part of the body, having to be invalided home.

The two sides' versions of the incident at Sheikh Abd el Aziz were, of course, contradictory. In any case it was true that the Israelis had opened with machine-gun and then three-inch mortar fire. They had no casualties, but the mortar fire wounded six Jordanians. I later had occasion to discuss this incident with Mrs Meir, who was very emphatic about Israel's intention to defend this sensitive area (near which there had been much hard fighting in the 1948 hostilities) by every means. She also asked me—possibly a rhetorical question—why the Arabs kept attacking Israelis. I said that in this case it seemed to me likely that some of the dispossessed Arab villagers from the area, who may have been among the Jordanian national guards in the Sheikh Abd el Aziz hamlet, had become infuriated at seeing the new Jewish immigrants from North Africa beginning the cultivation of the lands that had formerly been theirs. Mrs Meir was very indignant at my introducing the refugee question into the discussions. I replied that she had asked me a question, and I had answered. It seemed to me to be symptomatic of a certain blindness to the human reactions of others that so many Israelis professed not to understand why the Arabs who had been driven from their lands should continue to hate and try to injure those who had driven them out.

Eventually observers were posted on the Israeli side, and there was no more trouble at Sheikh Abd el Aziz. I had presented strong protests by the Secretary-General both to the Jordanian Government and the Government of Israel. Mrs Meir objected strenuously to both protests being couched in similar terms. I pointed out that the protest was against the breach of the cease-fire promise—that Israel might have resolved the difficulty by agreeing to the posting of UN observers, instead of opening up with her three-inch mortars.

CHAPTER 12

The Armistice crumbles

ON July 26 President Nasser announced the nationalization of the Suez Canal.[30] This act of defiance of the West shook the foundations of peace in the Middle East. I have pointed out that it was the Three Powers, France, the United Kingdom, and the United States, standing behind their Declaration of May 1950, that really provided what strength there was behind the Security Council resolutions concerning relations between Israel and the Arab states. It was the diplomatic efforts of these Powers, and their ability to apply economic sanctions, or in the last resort military sanctions, that had made it possible to be confident that, even though more and more of the provisions of the armistice agreements were being disregarded, war between the parties could be prevented from breaking out.

Now Egypt had seized a very important property mainly owned by the British and French nations. This act bore even more serious implications. Great Britain, France, and other European nations were all more or less dependent on Middle Eastern oil for transport and industrial power. Egypt was now in a position to cut off this vital fuel without warning. The position appeared intolerable to the British Government, and in early August it began to concentrate troops and air-force units in Cyprus. French troops followed towards the end of the month. The Western Powers began negotiations and held conferences, trying to undo the effect of Egypt's nationalization of the Canal, and to devise a system of international control of its operation. Egypt resisted all suggestions towards the establishment of such a system, and received the strongest backing from the U.S.S.R. in her resistance. No doubt Nasser had been promised this support before he took the step of nationalization.

It was abundantly clear that in these circumstances neither the United Kingdom nor France would be ready to apply pressure or support in the Security Council measures to oblige Israel to comply with the General Armistice Agreement with Egypt, or to give effect to any of the measures recommended in the Council's resolutions of June 4, which Israel was either evading or refusing. Israel, of course, had a special interest in the freedom of passage through the Suez Canal. Although her efforts to get herself included in the conferences about the Canal failed, it was remembered that Egypt had continued to refuse Canal transit to Israeli shipping in spite of the Security Council resolution of 1951, without consequences to herself—largely because of Russian support. It had to be reckoned with that Egypt would probably act in a similar way with the shipping of any other country with whom she had a quarrel, if she thought it safe to do so.

War plainly threatened. In an interview I had with Colonel Gohar in Gaza on June 3, he expressed apprehensions that Israel was preparing an aggression. He suggested the Israelis had begun the usual publicity build-up, by a Press campaign exaggerating the importance of the incidents which had occurred in the Gaza and El Auja areas, and were combining this with aggressive patrolling, to provoke incidents. I advised him that, if the Egyptian authorities believed this to be true, they should be most careful to give the Israelis no cause or excuse for retaliation. It was essential that they issue stringent orders against opening fire on Israeli patrols or individuals in ICT, and that they repress all infiltration.

Early in July an incident had happened in the Gaza Strip which was bound to have repercussions. The Egyptian officer in charge of intelligence in the area, Lieutenant-Colonel Mustafa Hafez, whose duties included recruiting *fedayeen* from among the Gaza refugees and sending them on missions into Israel, was killed by a bomb which had been sent to him in the form of a parcel. This was on July 13. On July 14 Colonel Salah Mustafa, the Egyptian military attaché at Amman, opened a parcel looking like a book, which purported to come from the Jordan-Israel Mixed Armistice Commission, and received severe wounds when the device exploded. He died a few days later. He also was supposed to have been organizing *fedayeen* raids from Jordanian territory.

The *Jerusalem Post* published circumstantial stories that Lieutenant-Colonel Mustafa Hafez had been the victim of revenge taken by refugees, who were supposed to have become embittered by Hafez' strong-arm methods of recruiting *fedayeen*, and the fact that many of the young men so recruited were captured or killed by the Israelis. When the news of the second assassination of Colonel Salah Mustafa came out, presumably the Israeli intelligence service had run out of invention, because no similar explanatory tale was published.

The Egyptians intimated that they had secured certain evidence indicating Israeli responsibility for Mustafa Hafez' death, but they never made a complaint about the incident to the Mixed Armistice Commission. The efficiency of the infernal machines, the synchronization of the attempts, and the quick news which Israeli papers had of the incidents combine to make it seem probable that the bombs were made in Israel. Doubtless the majority of Israelis who read about the matter felt that a fitting revenge had been wreaked on those who had been sending terrorists into Israel, while they themselves remained in imagined safety in Gaza and Amman. One can admit that this attitude would not be unnatural ; nevertheless the act clearly was in contravention of the assurances which Mr Ben-Gurion had given that Israel would refrain from all kinds of hostile activity. Doubtless he knew nothing about it, except what he read in the papers.

As the summer wore on, incidents between Israel and Jordan were of almost daily occurrence. It was between these two countries that the tension now seemed greatest, and there was danger that the chain of incidents and reprisals would lead to war. In the two months from July 29 to September 25 Israel lodged fifty-nine complaints with the MAC, concerning crossings of the demarcation line by military or civilians, or firing across it. Nineteen Israelis had been killed and twenty-eight wounded as a result of these incidents.

During the same period Jordan lodged sixty-three complaints on the same kind of infractions of the GAA (besides 147 complaints of overflights), and seventy-two Jordanians were killed and twenty-four wounded, mainly as a result of Israeli retaliatory actions.

The first reprisal occurred as a result of an incident in the Idna-Dawiyima area—about fifteen kilometres west of Hebron. An Israeli unit was carrying out map-reading exercises very close to the demarcation line—a very stupid business. As mentioned previously, I had several times protested against the Israeli practice of conducting military exercises close to the demarcation line. On this occasion the Jordanian national guard opened fire on them, and in the ensuing fight six Israeli soldiers were killed and three wounded. A bad feature was that the Jordanians, to make it appear that the Israelis had actually crossed the line, dragged some of the bodies into Jordan. Such tampering with bodies usually resulted in accusations in the Israel Press that the Arabs had mutilated them, though not on this occasion.

It is interesting to note that in the September 11 issue of the *Jerusalem Post* which reported this clash Foreign Minister Golda Meir was reported as having told Drew Pearson, the American columnist, that " for Israel to initiate a war against Egypt a change of Prime Minister, Foreign Minister, Knesset, and probably in the whole spirit of the country would be required."

Mrs Meir may or may not have known about the Army's plans for chastising the Jordanians for the Dawiyima incidents, but in any case towards midnight a force about a battalion strong crossed the demarcation line, and blew up the police-post at Rahwa, on the Hebron-Beersheba road several kilometres inside Jordan, killing five Jordanian policemen and ten soldiers. A school building, built with UNRWA funds and just completed, was blown up, and an ambush some kilometres along the road towards Hebron killed another five Jordanians and wounded three.

During the evening of September 12, in an unconnected incident, a group of marauders whose tracks were followed to Jordanian territory killed three guards at an oil-drilling camp in the Negev. These guards happened to be Druses, and after the subsequent retaliation the Israeli Press seemed to take a good deal of satisfaction in complimenting the security forces on how they were protecting the lives of the Arab citizens of Israel. There had been another bad incident in the Negev on August 16 when some fifteen armed men from Jordan ambushed a bus and two escorting jeeps going to Eilat. One woman passenger and three of the escorting soldiers were killed, and seven Israelis were wounded. The Druse incident loosed another reprisal. On September 13 a large Israeli force attacked and destroyed the police-post at Gharandal, and a school close to it. Nine Jordanian policemen and two civilians were killed, four policemen and two civilians wounded.

A few days later an extremely serious incident occurred. An archaeological congress was being held in Israel, and as part of the programme some one hundred of its members were taken to Ramat Rahel, at the tip of the Israeli salient south of Jerusalem, to view some recent excavations. A very innocent expedition, but in the existing state of tension with Jordan it was hardly prudent to lead so many Israelis and visitors right up to the demarcation line, while loudspeakers roared out in Hebrew. A few hundred yards away, to the south, stood the monastery of Mar Ilyas (St Elias) garrisoned by the Arab Legion. Suddenly fire was opened by a Bren gun from the Arab position, and when it ceased three of the archaeological group had been killed and seventeen wounded, one of whom died later.

This was grave indeed, and a dangerous reaction from the Israelis was almost certain. The Jordanians promptly put out a *communiqué* stating that one of the soldiers at Mar Ilyas had, " in a sudden fit of insanity, opened fire on the Israeli crowd." The Israelis claimed that more than one machine-gun had opened fire (of which the MAC investigation found no conclusive evidence), and scornfully rejected the plea of insanity, claiming that that was the common excuse of the Arab who had on impulse done something he should not have done.

In the subsequent MAC proceedings the Jordanians stuck to their excuse for what had happened, and offered to produce the soldier for examination by a neutral psychiatrist. We felt we could not reject the Jordanian plea out of hand, and we had arranged for an Armenian psychiatrist to come from Beirut, but the Israeli delegation to the MAC would not take any further part in the proceedings.

Later I heard, in an indirect way, that the soldier who had done the firing, and who was promptly arrested by the Jordanians, had had his brother killed by the Israelis in the attack on Rahwa. He had lost his head, and in an excess of rage had taken his own revenge—according to the Arab tradition. This, in retrospect, seems to me the probable explanation.

I tried, though without much hope, to avert a retaliation by the usual pleas to the Israeli Government. Perhaps it might have been averted but for two other incidents which followed in rapid succession. In the first an Arab penetrated into Israel territory, on September 24, and shot a girl picking olives near the Aminadav settlement, a few kilometres south of Jerusalem. On the same day a tractor-driver was shot in the Maoz Haiyim area, near Beisan, and his body dragged across the river. A second driver was wounded. This made it inevitable that the Israelis would retaliate. The operation began about half-past nine on the night of the 25th. Warnings had reached us, and UNMOs had seen ambulances and other vehicles moving towards Mevo Betar. We warned the Jordanians and, without success, tried to reach responsible officials at the Ministry of Foreign Affairs in order to try to stop the impending action.

The morning after I visited the places attacked, Sharafa police-post near Husan and a school near Wadi Fukin. The preceding night, while the raid had been going on, General Abu Nuwar sent a message to suggest that I should go out to the Husan area, to see for myself what was happening. I did not treat this suggestion as a very practical one. Colonel Saadi, head of the Jordanian delegation to the MAC, had just refused my offer to send out observers. He very sensibly said that he and they could learn nothing in the darkness and confusion, and it would be better to wait until light. We went out together in the morning, and Lieutenant-Colonel Christian Moe, Chairman of the HJKIMAC, came with us. We drove out past the hamlet of Al Khadr—the Arabic name for St George. There is a Greek monastery there, dedicated to the saint. The local inhabitants believe that he has powers to cure insanity. On this occasion he did nothing for the safety of the Arab Legion and national guard men who held and tried to reinforce the police-post. The protection of the British alliance must have seemed as remote and ineffective as the protection of the English patron saint to those villagers.

A little before we reached the hill on which the Sharafa police-post had stood we stopped to look at the remains of a jeep, which had been ambushed and destroyed by fire. Captain Abdullah Baha El Din, who was going forward in it to reconnoitre, had been taken out of the vehicle and shot, with his driver. Presently Colonel Izzat Hassan, commander of the area, arrived with some other Legion officers, and an elderly civilian, very dignified in his white linen suit and Turkish-style Astrakhan cap. Colonel Hassan told me that he was the father of the young captain who had been killed. I said, in my fragmentary Arabic, how sorry I was, and the Legion officers chorused their condolences. " Hukm Allah [It is God's will]," murmured Colonel Saadi.

Almost certainly Captain Baha El Din and the thirty-eight other Jordanian men killed in this reprisal had had nothing to do with the shooting of the four Jews in the crowd at Ramat Rahel, or of the young girl from Aminadav picking olives, or of the Jewish tractor-driver near Beisan. Yet they and the six innocent Jewish victims paid the penalty of the code, very ancient in this land, that calls for revenge to be taken for blood spilt.

We drove on and looked at the ruins of the police-post. A tremendous charge of explosive must have been used ; not one stone lay on another, and debris was scattered over hundreds of metres. The dead had been taken away, after having been seen by the UNMOs investigating the incident. We went on to Wadi Fukin, a small village in a valley where water sources made it possible to cultivate field crops, olives, and figs. The village had long been deserted by its inhabitants, because of its position right on the demarcation line, below a *kibbutz*, Mevo Betar, occupied by Israelis belonging to the Herut Party, many of them former Irgun Zvi Leumi and Stern group men, ruthless fighters. Wadi Fukin had been raided in 1953, and, though its inhabitants still worked their fields, they went there only by day.

A Government school had stood on a hill a kilometre to the east of the village, and this the Israelis had also razed with explosives. It had been attended by children from the near-by villages of Husan and Nahhalin. Presumably the Israelis had adopted this practice of blowing up schools because they would be empty at night, and the reproach of killing women and children would not be incurred, while the ruins would still stand as a witness and reminder of Israel's wrath.

On September 14 I had written a memorandum to the Secretary-General giving my view of the situation at the time, in which I offered the opinion that the dispute about the Suez Canal would govern all developments in the Middle East until it was settled. The memorandum continued :

> I think that if hostilities between the disputants in the Suez Canal question should break out, Israel might try to settle some accounts with the Egyptians. She might provoke a situation where she could attack—with self-justification, at any rate—the Egyptian forces remaining in the El Arish-El Quseima-Rafah area. The UNMO investigating the recent El Quseima incident passed through this area and noted that many of the camps appeared vacant. It appears highly probable to me that the Egyptians have withdrawn two of the three divisions they had in this area, using the troops withdrawn for defence against possible attempts to occupy key points on the Suez Canal. The Israelis, therefore, might find this a good opportunity to deal with the remainder of the El Arish concentration, thus securing hostages to force a peace settlement. I do not think that the Israelis would like to go into the Gaza Strip directly and become responsible for the refugees there, but if the Strip were cut off from Egypt, obviously very grave difficulties would arise in this area.
>
> I don't think Israel will attack Jordan, except in the way of retaliatory raids such as those of Rahwa (12 Sept) and Gharandal (13 Sept). But if Jordan stages a large counter-retaliation, then Israel might reply by attacking and occupying certain points of vital importance. . . .
>
> . . . It also seems clear that as the Israelis might desire to take offensive action in certain circumstances, they are interested to prevent this becoming known, and therefore will try to restrict the movements and liberties to observe and report of the UNMOs in every way.
>
> In the meantime, they are vigorously applying their policy of immediate retaliation against acts of sabotage in Israel, or those resulting in loss of Israeli lives. . . . They apparently feel quite free to carry out this policy, knowing that Egypt is not in a position to react vigorously against it, and neither is Jordan, lacking support from Egypt. . . . The Israelis further know that in present circumstances neither the U.K., nor France, nor the U.S. is likely to place heavy pressure on them, either to conform to the Security Council resolutions or to refrain from their arbitrary retaliations.

Mr Hammarskjöld replied in a long letter of September 19, saying that he agreed generally with my analysis, but that we should have to accept the fact that for the time being all our problems would develop in the shadow of the Suez crisis, and that the possibilities of dealing with them would be affected by considerations going far beyond the confines of the region. This letter indicated that in the circumstances existing it was almost impossible for him, as Secretary-General, to avert the threat I had pointed out.

On September 27 the Secretary-General submitted a report to the Security Council, recording how little progress had been made in implementing the recommendations of its resolutions of April 4 and June 5, 1956, and drawing attention to the dangers of the situation. The cease-fire promised by all parties in May had not been observed ; and the danger of a chain reaction of violence leading to open hostilities was great. He referred to the restrictions of movement of the United Nations Military Observers, and their implications, which were spelled out in my report to him, which he annexed. I had written :

> The maintenance of observers in the El Auja Demilitarized Zone, with freedom of movement and to transmit messages to the Chairman of the EIMAC and to UNTSO by speediest means, is essential in order to fulfil the duties imposed on UNTSO by the Security Council resolution of June 4, 1956. The strategic importance of the roads radiating from El Auja is such that if one side or the other should contemplate aggression on a large scale against the territory of the other, primary or secondary lines of operations would certainly be established through the demilitarized zone. If either side entered the Demilitarized Zone with forces on an offensive scale, this would be *prima facie* evidence of aggression. The presence of UNMOs, therefore, is a deterrent against aggression and their withdrawal from the area would be a removal of this deterrent.

As to the situation along the demarcation line round the Gaza Strip, I said :

> The observation posts have been established, and five to seven posts are manned daily. . . . The presence of these observers has not always deterred the Parties from opening fire across the Demarcation Line, nor from crossing it. Whenever such incidents have been observed, protests to the Party which has violated the Armistice Agreement have been made, but these protests have not prevented other incidents occurring. . . . The failure to mark the Demarcation Line clearly and the failure to accept the proposals for separations of the Parties' forces . . . are regrettable, as they might have gone far towards preventing the occurrence of so many breaches of the cease-fire.

(Israel had blocked the marking of the line, as mentioned on page 154.)

Some of the Israeli patrols which the UNMOs had seen approaching the demarcation line were neither protecting settlers working in the fields nor preventing any infiltrators from crossing. Thus the assurances which Mr Ben-Gurion had given about the conduct of these patrols were disregarded by the Israeli troops on the ground.

My report also detailed the incidents between Egypt and Israel during the month of August. The most important of these were :

on August 14 an Israeli truck was blown up by a mine near Sde Boker and its driver slightly wounded, and on August 16 a truck was mined and five of its twenty passengers wounded in the same vicinity. As Sde Boker was the *kibbutz* in the Negev where Mr Ben-Gurion had lived during his temporary retirement from politics, and where he occasionally went for rest and relaxation, it was a sensitive spot.

During the night of August 16–17 an Israeli group of from fifteen to twenty armed persons entered Egyptian-controlled territory near Deir el Balah. There was an exchange of fire between this group and an Egyptian post, and later an Egyptian patrol. Three soldiers of the patrol were killed. On the road from Rafah to Gaza a jeep carrying a doctor, four medical orderlies, and a driver was ambushed by another Israeli group. The jeep was set on fire by a mine, and all its occupants were killed by small-arms fire at close range. Another Israeli patrol crossed the International Frontier from the El Auja demilitarized zone and destroyed a jeep, at the same time wounding an Egyptian soldier.

There had also been a great many firings across the demarcation line surrounding the Gaza Strip, most of them centred round the Nuseirat and Beit Hanun areas. There were other incidents in the vicinity of El Auja. Some of the Israel incursions there had been in strength approaching a company, according to Egyptian complaints. The situation was very bad, and it seemed that full-scale hostilities could be set off by one of these incidents spreading and continuing, each side reinforcing their troops engaged. I had warned of such a possibility several times before ; but now the danger seemed closer and more obvious, and there was no Great Power which would act to check the collapse of the armistice.

On October 3, following the Ramat Rahel incident, and the MAC meeting about it, in which the Chairman had sided with the Jordanian delegation in the proposal to examine the mental state of the soldier who had fired on the archaelogical group, the Israeli authorities announced that they could not participate in any more discussions of cases in the MAC, as they found such proceedings useless. They would, however, continue to make complaints for the record. A statement in the *Jerusalem Post* of October 4 said that this decision was taken following " the recent travesty of justice in the discussion of the Ramat Rahel attack." The statement went on : " As regards the UNTSO, not only did it not succeed in deterring the Arab countries from their attitude of aggression, but it even failed in its responsibility to draw a distinction between attacker and attacked, between the party which refuses to live up to its obligations under the UN Charter and under the GAA and the party which demands the fulfilment of these obligations in their entirety."

The Israelis never seemed to have any doubts as to the righteousness of all their actions.

A day later, on October 5, the Foreign Ministry informed me that Israel in future would not agree to UN observers' taking part in the investigation of incidents which occurred inside Israeli-controlled territory. I protested, but the decision was confirmed in writing by Mrs Meir, the Minister of Foreign Affairs. I thereupon reported the matter to the Secretary-General, who published it as a document to the Security Council, and subsequently commented on it, in his report to the Council on the Qalqilya incident, as follows :

> In this document the Chief of Staff . . . states that at present the situation is that one of the Parties to the GAA makes its own investigations, which are not—and cannot be made—subject to check or confirmation by the United Nations Observers, publishes the results of such investigations, draws its own conclusions from them, and undertakes actions by its military forces on that basis. I endorse the view of the Chief of Staff that this is a dangerous negation of vital elements of the Armistice Agreement.

This, translated into language for the reader who is not a diplomat, could explain that the Israelis would in future carry out retaliations, or more extensive operations, in respect of whatever misdeeds their own police or military forces found or alleged that the Arabs had committed. They would not submit to any restraint, nor even any independent assessment of the implications—or even the existence —of the evidence on which they claimed to judge their opponents and find them guilty. Very soon afterwards they also refused to allow UNMOs to take part in investigating incidents involving men coming from Egyptian-controlled territory. The way was thus open for them to elaborate or manufacture a *casus belli* against Egypt whenever they found the opportunity ripe, and it was not long before it ripened. But in the first half of October it looked as if their enmity was concentrated mainly against Jordan ; it seemed that an Israeli attack was most likely to fall upon her.

In this connexion a leading editorial in the *Jerusalem Post* for October 7, 1956, said : "Jordan is the sick man of the Middle East, and Israel has the major misfortune to find herself next door to his disintegrating body." The rest of the article went on to analyse briefly the course of events since the loss of British influence on Glubb's dismissal, and advanced the statement that " it has been known in Israel for a considerable period that the recent attacks, including . . . have been carried out under Egyptian orders." This enabled Egypt to strike at Israel without incurring retaliation, and it was difficult to prove Egypt's responsibility in the matter. The repercussions of the Israeli retaliations on Jordan greatly disturbed the people, and weakened the Government's control still further. The article ended : " If Jordan crumbles, Israel will not sit with folded hands, and Egypt will not inherit."

On the same day, October 7, I had a conversation with Mr Peter Westlake, *chargé d'affaires* of the British Embassy in Tel Aviv at the time, and he told me, when I spoke of the danger I saw of the increasingly severe Israeli retaliations developing into an attempt to seize and hold Jordanian territory, that any such attempt would bring the Anglo-Jordanian treaty into operation. But there were two more developments before the British Government issued an official warning.

The last, and most severe, of the retaliatory actions taken by Israel against Jordan was at Qalqilya, on the night of October 10–11. This was triggered by the murder of two Israeli workers in an orange-grove near Even-Yehuda, about ten kilometres north of Qalqilya. They were shot by two men with sub-machine-guns, in broad day-light, and the Israeli papers stated that each had an ear cut off—presumably for the murderers to take back as proof they had fulfilled their mission.

The Israeli reprisal attack was centred on the Qalqilya police-post, and did not differ greatly in plan from the previous actions at Rahwa, Gharandal, and Sharafa, except that, the station being in a built-up area, it was more difficult for the Israelis to avoid inflicting casualties on the civil population. They used heavy artillery-fire to cover their attack, which eventually succeeded in blowing up the post. The bodies of forty-eight dead Jordanians were seen by UNMOs, forty-three of them police and military. There were also many wounded. In this action, however, the Arab Legion reacted more successfully than it had done before. The reinforcements they sent up got some of the Israeli columns into difficulties. The Israelis reported eighteen killed. The number of their wounded was not made public.

I included, as an appendix to my report on this incident, statistics of the casualties suffered by the several parties to the GAAs during 1955 and from January to the end of September 1956. Prior to 1955 no regular statistics had been kept. The statistical tables are too detailed to be reprinted in this book, but are available as a Security Council document. In brief, they showed that in 1955 Israel had thirty-nine military personnel killed and 131 wounded ; twenty-four civilians killed and forty-one wounded. In the same year the Arab states had 246 military killed and 187 wounded ; fifty-one civilians killed and thirty-five wounded. During the nine months of 1956 Israel had twenty-two military killed and forty-one wounded, thirty-six civilians killed and nineteen wounded, while the Arab states had ninety-seven military killed and forty-three wounded, 102 civilians killed and 154 wounded. All the killed were not seen by UNMOs, but the evidence was carefully checked, and I believe the figures are substantially correct. The Israelis in the course of their retaliatory actions probably had considerably more military personnel wounded than they acknowledged, but they did not publish the figures, nor give any evidence to UNTSO. The grand total for the twenty-one months showed that Israel had 121 killed, while the Arab states had 496 killed. Israel's retaliatory policy had piled up an impressive balance of corpses in her favour.

For some time the Jordan Government had been negotiating for Iraqi troops to enter Jordan, to reinforce the Arab Legion in case extensive hostilities were launched by Israel, and perhaps to provide a deterrent. The first negotiations broke down, apparently on the question of command. The Iraqi General Staff and Government were apparently unwilling to place their troops under the command of General Ali Abu Nuwar. Their reluctance was perfectly understandable. On October 12 Israel issued a statement through the Ministry of Foreign Affairs that the proposed placing of Iraqi troops in Jordan " would be a direct threat to the security of Israel and the validity of the Israel-Jordan Armistice Agreement."

I reported on October 15 to the Secretary-General on the Israeli reactions regarding the possible entry of Iraqi troops into Jordan. My political and legal advisers told me that such a move would not invalidate the Jordan-Israel GAA, as Israel had publicly claimed. The only provisions relating to Iraq in that agreement were that the Iraqi troops would move out of the sector of the front which they were then holding. There was no proviso that they had to move out of Jordan territory entirely, or were prohibited from re-entering it. Therefore Israel could not claim the GAA was broken unless the Iraqi troops moved back into the same sector. I suggested to the Secretary-General that it might be advisable to inform Israel of United Nations views on what the legal position would be, should the prospective move of troops take place. He replied the same day, saying that he did not feel it was wise, in the very delicate and dangerous situation, to come out with contingent interpretations of the point in the GAA. However, it could be publicly stated that any questions arising out of an Iraqi troops move, if it materialized, would have to be settled in strict observance of the procedures prescribed in the GAA and the UN Charter. That meant Israel could take up the question in the Mixed Armistice Commission, or the Security Council. It proved unnecessary to make any such public statement, either at Jerusalem or New York, because of diplomatic action taken by the United Kingdom, apparently supported by the United States, and rather less positively by France.

On October 12, according to the *Jerusalem Post* of October 14, Mr Westlake sought an interview with Mrs Meir and told her that H.M.G. rejected the Israeli statement quoted above, and drew Israel's attention to the fact that any act of hostilities " would automatically bring the Anglo-Jordan security treaty into play."

The London *Times* of October 15 quoted Mrs Meir's further statement of October 13 that " Israel was determined to meet the threat to her integrity " which, she said, a movement of Iraqi troops into Jordan would constitute. This was taken to mean that if Iraqi troops moved in, Israel would invade Jordan. The *Times* article went on to say :

> It has often been argued that some Israel military advisers would like to seize a pretext to straighten their Eastern frontier up to the line of the river Jordan. Such action might have a swift military success against the Jordan Army if it were unsupported. The Jordan Army is at present largely deployed on the West Bank of the Jordan, for political rather than strategic reasons, and it is common knowledge that internal dissensions since the removal of Glubb Pasha have weakened it as a fighting force. After Mrs Meir's statement it was feared, therefore, that the Israel Government might decide to risk open aggression against Jordan in the hope of establishing in practice a new and more favourable armistice line from which to negotiate ultimately a final settlement. . . . The Israel Government has, however, received through the British Embassy a very clear indication that Britain would be bound to come to the assistance of Jordan if King Hussein invoked the Anglo-Jordanian Treaty.

The article concluded by mentioning that the Israel Government had recalled its ambassadors from London, Paris, Washington, and Moscow for consultation. According to the brothers Bromberger in *Les Secrets de l'Expédition d'Egypte*, it was at this juncture that the Israelis decided on their invasion of the Sinai—" C'est alors que Tel Aviv prit la décision du raid purgatif dans le Sinai "—and proceeded to co-ordinate plans through emissaries in Paris. While one does not endorse the Brombergers as a first-class historical authority, it certainly seems that it was about mid-October that the fateful decision was indeed taken by Israel—by Ben-Gurion and his colleagues, or perhaps a chosen few of them. I do not propose to debate here the question of collusion between Israel, France, and Great Britain prior to the Sinai invasion and the Port Said expedition, which has been sufficiently discussed in several other books besides the Brombergers', and which will have to wait for a final verdict on the publication of evidence not presently available.

CHAPTER 13

Israel Invades Egypt:
October 29, 1956

Maps 4 and 6

On October 27 it became publicly known that the Israeli Defence Forces were mobilizing. This had already been reported to Washington by the U.S. Embassy. President Eisenhower sent an urgent message to Mr Ben-Gurion counselling him to avoid anything " which might endanger the peace," and followed it by a second message in more pressing terms, which was delivered at 5 A.M. on the 29th. But Israel's decision had already been taken, and the deployment of her forces for the invasion of the Sinai went on without interruption.

On October 28 (a Sunday) the Israeli Ministry of Foreign Affairs published a statement about the mobilization. To conceal the intention to attack Egypt it was explained that reserves had been called up because of *fedayeen* attacks and because of the recently concluded military alliance between Egypt, Jordan, and Syria which provided for a unified command under Major-General Abd El Hakim Amr. The alliance had been celebrated with the usual fantastical Arab oratory, whose theme was the recovery of the Arab homeland in Palestine and the extirpation of the State of Israel. The third reason given for the mobilization was the presence of Iraqi troops close to the Jordanian border and the fact that ". . . the Arab armies are always mobilized, because their forces consist entirely of regular soldiers ; while in Israel the regular army is small. . . . Our defence forces consist of reserves, and it was essential to mobilize a number of reserve battalions and station them on the borders, to block any possible attack." The *communiqué* concluded sanctimoniously : " Let us stand firm . . . confident in the justice of our cause and in our strength, and knowing that the Guardian of Israel does not slumber nor sleep."

All this was, of course, mere camouflage, but it served its purpose for the thirty-six hours that elapsed until the attack was launched.

I must confess that prior to October 28 the reports of the mobilization did not excite me greatly. During my term as Chief of Staff UNTSO the Israelis had several times mobilized a portion of their reserves, usually followed by reports from the U.S. military attaché at Tel Aviv that the situation was dangerous and war a possibility. So, on this occasion, I thought that it was just a repetition of previous false alarms. UNMOs in the Beersheba area had reported increased activity of the Israeli troops in the area, but not to a degree that pointed to an immediate Israeli attack.

As the preceding chapters show, Israeli hostility during the preceding months had been directed mainly against Jordan, and it had seemed that they might seize a suitable pretext to attack that country, at least to the extent of cutting off Latrun and seizing territory to the north of Jerusalem to make a corridor to Mount Scopus. But the British warning that attack on Jordan would bring the Anglo-Jordanian treaty into operation had seemingly averted this danger. A change of front to attack Egypt did not seem to be an immediate prospect. I underestimated the Israeli determination to break the ring of hostility that surrounded her, and perhaps overestimated the sincerity of Mr Ben-Gurion's public announcements that Israel would never engage in a preventive war. This was in spite of the fact that I had foreseen the event as referenced by my memorandum of September 14 to the Secretary-General. (See page 169.)

There were other preoccupations for UNTSO too. The Arab countries had announced a " strike " for Sunday the 28th because of the French capture of five Algerian rebel leaders, who had been taken from an airliner some days before. Trouble was anticipated, and we had arranged for all dependents to be moved out from the Arab side of Jerusalem and for the protection of UN property, and for the military observers on duty to avoid becoming involved in crowds. During the riots of the previous December and January in the Arab Jerusalem, UNTSO personnel and dependents had not suffered, except for a few stones being thrown at jeeps, but the attacks on the American, French, and Italian consulates, and on some French nationals, had shown the necessity for a plan for the protection of UN people from the excesses of the mob. Also, owing to the disturbed conditions which had existed for some time in the Middle East, plans had been made for the evacuation from Israel and the surrounding Arab states (except Lebanon) of the dependents of UN military and civilian personnel—not only UNTSO but also UNRWA, Technical Assistance Board, and other UN organizations.

However, on Sunday the 28th, all arrangements were complete ; and furthermore we had been assured by the Jordanian authorities that the demonstrations would be kept under control. So there seemed no reason why I should not go for a swim in the Mediterranean—about the only form of recreational exercise I could take. I drove to Caesarea, where the rocks favoured skin-diving.

On the way there, and back, I noted signs of a mobilization beyond anything previously seen : large numbers of civilian trucks parked in fields near Jerusalem and · Ramle, giving the impression of improvised transport companies, which had been busy the previous night and were getting ready to go again.   There was other military traffic on the main Tel Aviv-Haifa highway, mainly armoured half-tracks going towards the south.   Based on my own observations, together with the reports of UN Military Observers, I wrote in my diary that the troop movements seen on the 27th and 28th indicated the shifting of approximately another division of Israeli troops to the Beersheba area.

According to Colonel Henriques, in his book *100 Hours to Suez*, the Israelis conducted their offensive with six infantry and two armoured brigades.   For some time previously the opinion of foreign military observers was that the Israelis had a force approximating one armoured and two infantry brigades in the Gaza-Beersheba-El Auja area.   If so, the additional force called up for the Sinai operations would be about as I estimated.   There may have been other units or formations mobilized to guard the Jordan and Syrian borders.   But I very much underestimated the speed with which they would put their plan into execution.

I reported on the Israeli mobilization to the Secretary-General on the 29th, and gave an appreciation of possible developments. It was clear that there was imminent danger of war.   The emphasis given to renewed Egyptian *fedayeen* actions as a reason for mobilization caused me to believe that the Israelis were planning a large reprisal, which they hoped would bring Egyptian counter-action, perhaps supported by Jordanian and Syrian operations.   This would confuse the issue as to who was the aggressor, and allow Israel to launch unrestricted warfare against Egypt, directed in the first place towards the destruction of the Egyptian forces in the El Arish-El Quseima area, and in the Sinai generally.

In fact the Israeli Government had decided to omit any intermediate steps, and to proceed directly to deal with the Egyptians, secure in the knowledge that a French veto would stop any Security Council sanctions being applied, and that the presidential election (on November 6) would prevent the United States from taking action in the matter alone.   However (according to Henriques), the operations were so designed that they could have been stopped after the first day or two, with objectives limited accordingly, if military or political developments were unfavourable.

At nine o'clock on the evening of October 29 a message was received from Major LeGrelle, of the Belgian Army, who was the observer on duty at El Auja, that he had been forcibly expelled by the Israeli Army at half-past five in the afternoon. This was immediately reported to the Secretary-General ; in clear, as together with the mobilization this expulsion of the UNMO indicated that Israeli offensive action had begun, though possibly only a large raid.

The ten-o'clock broadcast of Kol Israel announced that " units of the Israel Defence Forces have penetrated and attacked *fedayeen* bases in the El Kuntilla and Ras El Naqb area, and have taken up positions to the west of the Nakhl road junction on the approaches to the Suez Canal." [31]

I had Colonel Byron Leary (my senior military assistant) telephone Lieutenant-Colonel Nursella, who was Israel Army Liaison Officer for Armistice Affairs with the Ministry of Foreign Affairs. Nursella confirmed the radio announcement, and further told us that this was not just a retaliatory raid, but that the Israel forces were going to stay in the Sinai. This was immediately reported to the Secretary-General.

I discussed with my advisers whether it would be useful to follow the customary practice of UNTSO when large-scale fighting had broken out between parties to the armistice agreements, and call upon them to order their troops to cease fire and withdraw behind the Armistice Demarcation Line. But experience had shown that the Israelis, when they made a retaliatory raid, would withdraw only when the operation they had planned was completed. It seemed clear to me, even without Nursella's information, that the operation was more than just a raid, and that the Israelis would disregard a cease-fire ' order ' of UNTSO. So I decided not to issue one.

However, about two o'clock the following morning I had a telephone call from Mr Andrew Cordier, Executive Assistant to the Secretary-General, in New York. He inquired about the situation, and I asked him whether he thought I should call for a cease-fire, giving the reasons why I had not already done so. Although agreeing with my doubts as to the response, he thought, nevertheless, that the call should be issued. So I drew up a letter to the Israeli Foreign Minister, Mrs Meir, and sent a message in the same terms to Cairo.

It proved impossible to reach either Lieutenant-Colonel Nursella, Mr Eytan, Director-General of the Foreign Ministry, or Mr Arthur Lourie, Assistant Director-General, to arrange for prompt transmission of this missive to the Minister. Eventually Colonel Leary went himself to the Foreign Office, and handed the letter to the junior official on duty, about four o'clock in the morning.

The Defence Forces' announcement of Israel's attack on Egypt

was accompanied by an apologia by the Foreign Ministry spokesman : " Israel this evening took security measure to eliminate the
Egyptian *fedayeen* bases in the Sinai Peninsula." The statement
went on to allege that within the last week twenty-four Israel
casualties, dead and wounded, had been caused by mines placed
by the *fedayeen* in the Southern Negev.

Nearly all of the casualties complained of resulted from one
incident. Two military vehicles were blown up in the El Auja
demilitarized zone, and first reports were that three soldiers had
been killed and twenty-seven wounded. Of course, the presence
of Israeli soldiers in this zone was in violation of the General
Armistice Agreement, and despite repeated demands by the United
Nations that Israel withdraw her troops from it. The Israelis,
furthermore, had refused to allow UNMOs to investigate this
incident, as well as others which the Foreign Ministry statement
included under the heading of *fedayeen* activities in the Negev. As
there was no impartial investigation of the facts, it was open to the
Israeli authorities, if they wanted a *casus belli*, to exaggerate or
falsify any incident, or even to invent incidents. In this case there
is no reason to believe that the incidents the Israelis complained of
did not take place. But there is no impartially ascertained evidence
that they did, either.

The Foreign Ministry statement also cited the blocking of the
Suez Canal and alleged Egypt had " gloried in the effort to en-
compass Israel with a ring of steel with the announced and flaunted
purpose at the appropriate moment of annihilating her, crowned a
few days ago by a Syrian-Jordan-Egyptian military command under
the Egyptian commander-in-chief."

In short, Israel was initiating the preventive war which Mr Ben-
Gurion had declared she never would, with the above as justification.
Reading this statement, I was reminded again of the words I had
heard attributed to Mr Ben-Gurion a year and a half before : that
the function of the Ministry of Foreign Affairs was to justify, in the
eyes of the world, the actions of the Israeli Defence Forces. Perhaps
he didn't say it, but in the following eighteen months anyone could
have said it, and with justice.

About nine o'clock on the 30th I spoke to Mr Eytan, asking when
I might expect a reply to my request for a cease-fire. He said that
Mrs Meir would see me about five o'clock in the afternoon, and
that no answer would be possible before then. She was at Tel Aviv,
in the Foreign Affairs Office at Hakirya, the Government village,
where the H.Q. of the Israeli Defence Forces were, and to which,
apparently, Mr Ben-Gurion had moved the effective seat of
government during the critical days.

When I did see Mrs Meir that afternoon, after some delay, I got no answer other than that there was shortly to be a Cabinet meeting which would decide upon the question. Although I did not know it at that time, the Israeli Government must by then have received the Anglo-French ultimatum, addressed to the Egyptians as well as to themselves, to withdraw their forces to a distance of ten miles from the Canal. So naturally they were not particularly concerned with the UNTSO cease-fire call. They had by then reported their forces as being within thirty kilometres of the Canal—presumably at the Mitla Pass.

During most of October 30 and 31, UNTSO was preoccupied with the problem of evacuating the dependents of UN personnel, and those officials of UN and allied agencies who were not obliged to remain at their posts. UNTSO had been made responsible for this operation for all Israel, for the UN Technical Assistance workers and dependents as well as the UNTSO people, and also for UNRWA international officials in Jerusalem on the Arab side. Evacuation of all but essential UNTSO personnel was decided upon, as it was expected that there would be bombing of Israeli cities by the Ilyushin jet bombers Egypt had acquired from Russia. The Israelis were very apprehensive of this, but, in fact, not a single bomb was dropped. Nevertheless, there was no telling how far hostilities might spread once they had begun. Although one might have discounted the effectiveness of the combined command of Jordan, Syria, and Egypt, it hardly seemed probable, before the event, that neither the Syrians nor the Jordanians would send a single soldier across the Israeli border.

By the 31st, after strenuous efforts, the dependents were evacuated. They were sent to Beirut, which was considered a safe area, some by road convoy, some by the UNTSO and UNRWA aircraft. United States nationals were being evacuated from Israel and Jordan at the same time.

Although the Israelis had not yet attacked the Gaza Strip, it seemed clear that it would soon be cut off from Egypt by an offensive in the direction of Rafah and El Arish, and later occupied. As the Egyptian-Palestinian garrison of the Strip comprised approximately two brigades of infantry, with some supporting artillery and mortars in strong defensive positions, a resistance of some duration seemed possible. In such a case rioting by the refugees and attacks upon UNRWA and UNTSO officials and officers could also be expected, such as had previously occurred after Israeli raids. Some time before, I had made an arrangement with the U.S. 6th Fleet to send landing-craft to Gaza to evacuate UN personnel if the situation became critical. This had been done through the U.S. naval attaché at Tel Aviv. During the 31st we warned the U.S. naval authorities that their help might soon be required.

On the night of October 31–November 1, the Anglo-French air forces began their attacks on the Egyptian aerodromes and Air Force. The following day I was mainly occupied with affairs in Gaza. In the course of the morning the Israelis had announced the capture of Rafah, thus cutting off the Strip from Egypt. Lieutenant-Colonel R. Bayard, U.S. Army, who was Chairman of the Egypt-Israel Mixed Armistice Commission, suggested that the Israelis should be asked again for a local cease-fire, and that the Strip and the refugees should be administered by the United Nations. M. Henri Vigier, my senior political adviser, made this suggestion to Mr Eytan at the Ministry of Foreign Affairs, who said he would put it to the Government which was still in Tel Aviv.

Later, Bayard reported bombing and mortaring of the Egyptian forward positions, and then of the town of Gaza. It seemed that the time had come for evacuating the UN personnel. The U.S. naval units had arrived off Gaza, and the EIMAC was in touch with them by radio. Bayard radioed that he was considering moving out during the night. I replied that he should not attempt that, unless in the last extremity, in view of the difficulty of a night evacuation off a beach without the most careful preliminary arrangements. It would be better to wait for first light.

Bayard also repeated his request that I should ask for a cease-fire. I said I thought it would be useless to do so, if the Israelis intended to attack in the morning, as seemed likely. They had been dropping leaflets, telling the local population and refugees to remain quietly in their homes, and if they did so the Israeli Defence Forces would not harm them. But I said that when the morning came I would ask for a cease-fire, if there seemed a chance that it would be accepted.

On getting reports from Bayard the following morning, November 2, that the Israelis were attacking, but the Egyptians were still holding out, I telephoned Mr Eytan, and asked that Israel agree to a cease-fire in the Gaza area. About 8.30 A.M., having consulted the military authorities in the meantime, he replied that the Egyptians would have to lay down their arms first—*i.e.*, surrender unconditionally. About 9.20 A.M. Bayard informed me that the Military Governor of Gaza, Major-General Digwi, had decided to surrender. Bayard passed this message to the senior Israeli delegate to the Mixed Armistice Commission, and I gave it to the Ministry of Foreign Affairs.

The MAC observers, following this, put the Governor into touch with the local Israeli commander, with difficulty, as there was still firing going on around Gaza. The Israelis thereupon obliged the Governor and his assistants, with some roughness, to go round to remaining Egyptian points of resistance, and order them to surrender.

The intermediary services of the UN observers in connexion with the surrender were scrupulously ignored by the Israeli Press. Apparently, casualties in the fighting were negligible on the Israeli side, and very light among the Egyptian and Palestinian troops. But with the Strip cut off, and with no hope of relief from the Egyptian forces then retreating rapidly across the Sinai, there was no point in continuing to resist and thus incurring further casualties among the troops, and probably among the civil population. The surrender was justified.

Meanwhile all the international UNRWA personnel, and the UNMOs with the exception of Bayard and seven others, had been taken off by the vessels of the U.S. 6th Fleet. These consisted of a couple of destroyers, a transport, and the necessary landing-craft.

Mr Eytan informed me that Israel would like UNRWA to remain in Gaza, and continue their services to the refugees. By this time the U.S. Navy vessels had sailed away. As Bayard said that the Israelis were re-establishing order, and that it should be all right for UNRWA to return after a short while, I passed these messages on to Mr Henry Labouisse, the Director of UNRWA, who was in Beirut.

Later in the day Lieutenant-Colonel Nursella asked for the UN personnel of the Mixed Armistice Commission to be withdrawn from the Strip, on the grounds that as the armistice no longer existed there were no functions for them. My first reaction was to agree with this proposal, but when I reported it to the Secretary-General he took a very strong stand against any withdrawal, pointing out that since the duties of UNTSO under the GAA were not suspended by the " present state of affairs," the personnel of UNTSO were required to remain at their posts. Accordingly, I informed the Israeli authorities that the UN personnel of EIMAC would stay in Gaza.

During the following days the Israeli Military Governor of Gaza imposed restrictions on the movement of the UNMOs, on the grounds of " security," and there was an attempt to close down the EIMAC radio-station ; in fact, on Bayard's refusal to hand over the equipment, Israeli soldiers broke down the door and took the transmitter away. As a result of a strong protest by the Secretary-General—the Israeli Government, if not the military, were in a somewhat more chastened mood by November 7 when this happened —Lieutenant-Colonel Nursella called on me to apologize for this action, on behalf of the Government of Israel. He said that the local commander had exceeded his instructions, and the equipment would be returned, which it was, after some delay.

The UN personnel of EIMAC remained in the Strip during the four months of the Israeli occupation, under Lieutenant-Colonel R. Bayard until he was recalled by the U.S. Army for another assignment and Lieutenant-Colonel W. M. Brown, New Zealand Army, took over. EIMAC, besides flying the UN flag from the mast of the MAC house throughout, was useful to UNRWA for transmitting messages and as a measure of moral support. The UN officers succeeded in making contact with a number of Arab residents, and encouraged them to hope for the restoration of the *status quo ante*. They were also able to send out logistical information which was useful to UNEF when it entered the Strip in the following March.

Lieutenant-Colonel Bayard rendered very valuable service to the UN during the period of the attack and surrender, and by his courage and firmness, in the face of great difficulties and considerable danger at times, maintained respect for the United Nations Truce Supervision Organization. He was well supported by the other military observers and UN personnel with him.[32]

CHAPTER 14

The United Nations Emergency Force is formed

I FIRST heard, about 11.30 P.M. on the night of November 4, that a United Nations force was to be formed and that I should have a part to play in it. Since the invasion had begun, transmitting communications from the Secretary-General to Israel and Egypt, and in the reverse direction, had become the principal business of UNTSO.

On this day I had been told by Mr Thomas Wikeley, the British Consul-General in Jerusalem, that the British Ambassador in Israel had assurances from Mrs Meir that Israel, despite the entry of Iraqi and Syrian troops, would not attack Jordan. I passed this information to Colonel Saadi, the senior Jordanian delegate to the Jordan-Israel Mixed Armistice Commission, my usual channel of communication with the Jordanian authorities. I stressed to him that Jordan was responsible under the General Armistice Agreement for preventing any acts of hostility by anyone within her territory, which, of course, included any foreign troops, and the importance of Jordan's keeping the peace, and preventing any incident which might lead to hostilities. Colonel Saadi said he would pass on this information and my representations to Major-General Abu Nuwar.

On this day also a convoy of UNRWA supplies and personnel entered the Gaza Strip, passing through Israel from Lebanon. Some UNMOs accompanied the convoy in their jeeps, to keep radio contact with the progress and help in any other way they could. The Israelis would not allow them to enter the Gaza Strip, in pursuance of their policy of blockading the EIMAC.

On November 2 the General Assembly, acting under the terms of the " Uniting for Peace " resolution of November 1950, had passed a resolution of which the principal operative clauses were the following :

1. *Urges* as a matter of priority that all parties now involved in hostilities in the area agree to an immediate cease-fire and as a part thereof halt the movement of military forces and arms into the area.
2. *Urges* the Parties to the Armistice Agreements promptly to withdraw all forces behind the Armistice Lines, to desist

from raids across the Armistice Lines into neighbouring territory, and to observe scrupulously the provisions of the Armistice Agreements.

This resolution gives the keynote of proceedings of the General Assembly during the next four months. During this period there were a number of other resolutions which, in essence, required that the three aggressor nations—and later Israel alone—should comply with the November 2 resolution. The resolution also forms the basis upon which the functions of UNEF were defined, after considerable debate and negotiation, and much hard thought on the part of the Secretary-General and his associates.

The next resolution passed by the General Assembly, in the early hours of November 4, requested the Secretary-General to submit a plan for a United Nations Emergency Force. Its operative paragraph was :

> Requests, as a matter of priority, the Secretary-General to submit to it within forty-eight hours a plan for the setting up, *with the consent of the nations concerned*, of an emergency international United Nations Force *to secure and supervise the cessation of hostilities* in accordance with all the terms of the aforementioned (2 November) resolution.

The phrases which I have italicized came to be very important in establishing the functions of UNEF. The November 4 resolution, submitted by the Canadian delegation headed by Mr L. B. Pearson, was adopted by a vote of fifty-seven in favour ; none against ; nineteen abstentions, which included the parties to the conflict, the U.S.S.R. and Eastern European Communist countries, Australia, New Zealand, South Africa, Laos, Portugal, and Austria. I have since been told that the idea of a United Nations force had been worked out at a luncheon meeting on November 3 between Mr Hammarskjöld, Mr Pearson, Mr Andrew Cordier, Executive Assistant to the Secretary-General, and Dr Ralph Bunche, Under-Secretary.

The message I received from Mr Hammarskjöld at 11.30 P.M. November 4, cited the resolution, and said he would have to submit the report it called for by Monday night (November 5). He said that the only technical possibility would " of course " be that the force would be put under my command, at least initially. Consultations about the formation of the force would be going on in New York. As he understood it, the functions of the force would be to secure the safety of the Canal, and to police the withdrawal of troops to the demarcation lines. He said he needed my views on the size, type, and equipment of troops I considered necessary. He mentioned the difficulty of organizing the force with the particular conditions which must apply in the choice of nations to furnish contingents. He also said that I must assume Anglo-French troops could not be used for the policing of the Canal.

Early next morning I sent off a lengthy reply giving my views. My suggestions as to organization were based on certain premises as to the political situation, some of which proved untenable, as things developed in the General Assembly. My premises were (a) that Egypt would agree to a force being stationed in the Suez Canal Zone " to secure its safety " (quoting from the Secretary-General's message) ; (b) that, if necessary, powerful sanctions would be applied to make the Israelis withdraw to their side of the International Frontier ; (c) that it would be politically possible to leave the Israelis in possession of the Gaza Strip, and make them responsible for the Arab population and refugees in it ; (d) that the space between the Suez Canal and the International Frontier (the old frontier between Egypt and Palestine) could be kept until the conclusion of peace as a demilitarized zone with only lightly armed Egyptian police-forces in it (besides the UN force).

Based on these assumptions, I stated that I thought the force should be so strong that it would be in no danger of being thrust aside, pushed out, or ignored, as the UN Military Observers had been in Palestine—mainly by the Israelis, but on occasion by the other parties. I thought such a force, in view of the strength of the armed forces of Israel and Egypt, would have to be about the size of a division, with a brigade of tanks, and attached reconnaissance and fighter-aircraft units—the whole organized as an operational force capable of fighting. I suggested that contingents should not be less than battalion size, as a force made up of many smaller units of different nationalities would be difficult to control, from the administrative as well as the tactical viewpoint.

Other specifications for the force were that the units constituting it should be organized and trained so they could operate as a unit. Units raised ad hoc would not be effective for some time. (This, of course, applied more to the ' fighting ' units than the administative.) Commanders and senior officers should be able to speak English or French well enough for military purposes— that is, to understand orders and make reports. The troops sent out should be ready to stay for a year, unless an earlier settlement between Israel and Egypt were reached.

It may be appropriate to anticipate events and to mention here how far it was possible to meet these recommendations. The units which actually came to form part of the force were, with a few exceptions, not trained to the point of being capable of operating as a battalion within a larger formation—that is, of carrying out the normal operations of war, attack, defence, etc. However, as it turned out, the UNEF was not called upon to carry out any very complicated operations, and the degree of training and discipline of the troops was adequate. The restricted standard of training was due to the fact that the rank and file of many of the contingents was made up of men doing their national service, which lasted a year to eighteen months. They had mostly done about six months when they arrived in the theatre—that is, had just completed their individual training, or at best training on the platoon level.

Offsetting the deficiency in the degree of training which I should have liked to see in the force was the fact that every nation sending a contingent seemed to have made a special effort to select officers and men who should be good representatives of their country's forces. I consider the personnel to have been of a very high standard. This probably was more important than the training. As a result there were very few disciplinary problems within the force, or conflicts between UNEF troops and the civil population.

As to the language specification, it turned out that nearly all the commanding officers and staff officers spoke pretty good English, which became the working language of the force. Of course, some of them found it difficult to write clear and comprehensive reports on operational and administrative matters, or fully to grasp complicated orders and instructions. But on the whole the language problem did not give rise to great difficulty on the officer level. Few of the rank and file, outside of the Scandinavian countries, could speak any other language than their own, so communication between the men of the various contingents was necessarily limited. But there was a general friendliness and, so far as I have observed, little international jealousy.

I had requested a strong force, containing armour and fighting aircraft, capable of carrying out operations of war. What UNEF turned out to be was something much less potent. Here we come to the limitations of which the Secretary-General spoke—particular conditions which must apply in the choice of nations to furnish contingents. What were the limiting circumstances? Two of the members of the Security Council, Britain and France, were labelled as aggressors, at any rate by the majority of the nations in the General Assembly. Their forces could not be used as part of the UNEF. Then, omitting nationalist China as not significant in the situation, the other two permanent members of the Security Council, the United States and Russia, while having the same general objective— i.e., the liquidation of the aggression against Egypt—were otherwise still in the same position of hostility, or incompatibility of policies which had hamstrung the operation of the Security Council since the founding of the United Nations. It was clear that no force would be workable if United States and Russian contingents were important components of it. Hence it was decided that the force would not include contingents of nations which were permanent members of the Security Council. The same factor made it inadvisable to accept contingents from any of the Eastern European Communist countries. They would be just as subject to Russian political control as the Russian Army itself.

It was equally deemed inadvisable to take contingents from " Mediterranean powers "—that is, Turkey, Greece, and Italy. The reason for this exclusion is not so obvious. Presumably, as these nations were important members of NATO, relatively close to the vital strategic area of the Suez Canal, their exclusion was a sort of counterbalance to the exclusion of the Eastern European nations.

There were left, as possible candidates to contribute contingents to UNEF, a relatively small number of member nations of limited military power, which, for the most part, had other commitments for the forces they had in being. Consequently, it would have been very difficult to organize a force of the size and characteristics I had specified. When the various nations eligible began to offer contributions to the force, these turned out mostly to be odd-sized units, usually smaller than the normal battalions I had requested. Nearly all offers were of infantry, practically no administrative units being proposed in the first instance. As speed in organizing the force and getting it into the theatre of hostilities was politically most essential, and as it was not open to the Secretary-General to insist on larger contributions from those nations which had made offers, the composition of the force had many of the disadvantages, from the military viewpoint, which I had hoped to avoid by my " specifications."

While, by and large, the United Nations Emergency Force accomplished its purpose in spite of its peculiar composition, I still feel that a stronger and more coherently organized force might have been a better instrument for the execution of UN policies.

At this point I should explain the assumption on which I based my recommendations for UNEF's organization. The first assumption was that Egypt would agree to the force's being stationed on the Suez Canal. Obviously, if the force was to be expected to " secure the safety " of the length of the Canal—and at the time the message was written the English and French were proposing that the international force should take over their self-assumed task of protecting the freedom of international navigation on the water-way—it would make a great difference whether Egypt would agree to such a task for the force, or whether the task would have to be carried out against overt or covert Egyptian hostility. It developed, of course, that the force had no protective task on the Canal, once the British and French had evacuated Port Said.

The assumption that sanctions would be applied, if necessary to make the Israelis evacuate the Sinai, was justified in the event. The Israelis did eventually evacuate the territory they had occupied, when it became clear to them that if they did not sanctions would be applied, including sanctions by the United States.

The third assumption, that it would be feasible to leave the Israelis in possession of the Gaza Strip and make them responsible for the Arab population there, was not politically realistic, as soon became clear. However, at the beginning of November, it seemed to me that as the result of the attack an opportunity had been created for solving an important part of the Palestine problem. The essence of that problem was the demand of the refugees to be allowed to return to their homes in what had now become Israel. A considerable part of them, some 210,000, were enclosed within the narrow confines of the Gaza Strip. The United Nations might have said to the Israelis : " You have captured the Strip and its population, including the refugees. Very well, keep the Strip and its population, but you must also settle the refugees that you have taken with the Strip, and whom you drove from their homes eight years ago."

The greatest difficulty in such a solution would have been to ensure that the Israelis would keep any engagements they might have made towards the refugees and other Arab inhabitants. Until they finally evacuated the Strip, in March 1957, they put about the impression that they would be prepared to absorb this population as the price of peace. But Israelis had a record of getting rid of Arabs whose lands they desired : the inhabitants of Majdal ; the Azazme tribe from the El Auja demilitarized zone ; and the Baqqara-Ghranname villagers from the demilitarized zone of the Syrian border. I have been credibly informed that what the Israeli authorities really had in mind, if they had been able to keep the Strip, was to absorb only about 80,000 of the Strip's population. The remainder would have been persuaded to settle elsewhere, perhaps in the Sinai Desert. That this is not a slander on the Israeli Defence Forces is, unfortunately, only too well attested by three separate incidents in which they took severe repressive measures against Arab civilians, killing large numbers of them. One of these incidents, the notorious Kafr Kasim case, was considered a crime by the Israeli Government, and the perpetrators were put on trial for murder. In the other two cases, which occurred at Khan Yunis and Rafah, the Israeli authorities did not admit that anything wrong had been done, nor did they take any action either by way of reparation or inquiry into the conduct of those responsible.[33]

While it may be interesting to speculate about what might have happened, it soon became clear that the solution was not politically possible in view of the temper of the majority of the UN General Assembly. Egypt would not hear of Israel's retaining the Gaza Strip, and the Afro-Asian bloc fervently supported Egypt in this, as in most of her other demands, and so did the Soviet bloc. The United States was primarily concerned to undo as much as possible of the damage to the position of the West in the Middle East and Asia caused by the ill-considered attack by Israel, France, and Britain on Egypt. Therefore in the end the United States used a great deal of pressure to get the Israelis out of the Strip.

On November 5 the Secretary-General made his first report to the General Assembly on the formation of the Emergency Force, announcing that Colombia, Norway, and New Zealand had offered to contribute troops. He recommended that a " United Nations Command " for the force should be set up ; the first elements of which could be drawn from the UNTSO, so that if the General Assembly approved, organization of a staff could be begun without delay. He also recommended that the Assembly should appoint me Chief of Command on an emergency basis, and that I should be authorized to begin recruiting a staff for the command.

The Secretary-General also asked for authority to take the administrative measures necessary for implementing the General Assembly's decision. He stated that he would ascertain from which countries troops could be withdrawn without delay, as well as which countries could supply contingents at a later stage. The General Assembly promptly passed a resolution (submitted by Canada, Colombia, and Norway) accepting the Secretary-General's recommendations.

It was on November 5 that the Allied force made airborne landings at Port Said. On November 6 the seaborne assault took place ; but the operations were terminated by the cease-fire which took effect at midnight that night. By that time the cities of Port Said and Port Fuad and the causeway as far south as El Cap were in the hands of the Anglo-French force.

November 6 was also the date of the presidential election in the United States. President Eisenhower's re-election by an over-whelming majority, though expected, was a relief to those who hoped for a firm and fairly consistent U.S. policy in the Middle East crisis.

On this day the Secretary-General made his second and final report on the plan for the Emergency Force requested by the General Assembly resolution of November 4. After discussion, the General Assembly passed a resolution on November 7 approving his recommendations generally, and authorizing action accordingly. This resolution is a key document for the functioning of UNEF, and accordingly is printed in full as Note 34.

Its third operative paragraph runs : " Concurs in the definition of the functions of the Force as stated in paragraph 12 of the Secretary-General's report." This paragraph begins by citing excerpts from the resolutions of November 2 (see page 186) and of November 4 (see page 187) and, referring to the latter, said :

> These two provisions combined indicate that the functions of the United Nations Force would be, when a cease-fire is being established, to enter Egyptian territory with the consent of the Egyptian Government, in order to help maintain quiet during and after the withdrawal of non-Egyptian troops, and to secure compliance with the other terms established in the resolution of 2 November 1956. The Force obviously should have no rights other than those necessary for the execution of its function, in co-operation with local authorities. It would be more than an observer corps, but in no way a military force temporarily controlling the territory in which it is stationed— nor, moreover, should the Force have military functions exceeding those necessary to secure peaceful conditions on the assumption that the Parties to the conflict take all necessary steps for compliance with the recommendations of the General Assembly. Its functions, on this basis, can be assumed to cover an area extending roughly from the Suez Canal to the Armistice Demarcation Line, established in the Armistice Agreement between Egypt and Israel.

In this statement of functions one should note particularly the phrase " to enter Egypt with the consent of the Egyptian Government." There was considerable argument between the Secretary-General and the Egyptian Government subsequently over the powers which this " consent " gave the Egyptians. They tried to make it mean that they had a right to say what nations should send contingents, where units of the force should be stationed, that their consent would be required whenever a unit was moved, and several other conditions which would have been hampering in the extreme, if they would not indeed have made the force an agency of the Egyptian Government, not of the United Nations. The Secretary-General in the end succeeded in making the Egyptian Government understand that such conditions could not be accepted.

The statement that the force is " in no way a military force

B.A.I.—13

temporarily controlling the territory in which it is stationed " would mean, *inter alia,* it would not have the powers of civil administration which an invading army has in occupied territory, such as the Allied Armies had in Germany in 1945, or the Israelis in the Gaza Strip during their four months' occupation. Then the meaning of the sentence following seems to be that the force would not be expected to attack and drive out any of the parties who did not obey the General Assembly's demands for withdrawal. This was a fairly obvious condition, when Great Britain and France had powerful forces in occupation of Port Said. The question of what powers or right the force would have to resist an attempt by one of the parties to the conflict to return to or reoccupy territory which it had vacated was not so clear, and at a later date was the subject of discussions between me and the Secretary-General, and between him and the Advisory Committee.

The resolution of November 7 had another important clause, establishing an Advisory Committee composed of representatives from Brazil, Canada, Ceylon, Colombia, India, Norway, and Pakistan, which, under the chairmanship of the Secretary-General, was to undertake planning for the force and its operation which did not fall within the responsibility of the Chief of Command. It was to be consulted in the framing of regulations and instructions to the force which the Secretary-General was authorized to issue, and was to continue to assist the Secretary-General in the responsibilities laid on him by the resolutions relating to the force. The Advisory Committee was empowered to request the convening of the General Assembly whenever matters of such urgency and importance arose as to require the General Assembly's consideration.

On November 6 I commenced canvassing the officers of UNTSO as instructed by the General Assembly resolution, to select a number who would be able to serve as an interim nucleus staff, pending the establishment of a regular staff of officers selected from the contributing countries. I also received a further message from Mr Hammarskjöld, officially notifying me of my appointment as Chief of Command by the Assembly, and informing me he proposed to place me on leave of absence from my appointment as Chief of Staff UNTSO while I was occupying the new position, and to appoint my principal military assistant, Colonel Byron V. Leary, USMC, as Acting Chief of Staff UNTSO during my absence. He also indicated I should have to come to New York for consultations on the setting up of the force.

On November 7 the Secretary-General instructed me to fly to Cairo for the purpose of establishing contact before I went to New York, and perhaps to negotiate with the Egyptian Government.

After some exchanges it was arranged that I should fly there on November 8. I had also cleared my passage with Sir Charles Keightley, the Commander-in-Chief of the Allied Forces. I had known Keightley from the autumn of 1944, when he commanded the British 5th Corps, and I the 1st Canadian Corps. The two corps operated side by side during the offensive up the Adriatic coast, and Keightley and I had often occasion to meet and discuss the co-ordination of our operations. We had always got on very well together, and I don't recall any disagreements. I mention this particularly because, after the Port Said evacuation, it was published in some newspapers that Keightley was one of the senior British commanders with whom I was supposed to have been at odds during the Italian campaign, according to the Canadian official history, which had been published a few months previously. In fact, my relations with General Keightley were most friendly throughout the period leading up to the Anglo-French evacuation, as were those with Lieutenant-General Stockwell, the British Commander in the Port Said area, whom I had not known before. I believe it may have had some influence in the relatively satisfactory outcome of the intervention of the UNEF in Port Said that Keightley knew me, and, I think, had confidence that I would carry out any promises I made.

No sooner had the cease-fire been established than the Egyptian Government began to complain that the British and French were violating it, that fighting was still going on in Port Said, and that the civil population and military forces were being attacked. I shall later give my opinion of what the facts were. These charges led to a decision to send ten UN Military Observers to the area, to observe compliance with the cease-fire on the part of all the parties. We selected these observers in Jerusalem, but when they were ready to go, with their jeeps and radio equipment, we ran into difficulty as to how they would get there. The simplest way would have been for them to have driven through the Gaza Strip and along the good road paralleling the sea from El Arish to El Qantara. However, the Israelis, when asked to facilitate this, while they did not actually refuse, delayed an answer, and finally suggested that they would put Israeli drivers in the vehicles while conveying the observers by sea. This was unacceptable, and we eventually arranged for the observers and their vehicles to be taken in a British landing ship, H.M.S. *Striker* from Haifa to Port Said, where they arrived on November 13. This was the first act of co-operation by the Anglo-French forces, and was a considerable encouragement. It also showed that they were not at all reluctant to have UN observers watching their actions in the Port Said area.

I flew to Cairo on the 8th in the UN's white-painted Dakota, as arranged. There were no difficulties. We saw some Allied jet aircraft flying along with us at one period, and many warships and transports below. The Egyptian coastline was crossed at Damietta as planned, and we landed at Cairo airport—the first aircraft to do so since the Anglo-French air attacks. The airport was little damaged ; some of the buildings seemed to have been hit by bomb fragments, and holes in the runways were being filled in. The wreckage of a certain number of military aircraft was still about.

Driving from the airport beyond Heliopolis to the Semiramis Hotel one was surprised that so little damage was to be seen. In fact, I recall only one place, which was the Military College opposite the Almaza military aerodrome, a few kilometres nearer the city than the International airport. There, apparently, a stick of bombs intended for the airfield had dropped short, or over, and destroyed one wing of the building and damaged another part. Several officer-cadets in training had been killed or wounded.

But elsewhere, through Heliopolis, Abbasia, and so to the Liberation Square by the Nile, there was no damage—evidence that the Anglo-French bombing had been confined to military targets, as their broadcasts had been claiming. Lieutenant-Colonel D. R. Ely, UNTSO Liaison Officer, and Mr King Gordon, Director of the United Nations Information Centre, who had met me, and who had been in Cairo throughout the air offensive, testified to the remarkable accuracy of the air attacks, mostly by low-flying fighter aircraft with rocket and heavy machine-gun. There had been a few stray bombs, but not many.

Cairo looked much the same, except that there was little traffic in the streets. One also saw, on the boulevards leading in from the airport, many tanks at the corners, behind walls and hedges, their guns pointing in the direction of the airport, which was also the road to Suez. I marvelled at these tactical dispositions at the time, but I have since realized that their presence might be explained in two ways. The first was that at that time the Government was concerned to show the people of the capital that the Egyptian Army still disposed of powerful forces. During this first stay in Cairo, and the next, a few days later, I was also puzzled to note tanks on transporters roaring and growling along the Corniche and across the Kasr el Nil bridge, accompanied by lorry-loads of infantry and occasionally artillery. Where were they coming from and going to ? After a day or so of this I concluded that they were going nowhere, but just parading around for the same purpose as the tanks were stationed on the boulevard.

The other reason for the presence of such a concentration of armour and other heavy weapons in the heart of the capital could have been that the Allies having declared that they would attack no centres of population, and having adhered to this policy, the Egyptian Army, which had suffered severely from air attacks by fighter aircraft on the roads from the Suez Canal Zone towards the west, had concluded that the safest places for its remaining armour were in the cities, towns, and villages.

My first interview was at 2.15 P.M. with Colonel Gohar, Director of the Palestine Affairs Department of the Foreign Ministry, who had met me at the airport. Our talk was to indicate to him the subjects I had to discuss with Dr Mahmoud Fawzi, the Egyptian Foreign Minister, whom I met at three o'clock. Up to this time, it is to be noted, Egypt had not declared that it would agree to UNEF's entering the country. The Secretary-General had sent a message to the Egyptian Government through its permanent representative at the UN, Mr Omar Loutfi, that the United Nations Emergency Force could be constituted without delay by calling on Canada, Colombia, Denmark, Finland, Norway, and Sweden to send contingents. He asked for an immediate answer as to whether Egypt would raise objections to participation of any of the countries mentioned in the force. He also asked that plans should be made with me for the landing and initial stationing of the force.

In our interview, at which Dr Fawzi was as calm, suave, and pleasant as ever, he first of all said that the Secretary-General's query would be answered in an hour or two, and he thought the answer would be satisfactory. He went on to state the Egyptian view that the force could operate in their territory only with their consent. Its function would be the carrying out of the resolutions of the General Assembly. The force would commence to operate close to the Canal, and would end up, in accordance with the General Assembly resolution, at the Armistice Demarcation Line. He expected the force to enter Port Said on the withdrawal of the Anglo-French forces. He made the observation, presumably as a bargaining-point, that as the Anglo-French forces had landed within forty-eight hours, they should be able to withdraw in the same period of time. I did not enter into argument as to this timing.

It was then arranged that I should talk with Colonel Gohar, Mr Hussein Aziz, Under-Secretary of the Ministry and an officer of the Eastern Command, to determine where the air-landing and assembly of the United Nations Emergency Force could take place. I was also to discuss the tasks of the UN observers in Port Said, Dr Fawzi stating that the Egyptian Government was informed the Allies were still attacking civilians and the Egyptian armed forces, though the latter remained strictly on the defensive.

I then left Dr Fawzi and talked to Colonel Gohar and the Under-Secretary about landing-fields and concentration areas. It appeared that the force should initially concentrate between Ismailiya and El Qantara, and land at the nearest suitable and serviceable airfield. Nothing definite was decided, pending the decision on the acceptability of the nations the Secretary-General was proposing to provide the initial contingents.

I got a considerable shock when, at my meeting with Dr Fawzi, he intimated that it might not be acceptable to Egypt that a Canadian contingent should form part of the United Nations Emergency Force. I pointed out the leading part which Mr Pearson had played in the General Assembly in the creation of the force, promoting a policy contrary to the views of not only the United Kingdom but also the other Dominions, and one which would be greatly to the advantage of Egypt. Fawzi said he understood Canada's independence in foreign policy and Mr Pearson's helpful efforts very well ; but the trouble was that Canadian soldiers were dressed just like British soldiers, they were subjects of the same Queen—the ordinary Egyptian would not understand the difference, and there might be unfortunate incidents. He said this was not a " firm answer " to the Secretary-General's proposal that Canadians should form part of the force, but wanted me to pass the thought on to Mr Hammarskjöld. I said I hoped no such regrettable decision as to exclude Canadian participation in the force would be taken. For one thing, I should naturally not be able to act as commander in such a case. Dr Fawzi was good enough to say that he hoped such a consequence would not follow ; the Egyptian Government knew me, and had confidence in my impartiality as a servant of the United Nations, etc.

The rest of the day passed with no word from the Egyptian Cabinet, although a message was received from the Secretary-General pressing for immediate decision, so that it would be possible to begin to move the first contingents of the UNEF into Egypt, and have at least a token force on the ground. A further message was sent to Dr Fawzi early the following day, the 9th, pointing out the danger Egypt would run of alienating general sympathy if she created difficulties in establishing the UN force in the theatre.

On the 9th I had another interview with Dr Fawzi at 12.30 P.M. He wanted additional information, presumably to enable President Nasser and his advisers to come to a decision. He said that he understood the need for speed, as expressed in the Secretary-General's urgent messages to him. But while Egypt had agreed in principle to receive the force, and would stand by that agreement, they wanted to understand what the function of the force was, in clearer terms than any yet formulated, including those in the Secretary-General's second report, before they could receive the troops on Egyptian soil and furnish the required co-operation. He wanted to know (a) if it was understood that when the force reached the Armistice Demarcation Line after evacuation of the Sinai by the Israelis, the areas to be occupied by the force would be agreed to by the parties concerned, (b) how long the force would stay in the ADL area, (c) after the withdrawal of the Anglo-French forces, what the UN force would do in the Port Said area. It was his view that they would have no·responsibility for the maintenance of law and order, which would be the function of the Egyptian Government.

I tried to impress on Dr Fawzi that Egypt should not lose the favourable opportunity to get the Israeli and Anglo-French forces to withdraw, as she might if she tried to provide against every possible contingency at this stage. Dr Fawzi then went to see President Nasser, and I radioed Mr Hammarskjöld for answers to Fawzi's questions.

Later in the afternoon I was told that President Nasser wanted to see me. I was conducted through the unlighted streets to the President's temporary office, which was in a building looking rather like a mosque, directly across the Nile from the Semiramis Hotel. Several echelons of sentries with fixed bayonets, backed up by machine-gunners, guarded the approaches to the blacked-out offices. I was taken in directly. The atmosphere was rather like that of an improvised field headquarters. The President was wearing an ancient grey cardigan, and looked rather tired, but still vigorous and confident.

He told me there was to be a meeting of the Cabinet at 8 P.M. which would discuss the entry of the UN force, but they could not come to a firm decision until he had answers from the Secretary-General to the questions which Fawzi had put to me earlier in the day. It seemed to me that the main difficulty was that the Egyptians suspected that the UN Emergency Force might remain in Port Said and elsewhere along the Canal after the British and French had left, and would constitute the international control which the British and French, and to some extent the other " users," had been demanding since the Canal had been nationalized. In the circumstances, the suspicions of President Nasser and his colleagues were not surprising. I told him that the Emergency Force was set up by the General Assembly, which would also determine its tasks. The General Assembly, in view of the attitude of its majority in respect of the then situation, would never permit the force to be used to compel the internationalization of the Canal. However,

President Nasser wanted specific assurance on this from the Secretary-General.

He also inquired where the force's elements would be located when it reached the Armistice Demarcation Line. I said I thought part of it should be in the area El Arish-Rafah, and part in the El Auja demilitarized zone.

The President rehearsed the arguments against inclusion of the Canadians in the force which I had previously heard from Dr Fawzi. He said it would be easy for agitators to incite some of the people against troops that looked like the British ; there might be nasty incidents, and he did not wish to become embroiled with Canada and the United Nations. I said I thought this was a risk which should be taken. I did not voice my impression, however, that the real reason Canadians were not desired was the fear that Canadian policy, while so far favourable to Egypt in the General Assembly, might later veer to the " Western " if not the British stand in regard to the control of the Canal.

I said to the President that I thought he could hardly expect, at this stage, to negotiate an agreement covering all possible future actions of the force and that it would be very advantageous to Egypt to have it set up as soon as possible. The General Assembly, by whose authority the force existed, could be trusted to safeguard the interests of Egypt in regard to its eventual employment. I said he should look on the nations proposing to contribute to the force as allies of Egypt, rather than potentially hostile foreigners. The presence of the force would help rectify the situation produced by the aggression and would symbolize the solidarity of the majority of the General Assembly with Egypt.

The President heard me attentively, but at the end repeated that it was necessary for him to have clarifications on the points discussed from the Secretary-General. The entry of the force would have to be explained to the people of Egypt. It would be better to take a little longer to get a clear understanding now, than to have difficulties later. The interview ended, and I reported by radio to Mr Hammarskjöld, hoping I should get his answers to convey to President Nasser the next day.

Late that night I got the Secretary-General's reaction to the Egyptian argument that Canadians should be excluded from the force. After pointing out the legal position that operations of the components of the force would be " insulated " from national policies, and controlled solely through the channel of authority, General Assembly to Secretary-General to Chief of Command, he directed me to convey to Dr Fawzi his view that it would be catastrophic if Egypt continued to make objections to having

Canada in the force, in view of the Canadian rôle in the whole politico-military situation. He could not possibly change his stand in this matter, and it would be most unfortunate if the conflict between him and Egypt should have to be brought out into the open.

The next morning I saw Dr Fawzi again, and gave him the answers I had received from the Secretary-General to the Canadian question and the others President Nasser had put the previous day. These answers were generally in accordance with the line I had been taking myself. In brief, they were that when the force reached the demarcation line the areas it would occupy would be agreed with the governments concerned. It was impossible to say how long the force would remain in the area, but as it was an *emergency* force, and linked to the situation described in the November 2 resolution, when that situation was liquidated the task for the force would be ended. If there was a difference of views with the parties as to whether the situation required the further presence of the force, the matter would be negotiated. It was the Secretary-General's view, in which he was supported in the debate following his second report, that when the Anglo-French forces had withdrawn from Port Said there would be no further function in that area for the UN force. Some staging and administrative areas would be required by the force in the Canal Zone.

I concluded my talk with Dr Fawzi by saying that I hoped that the Government of Egypt would be able to notify the Secretary-General very soon of its agreement to the composition of the force, and its entry into Egyptian territory. The President had told me that once the main decision was taken, the Egyptian authorities would co-operate in providing airfields, quarters and other necessary administrative facilities.

As it appeared that the negotiations could not be advanced further that day, I flew back to Jerusalem about noon, intending to return on the following day with the interim staff that I had assembled from the military observers with UNTSO.[35] However, Gohar sent me a message saying that nothing could be settled until the 12th, so we delayed our departure until then.

By November 8 an advisory group of military representatives of nations intending to contribute to the United Nations Emergency Force had been set up at New York. They soon sent me a formidable list of points upon which they needed information.[36]

When I received this questionnaire I was in the middle of the discussion as to whether the United Nations force would be able to enter Egypt at all. It was not possible to answer some of the questions until the regular UNEF headquarters-staff had been set up and was functioning.   Other questions were settled when I went to New York.

On November 8 I had received a message confirming my appointment " on an emergency basis " as Chief of Command of the Emergency International United Nations Force.   In my reply I suggested that when an opportunity offered to do so, the official title of the force should be changed to the " United Nations Emergency Force " (on the grounds that " International " in the title was redundant) ; and that my title should be " Commander, United Nations Emergency Force," because the title " Chief of Command " was unknown in the terminology of British or American military organization (or that of any other nation, so far as I know), and it might create ambiguity in regard to my functions.   These titles were adopted in an official document of the Assembly a week or so later.

On November 10 I sent a message to United Nations headquarters stating what administrative and technical units would be required in addition to infantry.   This question was dealt with when I was in New York.

I also asked for senior officials of the Legal and Finance departments to deal with the many problems in these spheres that were bound to arise.   I pointed out the importance of providing the UNEF regular headquarters, when it should be set up, with adequate numbers of trained military clerks, able to work in the English language.   (We never did get more than a few such clerks, and the main load of clerical and secretarial work was carried by women secretaries of the UN international service, plus locally recruited civilian personnel, who had been working for British military and commercial organizations, and were unemployed.)

Following an exchange of messages about advance parties for certain contingents of the force, I was informed on November 10 that approximately fifty officers and men each from the Danish and Norwegian contingents were being carried in U.S. military aircraft to the staging area at Capodichino airfield, Naples.   Similar advance parties of the Canadian, Colombian, Finnish, Indian, and Swedish contingents would follow.   These advance parties would be sent on by chartered Swissair aircraft from Naples to Egypt.

Even assuming that the difficulties the Egyptians were making about the composition of the force would be settled quickly, I was not very happy at the prospect of troops being flown in to Egypt before proper preparations had been made to receive them. However, it was very urgent at that time, Mr Hammarskjöld and his advisers believed, to get some United Nations troops into

Egypt at once. It was felt that it would be a race between the UNEF's getting established on the ground and 'volunteers' from Russia, Communist China, and other similarly oriented countries' arriving in Egypt to assist the Egyptian forces to expel the invaders. It was thought quite possible that such volunteers might be sent, and that the Middle East might develop into another Korea, with the forces of the West, nominally under the aegis of the United Nations, ranged against the forces of the Communist countries and deployed in Egypt and possibly other Arab countries. When one looks back it seems improbable that such a development could really have occurred, but in early November the danger appeared very great and there was no time for a cool assessment of military probabilities at UN headquarters. Certainly, no one knows what might have happened if the UNEF idea had not been conceived and energetically developed as it was by the Secretary-General, the representatives at UN of the leading countries participating in it, and the United States. In moments of great danger in war, the most important thing is to *do something*—to have *some plan* and put it into execution quickly. Later analysis may show that the plan was not the best possible in the circumstances, but the view commonly held by soldiers, that an indifferent plan, speedily and energetically executed, is better than a perfect plan put into execution too late, certainly held true in the politico-military situation of early November 1956. In an historical review of events, criticism of what was done must always be tempered by this thought. Still, even criticism of operations which resulted in success is valid if it points a lesson as to how the same success could be obtained another time with less cost and effort.

On November 11 I received a message from New York intimating that it had been decided to announce that agreement on the arrival in Egypt of the United Nations Emergency Force had been reached between the Secretary-General and the Egyptian Government, and that the first group of the UN force would go to Egypt on November 12 or 13. It was the intention of the Secretary-General to visit Cairo at the very first stage of the operation for discussion of details with the Egyptian Government. The " details," in fact, were the very important points of principle : whether Egypt would agree to the entry of the troops of certain countries, and also whether Egypt had the right to withdraw her consent to the force's presence.

Egypt had by this time agreed to the participation of Colombian, Swedish and Finnish, Indonesian and Yugoslav forces, observing that these countries " were not entangled in military pacts with the aggressors." This was in reference to an objection which Egypt had

advanced against the inclusion of Danish and Norwegian contingents
—*i.e.*, that they were members of NATO, along with France and
Great Britain.   This caveat had a strong Russian smell about it.
At this time consultations of Nasser, or Ali Sabri, his right-hand
man, with the Russian Ambassador were very frequent.   The
Secretary-General reacted against this attempted exclusion in the
strongest terms, saying that if Denmark and Norway were kept out
Sweden and Finland would probably not join in either, and without
Scandinavian participation there was a strong probability that
UNEF could not be organized at all.

Having been informed that President Nasser would see me on
the 12th, I flew to Cairo that day with the UNEF headquarters
nucleus staff.

At 12.30 P.M. I saw President Nasser, and we talked for about
an hour.   He gave me a message to send to the Secretary-General,
in cordial terms, accepting Danish and Norwegian participation,
and suggesting the force be composed of Colombian, Danish, Finnish,
Norwegian, Swedish, Indian, Indonesian, and Yugoslav contingents.
Canada was still left out.   We talked for some time about this, but
we both only repeated previous arguments.   He was friendly and
agreeable in his attitude throughout, and appeared very willing to
co-operate, apart from the composition of the force.   He said that
he hoped Mr Pearson would understand his position, and that there
was no prejudice against Canada.

President Nasser was extremely hoarse, having just made his first
major speech since the attack on Egypt at the El Azhar mosque.
In it he gave his interpretation of the events of the previous fortnight,
and endeavoured to convince the Egyptian people that Egypt had
not, in fact, suffered severe military losses.

At this meeting the President introduced to me Brigadier Amin
Hilmy, the officer he had designated chief liaison officer to the
UNEF, and said that he would arrange for landing-facilities,
quarters, barrack stores, and any other help the force might immediately require.   It was agreed that the best airfield for landing
the troops would be Abu Sueir, about twenty kilometres west of
Ismailiya.   This was an air station built by the British, which had
been quite heavily damaged during the Anglo-French air offensive.
However, the runways were serviceable.   The barracks surrounding
the field were extensive, and would serve as initial accommodation
for the first arrivals.

The President made a very fortunate selection of Brigadier Hilmy
as the force's chief liaison officer—that is to say, the officer through
whom we would work in our dealings with the Egyptian Army and

Air Force, and in most of our dealings with the Egyptian Government and local authorities. Brigadier Hilmy had extensive experience in staff appointments and also in dealing with other departments of the Egyptian Government. His previous appointment as Chief of Staff of the Eastern Command carried over authority which enabled him to get action which otherwise might have been slow and difficult. However, it was his personal character which made him particularly suitable. Courteous, friendly, and good-humoured, he also was quick in action and showed an ability to get results, to produce the co-operation UNEF needed. He appeared to take very seriously the orders to give UNEF every co-operation, which he told me he had received personally from the President (they had been instructors at the Egyptian Staff College together). Of course, from time to time there were arguments and difficulties, but one felt in dealing with him there was always goodwill, and a sincere intention to treat UNEF as one would treat an ally in wartime, at the least. His help to the UNEF was invaluable, and one does not like to think of the difficulties we might have met had an officer of another type been appointed.

Leaving Lieutenant-Colonel C. F. Moe as my deputy, with the other officers of the improvised nucleus staff, I flew back to Jerusalem that day, preparing to take off for New York on the morrow. By this time the Secretary-General had decided to come to Egypt, as announced, and I was to meet him on November 14 in Rome for clarifications and instructions.

CHAPTER 15

Organizing in New York

ON November 13 I flew from Lydda (airport of Tel Aviv) to Rome, where General Ferdinando Raffaelli, Chief of the Italian Air Staff, kindly met me. The Italian Air Force had given UNEF Capodichino airfield at Naples to use as an air-transfer point. The UNEF contingents arrived in huge C-124s of the U.S. Military Air Transport Service, deplaned, and later were emplaned for Egypt in the DC-6s of Swissair. Capodichino became the advance base of UNEF in Europe, under the general management of Mr Virgil de Angelis of the UN Secretariat. The Italian Air Force was extremely helpful and co-operative in providing accommodation and other facilities for UNEF.

Capodichino was also the point of contact with the U.S. supply line. Rear-Admiral Clarence Ekstrom, Commander U.S. Naval Activities, Mediterranean, was the officer made responsible for organizing support for UNEF. The United States, though sending no military personnel into the theatre of UNEF's operations, because of the restriction against permanent members of the Security Council's participating in UNEF, had promised " logistic support " for the force, meaning that they would help with transport, supplies, and equipment. UNEF experienced many difficulties in getting supplies of all sorts. This was not due to any lack of goodwill or energy on the part of the U.S. officers with whom we had to deal, but essentially the difficulty inevitable when a very large and complex machine, designed to support the U.S. forces in Europe and their allies, was expected to provide for the wants of a relatively small, heterogeneous force of unique character.

I expected to meet the Secretary-General on the 14th, but word came that his departure had been delayed by the Hungarian rebellion crisis which was boiling up in the UN. On November 14 I was flown to Naples in an Italian Air Force DC-3 and inspected the advance parties of the Norwegian, Danish, and Colombian contingents—the first sight of the troops I was to command. I was impressed by the good appearance of the men who composed these parties. I was also glad to meet Lieutenant-Colonel G. K. Wade and other officers of the Canadian advance party.

While waiting, I prepared a memorandum for the Secretary-General, pointing out, among other things, that it would be necessary for UNEF to have a secure base and lines of communication if it were to operate without fear of Egyptian interference. According to the rôle foreseen for the force, it would eventually be deployed along the Armistice Demarcation Line between Egypt and Israel, and its line of communication would stretch back across the Sinai to the airfields in the Canal Zone and Port Said, which would eventually have to be the port of entry for its supplies and equipment.

It is axiomatic that a military force can function only if it is supplied with food, and the fuel and lubricants for the mechanical transport on which it depends for all its movements, plus munitions to replace those used up in operations. While in certain circumstances small forces can live off the country for a short while, any extended military operations in modern times require that the force shall be assured of a constant and adequate replenishment of these items, which come to it over its line of communications from its base. If this line of communications is cut, or the flow of supplies is stopped, then after a longer or shorter interval the operations of the force will stop also. The first preoccupation of a commander must be to ensure that his lines of communication are protected, and that the essential supplies for the force will continue to come up.

The problem before me was : how were Abu Sueir airfield and Port Said, the prospective UNEF bases, and the lines of communication between them and the eventual position of UNEF to be guarded ? It was now clear that UNEF was to be a relatively small force. It could not detach troops to the bases and along the lines of communication of a strength which could prevent interference with the supply line by guerrillas such as the Egyptians had harassed the British with in the Canal Zone, let alone resist intervention by the Egyptian armed forces. By its terms of reference UNEF could not be an occupying force. It was therefore obvious, as soon as the problem was examined, that UNEF could only operate in its intended theatre if Egypt co-operated by allowing free and unhampered use of base facilities and passage by road and air over the lines of communication. Thus, the military realities of the situation brought one to the same conclusion as the legal approach. The legal position, created by the General Assembly resolution, was that UNEF could enter and operate on Egyptian territory only with Egypt's consent. A United Nations force capable of acting *without* Egypt's consent—that is, in spite of her possible hostile action—would have had to be about the size and strength of the Anglo-French forces which had commenced the invasion.

In early November, however, I had considerable misgivings over the prospect of operating with lines of communication completely subject to the goodwill of one of the combatants. I had in mind many interferences with the observers of the Truce Supervision Organization which had rendered it ineffective at critical times. It seemed to me that there was a danger that the General Assembly, by failing to provide a big enough force, and failing to express a firm enough attitude towards *both* parties, had created the danger that the UNEF might be thwarted, and in the end prove no more effective than the observer organization. However, I gradually realized that the force would achieve useful results, not by the exercise of military force, but so to speak as a political counter— that its moves and acts were dictated by a delicate balance of political pressures, whose resultant force it registered.

Mr Hammarskjöld arrived in Rome late in the afternoon of November 15. In about an hour's conference he explained some of the principles upon which the force was intended to function, and took note of some of the points which had worried me as to the force's relation to the Egyptian authorities. Then I took off for New York, and he for Naples. He went on to Egypt in the UNEF airlift, with detachments of Colombian and Norwegian troops, arriving at Abu Sueir in the morning of November 16.

The Secretary-General was accompanied by Dr Garcia Robles, of the Political Affairs department of the United Nations Secretariat, whom he had nominated as my political adviser, and Mr George Ivan Smith, the Director of the United Nations Information Centre in London, who came to lend a hand in the delicate and vital questions of publicity. These were United Nations officials of the highest calibre, whom I was fortunate enough to have associated with me during the early days of UNEF. They were equipped by experience to deal with many of the difficult problems which pressed upon me as commander.

I landed at Idlewild airport, New York, on the morning of November 16 and soon after was plunged into conferences with Mr Cordier, Dr Bunche, and the committee of military representatives of the participating countries.

The result of the Secretary-General's negotiations in Cairo was awaited with anxiety, in particular the outcome of the argument about the inclusion of a Canadian contingent in the force. His view as to what would happen if Egypt insisted on excluding the Canadians has already been recorded. After a difficult negotiation he was able to secure President Nasser's consent, but at first only for bringing in administrative elements and a transport squadron of the Royal Canadian Air Force, which had also been offered by Canada.

I have mentioned that both Dr Fawzi and President Nasser

had argued that, in spite of Canada's constitutional independence, and the proof of it given in her attitude in the General Assembly, Canadian soldiers were also " soldiers of Queen Elizabeth," whom the Egyptian population would be incapable of distinguishing from the British invaders. Shortly after these discussions I found out that the unit selected to represent Canada had been the Queen's Own Rifles ! There is no regiment in the Canadian forces that I respect more than the Queen's Own, but it did seem an unlucky chance, in view of the Egyptian argument, that out of Canada's six regular infantry regiments this one had been selected.

The committee of military representatives of the contributing countries had prepared, for me to answer, a list of sixteen questions, with sub-headings, covering the following points : general organization of the force and its headquarters ; whether the equipment of the contingents was suitable ; what accommodation was available in the theatre—barracks, tents, stores, hospitals, etc. ; what could be procured locally in the way of food, fuel and lubricants, labour, repair facilities and so forth ; what ports of entry, airfields, rail and road transport could be used ; where the force H.Q., the troops and the logistical base would be located ; whether there was a field bakery UNEF could use ; what arrangements should be made for supply of rations, clothing, spare parts, and ammunition which were peculiar to the several contingents ; rest areas ; arrangements for the handling of mail ; interpreters ; special equipment needed for road repair, ports, and airfields ; arrangements for pay in local currencies, and equalization between the varying rates of pay of the contingents ; the legal status of the force, disciplinary powers and powers of command ; Press correspondents ; requirements for special clothing for the climate in the theatre of operations ; and, finally, what should be put in a booklet of information for the troops.

The scope of these questions indicate how little information UN had, compared to what would be available normally to a military staff planning an expedition. It will explain some of the initial delays and confusion in UNEF's operation. I gave such answers as I could, but these were mainly restricted to my views on what the organization of the force should be, and how the main administrative problems raised should be dealt with in principle. Obviously, many of the questions asked would require work on the ground by a competent staff, in liaison with the Egyptian authorities, and as yet such a staff did not exist. But eventually UNEF had to deal with all the problems which were raised at this conference. It was done as we went along, and as the problems became sufficiently pressing to require action.

B.A.I.—14

I stayed in New York until 6.30 P.M. on the 19th, and in those four days the main outlines of the organization of the force had been determined. I left brief memoranda on the points upon which action or further decision was required with Mr Cordier, Dr Bunche, and Major-General A. E. Martola. General Martola, a retired officer of the Finnish Army with a distinguished fighting-record and also with a wide organizational experience in civil life, had been appointed as Special Military Adviser to the Secretary-General— that is to say, as his principal military assistant on UNEF matters at United Nations headquarters.

Based on what contingents seemed likely to become available, my recommendation as to the overall organization of the force was that it should consist initially of six infantry battalions, as this seemed to me to be the minimum needed for stationing along the Armistice Demarcation Line, the force's final task as outlined in the General Assembly resolutions. As of November 18, India and Canada had each offered a battalion ; Denmark and Norway had proposed to join together to provide another battalion ; and it was hoped that Sweden and Finland would come together in a similar arrangement. Colombia proposed to send a battalion, less two companies. It therefore seemed necessary to make up the Colombians to a complete battalion, by incorporating troops from some other country, unless the Colombians themselves were prepared to make a greater effort and get another battalion from another country to make up the six. Yugoslavia was contributing an armoured reconnaissance unit.

The eventual infantry components were : an Indian battalion [3rd Battalion, Parachute Regiment (Kumaon)] ; a Danish-Norwegian battalion ; a Swedish battalion of two companies about 450 strong ; a Colombian battalion of two companies about 550 strong ; a Finnish company about 250 strong ; an Indonesian battalion of three companies, 600 strong ; and a Brazilian battalion of three companies, 500 strong. But this organization was not complete until January, when the Brazilians joined UNEF after a further negotiation with the Egyptian Government.

I recommended that there should be only one headquarters for the force until the whole six battalions were operational, when it might be desirable to form also two regimental group headquarters. (These were never formed.) The immediate problem was to organize UNEF headquarters which was at the time only an improvisation manned by a few UNMOs temporarily posted from UNTSO.[35] I suggested that the nations which were contributing to UNEF should be asked for names of officers suitable to serve on the staff ; they should have had staff training and experience, and a good working knowledge of English. My first recommendation was for a staff of four branches : Personnel, Operations and Intelligence, Logistics, and Stores and Equipment. A three-branch organization was finally adopted : Personnel, Operations plus Intelligence, and Logistics. However, civilian personnel from the UN Secretariat were posted to UNEF for procurement of stores and equipment, finance and general administration, especially control of expenditures in accordance with UN financial regulations and practice. I also asked for a senior medical officer, familiar with problems of medicine and hygiene in the Middle East.

I further recommended that a channel for supply of rations should be organized immediately. While as much of the fresh rations as possible should be procured in Egypt (to save shipping) a reserve of a month's pack, or preserved, rations should be constituted in the force's base in Egypt as soon as possible to guard against possible interruption of the supply line.

The U.S. liaison group had suggested that a base organization should be established at Naples, which would be the point of delivery of the stores, supplies, and equipment which the U.S. had promised to provide for UNEF—the " logistic support." As things developed it was found unnecessary to establish such a base. No stores or equipment were held under UN control at Naples, except a limited quantity of things so urgently required that they had to be forwarded by air, which the RCAF could safeguard.

I recommended that each nation which supplied a contingent should also provide military police, equal to 1 per cent. of its strength, to be organized into a combined military police detachment for the force, on arrival in Egypt. I suggested that contingents should also bring some ordnance personnel, who would be able to look after their own special stores and equipment in the depots.

One crucial problem was to provide mechanical transport for the force. The first elements, coming as they did by air, brought nothing but a very few jeeps and one or two $\frac{3}{4}$-ton trucks which could be lifted in the U.S. C-124s and the Canadian C-119s. Some contingents, coming later by sea, were able to bring their own transport, but for most this would not be possible. (The Yugoslavs, Canadians, Brazilians, and Indonesians brought their own mechanical transport.) Meanwhile it was very urgent to obtain the essential transport for the other contingents which were already on their way. The Indian infantry battalion and the Norwegian medical company would bring no vehicles at all with them.

In one of the communications from Mr Selwyn Lloyd, the British Foreign Minister, to the Secretary-General it had been stated that the British Government welcomed the creation of the UNEF and would be prepared to assist in its operations. Dr Bunche and I had a meeting with Mr Selwyn Lloyd and his military adviser, Brigadier Rowlandson, during which we raised the question of whether the United Kingdom could furnish some mechanical transport, as well as other stores needed by UNEF. They had agreed in principle to do this, subject, of course, to approval by the British Cabinet. Thus, when I got to Port Said and met General Keightley, commander of the Allied force, among the first items of business was seeing what vehicles and stores the ' enemy ' could furnish to the United Nations Emergency Force which, while not supposed to drive the invaders out, at least was politely to usher them out. Looked at in one way, this transaction had a distinctly Gilbertian aspect, but it was quite logical in view of the British decision that when a United Nations force was formed they would withdraw with a good grace. The vehicles and stores were sold to UNEF at a valuation, and facilitated the British withdrawal, as it was not necessary to back-load them by sea. The stores and particularly the MT vehicles so obtained were invaluable to UNEF in the early days, and the force would have been in great difficulties without them.

I have mentioned that vehicles were required by the Norwegian medical company. In a message from Cairo after a brief visit to Abu Sueir, where the advance parties of the contingents were being brought in as rapidly as possible by the Swissair lift, Mr Hammarskjöld pointed out that it was very important to provide troops for medical service and supply duties at the earliest moment. I was glad to see him recognize the necessity for providing adequate administrative troops, as the earliest emphasis had been on sending as many infantry as possible as quickly as possible, and from as many different nations as possible. This, of course, had many advantages from the political viewpoint, but it produced a military administrative headache.

The normal practice in sending a military expedition overseas depends upon whether it has to fight to get ashore or to descend from the air, or whether it is to be deposited at an advance base in friendly hands, to concentrate prior to beginning operations. The operation of sending UNEF to Egypt corresponded roughly to the latter condition, in which the military practice is to send first a sufficient number of administrative troops to provide for the feeding, quartering, and supplying of all necessities to the fighting portion and the rest of the force as it arrives. But the reverse procedure was followed in UNEF's descent upon Egypt, and happened because of the way in which UNEF was conceived, created, and organized. One can only praise the remarkable feat of organization performed by the Secretary-General, his immediate assistants, the UN Secretariat, and the military authorities of the contributing and co-operating countries in landing advance parties of the force in Egypt only eleven days after the General Assembly had resolved to create it. But the difficulties and delays which ensued point out the necessity of studying its experience and determining procedures to avoid these troubles, in future, if there should ever be a similar United Nations military operation.

A result of the Secretary-General's message was to cause the quick acceptance of the Norwegian offer of a medical company, one of the relatively few offers of supporting troops which had been made. This unit was rushed out by air with a high priority and was functioning at Abu Sueir when I got there on November 22. The commanding officer reported with satisfaction that it had performed its first emergency operation—an appendectomy on a Colombian soldier who had been taken ill on the aircraft.

While in New York, I also requested that UNEF headquarters should be asked whether the troops arriving had brought adequate cooking equipment with them and, if they had not, to make recommendations for supplementing it. When I reached Abu Sueir I found that several of the contingents first arriving had no stoves or utensils with which to cook their food. Fortunately the Egyptians were able to provide a number of new Czechoslovak travelling kitchens, which provided for the troops' need in this respect until they could be issued with cooking equipment of their own.

I pointed out that the engineer detachments which Yugoslavia and Canada were sending should be equipped with a good scale of mine-detecting and clearing equipment. I knew that many minefields existed in the Sinai and the Gaza Strip, and that they would give us a good deal of trouble. This turned out to be the case, and mine explosions caused more casualties and hazard to the force than anything else.

The advance party of the Canadian supporting administrative troops had been flown from Canada in an RCAF North Star. In Canada, ready to be flown out, were the remainder of the administrative troops, something over 200, held up until the impasse with Egypt could be resolved by Mr Hammarskjöld.

A Swedish advance party of 50 officers and men was to be airlifted to Naples on the 18th, and the Norwegian medical company of 230 officers and men, mentioned above, was also expected to commence moving to Naples the same day. Five hundred more Colombians and 500 more Indians would be airlifted to Naples in the next fortnight, and about 200 Finns by November 28.

By November 17, happily, the Secretary-General had been able to get the Egyptian Government's agreement that Canada should supply a transport squadron of C-119 aircraft to lift troops from Naples to Egypt, and also that the administrative elements organized for the support of the Canadian infantry battalion should come to fill the very urgent need for administrative troops. It had not been possible to get agreement for the dispatch of the Queen's Own Rifles.

During the discussions of my four days in New York I was naturally much concerned to settle arrangements for the provision of the administrative and supporting troops of the force. The first essential was an intercommunication unit (signal corps) to provide radio and line communication as well as dispatch-rider service between headquarters of the force and its components. The following would also be needed : several platoons of mechanical transport (each about thirty $2\frac{1}{2}$- or 3-ton trucks) for general duty ; a service corps unit to handle food and other supplies at the base and distribute them to the troops ; ordnance corps to look after stores and equipment at the base ; a mechanical transport repair workshop company ; and an engineer unit to direct and supervise essential services for quartering the force—repair of buildings, provision of water and electricity—and also to handle the very vital operational task of mine clearance.

I requested that all contributing nations and those who had offered to contribute should be asked whether they could provide any of the units enumerated. The detachments which Canada had organized for the support of the Queen's Own Rifles were immediately available. They were, of course, not large enough to support a force of six infantry battalions.

It would also be necessary to have a small group of light aircraft, and perhaps DC-3s, for reconnaissance and intercommunication when the force began to operate over the wide and inhospitable spaces of the Sinai Desert. In the early stages it was intended that Norway would provide the light aircraft, but difficulties of transporting or flying these out proved too great, and in the end the Royal Canadian Air Force produced air transport units. Arrangements had already been made that the RCAF would provide an augmented squadron of fourteen C-119s—flying boxcars—for the airlift from Naples to Egypt.

On Sunday, November 18, after the agreement of Egypt to the participation of Canadian Air Force and administrative troops had been obtained by the Secretary-General, the Chief of the Air Staff, Air-Marshal C. R. Slemon, and the Chief of the General Staff of the Army, Lieutenant-General H. D. Graham, came down to New

York. I had a talk with them which laid the foundation for the increased contribution in air force and administrative troops furnished later.

In particular, detailed studies were put in hand of the sort of signals unit which would be needed for the force. Eventually Canada provided a signals unit of some 185, all ranks, with excellent mobile radio equipment which provided very good intercommunication service in the Sinai and the Gaza Strip. India also provided a signals section which performed very useful service. However, as the working language of the force was English, it proved that thorough familiarity with that language was necessary for efficiency in the intercommunication service. This is also a requirement in the radio service of the United Nations, whose very skilled and experienced operators are drawn from a very large number of nations. The UN international radio service provided the intercommunication between UNEF headquarters, first at Cairo then at El Ballah (near the Canal) and finally at Gaza, to New York through Geneva, to Jerusalem, to Cyprus until the Anglo-French operations were liquidated, and to Naples. It also handled, in the early stages until the Canadian signal company got its equipment and personnel in the *Magnificent* and could take over, a large proportion of the communication needed between UNEF headquarters and the subordinate units.

While in New York I had several conversations with Mr L. B. Pearson, the Canadian Secretary of State for External Affairs, and before I left wrote him a letter stating that as a result of my studies and discussions with military representatives at UN headquarters, I had concluded that the most urgently required and valuable contribution which Canada could make at the time would be the air transport squadron of the RCAF and administrative elements for the force. It may be thought that this was merely making the best of an awkward situation created by President Nasser's obduracy in refusing to accept a Canadian infantry battalion. However, in the light of subsequent experience, I feel that Nasser's refusal was a blessing in disguise, for the administrative and supporting troops Canada provided then and subsequently were absolutely essential, and the force could not have operated without them. It was not feasible for other contributing nations to furnish technical and administrative troops of the kinds needed, as was proved by the lack of response to the request for such contributions which had been sent out by the representatives on November 10.

I would have been extremely glad to have a Canadian infantry battalion in the force ; but if the choice had been between the infantry battalion and the technical troops I should have been obliged to take the latter. In effect, it was such a choice, because the ceiling of the Canadian contribution had been set by the Cabinet at such a figure that both could not have been sent.

On November 18 the Secretary-General had sent a message from Cairo referring to persistent reports that fighting was continuing between the troops occupying Port Said and the civilian inhabitants, with a daily death toll. These reports came from people who had escaped from the city, from others still in it who had some secret means of communication with the Egyptian Government, and from one or two international pressmen. The Secretary-General thought I should arrange for additional observers, and for putting at least a company of UNEF into the city at the earliest possible moment. It was feared that if these stories of atrocities continued with no contradiction from a neutral source, public opinion in Egypt might become inflamed, and attacks on foreigners might result. I accordingly sent a message to Lieutenant-Colonel C. F. Moe, who was acting as commander during my absence, instructing him to obtain information on the exact state of affairs. He was also to see how soon a UNEF company could be got into Port Said.

On the 19th a reply was received from Lieutenant-Colonel Moe saying that between 2 P.M. and 5 P.M. on the 18th Captain de Ghellinck, Belgian Army, an UNMO, had gone around the streets, airfield, and outskirts of Port Said. He reported the situation "normal," shops open, people walking in the streets without restriction, the water and food situation good. It was also reported that the civil population was calm, and that there was no evidence of tension between the civil and military authorities.

On November 19 the Secretary-General returned to New York and immediately was plunged into a welter of business. All the important people in the UN Secretariat and delegations seemingly wanted to see him at once. About noon he held a meeting of the Advisory Committee, at which he explained the results of his negotiations with the Egyptian Government. These were summarized in two aides-mémoire, the principal points of which were as follows.

It was noted that Egypt accepted the General Assembly Resolution 394 of November 5, establishing an Emergency Force " to secure and supervise the cessation of hostilities in accordance with all the terms of the Resolution of 2 November 1956." It was further noted that General Assembly Resolution 395 of November 7 approved the principle in the Secretary-General's report that the force could not be stationed or operate on a country's territory without its consent. Advance groups of UNEF had been received by Egypt after agreement as to their arrival. The Government of Egypt declared that in exercising its sovereign rights on any matter concerning the presence and functioning of UNEF it would be guided, in good faith, by its acceptance of the resolution of November 5 (creating UNEF), while the Secretary-General, for the United Nations, declared that the activities of UNEF would be guided, in good faith, by the task established for the force by the resolutions mentioned. The Government of Egypt and the Secretary-General further agreed that they would proceed at once to explore jointly concrete aspects of the functioning of UNEF, including its stationing and the question of its lines of communication and supply.

I assume the last phrases resulted from the Secretary-General's inquiries as to these points, perhaps prompted by the memorandum I had given him in Rome.

The Secretary-General, in a note explaining some of the terms of the aides-mémoire, examined the question of whether the UNEF would have any function in regard to the opening of the Canal to navigation, because of the inclusion in the resolution of November 2 of a clause which stated ". . . *urges* that, upon the cease-fire being effective, steps to be taken to reopen the Suez Canal and restore freedom of navigation." He inferred that as this resolution was passed before the United Nations Emergency Force was established, the General Assembly could not have specifically intended that the UNEF would have duties in this respect. Therefore, while it might have some duties in connexion with this object of the General Assembly's resolution, they could be undertaken only in conformity with the general principle that Egypt's agreement to any actions of the force would be necessary. It followed that the force could have no functions in Port Said or the Canal area, after the withdrawal of non-Egyptian forces, unless such functions were based on freely negotiated agreement with the Egyptians.

The Secretary-General's view, put in clearer terms in another document, not attached to the aides-mémoire, which was discussed at the Advisory Committee meeting, was that in the debate that preceded the adoption of the resolution of November 7 on the force, it was made very clear that the United Nations Emergency Force would in no way ' take over ' from the Anglo-French forces. If the force was to function only with the consent of the Government of Egypt it could obviously not be considered as an instrument of enforcement directed against the Egyptian Government. The Secretary-General interpreted the intention of the General Assembly as that the clearing of the Canal should be arranged for, and that this should be correlated with, but not subordinate to, the establishment of the force. Further, efforts to reach an agreed solution of the operation of the Canal should be resumed, as indicated by the American draft resolution on the subject.

It was also stated, in one of the aides-mémoire, that the area which the force would occupy at the Armistice Demarcation Line, after withdrawal of the Israeli forces behind that line, would be subject to agreement, as would the question of appropriate staging areas for the force. The Secretary-General also declared that it was his intention to negotiate with the Government of Egypt concerning any additions of new nations to the list so far agreed upon to constitute the force.

Arrangements had been made for me to leave in the late afternoon of November 19 to return to Egypt and take over command of the force. At the meeting of the Advisory Committee no confidential conversation with the Secretary-General was possible. He, Mr Cordier, Dr Bunche, and I had lunch together, but there was no chance for the unhurried talk I should have liked in order to clear my mind as to my task and general responsibilities. It is the practice, when a commander is sent out with a military expeditionary force, to provide him with a general instruction as to what he is expected to achieve, what his relations should be with allies or the authorities of the country in which he is to operate, and other guiding principles for his action. Of course, in the circumstances, it was impossible for such a document to be drawn up by the UN Secretariat, since so many matters relating to UNEF were improvised, and so much was dependent on political conditions, which were fluid and in the course of development. I understood this, but my difficulties were increased by the absence of a definite instruction as to how it was intended that the force would be constituted and would function, and its relations to the Egyptian authorities.

CHAPTER 16

The UNEF in Port Said

ARRIVING at Naples on November 21 *via* Lisbon and Rome, I had an interview with Admiral Walter Boone, U.S. Navy, Commander-in-Chief Eastern Atlantic and Mediterranean (CINCELM), Rear-Admiral Clarence Ekstrom, Captain D. C. Brown, and others of his staff officers. The staff officers had produced a memorandum setting forth the principles and general arrangements under which the United States' logistic support for UNEF would be provided. The function of the United States Navy Support Activity Command, located at Naples, was to help the NATO allies of the United States in this region with equipment, munitions, and other kinds of reinforcement of their military power. The command was thus well adapted to look after the wants of UNEF. Their proposals were quickly agreed upon, and, after an exchange of letters between H.Q. CINCELM, H.Q. UNEF, and United Nations headquarters in New York, were ratified. The U.S. naval officers of the Support Activity Command were extremely helpful to UNEF and seemed anxious to meet all our demands.

On November 22 I flew to Abu Sueir, and, after inspecting the Danish, Indian, Norwegian, Swedish, and Yugoslav advance parties there, drove to Cairo where the temporary headquarters of UNEF had been set up. A large apartment had been rented in the Garden City quarter of Cairo, near the Semiramis Hotel. As the staff built up, space became a problem in these temporary offices, and people were trying to work two and three at a desk. However, in less than three weeks we had moved out to a new headquarters at El Ballah, near the Canal.

At this time intercommunication was a major difficulty for UNEF. We were entirely dependent on the UN international radio service, which linked Cairo to New York through Jerusalem and Geneva. We also communicated with Naples through Geneva. Communication through this link was slow and uncertain, and caused many difficulties through our not knowing when airflights would arrive and what they were carrying. After several weeks we were able to set up a UNEF station at Naples which eliminated this trouble. We also set up a link to Abu Sueir, as the Egyptian telephone system was overloaded and inadequate for our needs. Motorola mobile radios were installed in a number of jeeps, which the ten

UNMOs had brought from Jerusalem, and proved invaluable for UNEF communication between the Egyptian lines and Port Said. Our messages to the Allied forces at first were sent to Cyprus, and there were frequent delays and errors owing to differences in radio procedure. Later we set up a UN station in Port Said as a link to the UNEF and Allied force headquarters there.

All this work imposed a very heavy load on the UN radio operators, who met the challenge most effectively, working extremely long hours at high pressure. That we were able to establish this inter-communication system so quickly was due largely to the foresight of Mr Paul Altorf, Chief Communications Officer of UNTSO, who had established a large reserve of communications equipment in the previous years at Jerusalem. This enabled the new stations we required to be set up quickly. Mr Altorf himself came to Egypt and superintended the setting up of the new station at El Ballah, to work to all the rearward and forward links in the force's system of communications. All this, of course, was before the Canadian signal unit arrived in H.M.C.S. *Magnificent*. The signal detachment of about fifty officers and men of the original Canadian base organization soon arrived, but the amount of equipment they had been able to bring by air was strictly limited.

In the previous chapter I mentioned that Lieutenant-Colonel Moe had been instructed to see whether a company of UNEF could be sent into Port Said. On return to Egypt I found that this had been accomplished on November 21. One company of Norwegians, under command of Major Wiik, had been taken in by train. The railway between El Qantara and Port Said had not been destroyed, and a train carrying Red Crescent supplies had previously passed over it. The UNEF soldiers had received a very warm welcome from the Port Said population, which encouraged us to hope that our operations would be successful.

Lieutenant-Colonel Moe noted that joint patrols of Allied soldiers and Egyptian police were keeping order in the city. He had suggested to the Secretary-General that UNEF should join in these patrols, as this seemed the most obvious way of using the company we had in Port Said. However, before I arrived, the Secretary-General had ruled out UNEF participation in mixed British-Egyptian patrols, for obvious political reasons, and suggested we should set up joint patrols with the Egyptian police as soon as possible. This required planning and consultation with the Allied force commander. It was not possible for the meeting to take place until Sunday, November 25.

At Abu Sueir we had huts and tents for six or seven hundred

troops. This accommodation was rapidly being filled up, and it was necessary to get more camp and barrack space. We also needed a headquarters for the UNEF which could be conveniently placed for controlling the operations in Port Said, the concentration of the force generally, and the first moves out into the Sinai when the Israelis began their withdrawal. With the assistance of the Egyptian liaison staff we found three camps, Ciba, Omar, and Karnak, and a new school building for headquarters conveniently located in relation to the three. The two first-named camps and the school were three kilometres or so from El Qantara, while Karnak was near the El Ballah station on the railway. We used El Ballah as the place name for both headquarters and camps. The camps had not been much used since the Second World War and were pretty dilapidated, needing much repair work before they could be occupied. This was pushed ahead, and we put troops in them pending completion of the repairs.

By November 24 we had decided on the final organization of the UNEF headquarters staff, and had received nominations of staff officers from the various contributing nations. It had been decided to have a colonel as Chief of Staff and lieutenant-colonels to head the Personnel, Operations, and Logistics branches. Each branch had from three to six majors and captains in it, apportioned among the nations contributing to the force. The first appointees to the senior positions were the following : Chief of Staff, Colonel Walter Lundqvist, Swedish Army ; Chief of Personnel, Lieutenant-Colonel Boris Ribaric, Yugoslav Army ; Chief of Operations, Lieutenant-Colonel Christian Moe, Norwegian Army ; Chief of Logistics, Lieutenant-Colonel Shavak Antia, Indian Army. All proved able, conscientious, and experienced staff officers.

The size of the staff and the ranks of the officers composing it may seem excessive for a force only 6000 strong. This would have been so if it had been a homogeneously organized and trained formation in a national army. But the force was in process of organization ; its international character made staff-work more complicated, and the headquarters would have to control nine subordinate units rather than the usual three to five. Also, UNEF headquarters would have to perform duties relating to its base and lines of communication for which there are separate staffs in national armies. Therefore a strong staff for UNEF was essential.

In response to an early recommendation that experienced UN officials to look after finance and purchasing should be sent out, UN headquarters sent Mr Thomas Clements (U.S.A.) for procurement duties and Mr Pieter Kien (the Netherlands) for the finance work. Soon after, Mr Thomas F. Power (U.S.A.) arrived to act as Chief Administrative Officer. He proved an admirable choice for the position. His regular post was as Resident Representative of the United Nations Technical Assistance Board in Persia, and he had held several other responsible administrative UN posts in the Middle East. He had great ability and drive, and the successful organization of UNEF in the theatre owed much to his work. No senior UN official from the Legal branch was available for some time, but fortunately the Canadian Department of Defence had sent an officer from the Judge Advocate-General's branch, Wing-Commander A. Cobus, who, as well as possessing the usual service law experience, had been working with the RCAF in NATO and hence was familiar with some of the legal problems which arise when a military force is established in the territory of a ' host ' country. Mr King Gordon (a Canadian in the UN service) acted as Public Relations Officer for the force.

On November 25 I flew to Port Said in the white UN DC-3 and landed at the Gamil airfield, which was where the British paratroops had landed on the 5th and fought their way into the town. From the air there was not much destruction to be seen, except for a relatively small area which had been ' burned out.' This area had been covered by a very poor class of wooden dwelling, and in Canada would have been called a shack-town. It had caught fire as a result of British naval fire against Egyptian self-propelled guns located near there, which were holding up the advance of the force assaulting by sea. This was the area in which most of the atrocity pictures had been taken.

I was met at the airfield by General Keightley, who had flown over from Cyprus, and Lieutenant-General Stockwell, commanding the 2nd Corps, and both received me in a very friendly fashion. I, and the officers accompanying me, got into the British cars, and we drove to Lieutenant-General Stockwell's H.Q., which was in the offices of the Suez Canal Administration overlooking the harbour. As we drove along, more of the destruction due to the fighting was to be seen, but this was nearly all confined to the avenues along the waterfront. The police-barracks between the airfield and the city, where the Egyptians had put up a strong resistance, was severely damaged, and all along the waterfront one could see the effects of the bombardment which had covered the landing of the commandos near the Canal. But, in sum, it was not very great—certainly not by the standards of anyone who had seen the cities of Italy or Germany which had been subjected to air bombardment during the Second World War. What other damage there was in the city, apart from a very few houses apparently destroyed by chance bombs, was around the inner harbour, where the former British Admiralty House had been burned out by fires started by rockets to dislodge the Egyptian troops, who put up a stout resistance there, and a few warehouses near the inner basins.

The most important question for discussion was how UNEF was to come into Port Said and fulfil its task of interposing between the Anglo-French forces and the Egyptian forces in order to prevent further hostile acts. One obvious measure was to put a unit of UNEF between the Anglo-French and Egyptian positions on the very narrow strip of land, little more than a causeway, which connected Port Said with the mainland near El Qantara. The British positions were at El Cap, and the Egyptian positions about five kilometres to the south of that station. I had previously discussed this with Colonel Gohar, for the Egyptian side, who had agreed in principle. At this conference the Allied commanders accepted the idea readily, and it was left to me to arrange details. The Allied commanders were also in favour of stationing UNEF troops in Port Said so that they would be between the Allied troops and the Egyptians and prevent incidents at the time of the eventual withdrawal.

They agreed to the entry of another company and the battalion headquarters of the Danor battalion into Port Said, with a detachment at Port Fuad on the east side of the Canal. I was under great pressure from New York at this time to build up the UNEF in Port Said as rapidly as possible, without any particular regard to unit organization. I, on the other hand, would have preferred only to commit the units of UNEF after they had completed concentration of their personnel and were organized to carry out whatever tasks they were given. Of this, more later.

As the proposal for joint patrols of Allied and UNEF troops and Egyptian police had been ruled out I suggested, and it was accepted, that separate areas in Port Said and Port Fuad should be designated in which the UNEF in co-operation with the Egyptian police should be responsible for security. These areas would be extended as more UNEF troops were brought in.

UNEF had been informed that the reconnaissance unit which was to form the Yugoslav contribution to the force would be transported to Egypt in two ships. We asked the Allies whether the ships could enter Port Said, and the Yugoslavs and their vehicles could disembark conveniently there. This was agreed to, and we also found that there would be no difficulties about using Port Said for disembarking equipment and supplies for UNEF generally, apart from the blocking of the harbour by the ships, cranes, and barges, which the Egyptians had sunk there. At this time, one could look from the veranda outside the office where we were holding our conference and see the sunken ships in the harbour, with the Anglo-French salvage-fleet working at their clearance. A channel had already been cleared, so that ships could go into the inner basins for unloading, and some passed while I was watching.

I have already mentioned the preliminary negotiations with the British to obtain vehicles and supplies for UNEF. We were told at this conference that we could have the complete quota of vehicles for a medical unit (the Norwegian medical company) and an infantry battalion (Indian Para Bn). Later we added to this list, and got a number of additional trucks and land rovers for H.Q. UNEF and for general transport work. The Allied forces also agreed to sell UNEF petrol, oil and lubricants, medical supplies and rations.

The attitude of the commanders and staff of the Allied forces was entirely co-operative. It seemed to me that they were expecting orders to withdraw before long, and would be relieved when they had them. They were not very sure if UNEF would work, or how, but they seemed very willing to give it a chance, and, indeed, to help it succeed. It was greatly to their interest that UNEF should be effective in this rôle. A withdrawal by sea, in the face of an enemy who is aware of your intention, is a very inconvenient and tricky operation, and can easily result in large casualties, loss of material and perhaps prisoners. It is true there was a cease-fire in effect at this time between Egypt and the Allies, but I don't think this alone would have given the Allied commanders enough assurance to have relaxed their precautions in withdrawing. The interposition of a neutral force between the Egyptians, including the underground or guerrilla fighters, and the Allies ensured a practically undisturbed withdrawal.

The Allies had been complaining of the propaganda emanating from Egyptian sources. This greatly exaggerated the damage in Port Said caused by the Allied attack, and alleged continued attacks on the civil population and various other horrors, which, unfortunately, are frequently suffered by the inhabitants of a theatre of military operations. The British and French suggested that UN observers, and perhaps I myself, should have a thorough look at anything in the city we pleased to, and make a report to the United Nations to tell the truth to the world. The Secretary-General, however, considered that it would be unwise for the UN to make public statements on the damage and current conditions in Port Said, as these might create further difficulties in the delicate and complex negotiations with the parties which were still proceeding.

In my message following this conference I reported to the

Secretary-General, for his own information, that I had driven through Port Said in an open jeep, first with the British, and then with UN observers. I reported the amount of visible damage, and that everything seemed quiet, though few shops were open. British and French troops had been allowed to go shopping, and were buying the usual souvenir goods from sidewalk merchants. The British informed me that the Egyptian police were keeping order well, that the sewage system had been repaired, that electric light and water services were functioning, and that there was plenty of food in the town. I qualified this by saying my observations were necessarily cursory, but that whatever had happened previously it should be possible to carry out the withdrawal without serious disturbances by the civil population.

It should be remembered that just before the invasion very large supplies of arms and ammunition had been distributed indiscriminately to young boys and women and anyone who would take them. The idea, which according to the Brombergers was very actively and effectively promoted by the Russian Consul there, was that there should be a desperate resistance by every last inhabitant, in the manner of Stalingrad. In the early days Egyptian propaganda represented that this indeed was taking place. In fact, the local population showed the good sense to do nothing of the kind. Great quantities of these arms were collected by the Allies. I was told that one battalion had collected fifty-seven lorry-loads, which had been dumped in the sea. Of course, a good many arms were retained and hidden, and this, in fact, was a source of worry to the Egyptian authorities when they returned after the evacuation, for, of course, criminals and other elements whom the Egyptians considered unreliable had got hold of weapons and ammunition. The Egyptian police, in particular, complained of the fact that whereas they had only ancient British First World War type rifles, mere children were handed out the latest and best Czech sub-machine-guns.

I visited the Norwegian company which was camped in the park, and which appeared in very good spirits, with conditions generally satisfactory. Up to that time they had no specific responsibilities in keeping order, but their presence had been welcomed by the people, and doubtless had an influence for good. Above all, it showed both the Allies and the population that UNEF was a reality, and that when it was built up in strength it could perform its allotted task of interposing between the combatants and " helping to maintain peaceful conditions."

On the following day, November 26, Mr Robles and I had a long discussion with Colonel Gohar on the rôle proposed for UNEF in Port Said. Gohar did not care for the idea of a limited area of responsibility, but seemed to think it would be possible for UNEF to take over the policing of the entire city at once, thus preventing any contact between the Allied forces and the population. I explained this was beyond UNEF's capabilities at that point. The next day, however, the Egyptians accepted my proposals, in particular for putting a company of UNEF between the Allies and Egyptian troops south of El Cap.

On November 28 I went to Abu Sueir and had a conversation with Lieutenant-Colonel G. K. Wade, the senior Canadian officer, who had been made commandant of the base area, and was endeavouring to establish order in the administrative confusion in the base area using the Canadian administrative troops which had arrived. At this time I was receiving rather peremptory cables from New York, urging me to hasten the bringing forward of troops from Naples and to get them into Port Said as quickly as possible. There was some criticism of stores being brought forward, instead of men. The object of the Secretary-General and his advisers was to establish as quickly as possible an effective showing of UNEF in Port Said in view of the political situation, but they did not allow for the administrative difficulties which the new-born force was facing. If the troops were to operate at all they had to have cooking equipment, blankets, weapons, and ammunition, and, above all, food. Up to this time, it had not been possible to arrange to procure rations for the force in Egypt. Therefore it was being fed on U.S. " C " rations which all had to be carried from Naples by airlift. This imposed a heavy load on the available aircraft. At one time the force reserve was down to 650 rations, not enough to feed the force for one day—that is, we were literally living from hand to mouth. This situation cleared up only when we got the stock of hard rations from the British, and organized procurement of perishable foods in Egypt, a week or so later.

On the same day I went to El Qantara, and with Brigadier Hilmy went to the forward Egyptian position, which lay along an embankment stretching west from the causeway, presumably designed to prevent inundation. From there, the way having been prepared by the UNMOs, I went over to the forward company of the Yorks. and Lancs. Regiment, which was holding the British outpost position. I saw the commanding officer of the battalion, Lieutenant-Colonel Halford, and made a tentative plan for the Danish company to come into the space between the two forces. This would have involved a slight retirement by each, as they were closer together than earlier information had indicated. In the event, it was only the British and French who withdrew about a kilometre, but the plan worked successfully, and in the ensuing period there were only minor incidents, owing to Egyptian patrols trying to come in from the flanks—areas, which, though mainly water, had some restricted paths across them. Seemingly some Egyptian units in the area had not received proper instructions in regard to observing the cease-fire.

During the next week I saw Stockwell and Keightley twice, and discussed the principles and methods for UNEF's operation during the process of the evacuation of the Allied forces from Port Said. Eventually, after several consultations, discussions with the Egyptian side represented by Colonel Gohar, and reference to the Secretary-General, the general principles were embodied in an aide-mémoire which was accepted by the Allied Command. The essential parts of this were as follows. UNEF troops would be stationed in Port Said and Port Fuad, and would assume responsibility in co-operation with the local authorities for " securing peaceful conditions for the civilian population " in conformity with the decisions of the General Assembly. UNEF would not interfere with the base establishments of the Anglo-French forces, nor with the roads essential for communication between them. It would be settled between the commanders of UNEF and the Anglo-French forces what roads would be so reserved, and the discharge of UNEF's responsibilities would not be impeded.

The plan which was agreed upon was that UNEF would take over responsibility for additional block areas in Port Said as soon as troops could be moved in. Also, as the Anglo-French troops which were disposed along the ' causeway ' south towards El Cap were withdrawn, additional UNEF troops would be put in, extending the buffer zone from below El Cap up to the Manzala Canal which was the southerly boundary of the city, and across which access was possible by only two bridges. The Indian parachute battalion actually carried out this task.

The UNEF would gradually take over the guarding of " vulnerable points " such as electricity generating plants, water-pumping and sewage installations, telephone exchanges, food warehouses, and so forth, where sabotage by misguided ' patriots ' could have had serious effects for the orderly life of the population. That precautions in this respect were not unnecessary was proved by the fact that on December 7 British patrols intercepted a group of young men who, having crossed Lake Manzala by boat, were conveying some 250 lb. of gun-cotton and gelignite as well as other munitions into the port. This was verified by UNMOs, and I complained of it to General Amr, who promised to do his best to prevent such incidents in future. However, no significant act of sabotage took place after UNEF entered Port Said.

When the evacuation reached its final stage the Allied forces would be withdrawn into a narrow perimeter, protected by a barbed-wire fence, in the northern parts of Port Said and Port Fuad close to the Canal entrance. Outside this, on the last day, UNEF would occupy a zone of several hundred metres. Civilians would be excluded from this zone, which would also be shut off by wire fences on the city side. By this time UNEF would have taken over responsibility for all vulnerable points outside this zone, as well as general " maintenance of peaceful conditions " in co-operation with the Egyptian police. It will be noted that we were careful not to say that UNEF would be responsible for " law and order," which would have been the normal phrase to have used, because the Egyptian side were very insistent that this was the prerogative of the local Egyptian authorities, probably fearing that UNEF might remain in Port Said overlong, if it had a pretext afforded by these words.

In fact, the co-operation with the Egyptian police, which were under the control of Mahmoud Riad, the Governor, was effective enough. The Governor had got in touch with Lieutenant-Colonel Carl Engholm soon after he had arrived with his Danor battalion, and complained that, while the normal police complement of Port Said was 1500 men, only 800 of these remained, the rest having become casualties during the fighting or having escaped. He asked that these be reinforced by additional men from Egypt. After some days General Stockwell agreed to 350 coming in. They were brought in by train, after being checked by UNMOs to make sure they were really police and not disguised *fedayeen*, and had only their normal armament of rifles. On the day of the evacuation a further large detachment was moved in, and it turned out that these police forces were capable of maintaining order after the evacuation, with no intervention by UNEF.

Shortly after the Danor battalion H.Q. moved in we began the practice of sending UNEF patrols in jeeps and on foot around certain districts, independent of either the Allied patrols or the Egyptian police. Strictly speaking, these patrols had no function, other than to show themselves, and get the people used to the idea of UNEF's being in the city.

On December 3 Mr Selwyn Lloyd announced the United Kingdom's intention to withdraw its forces from Port Said. He said that the British and French governments had instructed General Keightley to seek agreement with me on a timetable for the complete withdrawal, taking account of the military and practical problems involved. The UN was to become responsible for the safety of any British or French salvage resources left at the disposition of the United Nations Suez Clearance Organization, and the Secretary-General had accepted this responsibility.

Following this, the Secretary-General instructed me to arrange for the earliest possible date for the completion of the UNEF take-over and Allied withdrawal. He had said that UNEF should be in position to assume its responsibilities in the Port Said area by the middle of December.

I discussed the time for completion of the withdrawal with Keightley and the other Allied commanders on December 5, and they said that this was dependent in the first place on shipping—there was a shortage of ships that could carry vehicles—also on weather, and the capacity of the docking and loading facilities at Port Said. They said they wanted to leave as quickly as possible, but could not do it in less than fourteen days—*i.e.*, the 19th would be the date for the completion of evacuation. We talked at some length, and the Allied staff officers even showed me the detailed shipping schedules on which the date was based. I told them that I had been instructed to press for withdrawal to be complete by December 14 and that I would report to UN H.Q. what their viewpoint was.

There were several messages exchanged between the Secretary-General and myself, and further discussions with the Allied Command, on the question of date of withdrawal. The main reason for pressing for an earlier withdrawal than that which the Allied Command had scheduled was that the Egyptians refused to allow any clearance of the Canal to be commenced before the withdrawal, and each day that the Canal remained closed was costing great sums of money.

This was the first of the occasions on which, after withdrawal had been accepted in principle, I was instructed to press the commanders of the invading forces to pull back more speedily. I found I had very little bargaining-power to enforce or persuade to such a withdrawal. Usually, when there are negotiations between the military commanders of two opposing forces, it is for the making of or during an armistice. The commander of the force which is victorious, or has the better military position, can oblige his opponent to accept terms under the threat of continuing or resuming hostilities, and so placing him in a worse plight than he already is in. In the situation vis-à-vis the Anglo-French forces in December, and vis-à-vis the Israeli forces later, there was no question of UNEF's being able to take offensive action, consequently it posed no military threat. Therefore I could do little but argue that the other side *ought* to withdraw more quickly. But the arguments for withdrawal were political arguments, and the ultimate sanctions forcing the withdrawals, though very real, were certainly not provided by UNEF. The negotiations were essentially political, not military, and it was for politicians to carry them on, not myself as a commander of a force having defensive powers only, and limited defensive powers at that. In the end, after negotiations with the Israelis over the withdrawal from the Sinai and the Gaza Strip had been going on for some time, this was recognized, and my subsequent conferences with General Dayan were confined to giving effect to decisions already reached between the Secretary-General and his aides and the Israeli representatives at the United Nations. Parallel negotiations usually were going on between United States and Israeli representatives, the Secretary-General and the Egyptian representatives, with other elements taking a hand from time to time. But this is to anticipate.

The Anglo-French withdrawal eventually took place on December 22—that is, three days after the date first mentioned to me by Keightley. I believe it could have taken place on the date mentioned, but was delayed because of the dispute which developed in regard to the use of the Anglo-French salvage-fleet in the clearance of the Canal.

I considered it necessary to keep the actual date of withdrawal as top secret. This had been communicated to me by the Allied Command, and in UNEF only the commanders of units in Port Said and staff officers immediately concerned knew of it. Of course, it was known by every one that the withdrawal would soon take place. But if the exact date had been known the underground elements in Port Said would have been encouraged to make attacks at that time, with resulting bloodshed. So when asked by journalists or others about the exact date of withdrawal I usually gave the impression that it would be rather later than the actual date.

I have mentioned that underground elements were in possession of large quantities of arms and ammunition, which could easily be hidden from the occupying forces and the police. From time to time there were incidents, after UNEF entered the city, and the attackers became emboldened when signs of early withdrawal became evident. I had urged Major-General Abd El Hakim Amr, Minister of War and Commander-in-Chief of the Egyptian forces, to suppress such activities and keep things quiet on the Egyptian side. Guerrilla operations might well delay the evacuation, and would probably result in many more casualties to the inhabitants of Port Said than to the withdrawing invaders. He saw my viewpoint, and I understood him to agree to do what he could.

Representations to the same effect were made by the Secretary-General to Dr Fawzi, representative of Egypt at the UN. The official reply to later representations which I made on the same subject was that the invaders had cut off Port Said from communication with Egypt, therefore the Government had no means of conveying instructions to anyone there, and so could not be responsible for what they did.

There were a few incidents of Allied patrols being attacked in the streets at night by small-arms fire and grenades. Two UNEF patrols, a Danor and a Swedish, were fired at and returned the fire, fortunately suffering no casualties. The worst incident took place two or three days before the withdrawal, when a bolder attack was made on a British patrol and a major was killed. This was in an area for which UNEF had not taken over any responsibility. The British opened fire on the buildings from which they had been fired upon, using tanks, and some thirty casualties to Egyptians ensued. After that, there were no further incidents until embarkation.

About ten days before the evacuation a young officer, Lieutenant Moorhouse, was captured and held as prisoner by some of the Egyptian underground. Lieutenant-General Stockwell complained to me of this breach of the cease-fire and we endeavoured, through Mahmoud Riad, the Governor of Port Said, and also through the Egyptian authorities in Cairo, to find where he was being held, and to procure his release. All inquiries were without result, the Egyptian authorities in Cairo claiming, as before, to have no control over what went on in Port Said.

A most unfortunate part of this incident was that the intelligence officer of the Danor battalion, Captain Wiik, in his efforts to find out where Moorhouse was, had got in touch with some shady characters living in the Arab part of the town. These fellows took him, alone, to a certain house and showed him, at some distance, a man dressed in British officer's uniform, who they assured him was Moorhouse. He reported this to me on the morning of the embarkation as I was talking to General Stockwell, and on the strength of this apparent evidence that Lieutenant Moorhouse was alive and well, though a prisoner, his parents were so informed.

It would appear that Captain Wiik, who spoke no Arabic and had no prior knowledge of the Middle East or things Egyptian, had been completely deceived. Wiik's contacts apparently wanted to obtain information concerning the condition of three important Egyptian officers detained by the British. He had handed over notes from these officers, which the British had procured for him, at the nocturnal interview when he thought he saw Moorhouse. He had asked for a corresponding note from " Moorhouse," but had been put off with excuses. The captors refused to turn Moorhouse over, saying they had orders from their underground commander to turn him over only to an Egyptian officer.

When the British had left I continued to press for the release of Moorhouse, as we thought him to be still alive. We several times requested Colonel Hassan Roushdi, who had been head of the Criminal Investigation Department in Port Said and who had returned to the city, to obtain Moorhouse's release, as well as putting similar requests to the Cairo authorities and to Brigadier Hilmy. This went on for about a week, with evasive answers from the Egyptian authorities to all our requests for investigation and action. Finally, on December 30, an item was published in an Egyptian paper that Moorhouse was dead. On the following day Brigadier Hilmy confidentially gave me an account of what had happened, so far as the Egyptian police had been able to discover.

Moorhouse's captors had intended to hold him for exchange against Egyptian members of the " resistance " captured by the British. When British troops moved in to search the area where he was held the captors tied him up and shut him in a cupboard. They were unable to return to the house for two days, on account of the British search activity, and when they opened the cupboard Moorhouse was dead. He was buried near the cemetery to the west of the city, and on January 2 his body was handed over to UNEF, identified, and sent back to England.

The affair excited a great deal of attention in the Press in England, and inquiries continued to be directed to UN H.Q. and so on to UNEF until the middle of January, by which time it was possible to report the facts given in summary above. It was a tragic and unnecessary death, and one felt particular sympathy for the young man's parents. But nearly a thousand Egyptians—soldiers, police, and civilians of all sexes and ages—had been killed in the fighting.

A more satisfactory business arose out of our early requests to Cairo for Moorhouse's release. Colonel Gohar, in the course of the discussions, mentioned to Dr Robles that the British and French were holding a large number of officers and men of the Egyptian forces and also a number of civilians as prisoners. Robles suggested that as the Egyptian Government was detaining in prison some four hundred and fifty of the personnel of the British contractors who had had charge of the military bases in the Canal area prior to the invasion, an exchange might be worked out. After several vicissitudes, and near failure at the last minute because the French had taken away a number of their prisoners by ship and had to turn round and bring them back, the exchange did take place, in the afternoon of December 21. A train from Port Said carrying the

Egyptian prisoners (about 185 in all) came out to El Cap station, where the train from Cairo *via* Ismailiya carrying the 450 contractors' personnel also arrived. After verification of nominal rolls of persons turned over, in the presence of UNMOs and under guard of the Indian battalion, the trains went their respective ways. The contractors' men were in very good spirits at getting out, although they had had nothing to eat all day. It was gratifying to think that UNEF had been able to be of help in this case. The Egyptian prisoners did not seem quite so happy ; possibly they were in some doubt as to the reception they would get in Egypt.

On November 29 the Yugoslav contingent had arrived at Port Said in two ships. I went to meet them with several staff officers and the Yugoslav liaison officer, Colonel Vojvedic. Lieutenant-General Stockwell was on hand and himself directed the launches that brought in the cables from the Yugoslav ships and got them tied up, as the officer who should have been in charge of this business was not on hand. Then we both went aboard and greeted the commander of the unit, Colonel Radosevic, and his senior officers. They appeared somewhat surprised to see General Stockwell, but with the hospitable production of coffee and *slivovitz*, all became friendly. The disembarkation took several days, the delay mainly being due to lack of suitable cranes for unloading their armoured cars and other vehicles. On December 3 the unit moved out and assembled at Omar Camp, one of the El Ballah group, within a hundred metres of UNEF H.Q.

On the previous day the Israeli Government had announced that it was withdrawing its forces fifty kilometres from the Canal. I had received instructions from the Secretary-General to follow up this retirement, and the Yugoslavs were the only unit I had free for the purpose. It was therefore necessary to order them to cross the Canal immediately, before they had any time to sort themselves out in their base camp.

The early moves to follow up the Israeli withdrawal across the Sinai will be described later, although these were going on simultaneously with the Port Said operations. All other troops but the Yugoslavs were engaged in Port Said, and they were none too many. Besides the Danor battalion which had three rifle companies, there were the 3rd Battalion Indian Parachute Regiment (Kumaon) of four companies, the Swedish battalion of two companies, the Colombian battalion of two companies, and the Finnish company. The clumsiness of the force's organization will be apparent from the above. There were four " battalions," but they had only eleven companies between them, instead of the sixteen which a normal infantry organization would provide. This meant that an undue portion of the manpower of the force was taken up by headquarters and administrative personnel within the battalion establishments, and there were less " G.I. Joes " to supply the guards, picquets, and patrols that were needed for UNEF's operations. I doubt that this factor was appreciated in New York, where it was from time to time pointed out that UNEF had in Egypt so many thousand men, and why was I not doing more with them than I was ?

Early in December I had talked with Lieutenant-Colonel Wade, the officer in charge of the Canadian administrative detachments, who had been made commander of the base area, and we had quickly agreed that there was an urgent need for more administrative troops if the force was to be able to operate effectively in the Sinai. So a message was sent off to the Secretary-General suggesting that Canada should be asked to send, instead of the infantry battalion originally proposed, a signal unit, an RCAF air communication squadron, a workshop unit (which no other nation had offered and which would be needed to keep the force's mechanical transport in operation), and two transport platoons. I also suggested that Canada might send an armoured reconnaissance squadron, which, as well as being a useful unit to have, would give Canada a representation in combatant troops. I discussed this proposal for a switch in Canada's contribution with Mr Herbert Norman, Canadian Ambassador in Cairo, who advised the Canadian Government of my views directly.

A message was received from Dr Bunche the next day agreeing to this proposal, and saying the preliminary response from Canadian representatives was favourable. The discussions I had had with the Chief of the General Staff and the Chief of the Air Staff when I was in New York had paved the way for this.

In subsequent telegrams, giving the requirements in more detail, some additional engineers, an ordnance detachment, provost, pay, postal, and movement-control detachments were also asked for. The total administrative group asked for came to about 50 officers and 900 NCOs and men. The number actually sent was about 200 less, but was adequate for the tasks required.

At this time additional contributions to the force to bring the total number up to about 6000 were being discussed. The countries which New York had selected as the most suitable contributors were Indonesia, Brazil, and Pakistan. I was instructed to get the Egyptian Government's agreement to these additional contributions to UNEF, as well as to the increased Canadian contribution. Dr Fawzi in New York had indicated a favourable atmosphere. I saw

Mr Ali Sabry, who was President Nasser's Chef du Cabinet and principal political adviser, on December 8 and 9, and at the second interview he informed me that Egypt had no objection to the proposed increase of the Canadian troops. The question of participation of the other nations was referred back to New York for negotiation.

These negotiations dragged on for nearly a month. Egypt accepted the Indonesian contribution at once, but objected to Pakistan and could not be argued out of it. The Brazilian contingent was agreed to only after a good deal of pressure. It appeared that the Egyptian attitude towards contributions from the several countries was determined by her general political relations with them and her opinion as to how far they supported her policies in the United Nations.

About December 19 Air Commodore Carpenter of the RCAF came to Egypt, and the establishment of the air transport and reconnaissance unit was decided upon. It was to consist of four C-119 aircraft to carry urgently needed freight, mails, and some personnel from Naples to Abu Sueir ; two DC-3s (Dakotas) to be based at Abu Sueir for medium-length flights, and where passengers and freight had to be carried within the theatre ; and four Otter aircraft. This was a light aircraft developed in Canada for use in the north country, which had good endurance and load-carrying capacity yet was able to land on relatively short and rough landing-strips. There were several officers who would have liked to see helicopters on the establishment, but these were ruled out on account of the difficulties of maintenance. Certainly the helicopter has many uses and is very handy, but they would have been rather a luxury in the circumstances in which UNEF was to operate. The establishment actually provided was adequate for the needs of the force. The Otters in particular performed very well in the desert, being able to land on strips that received very little preparation and, in emergency, in places on the desert which had been picked out from the air.

On December 8 Lieutenant-General Raymond A. Wheeler, U.S. Army (ret.), who had been appointed chief of the UN Suez Clearance Organization, came to Egypt. How this organization got the Canal clear for traffic much sooner than anyone believed possible is one of the most satisfactory performances of the United Nations during the Suez crisis. However, the operations of the Clearance Organization and UNEF were almost entirely separate after the early days when we gave some assistance in intercommunication and administrative matters.

At first it was thought that UNEF might have to provide protection for the salvage-vessels employed in the Canal clearance. It was believed that the population along the Canal might be badly disposed to foreigners after the invasion. Of course, protection would especially be needed for the British and French salvage-craft which it was at first expected would be a large element in the UN salvage-fleet. There was a great deal of acrimonious argument as to the use of the Anglo-French salvage-organization. The Egyptians wanted none of it, and fought the proposal to use it bitterly. The British and French were sure that without using the resources which they had assembled there would be great difficulty in clearing the Canal, and completion would be much delayed. Eventually it was agreed that about ten of the Anglo-French vessels would remain, that their naval crews would be dressed as civilians and would be protected by small detachments of " civilian guards " recruited from the Swedes and Finns of UNEF. There were only eighty of such guards, all told. They wore civilian clothes (which UNSCO had provided with some difficulty), with the UNEF blue beret and arm-band. No incidents occurred in which they had to use force, and with the " phasing out " of the British and French elements after about six weeks the guards returned to their duties as UNEF soldiers.

The British and French seemed to blame General Wheeler for the rejection of their offers to help in the clearance of the Canal, and for a while he was the target for a good deal of abuse in the British Press. He did not take this very kindly, having, like most successful generals, a fair amount of fire in his belly ; so the discussions with the British and French admirals with whom he had to negotiate were, I gathered, fairly pyrotechnic on occasion. General Wheeler, with whom I came to be on very friendly terms, remarked to me that he didn't like this at all, as he had always got on very well with the British in India where he had served most of the Second World War, being at one time Deputy to Lord Mountbatten. For these services he had been granted the K.B.E. and the K.C.I.E. ; so the British should really have referred to him as Sir Raymond Wheeler.

I recall that in his first Press interview after his arrival in Egypt he was reported to have said, " I'm here to do an engineering job ; I have nothing to do with politics." He was never more mistaken ! Most of the difficulties he encountered were political, but these sorted themselves out as the withdrawal progressed, although the Egyptians held up the work of raising the last obstacle, the tug *Edgar Bonnet*, sunk just above Ismailiya, under the pretext that it was mined, until the Israelis moved out of the Gaza Strip and Sharm El Shaikh—that is to say, they would not allow the Canal to be opened, which was a prime object with the Western nations and many Asian nations, until the Israelis were made to comply with the General Assembly resolution that they should withdraw behind the Armistice Demarcation Line. But this was only the last of several political ' obstructions ' that had to be removed before the Canal could be opened.

I have mentioned the blue berets worn by the Finns and Swedes as civilian guards on the salvage-ships. This brings up the subject of uniforms for UNEF. From the first it was an idea of the Secretary-General that there should be a distinctive uniform for the force, but it was obviously impracticable to outfit the contingents with a common uniform in the early days, when everything had to be done as quickly as possible. Afterwards, when the matter was studied further, it was felt that it would be an unwarranted expense ; besides, most contingents preferred to retain their national uniform, of which they were naturally proud. It was contemplated that every one would be issued a summer uniform, but here again the same factors operated, and it was issued by UNEF only to those contingents that did not have a summer uniform of their own suitable for the climate of the theatre. The Indian summer uniform, bush-jacket, shirt and trousers of medium-green cotton material, was chosen as standard.

The problem of distinguishing the UNEF troops from the troops of the several combatants was solved by providing them with a distinctive headdress of United Nations blue. The first suggestion was a blue beret, and eventually these were issued, but in November none of this colour was to be had through commercial sources, and they had to be manufactured specially. In the interim some one had the bright idea of taking the plastic liner of the American steel helmet and enamelling it UN blue. It worked very well ; the U.S. naval authorities in Italy produced the requisite numbers of blue bonnets as they were needed, and the UNEF troops moving into Port Said were clearly identified by them. A great many United Nations flags were also used to identify our vehicles and buildings.

When the next summer came a lighter headdress was brought into use. It was of the ski-cap type, similar to that worn ordinarily by some of the Scandinavians. It was, of course, UN blue in colour, had a good peak, and a flap that could be let down to protect the back of the neck from the sun. It was comfortable and popular with the troops.

When I had been in New York it had been put to me that as a United Nations general I ought to have a special uniform and not wear that of any particular nation. The Secretary-General was firmly of this opinion. There was an additional reason in that as Chief of Staff UNTSO I had worn the uniform of a Canadian major-general, which is exactly the same as that of a British general except for small brass " Canada " emblems on the shoulder-straps. When I landed in Port Said there was nothing in my dress to distinguish me from Generals Keightley and Stockwell except the United Nations brassard and the United Nations shoulder-patches. This, understandably, could have had adverse psychological effects on the Egyptians and perhaps within the force. So, although I delayed for some time, I eventually had a uniform made.

Bearing in mind the criticisms levelled at certain eminent generals who were reputed to have designed special uniforms for themselves, I tried to make mine as sober as possible, but nevertheless some of the Press had their fun out of it. The design was basically the same as the uniform worn by the security officers (guards) of the United Nations, at New York H.Q. and in missions abroad. For badges of rank, which had to be different from that in use in other armies, I used the UN symbol of the world surrounded by a wreath of olive-leaves, with a broad band of gold braid underneath. It had gorget patches of UN blue, with olive-leaf embroidery instead of the usual oak-leaf. At first I felt somewhat self-conscious in this new garb, after forty years of khaki, but soon got used to it.

On December 22, the day set for the evacuation, I went up to Port Said, where I met General Stockwell in the small perimeter which the British were holding near the waterfront just by the Casino Palace Hotel, which had been used as a casualty clearing station and had suffered a good deal of superficial damage. It was a beautiful bright day, and all was quiet in the city. There was not much to talk about ; General Stockwell thanked me for the harmonious way in which the unprecedented operation had been carried out. I thanked him for the co-operation given to UNEF, especially in the sale of vehicles and stores. He was warm in praise for the way Lieutenant-Colonel Engholm, who had been in command of all the UNEF troops in Port Said, had carried out his task, and was complimentary as to the conduct of the UNEF troops generally.

Presently General Wheeler came up, and after we had talked for a while we took his motor-launch and made a tour of the harbour, especially to see the Anglo-French salvage-vessels, which had been moored together in the outer basin on the Port Fuad side. British cruisers, destroyers, and other naval craft, as well as tank-landing ships and other transports, and a number of French vessels, were either lying alongside the docks or at anchor in the outer harbour or just outside. From time to time jet fighters screamed overhead, at low altitude, to remind the Egyptians that the Allied air power was still ready to counter any resumption of hostilities. But all was very quiet as the British regular soldiers went about the final tasks of embarkation (and there was little that remained to be done) with the quiet precision which denotes well-trained and disciplined troops.

It made a great show of military power, and yet—they were getting out. Attending their departure was the tiny half-organized and lightly armed United Nations Emergency Force. It was an historic day, perhaps marking the last time that an Empire (here two Empires in association) would seek to impose its will by force on a weaker nation. It marked the end of an epoch. Perhaps only the end of an epoch for Britain and France, for they were really withdrawing under the pressure of greater Powers than themselves.

Some Frenchmen had wired a *tricolore* to the hand of the De Lesseps statue, standing high overlooking the entrance to the port. It was a forlorn gesture.

By midnight I received the code-word from Engholm that the last Allied ships had cleared the harbour. The next day control was handed over to the Egyptian Governor, Mahmoud Riad, and we began to withdraw the UNEF troops, to redeploy for the advance across the Sinai. There had been fears of riots and attacks against foreigners, especially the French religious and educational establishments. UNEF had put guards over them. There was no such trouble, however, and much credit must be given to the Egyptian authorities for this. A strong body of troops, comprising a regiment of tanks on carriers, a battalion of armour-carried infantry, artillery, and numerous other detachments started to roll into Port Said during the afternoon of the 23rd. It was explained to me that the purpose was to ensure strong support for the police and law-enforcement agencies, as many unreliable elements possessed arms. I suspected that it may have been in the minds of the Egyptian Army Command to put this powerful force into the port at once, to ensure that UNEF did not remain in possession—a possibility of which they had been very suspicious in the beginning. Of course we had no such intention.

There were no breaches of the peace, and no overt persecutions. The crowds released their emotions by parades, speeches, and by blowing up the statue of De Lesseps—at the third attempt. Perhaps a symbolic act also, showing the desire to ignore any benefits brought to the country by the foreigners who for a period had ruled over them by right of superior force.

CHAPTER 17

UNEF crosses the Sinai, and waits at the Border

Map 6

ON December 2, 1956, the Government of Israel announced that its forces would begin withdrawing from the Sinai. Their withdrawal continued by stages throughout the months of December and January. Each stage of withdrawal required negotiation—in New York between the Secretary-General and his assistants and Mr Eban, the Israel permanent representative at the United Nations, and in the theatre between General Dayan and myself. There was a considerable amount of haggling as to when, and how far, the Israelis would move back at each stage. They inclined to drag their feet—in part because the soldiery and the public were disappointed at having to give up their 'conquests,' and in part because the Government of Israel wanted to hold on to the territory they occupied until they had received a satisfactory settlement of their claims in regard to the Gaza Strip and Sharm El Shaikh, the former Egyptian fortified position which controlled passage through the Strait of Tiran.

The initial, unnegotiated withdrawal was to a line roughly fifty kilometres east of the Canal, then south-west to Sudr on the Gulf of Suez. It was followed by two intermediate stages, and three other main stages.

Stage 1a, on December 31, was a withdrawal on the North and Centre * roads to about five kilometres east of El Mazar station, and Bir Rod Salem, the former of which the Yugoslavs occupied. Stage 1b, on January 6, was to a point ten kilometres west of El Arish, the rest of the line remaining unchanged.

Stage 2 saw UNEF advance on January 7, 1957, following Israeli withdrawal to a line from a point five kilometres west of El Arish-Bir Hasana-El Themed and a road junction thirty-five kilometres north-west of the St Catherine Monastery, and El Tor, which was occupied on January 8.

Stage 3 : On January 15 the Israelis retired behind a line running

---

* For convenient reference UNEF named the roads crossing the Sinai as follows : El Qantara-El Arish-Rafah : North Road. Ismailiya-El Auja : Centre Road. Suez-El Nakhl-Ras El Naqb : South Road.

due south from a point on the North Road twenty-five kilometres east of El Arish, to a point about forty kilometres north of the southern tip of the Sinai peninsula, thence south-west to a point on the road about thirty kilometres south-east of El Tor.

Stage 4 saw the Israeli retirement on January 22 to the line of the International Frontier, except at Rafah in the north, where they remained five kilometres to the west of it, owing to the local circumstance that Rafah Camp straddled the line, and it would not have been convenient, or allowed good control, if the Israeli Defence Forces and UNEF had divided the camp between them.   Also, Israel retained a strip about twenty-five kilometres in breadth parallel to the shore of the Gulf of Aqaba, from the International Frontier in the north, down to the point thirty kilometres south-east of El Tor, which had been the limit of retirement in the previous stage in this sector.   This was to allow land communication with the garrison which they still kept at Sharm El Shaikh.

There was no further withdrawal until the Israelis finally vacated the Gaza Strip on March 6, 1957.

To work out this programme of withdrawal, General Dayan and I met a number of times at El Arish and Lydda.   At these meetings we arranged the details necessary to ensure that there would be no unforeseen contact between the Israel forces and UNEF, which might have led to misunderstanding and even opening of fire.   No such incidents did occur, due to the plan we agreed upon.   Successive lines were designated behind which the Israel forces would withdraw by certain dates and times ; thereupon the UNEF would follow up to a line approximately five kilometres to the west, and would halt there until the next move forward.   UN Military Observers, in their white jeeps and carrying the UN flag, preceded the UNEF columns, making contact at each stage with the Israelis, and ensuring that each side ended up at the locations decided upon.   UNEF's advance and the Israelis' retirement were along the three main routes across the Sinai ; North, Centre, and South roads, as shown on the map. Only light elements, about a company strong, were sent along each route, owing to difficulties of supply, particularly of water-supply in the desert, and the destruction of the roads which the Israelis had carried out before their withdrawal, which necessitated considerable detours by the UNEF transport.

When the Israelis began pulling back on December 3, UNEF was still in the process of concentrating, and the priority task for nearly all the troops I had at disposal was to help secure the orderly evacuation of Port Said.   The Yugoslavs had just arrived, fortunately with complete unit transport ; they also had an engineer detachment.   I have told how they were immediately pushed across the Canal, to follow up the Israelis. Until after the Port Said evacuation was completed (December 23), the Yugoslavs were the only UNEF troops in the Sinai, with detachments on the North, Centre, and South roads, as well as on the road running along the eastern shore of the Gulf of Suez, towards El Tor. This was an extremely wide dispersion for a unit of battalion size, but its organization and equipment as an armoured reconnaissance battalion enabled it to carry out its task. The main difficulties the Yugoslavs encountered, and continued to encounter during their advance along the North Road until they passed El Mazar, was in making tracks over which their vehicles could pass in the sand-dune country of the north Sinai, and in clearing those tracks of mines. The Israelis had planted a number of minebelts, presumably as protection against a possible Egyptian counter-attack. They gave us full and accurate information as to where these minefields were located, but inevitably there were a number of scattered mines whose position was unknown; so the advancing UNEF troops had to prod laboriously for mines (which were of the plastic variety) over every foot of the routes they traversed.

After the Allied evacuation of Port Said, UNEF was redistributed for the advance across the Sinai, the Yugoslavs being concentrated on the northern route, and the other routes being allocated to one unit each. UNEF was still greatly hampered by lack of transport ; and it was not until the arrival of a shipload of vehicles at the end of December, provided from U.S. sources, and which had been ordered early in November, followed by the arrival of H.M.C.S. *Magnificent* with the Canadian technical and administrative troops and their full complement of vehicles, that the force began to dispose of reasonably adequate transport. Modern military forces must have enough mechanical transport, if they have to operate over distances of more than a few miles from their base, and UNEF was about to operate in a very extended theatre. One of the more difficult problems in making UNEF truly operational was to collect the transport, ship it by sea to Port Said, and put it in running order. A national army undertaking an overseas campaign has to plan elaborately to ensure that the necessary fighting and administrative vehicles will be shipped so as to join up with the units to which they belong at the proper time and place. At the time it was decided to organize UNEF the United Nations had no stock of vehicles, no expert planning staff, no military transport organization. One would hope that this lesson, as a result of the experience of UNEF, and in the Congo, has been learned, and will be applied if other UN forces have to be organized in the future.

The build-up of UNEF continued with the arrival of an

Indonesian battalion, about 600 strong, early in January 1957, and of a Brazilian contingent, about 550 in number, which came on February 2, 1957, in a Brazilian troopship, carrying their vehicles with them. The last unit of UNEF to arrive was a Canadian armoured reconnaissance squadron, towards the end of March, a small " fighting " unit to add to Canada's essential contribution of technical and administrative troops.

As the Israelis withdrew across the Sinai, they began a systematic destruction of the surfaced roads, the railway, the telephone-lines, and what few buildings there were along the railway, and at one or two road-junction points. God had scorched the Sinai earth, and His chosen people removed whatever stood above it. They doubtless hoped by this operation to prevent the Egyptians from re-establishing their forces on the border of Israel, in the El Arish-Rafah-El Quseima area in the same strength as they had been before the invasion. When UNEF found out what was going on Mr Hammarskjöld protested vigorously to the Israel Government, that this destruction was a breach of the undertaking they had given to facilitate the efforts of UNEF directed towards maintaining peaceful conditions, and it certainly was not co-operation to destroy the roads by which we had to advance. Shortly thereafter the destruction of the road and railway was stopped. But by that time the roads from about twelve kilometres east of the Canal, the limit of the Israelis' advance, for a distance of about seventy kilometres eastward had been thoroughly demolished. There was no further destruction of the North Road, through El Arish to Gaza, but when we arrived at El Arish we found that the surfaced roads running laterally through Abu Aweigila and El Quseima to El Auja had all been destroyed, as well as all buildings in those places, and most of the military buildings around El Arish.

As UNEF did not dispose of engineer resources large enough to rebuild the destroyed communications with the necessary speed, we had to call on the Egyptians for assistance. They quickly organized large gangs of labourers, directed by a few engineers, who restored a temporary surface to the North Road, which enabled us to get essential UNEF transport over it. Soon thereafter they got the railway working again to El Arish. To restore the surface of the roads to good motorable condition took a good deal longer, but it was gradually completed in the next few years.

The main principle upon which UNEF operated was to interpose itself between the armed forces of the two sides, and so to prevent hostile acts, which could have restarted the fighting. It was clearly desirable to keep the main bodies of Egyptian and Israel troops as far as possible away from each other. As we had no means of controlling how the Israelis disposed their troops behind the screen with which we were in contact, this involved persuading the Egyptians not to return to the Sinai in force. The Secretary-General negotiated a sort of gentleman's agreement to this effect in December 1956, with Dr Fawzi. It probably was not inconvenient to the Egyptians at that time, as they had a good deal of reorganizing and re-equipping of their forces to do as a result of the campaign. Also, the destruction of communications and quarters made it difficult to maintain troops in the forward area. So they found it sufficient to send back the civil police who had kept order in El Tor and El Arish, the only populated places in the Sinai, and also units of the frontier force, a paramilitary organization whose duty was controlling the Bedouin and preventing smuggling. The Egyptians also sent a small military force, of about a battalion group, to El Arish later, claiming that the civilian administration needed this backing to their authority.

I would have preferred that the Egyptian armed forces in the Sinai should have been kept to this minimum, but the United Nations had no authority to prevent the Egyptians from sending their troops into the territory if they chose to do so. It was within their boundaries, and none of the General Assembly resolutions had placed any restrictions on what they could do in it. So, in the course of the next three years the Egyptians gradually built up the number of their troops in the El Arish-Abu Aweigila area, but they remained much below the strength kept there in 1956.

The advance of UNEF had been through the depopulated waste of the Sinai, so the arrival at El Arish and its take-over from the Israelis was something of an event, marking the end of a phase. Detailed arrangements for the take-over had been made, so that when the Israelis moved out of one end of the town, the Yugoslavs would move into the other, and so avoid any interval of public disorder which might involve shooting and the paying-off of old scores—perhaps violence against those suspected of having collaborated with the Israelis. However, the arrangements worked very well, and there were no disturbances. The population demonstrated its joy on liberation, and welcomed UNEF with manifestations of friendliness. The Captain of H.M.C.S. *Magnificent*, Fraser-Harris, flew me in his helicopter to El Arish, where we arrived just as the long line of Yugoslav armoured cars and personnel-carriers began to move in, and were being met by clumps of celebrating Arabs.

The pilot set the helicopter down in a large sandy lot at the edge of town, and in a minute it was surrounded by cheering Arabs. Fraser-Harris jumped out, to try to push them back out of danger of having their heads chopped off by the whirling rotor-blades, and was promptly embraced and kissed by three or four large and rather dirty Arabs. He hastily disentangled himself from his admirers, and got back into the helicopter, which rose and came down again in a place where we could be protected from the crowd's enthusiasm by the Yugoslav troops.

I went in an UNMO jeep to municipal headquarters, moving slowly through crowded streets, with a Yugoslav soldier fending off the numerous celebrants who wanted to be passengers. Eventually we got into a room filled to bursting with an assortment of officials and citizens, from ancient and gentle-mannered sheikhs (religious leaders) to small boys, and a large detachment of gloomy Egyptian officials who had been expelled from the Gaza Strip by the Israelis a few days before. The street in front of the building was swarming with grinning and shouting inhabitants. In a small cleared space a gap-toothed grandmother was performing a kind of victory dance, vociferously encouraged by the crowd, while in the doorways of houses near by, other women (strictly unglamorous types) had appeared, emitting the shrill ululations of triumph.

We in UNEF had not been sure of what kind of reception we should have, and we were very heartened by the first surge of enthusiasm. We felt that we were really being received as liberators, and the Yugoslav colonels, Radosevic and Vojvedic, and their troops were very happy. They deserved this cordial greeting after their long struggle across the sand-dunes.

However, there were features to the demonstration that were significant, in the light of what happened later. For one thing, a great deal of the shouting, after the first half-hour, was done by groups of schoolboys, under the direction of young men who seemed to be schoolmasters, sometimes carried aloft of the group on the shoulders of some of its members, in a technique whose origins are well known, and which became distressingly familiar to us after the entry into the Gaza Strip. The principal chant was " Yahya Tito, Yahya Tito ; Yahya Nasser, Yahya Nasser " (" Long live Tito ; long live Nasser "). Towards the end some one discovered who I was, and, with the traditional Arab politeness, they threw in an occasional " Yahya el Jineral Beernz."

About the end of December the Egyptians raised the question of an exchange of prisoners. I took this up with General Dayan, and after a period of negotiation, with the parties between whom we were mediating each suspecting the good faith of the other, the exchange began on January 21, 1957. It was carried out at a point a few kilometres west of Rafah Camp, approximately on the line of the forward posts of UNEF. The operation took a week or so ; we had to transport the released Egyptian prisoners of war in our trucks to railhead, some fifty kilometres back. They came in batches of about 500 a time, and there were nearly six thousand of them in all. When half the Egyptian prisoners had been handed over the Israeli prisoners were returned. There were only four of them, and three of these had been taken in raids and counter-raids in the autumn of 1955.

The long pause between UNEF's arrival at the International Frontier on January 22, 1957, and its entry into the Gaza Strip on March 6 was occupied with political negotiations and manœuvring in the United Nations General Assembly and at Washington. A summary of these complex and often tedious proceedings will be necessary in order that the reader may understand why the power of UNEF was so limited once it moved into the Strip.

On January 19 the General Assembly passed a resolution reiterating its demand that the Israelis evacuate the remaining positions they held in the Sinai and the Gaza Strip, and withdraw beyond the Armistice Demarcation Line. On January 23 Mr Ben-Gurion gave Israel's reply in a Knesset speech. After reciting the Israel apology for the invasion of Egypt (see page 181), which he characterized as an act of self-defence, he said that Israel must have specific guarantees for the free passage of her shipping through the Strait of Tiran and to Eilat, before she would evacuate Sharm El Shaikh and the strip along the shore of the Gulf of Aqaba through which ran the road which was her line of communications to the place. He also said that Gaza was not part of Egypt ; that the United Nations force by its very character would be unable to prevent the organization of *fedayeen* by the Egyptian authorities in this area, or prevent *fedayeen* incursions into Israel territory. The entry of the UNEF into the Strip would result in a deterioration of the security position of the Israel settlements on the borders of the Strip, and in fact everywhere within Israel's limited area. However, in consideration of the position taken by the Assembly, Israel would not maintain armed forces in the Gaza Strip. But for the good of the inhabitants and their neighbours the Israel administration would have to remain while a suitable relationship was established between it and the United Nations.

On January 25 Mr Hammarskjöld reported to the General Assembly, rejecting the idea that an Israel administration should remain in the Gaza Strip, which had been placed under Egypt's control by the General Armistice Agreement. He also observed that any changes which the General Assembly might propose in the position in the Strip which differed from that created by the GAA, and widening of the United Nations' administrative responsibilities in the area, would have to be based on agreement with Egypt.

The Secretary-General proposed that the UNEF should be deployed along the demarcation line in accordance with his second report (of November 6, 1956), which had been endorsed by the General Assembly. This would mean that it would have units in the Gaza Strip and also opposite the El Auja demilitarized zone. If the zone were actually demilitarized as provided for in Article VIII of the GAA—*i.e.*, evacuated by the Israelis—it would also be possible for UNEF to be stationed in it, but this would require another decision of the General Assembly and the consent of the parties to the GAA.

As for the Gulf of Aqaba and the Strait of Tiran, he said that the withdrawal of the Israel forces from this area would be followed up by UNEF, as elsewhere, and that it could help in maintaining quiet, but could not be used " so as to prejudge the solution of the controversial questions involved." He further said that in international law the character of the waterway might be considered to entail the right of innocent passage through its waters. However, a legal controversy as to the extent of the right of passage existed.

Mr Eban addressed the General Assembly on January 28, stating the Israel position, essentially as it had been given in Mr Ben-Gurion's speech of January 23. (See page 246.) Israel demanded assurances against any interference with her shipping before she would withdraw from Sharm El Shaikh.

Who was to give Israel these assurances? Obviously she hoped to obtain them primarily from the United States. Mr Cabot Lodge, however, in a speech just before Mr Eban's, had said, " The U.S. thinks that Israel must withdraw its forces without further delay." He supported the proposals of the Hammarskjöld report, and the suggestion that UNEF be deployed on both sides of the demarcation line. As for the Tiran Strait, he thought UNEF should be stationed there after the Israeli withdrawal. But the assurances sought could only be given effect—and should be given effect—after Israel had complied with the Assembly resolutions.

About a week passed, during which there were negotiations among the representatives of the nations which had taken a leading part in attempting to find a solution to the situation created by the Israel invasion of Egypt. Eventually, two resolutions were sponsored by Brazil, Colombia, India, Indonesia, Norway, Yugoslavia, and the United States, and on February 2 were passed by the General

Assembly. The first of these deplored that Israel had not completed its retirement behind the Armistice Demarcation Line despite the repeated requests of the General Assembly, and called upon her to withdraw without further delay. The second resolution approved the Secretary-General's report, called upon the governments of Egypt and Israel scrupulously to observe the provisions of the 1949 General Armistice Agreement, and stated that the maintenance of the armistice agreement, after the Israel withdrawal, required the placing of the UNEF on the Armistice Demarcation Line, and the implementation of other measures as proposed in the Secretary-General's report.

Mr Cabot Lodge, who was the principal speaker sponsoring the resolution, declared, " In all seriousness and solemnity, I cannot predict the consequences which can ensue if Israel fails to comply with the will of this Assembly as expressed in the resolutions." This was generally regarded as a threat to apply sanctions.

Dr Mahmoud Fawzi said that UNEF was not in Egypt to resolve any question or to settle any problem, but to put an end to the aggression committed against Egypt and to secure the withdrawal of the Israel forces behind the demarcation line. UNEF after this withdrawal must take up positions on both sides of the line, and Egypt's consent was an indispensable prerequisite to the entry, stationing and deployment of the force.

Other interventions in the lengthy debate set forth the attitudes of different important national blocs with regard to the UNEF. These set the limits on UNEF's action after entry into the Strip, and explain the lack of progress towards the solution of the basic difficulties inhibiting peace between the Arabs and Israel. Summaries are given in Note 37.

On February 3 the Israel Cabinet met and decided to reject the demands of the Assembly resolutions, and stand by its previous position. The essentials of this were : not to withdraw from the Gaza Strip, and not to withdraw from Sharm El Shaikh until freedom of Israel shipping to pass through the straits was guaranteed. Israel thus defied the opinion of the world, as expressed by the General Assembly. The first of the February 2 resolutions had been passed by seventy-four votes in favour, Israel and France against, Luxembourg and the Netherlands abstaining. The second resolution had been passed by fifty-six votes in favour, none against, and twenty-two abstentions—the Arab bloc, the Soviet bloc, Israel, France, and the Netherlands.

The Arab-Asian bloc now began to press for, and other nations began to consider applying sanctions against Israel. The United

States had already applied a kind of sanction, by cutting off all aid to Israel from governmental sources ; and this had a serious effect. On February 4 the *Jerusalem Post* published an article, based on information from the Finance Ministry, in which it was stated that as a result of losing the U.S. aid Israel would have to reduce its budget by £I 90 million ($50 million) out of a total budget of £I 850 million. Israel would not receive the expected $25 million grant-in-aid, nor U.S. agricultural surpluses, from which she had expected to benefit in the amount of $30 million, nor any of the hoped-for export-import bank loan of $75 million. It would mean a reduction in the standard of living. On February 6 the *Jerusalem Post* reported the projected budget cut as £I 100 million, and that 2500 civil servants might have to be released as a measure of saving. The increased expenditures due to the Sinai campaign and its consequences, combined with the cutting off of U.S. aid, intensified the inflationary pressures always present in Israel, and the danger was seen by economists as acute.

On February 5 Mr Dulles told a Press conference that the U.S. would give serious consideration to a UN call for sanctions against Israel to support its resolutions calling for Israeli withdrawal. However, he said that the U.S.A. would not take unilateral action. On February 10 it was divulged that Mr Ben-Gurion had refused an appeal by President Eisenhower that the Israel forces should be withdrawn.

On February 9 (a sabbath) mass meetings had been held in many cities, towns, and villages in Israel to demonstrate the nation's determination to hold to her demands, in spite of the threat of sanctions. Resolutions were passed which said, " The citizens of Israel . . . strongly protest the attempts being made in the Assembly and other UN institutions to strike at Israel's security and equality of rights by an act of discrimination which constitutes a violation of the principles of the Charter." Many of the speakers expressed hostility towards Mr Hammarskjöld, who had been pilloried in the Israel Press as an enemy of their country and a friend to Nasser.

The situation now was that the General Assembly was insisting that Israel obey its reiterated demand to withdraw her forces behind the Armistice Demarcation Line ; whereas Israel refused to do so unless she retained the civil administration of Gaza and was given guarantees for free passage through the Tiran Strait— guarantees which would be effective only if given by the U.S.A. The Arab-Asian bloc, backed by the U.S.S.R., had begun to demand sanctions against Israel because of her non-compliance, and no such sanctions could be effective, or even be voted, unless the U.S.A. was to participate in them. The U.S.A. had promulgated the Eisenhower Doctrine, in an effort to re-establish among the Arab states a measure in Western influence, which had been wrecked by the Suez adventure. It was necessary to break the deadlock quickly, as the Egyptian Government was holding up the clearing of the Suez Canal until the Israelis withdrew ; and each day the Canal remained closed meant an enormous cost to the economies of the United States' west European allies. The U.S. Government, therefore, was faced with most difficult decisions. Needless to say, all the resources of Zionist influence in the United States, and they are great, were mobilized to induce the Government to give guarantees to Israel and abstain from sanctions against her.

From February 4 to February 10 there were negotiations and an exchange of letters between the Secretary-General and Mr Eban, the Israel representative, and on February 11 the Secretary-General reported to the General Assembly that these negotiations had produced no result. He also gave the following warning in regard to the proposal to apply sanctions against Israel :

> The Charter has given to the Security Council means of enforcement and the right to take decisions with mandatory effect. No such authority is given to the General Assembly, which can only recommend action to Member Governments, which, in turn, may follow the recommendations or disregard them. . . . If . . . collective measures were to be considered . . . the effect of such steps, while supporting efforts to achieve peaceful solutions may perhaps . . . be introducing new elements of conflict.

This may be read as a caution that some states might not support sanctions against Israel, which would therefore be of doubtful effect.

No report of the negotiations and pressures required to induce Israel to comply with the resolution calling for withdrawal of her forces from the Gaza Strip and Sharm El Shaikh would be complete without a reference to the television address given by President Eisenhower on February 20. By this time the Israeli " justifications " for their attack on Egypt, and their current refusal to withdraw to their former limits, had obtained wide acceptance, it seems, in the United States ; and many politicians of both parties were talking against imposing any sanctions on Israel. The President felt it necessary to explain the situation, as he saw it, to the American people. I have selected a few key passages from the speech.

" The future of the United Nations and peace in the Middle East may be at stake," he began, and then went on to explain the importance of the Middle Eastern issues to the American people, and recalled the position taken by the United States in the crisis of the previous November. He stated that

> Britain and France have withdrawn their forces from Egypt. Thereby they showed respect for the opinions of mankind. . . .
> . . . the United Nations must renew with increased vigor its efforts to bring about Israeli withdrawal. . . . Repeated, but so far unsuccessful efforts have been made to bring about a voluntary withdrawal by Israel . . . both by the United Nations and the United States. . . .
> But Israel insists on firm guarantees as a condition to withdrawing its forces of invasion. . . . Should a nation which attacks and occupies foreign territory in the face of United Nations disapproval be allowed to impose conditions on its withdrawal ?
> If we agree that armed attack can properly achieve the purposes of the assailant, then I fear we will have turned back the clock of international order. We will have countenanced the use of force as a means of settling international differences and gaining national advantages. . . . If the United Nations once admits that international disputes can be settled by using force, then we will have destroyed the very foundation of the organization, and our best hope for establishing a real world order.

On February 22 Mr Hammarskjöld supplemented his report of February 11 by the following statement :

> The Secretary-General states with confidence that it is the desire of the Government of Egypt that the take-over of Gaza from the military and civilian control of Israel in the first instance would be exclusively by the UNEF. It may be added that the Government of Egypt has the willingness and readiness to make special and helpful arrangements with the United Nations and some of its auxiliary bodies, such as UNRWA and UNEF. For example the arrangement for the use of UNEF in the area should ensure its deployment on the armistice line at the Gaza Strip and the effective interposition of the Force between the armed forces of Israel and Egypt . . . [to assist in] putting a definite end to all incursions and raids across the border from either side. Furthermore, with reference to the period of transition, such other arrangements with the United Nations may be made as will contribute toward safeguarding life and property in the area, of providing efficient and effective police protection : as will guarantee good civilian administration ; and as will protect and foster the economic development of the territory and its people.

On February 26, when the General Assembly again met to deal with the question, the Secretary-General issued a note to inform it of the position after further negotiations outside the United Nations, which had shown some promise of breaking the deadlock. But the statement showed that the dispute was still unresolved. In answer to specific questions from Mr Eban, the Secretary-General had said that before the UNEF was withdrawn from Sharm El Shaikh, as a result of Egyptian insistence or otherwise, an indicated procedure would be for him to inform the Advisory Committee on the United Nations Emergency Force, which would determine whether the matter should be brought to the attention of the Assembly. Mr Eban had stated that Israel remained totally opposed to the resumption of Egyptian civilian or military control of Gaza, and asked whether a *de facto* United Nations administration in Gaza as referred to in the Secretary-General's February 22 statement would exclude Egypt's return to the Strip. The Secretary-General replied that he could neither annul nor detract from any rights existing under the armistice agreement. His statement indicated practical arrangements within the framework of Egyptian control of the territory as established by the agreement, and could, therefore, not be understood as limiting Egyptian rights.

Mr Eban also said that he did not consider the question of stationing UNEF on both sides of the demarcation line and in the El Auja area was related to the problems of the Gulf of Aqaba and Gaza.

The last days of February saw a series of conferences between the indefatigable Mr Eban and Mr Dulles, and Mr Hammarskjöld, as well as many other discussions between these three diplomats, or their assistants, and the delegates of Egypt and other member nations who had taken a leading part in the debates and negotiations. The Israeli Cabinet held numerous sessions. At last, on March 1 in the General Assembly, Mrs Meir, Israel's Foreign Minister, announced that Israel would withdraw from Sharm El Shaikh and the Gaza Strip, in compliance with the demands of the February 2 and previous General Assembly resolutions.

However, she stated that Israel's withdrawal was made on certain assumptions. She cited Mr Dulles' memorandum to Mr Eban of February 11, concerning the right of free and innocent passage in the Gulf of Aqaba, and asserting the United States' intention to exercise that right. She also recalled the statements of the U.S. representative in the General Assembly on January 28 and February 2, to the effect that it was essential that units of the UNEF should be stationed at the Strait of Tiran to ensure the separation of the Israeli and Egyptian forces. She said that the Israeli Government was concerned that UNEF troops might be withdrawn, in circumstances which might again permit interference with free and innocent passage, which would menace peace and security. But her Government had noted the assurance by the Secretary-General, on February

26, that before the UNEF troops would be withdrawn he would consult the Advisory Committee on UNEF, which could refer the question to the General Assembly.

The Government of Israel would also withdraw all her forces from the Gaza Strip, on the basis of the following assumptions : that when the Israeli forces withdrew UNEF would be deployed at Gaza, and that the transfer of military and civil control from the Israelis would be exclusively to the UNEF. Israel trusted that these responsibilities of the United Nations in the administration of Gaza would be maintained until a definite agreement as to the future of the Gaza Strip could be reached. Israel declared that if the situation in the Gaza Strip should revert to the previous conditions she would resume full liberty of action to defend her rights.

The Government of Israel proposed an immediate meeting between General Dayan and myself in order to concert measures to allow the United Nations to assume its responsibilities in Gaza.

Other statements made in the General Assembly are significant in view of subsequent events. Mr Cabot Lodge, the U.S. delegate, spoke immediately after Mrs Meir and said that the U.S. took note of the declarations in the Israeli representative's speech, but did not consider that these declarations rendered the Israeli withdrawal conditional. The declarations either restated what had already been said in the Assembly, or by the Secretary-General in his reports, or else expectations which did not seem unreasonable, in the light of previous decisions of the Assembly.

Later, Dr Fawzi, the Egyptian representative, spoke. He said that he understood that the General Assembly was unanimous in counting on a complete and honest application of its resolutions demanding the immediate and unconditional withdrawal of Israel. This position, the only one the General Assembly could take, remained unaffected. Nothing that had been said in the Assembly or elsewhere could alter this fact or condition its validity, nor could it affect the scope and legitimacy of the rights of Egypt and the Arab population of the Gaza Strip.

These observations in themselves were not incompatible with the Secretary-General's statement of February 22 ; but it is certainly to be remarked that Dr Fawzi did not publicly commit Egypt to the position outlined by the Secretary-General.

Some light on the attitude of Egypt and the Arab states with regard to the administration of the Gaza Strip after the Israelis had withdrawn can be gathered from the reaction to the proposal for a measure of internationalization which was made by Mr Pearson on February 26. After saying that Israel must first of all withdraw from the Strip in accordance with the decisions of the General

Assembly, he cited the Secretary-General's February 22 statement indicating that the Government of Egypt would agree to the United Nations taking over peace-keeping and administrative functions within the Gaza Strip during a transitional period. These propositions were common ground.

Then he proposed a further extension of United Nations' functions and responsibilities.

> . . . after Israel's withdrawal, the United Nations should by agreement with Egypt accept responsibility to the maximum extent possible for establishing and maintaining civil administration in the territory ; in fostering economic and social welfare, in maintaining law and order. . . . To co-ordinate and make effective arrangements to this end the Secretary-General might decide to appoint a United Nations Commissioner for Gaza . . .

Mr Pearson's proposals were replied to by Abd El Moneim Rifai, the Jordanian representative, the same afternoon. He said,

> Mr Pearson . . . is trying now to take the Gaza Strip away from its Arab administration and put it under an international régime. He is trying not only to make such a major change in the status of the territory under consideration, but also to widen the functions and tasks of the United Nations Force in such a way that it will become able to solve territorial problems. This definitely goes far beyond the functions of the force, which functions should not touch on any controversial issue political or legal in nature.

He then went on to cite statements made in the Assembly by Mr Krishna Menon and agreed to by Mr Cabot Lodge which denied that UNEF could have any such function.

From the attitude expressed, it could well have been forecast that any attempt to establish a United Nations civil administration in the Gaza Strip would not be successful.

CHAPTER 18

UNEF enters Gaza

Map 3

UNTIL Mrs Meir announced in the General Assembly on March 1 that the Israeli forces would be withdrawn from the Gaza Strip, I had received no instructions that UNEF would be responsible for civil administration in the area. In a message sent on January 20, I had asked for a forecast of the functions of UNEF when it finally reached the Armistice Demarcation Line, and how long it would stay there. But owing to the confused political situation at that time, the Secretary-General was unable to give me a definite answer. As will be clear from the account in the last chapter of the bargaining and pressures during the month of February, it was not certain until the very last whether Israel would indeed withdraw; and, if she should, on what terms the withdrawal would be made, or to what extent the United Nations could undertake civil administration. Therefore little could be done in the way of planning for this aspect of UNEF's duties.

Of course we at UNEF headquarters had read the reports of the discussions in the General Assembly and elsewhere, and at our regular staff conferences had talked about what sort of administrative duties in the Strip we might have to carry out. We had dealt with the Governor of Port Said on certain administrative matters, but when we 'liberated' Port Said, El Tor, and El Arish, the only three centres of population we had yet entered, it had been understood that the Egyptian civil authorities, including police, would begin to operate very quickly after the invaders had departed, and UNEF had established itself. This had happened in all of these places.

UNEF had also obtained information about conditions in Gaza through Lieutenant-Colonel R. Bayard, Chairman of the Egypt-Israel Mixed Armistice Commission in Gaza when the Israelis invaded, and Lieutenant-Colonel W. M. Brown who succeeded him. Thus we knew something about popular feeling there, how the local administration functioned, and the names of some of the notables who had held office in former and existing municipal councils. We also received special information which UNEF would need on entry, relating to buildings for headquarters, hospitals and stores, camping-sites, vulnerable points, and so forth.

We had tried to get copies of the manuals dealing with the system of military government set up by the Americans and British in occupied enemy territories towards the end of the Second World War, but did not succeed in getting them in time. We considered a staff organization to deal with civil affairs, on the lines of that set up in the Second World War, so far as we could remember it. This would have required quite a number of additional officers or United Nations officials and subordinate staff. In view of the uncertainty, we did not propose to UN H.Q. that such additional staff should be recruited. We had to await developments.

I had gone to Cairo on March 1, and first heard from the Associated Press that the Israelis had announced that they would withdraw. This was about 11.30 P.M. local time, or 4.30 P.M. Eastern Standard Time. About 3.30 A.M. on March 2 I received instructions from the Secretary-General to meet General Dayan as soon as possible, to concert arrangements for the Israeli withdrawal and UNEF take-over. General Dayan set a meeting for 2.30 P.M. at Lydda, but cancelled it before it could take place, saying that he had not been given final instructions by his Government, and must postpone our meeting until he received them.

During March 2 there were reports that the Israeli Cabinet was in session, reconsidering its policy. They were dissatisfied with the speech of Mr Lodge, the U.S. delegate, in the General Assembly. He had said, in regard to Mrs Meir's statement of Israel's " understanding and expectations " (see Chapter 17, page 252) that these were not to be taken as " conditions " for the Israeli withdrawal, but that they seemed to be " not unreasonable." This half-hearted phrase was, so it was said, substituted at the last moment for the word " legitimate." As the Israelis had been counting on full U.S. support for ensuring that the " assumptions " would indeed be realized, the Government and public were resentful. So the Cabinet debated whether, with so little assurance of attaining the objects for which they claimed they had gone to war last October, they ought to pull out their troops. The political implications for Mr Ben-Gurion's Government were obvious. It was being rumoured that the Ahdut Ha'Avoda and Mapam parties were considering withdrawing from the coalition if the Israeli forces came out of the Strip without a valid guarantee that the Egyptians would not be permitted to re-enter.

I sent a message to the Secretary-General asking what I should do if, when UNEF had taken over control of the Strip, the Egyptian authorities should ask me to allow the return of an Egyptian Governor, administrative officials, and police, as they had done at El Tor and El Arish. What was I to say to General Dayan if he asked whether I would admit any Egyptians to the Strip? I said I understood that no final policy had yet been formulated, but what was the answer for the next few weeks? I knew that the take-over was to be exclusively by UNEF " in the first instance," but how long was the first instance to last?

Mr Hammarskjöld replied the next day, referring to Mr Lodge's statement that Israel's withdrawal must be considered as unconditional. I was not to discuss with Dayan what would happen after the initial take-over. The future of the Strip would be determined within the framework of the GAA.

I was to assume that UNEF would be responsible for all administration for the couple of weeks necessary to negotiate more definite arrangements with Egypt. Our authority in Gaza must be derived from Egypt as the power " in control " (according to the GAA) and, of course, not from Israel as the power in military occupation.

On receipt of these instructions, we began to bring our tentative ideas on civil administration into more definite form. Of course, the problem of taking over the Strip from the Israeli military force, and ensuring that there was no civil disturbance, rioting, or other violence, was uppermost in our mind. We anticipated that if this could be ensured, there would be time to tackle the other problems of civil administration of the Strip and to get any expert assistance that would be needed through United Nations. This, of course, was based on an assumption that the local Arab authorities—police, minor officials, town and village councils, and *mukhtars* would co-operate with UNEF.

Our plans for taking over from the Israelis, the order in which the troops would move in, the parts of the Strip they would occupy, the important buildings and installations they should guard, and the methods of controlling any tendency towards mass movements, had been worked out by the UNEF staff some time before. The units had been instructed as to their probable tasks and were positioned so that they could move in quickly when orders were given.

There were certain portents of the opposition which was to arise to UNEF's taking over of the civil administration. We did not give any great weight to them at the time, but, in the light of later events, they were significant. The first sign was that as soon as UNEF moved up close to the boundary, on January 22, many refugees from the Strip began to filter out to El Arish. Apparently the Israelis at first made no serious effort to stop people from the Strip moving out in this way, and every day one might see hundreds of Arabs, mainly youths or young men of military age, trekking along the main road from Rafah towards El Arish. Indeed, so many came out that to feed them became a difficult problem for the Egyptian authorities. They nearly all held refugee cards, entitling them to rations and the other limited benefits distributed by UNRWA. The Egyptian authorities wanted UNRWA to feed these people in El Arish, but this was impracticable. Neither the Egyptians nor UNRWA nor, of course, UNEF, wanted to see this exodus, but the Egyptians were not prepared to take a strong stand and issue instructions against it. UNEF could not drive the exodus back into the Strip, nor indeed stop the movement. So we were able to do nothing more than search them for arms, and hope that no trouble would ensue.

After a while, when the refugees found that there was nothing for them at El Arish except a very scanty distribution of food from the Egyptians, a reverse migration set in. Again, the Israelis did not, rather surprisingly, take effective measures to stop this movement until a week or so before they finally evacuated the Strip.

The large number of able-bodied young men seen walking to El Arish had made me think that they were either *fedayeen* or members of the Palestine Army who had " gone underground " during the Israeli occupation and now were moving out to be reorganized by the Egyptians. However, we saw no specific signs of this, and if the Egyptians were doing anything of the kind, they sent the young men back to Egypt for processing. But it is certain that with all the traffic back and forth the Egyptians had an excellent opportunity to send instructions and orders into the Strip as to what attitude its population was to adopt towards UNEF after the Israelis had gone. And it seems certain that the demonstrations and disturbances which followed shortly after our entry must have been organized in this way.

On March 4 Lieutenant-Colonel W. M. Brown (New Zealand Army), who had succeeded Lieutenant-Colonel R. Bayard (U.S. Army) as Chairman of the MAC in Gaza, reported that meetings of troublesome and youthful pro-Nasser elements were being set up. This information proved very accurate.

On March 4 I flew up in an Otter from El Ballah H.Q. to El Arish to discuss final arrangements for the move into Gaza with Colonel Lundqvist, the Chief of Staff. At 2.30 P.M. I got an urgent request from General Dayan to meet him at Lydda that afternoon. After an exchange of messages I flew on to Lydda, and found Dayan waiting there for me. He had apparently been ordered by his Government to get his troops out of the Gaza Strip and Sharm El Shaikh as quickly as possible, and made no difficulties of any sort. The contentious questions I had feared and sought instructions about were not raised.

General Dayan suggested that UNEF should take over from the Israeli forces in the camps and towns in the Strip during the hours of darkness, when a curfew was in force, and all inhabitants had to be indoors. This coincided with my ideas, so we arranged that the take-over should take place during the night of March 6–7. However, some Israeli equipment and the troops guarding it at Rafah Camp could not be removed until the afternoon of the 8th. They could then withdraw directly to the east, by a route that would not taken them through the length of the Strip.

Owing to the difficulty of the route from Sharm El Shaikh to Israel territory, the withdrawal from there could not be completed before March 8. This time was accordingly set for the Israelis to be out, and the Finnish company to move in. A number of non-running Israeli vehicles would have to be left, under a small guard, until a vessel could take them away.

All Israeli administrative personnel would move out of the Strip when the troops did. We discussed how they could " hand over " to the UN administrative personnel whom we were in the process of assembling. We agreed on a conference on March 6 at the meeting point of UNEF and IDF west of Rafah. Owing to disturbances in the Strip, it was not possible for the Israeli administrators to get there, and the meeting was eventually held at Lydda on the morning of March 7.

As it was too late in the evening on the 4th to fly back to my H.Q. at El Arish or El Ballah when the conference with General Dayan had ended, I went to Jerusalem by road, and stayed overnight. I was able to meet there Mr Leslie Carver, Deputy Director of UNRWA, and we discussed how civil affairs in the Strip could be administered when the Israelis left. We decided tentatively on a division of responsibilities between UNRWA and UNEF. I then returned to my H.Q. at El Ballah by air.

On March 6 groups of refugees in the Strip broke the imposed curfew and, excited by the imminent departure of the Israelis, began some shooting, which was vigorously repressed. This upset the plans for daylight reconnaissance of their areas by representatives of UNEF units. However, about dusk word was received from the Israelis that they were ready to go ahead with the planned handover, and our units, which had been halted along the road west of Rafah, began to move in. All went smoothly and the Danor battalion was in Gaza by 9.30 P.M. At the same time Colonel Lundqvist, the Chief of Staff, set up an advanced H.Q. in the EIMAC building in Gaza, which had radio communication with UNEF main H.Q. in El Ballah. By 3.35 A.M. on March 7, I was able to report to the Secretary-General that UNEF troops were in position in all camps and centres of population in the Strip. The last Israelis, except for those in Rafah Camp, were out by 6 A.M.

The main H.Q. at El Ballah was now 240 kilometres by road from the troops in Gaza, and it became necessary to move it up as quickly as possible. This was not very easy, owing to shortage of transport, and the bad condition of the North Road over a good part of its length. Those vehicles not having four-wheel drive had to be sent by rail. We decided to commence the move on March 10 when the key personnel moved up. It was carried out according to plan.

On March 7 the meeting on civil administration questions was held with the Israelis at Lydda. The main subjects were currency and banking, police and legal matters, posts and telephones, railway operation, disposal of the orange crop, continued movement of UNRWA food and supplies for the refugees, which during the Israeli occupation had been shipped through Haifa, and of which there was a large stock in that port. The Israelis offered to sell us goods and services which UNEF might require.

We had, with UNRWA, assembled a group of ' experts ' to deal with these several questions, some from our own staffs, some from the UN Technical Assistance experts in Egypt. However, events marched very rapidly, ending in the Egyptians' resuming responsibility for the civil administration of the Strip within a week. Thus the team of civil administrators, or experts, got little opportunity to show what they could do.

The Israeli troops in Rafah Camp moved out by 4.45 P.M. on the 7th, ahead of their schedule.

On March 8 I flew up to Gaza. The main street was filled with processions of demonstrators. While we had at first thought that the parades which had been taking place since the liberation of the Strip were more or less spontaneous manifestations of joy at being freed from the Israeli occupation, I observed that the banners they carried and the slogans they shouted were in favour of the return of the Egyptians, and acclaiming President Nasser. I noted in my diary at the time that they showed obvious signs of outside organization. However, in reporting to the Secretary-General on that day, I said that, while there were many problems to be dealt with in the Strip, I believed they could be handled if co-operation from both sides (Egypt and Israel) continued as it then was, and there was no agitation from outside. This turned out to be an illusory hope. However, in spite of the noisy demonstrations, I saw no cause to fear that UNEF could not fulfil its task of maintaining peaceful conditions " in the first instance," and to carry out any more extended duties that should be decided upon.

I had issued the following proclamation, or notice, which had been approved by UN H.Q. :

> I, Major-General E. L. M. Burns, Commander, United Nations Emergency Force, inform you that the Israeli Defence Forces are withdrawing from the Gaza Strip and the United Nations Emergency Force, acting in fulfilment of its functions as determined by the General Assembly of the United Nations with the consent of the Government of Egypt, is being deployed in this area for the purpose of maintaining quiet during and after the withdrawal of the Israeli Defence Forces.
>
> Until further notice the UNEF has assumed responsibility for civil affairs in the Gaza Strip.
>
> I call upon all the people of the Gaza Strip to help the Force to carry out its responsibilities and to assist the Force to maintain quiet.
>
> UNRWA will continue to carry out its responsibilities and will continue to provide food and other services as in the past. UNEF and UNRWA will do their best to relieve pressing needs which may arise from the present situation.
>
> You are to remain quiet.
>
> You are to remain law-abiding and orderly.
>
> You are not to carry arms or explosives of any kind.
>
> You shall continue to observe the present curfew hours until further notice.
>
> When you are in need, you should see your local civil leaders, Mayor, Mukhtar, or Camp leader, who have been called upon to co-operate with the Force.

This notification to the Gaza populace was translated into Arabic, and distributed when the UNEF units moved in.

The Secretary-General had arranged to send Dr Ralph Bunche to Egypt to have preliminary talks with the Egyptians on the arrangements for the control of the Strip. He was expected to arrive on March 9 or 10. The Secretary-General also planned to come himself, some time after March 20.

On March 9 I received a message from Colonel Lundqvist, the Chief of Staff, who was in charge of the H.Q. at Gaza, that Egyptian agitators were active in the Strip, and that he had issued a ban on demonstrations and meetings. I reported this to the Secretary-General, and also that Brigadier Hilmy had said that he was going up to Gaza on March 11 and would open the post-offices there. I asked whether the Egyptians had promised the Secretary-General to stay clear of the Strip for any specified period.

The three principal Egyptian agents directing the agitation after UNEF's entry came in as journalists. Their names were Ahmed Said, Sami Daud, and Lutfi Abdel Qadir. Their credentials as journalists had seemed in order. The principle upon which the UN Information Services with the force worked was that any journalist in Cairo who represented a responsible newspaper or other medium of information was allowed to go in the areas where UNEF had control. This applied to representatives of Egyptian papers, of course. Naturally, there was a great influx of journalists into the Strip with UNEF, and the above-named persons came in with the rest.

In view of this disturbing news from Gaza, I decided to fly up on March 10 and have another look at things myself. I arrived at the police-station, where we had set up our advanced head-quarters, and to which the main H.Q. from El Ballah was in process of moving. Colonel Lundqvist, other officers, and I began a discussion with Mr Carver, Mr Lucas, and Mr Jamieson of UNRWA on civil administration in the Strip. Our talk was interrupted by a growing hubbub from outside, and we saw that a crowd of demonstrators, nearly all young men and youths, possibly two hundred in all, were clamouring to get in the gate that led to the entrance of the building. It was not clear what they wanted, certainly not to the Danish and Norwegian military policemen who were guarding the gate. With some difficulty the MPs got the gate shut, arrested one or two of the leaders of the disturbance, and put them in the jail which adjoined the police-station at the rear. We afterwards found out that the ostensible purpose of the demonstrators was to hoist an Egyptian flag on the flagpole in place of the United Nations flag which was flying there. But the only thing clear at the time was that they wanted trouble.

Things happened rapidly thereafter. The crowd grew noisier and more aggressive, tried to shove the gate open, and it seemed likely that in a short while they would force their way in, either through the gate or the barbed-wire fence which enclosed the buildings. I told Colonel Lundqvist that the guard had better use tear-gas bombs to clear the crowd, and found he had already given the order for this. In a minute or two the Danors began to throw the bombs. The crowd scattered quickly, though a few bold spirits tried to kick the bombs back. A reserve platoon of the Danors now arrived and quickly advanced on the crowd, which was now standing a little way off on the main road out of the effect of the tear gas. The Danors fired rifles and sub-machine-guns over their heads, and the demonstrators removed themselves on the run. Firing over the heads of a crowd is not a recommended method of dealing with riots, but in this case it worked. The demonstrators made a half-hearted attempt to gather again, and were again dispersed in the same way. They showed no desire to close with the young Scandinavian soldiers.

That ended the episode, and by 11.30 A.M. all was quiet. It was reported then that there were no casualties among UNEF troops or rioters, but later we found out that one young Arab, Mohammed el Moushref, had been struck by a bullet, apparently a ricochet. As usual, it was a more or less innocent bystander who suffered. From the evidence we were able to collect later he had not been one of the demonstrating crowd but had just arrived on his bicycle to see what was going on. He died two days later.

The situation having been got under control I left for Abu Sueri to meet Dr Bunche, who I hoped would be bringing some clearer indications of the policy which UNEF was to follow than we had up to then.

Dr Bunche arrived at Abu Sueir by RCAF airlift from Naples in the early afternoon. I brought him up to date on recent events and the connected problems. Brigadier Hilmy was there and we had a short conference together. One of the important subjects we discussed was the refusal of the Egyptian authorities to allow the 56th Canadian Armoured Reconnaissance Squadron to enter the country. The Egyptian authorities had been informed some months before that this small unit, about 100 strong, would be brought out from Canada to join the rest of the contingent, and no objection had been raised.

Dr Bunche and I gathered that the refusal was due to political causes. The Egyptians had been annoyed by Mr Pearson's suggestion in the United Nations that the Gaza Strip should be internationalized and controlled by the United Nations. Also, Mr St Laurent, the Canadian Prime Minister, had made some remarks in the House of Commons which had been construed by the Egyptians as a suggestion that if they did not consent to the opening of the Canal, force might be used against them. I had sent orders to stop the forward movement of the unit, the leading elements of which were already in Naples. It was necessary to clear up this trouble at once as the reaction of the Canadian Government and people would have been very serious had the Egyptian veto to the entry of the unit been maintained. This was particularly so as there had been much Canadian resentment following the original difficulties about the inclusion of Canadian troops in UNEF. The present matter was, of course, immediately reported to the Secretary-General, who took vigorous action with the Egyptian Government. In a few days the matter was straightened out and the Egyptians withdrew their objection. The unit arrived in Abu Sueir by March 20.

Dr Bunche and I went to Cairo and spent the night there. I was kept awake thinking of the demonstration and the action the troops had had to take against the mob, and what it purported in regard to the task which UNEF was supposed to carry out.

Up to this time we had been making our plans on the assumption that the local officials and notables would co-operate with UNEF. But it now became clear from the parades and demonstrations, and the day's serious incident, that there was a definite agitation against control of the Strip by UNEF, and in favour of the return of the Egyptians. This much was clear from the banners put up in the streets, and the slogans shouted by the paraders. The demonstrators who were mainly schoolboys and young men were, perhaps, not numerous compared to the total population, but there was no counter-demonstration, nor was there support from any of the former members of the local councils or others to whom we had spoken for the idea of a UN administration without Egyptian participation. I was forced to think of what the situation of UNEF, some 5000 in all, would be in a hostile population of 300,000.

If these troops had been part of an army of occupation, and severe measures of repression could have been used, no doubt overt disturbances could have been stopped quickly. But there was no promise of co-operation from police or anyone else if UNEF should act in such a way. Once the problem was considered, it was plainly impossible to think of UNEF's checking disorders as the Israelis had done, by shooting enough rioters to cow the rest. It would be contrary to the whole idea of UNEF and the United Nations approach to the problem, and no doubt several contingents would have been withdrawn if such a policy had been tried.

In our attempt to enlist the co-operation of some of the more important local inhabitants who had been councillors, the police, and the engineers who were responsible for running the water-pumping and electric-light plants—key people in the administrative organization—we had met a very reserved response. They were not going to commit themselves. After a day or so, a sort of formula in their replies emerged : that they would co-operate with UNEF in essential public services, but it was to be understood that their first loyalty was to the Egyptian administration, when it should be resumed. The streets were spanned with banners bearing such announcements as " Egypt is our Mother," " We will never be separated from Egypt."

We knew well enough that there was a certain party among the local inhabitants who did not love the Egyptians greatly and who, if given time and favourable conditions, might have preferred to run their own affairs under UN auspices and protection. But this party was certainly neither strong nor courageous enough, nor so organized as to be able to come forward and offer to co-operate with UNEF and UNRWA indefinitely in the absence of the Egyptians. No one could blame them. To them the signs were all pointing the other way—that is, towards a resumption, sooner or later, of Egyptian control.

It was perfectly clear from the attitude of the crowds that, whatever they wanted, they did not want rule by outsiders. There were slogans against colonialism and imperialism (the Arabic word *ista'amar* is translated as either of these " isms "). They might not have particularly desired to be governed by Egyptians, but the Egyptians who called themselves Arabs (although not always accepted as such by the Palestinians) were better than any " white " foreigners.

A good many of the slogans showed U.S.S.R. propaganda origins—notably denunciations of the Eisenhower Plan, which certainly had little connexion with the Gaza Strip, and whose purport the shouting schoolboys probably understood about as well as they did Einsteinian equations. This did not necessarily mean that those who shouted the slogans were Communists, but did show that the Communists knew how to devise propaganda which was swallowed with relish by Arab nationalists.

UNEF and UNRWA were under a great disability in trying to set up a civil administration ; we had only a handful of officers who could speak Arabic, not nearly enough for all the business that needed to be done in that language. It is true that there were plenty of Arabs who could speak English well enough to act as translators, but they suffered from the same doubts as former officials and municipal leaders : they did not wish to compromise themselves by too enthusiastic co-operation with the UN for fear of reprisals when the Egyptian administration should be resumed, and doubtless because of threats from some of the more violent demonstrators and agitators against a UN administration. We could never be sure that in translating they would convey exactly what we meant, nor that we should get the exact translation of the statements of those Arabs with whom we were communicating. This would be true, certainly, when the subject under discussion was a delicate one.

Having more or less sorted out these ideas in my mind, I imparted them to Dr Bunche next morning as we were on our way to Gaza by air. We produced together a message to the Secretary-General to try to make it clear that the situation was developing in a way very different to that which he and his advisers at UN headquarters had hoped for.

In this message we pointed out that the population was in a state of excitement and uncertainty and that demonstrations such as those on March 10 could easily get out of control. There was a danger that UNEF in self-defence might have to use more forceful methods which would result in a great commotion and outcry. We pointed out that the Egyptians apparently wanted to force the issue of their return to Gaza as indicated by Hilmy's request to take a group of some five of his officers up to Gaza with him. It might not be possible to keep the situation under control until the 21st when the Secretary-General was scheduled to arrive in Egypt. We hoped he could get there sooner. It was our opinion that the fundamental problem in Gaza was to provide an Arab government and that circumstances indicated that the Egyptians must at least have nominal authority in it.

When we arrived at Gaza all was quiet enough. We had a conference with Mr Carver of UNRWA and Colonel Lundqvist, Mr Power, and others concerning civil administration.

I remained in Gaza to which the bulk of UNEF headquarters had now moved while Dr Bunche went back to Cairo. While he was on the way we received news in Gaza that the Egyptian Government, taking the excuse that there were disorders in Gaza and that UNEF had fired on the population, which it had no right to do, announced the appointment of an Administrative Governor and stated that he would take up his functions at once. While in our message we had stated our view that there would have to be Egyptian representation in the administration of the Strip, we were astonished by the announcement of the appointment of a Governor, which came as a shock to Mr Hammarskjöld and most of the United Nations.

After receiving this news I sent a message to the Secretary-General following up the previous one in which I said that I hoped that in spite of the impossibility of United Nations being entirely responsible for administration in the Strip and the development about the Governor he could obtain assurances from the Egyptians that (a) no Egyptian troops would be sent into the Strip, (b) no fedayeen activities would be allowed or countenanced, (c) disorders would be repressed and steps be taken to round up the large quantities of arms and explosives which we knew were in the hands of the people, and finally (d) free passage of UNRWA food reserves from Haifa would be allowed and the Egyptian authorities would fully co-operate and not interfere with the UNRWA functions.

On March 11 also I saw Munir el Rais, who had been Mayor of Gaza prior to the Israeli occupation and had been imprisoned by them and released by us when we took over the jail. He had made a few requests regarding the re-opening of banks, the release of certain prisoners, and so forth. He and other members of previous councils of Gaza had come together and were discussing what they should do, but their attitude towards UNEF was very cautious, as described previously. On this occasion he seemed satisfied by the assurance that UNEF was not there to " internationalize " the Strip, but merely to fulfil the tasks imposed by General Assembly resolutions, and he showed a co-operative attitude, within limits.

On the 12th we received a message from the Secretary-General giving instructions as to the line Dr Bunche was to take in negotiations with Egyptian authorities, pending his arrival, and agreeing to the necessity for assurances from the Egyptians on the points mentioned in the paragraph above.

Dr Bunche saw Brigadier Gohar on the 12th and discussed several of the questions raised by the Egyptian appointment of a Governor.[38] Gohar said it was their intention to send the appointee, Major-General Mohammed Abd el Latif, with a staff of nine or ten administrative personnel to the Gaza Strip on the 13th. He inquired whether UNEF would resist their entry. Bunche, of course, told him that UNEF had no mandate to do any such thing, whereat Gohar seemed rather relieved. It was arranged that Bunche should see President Nasser on the following day.

On March 12 I visited the Colombian battalion at Khan Yunis and the 3rd Para Bn at Deir el Balah. There were no difficulties with the population at either place. When I returned to Gaza I heard of the death of Mohammed el Moushref, the young man wounded in the incident of the 10th. I saw Munir el Rais and asked him to help in keeping things quiet. It developed he had already done a good deal to prevent the funeral's being made into a riotous demonstration. I issued a Press statement regretting the death of El Moushref, and saying we were not in the Strip to fight with Arabs but to prevent hostilities.

On March 13 Dr Bunche saw President Nasser. His instructions were to try to get the Egyptians to delay sending the Administrative Governor into the Strip, and any other action which would make more difficult the setting up of a régime of shared responsibility between the Egyptians and the United Nations in the Gaza Strip. Dr Bunche was to press strongly for assurances that there would be no countenancing of *fedayeen* activities by the Egyptian authorities, and to try to obtain a gentleman's agreement that no Egyptian troops would be sent into the Strip. President Nasser accepted the last two points, but insisted on sending General Abd el Latif in, saying all had been arranged for March 14 and could not be cancelled. Dr Bunche was able to get President Nasser to agree to the entry of the Canadian armoured reconnaissance squadron which had been held up because of Egyptian objections, as related.

The United States Ambassador, Mr Raymond Hare, saw

President Nasser on the same day, with roughly the same purpose as Dr Bunche, but he too was unsuccessful.

Major-General Mohammed Abd el Latif made his entry into the Strip as Administrative Governor about 6.30 P.M. on March 14. It was rainy and dark, but there were enthusiastic crowds to greet him. As usual, there were some who used the occasion of general public rejoicing to further their own ends. Brigadier Hilmy, who was accompanying the group, riding in a jeep, observed one character shouting " Yahya Nasser " with immense enthusiasm. Too late, Hilmy also observed that this patriot had lifted the small valise containing his personal belongings from the jeep, and made off with them in the crowd, still loudly proclaiming his fealty to Nasser.

The next morning, it being fine, a procession formed and proceeded to the Governor's office, which was some hundred yards past the police-station on the main road towards the sea. There they halted, and there was shouting of slogans and speeches. General Abd el Latif spoke, and at one point when a section of the crowd was chanting that " UNEF must go " he silenced them, pointing out that UNEF was there with the consent of the Egyptian Government and should be treated with traditional Arab hospitality. This coincided with an official statement issued in Cairo by Abdel Kader Hatem, Director of Information, that full co-operation marked relations between UNEF and the Egyptian authorities, and that Egypt was doing what she could to help UNEF carry out the duties placed on its shoulders by the UN resolutions, also that the inhabitants of the Gaza Strip looked on UNEF as a friendly force and co-operated with them for the sake of peace, and in order that the mission entrusted to them by the UN might be realized.

This represented a sudden and drastic change of attitude from the public statements of the previous days, when UNEF had been denounced for firing on the Gaza inhabitants and seeking to coerce them, and so forth. When Mohammed el Moushref had been wounded the story in a Cairo paper had been that he had been shot by a Canadian while climbing up the flagpole. There was an attempt in some Press quarters to make the Canadians the villains of the UNEF at this time.

The switch in the " public information " line may have been made because President Nasser and his colleagues feared that there was a tendency to go too far in hostility to UNEF, and a danger that if it was not checked the force would be withdrawn, leaving the Egyptians to face the Israelis with their own resources—which at that time they were not at all anxious to do. The Strip might have been reoccupied by Israel, as the least serious consequence. Egypt had achieved her prestige-point of sending in a Governor and resuming the administrative control of the Strip, and it probably seemed judicious for them not to push their good fortune too far.

This is perhaps a convenient point to review or summarize the development of the situation regarding the civil administration of the Strip from the Secretary-General's statement of February 22 until the Egyptian Governor's entry into the Strip and assumption of functions on March 14.

If we look back to what Mr Hammarskjöld stated to the General Assembly on February 22 we note that the Government of Egypt was said to desire that the take-over from Israel would be *exclusively* by UNEF *in the first instance*. There was no definition of how long " the first instance " would endure. Then the Egyptian Government was said to be ready and willing to make arrangements for UNEF to be deployed between the armed forces of Egypt and Israel. UNEF and UNTSO (the auxiliary bodies of UN referred to) would help towards putting an end to all incursions and raids from either side. With reference to the " period of transition " (undefined) other arrangements would be made, envisaging United Nations contributing towards safeguarding life and property and providing police protection, guaranteeing good civilian administration, developing the UN refugee programme, protecting and fostering economic development.

Neither in this statement nor later, did the Secretary-General or the representatives of Egypt promise that no Egyptian administrative personnel (or military personnel) would re-enter the Strip, in spite of extreme Israeli efforts to obtain such assurance. Such a promise would have been politically impossible to President Nasser's Government. It would have amounted to an abandonment of Egypt's rights in the Strip, set forth in the armistice agreement. And these really were legal rights, as unequivocally stated by the Secretary-General on several occasions. Worse, from the viewpoint of Egypt's pretensions as champion of the Arabs, and particularly the Arab refugees in the Strip, it would have been taken as an abandonment of their cause. The prestige and perhaps the survival of Nasser's Government depended on reasserting Egypt's rights in the Strip. Later information came to us that President Nasser had disagreed with the wording of the latter half of the Secretary-General's statement of February 22 (the part dealing with arrangements after " the first instance ") and had told Fawzi he could not accept it. But this rejection by the President never reached the Secretary-General. It seems that the U.S. State Department apparently considered the Egyptians to be more committed to the principles of the statement than the UN negotiators did.

The question of timing remains. Here Mr Hammarskjöld hoped

that the assurances he received covered a longer time than they did in fact cover. He hoped, certainly, that UNEF and UNRWA would remain in exclusive control until the negotiations he expected to have in Cairo about March 21. He was certainly disappointed ; whether he was deceived also, only he and those who gave him assurances on behalf of Egypt can say. But in the last days of the negotiation for the Israeli evacuation he was in no position to insist on more definite self-denying promises from Egypt, which in the eyes of the majority of the members of the United Nations was the injured party, the victim of aggression from which un-favourable terms should not be extorted to satisfy the aggressor.

The great gap in the discussions and negotiations about who should control the Gaza Strip was that the General Assembly had no effective means of consulting the wishes of the people most affected, and those were the Arab residents and refugees in the Strip. Obviously they could not be consulted while Israel was in possession. Suggestions backed by very little evidence had been put about that the Strip population would prefer UN administration to the previous Egyptian régime. But once the Gaza inhabitants were free to make their views known, they made it clear, as described in the previous pages, that they wanted the Egyptians back. The reader may feel that they were unwise in their choice, and that it would have been better for the solution of the Palestine problem, and the refugees themselves, if they had chosen an administration under UN auspices. But certainly their mood at the time was quite otherwise, and the United Nations has no authority under the Charter, or moral justification to take over the government of fragments of peoples, especially if those people's wishes run in a different direction.

There is little to record of the period that intervened until the Secretary-General arrived on March 21 for his conferences with President Nasser and Dr Fawzi. I began to regroup the units of UNEF, of which, up to March 15, about three-quarters of the strength was guarding the various vulnerable points, such as police-stations, power and water-pumping installations, UNRWA food stores, and were posted at convenient points to provide reserves for suppressing disorders. The remaining quarter was disposed along the demarcation line to carry out UNEF's task of stopping in-filtrators. As the local police were now prepared to take responsi-bility for most of the tasks of preserving order, it was possible to reverse this proportion and get the bulk of the force out along the demarcation line. We still had to keep guards over UNEF stores, equipment, headquarters, and other important points. Also we had the responsibility of protecting UNRWA lives and property, if they should appear in danger from riotous assemblies.

We decided that El Arish would be the UNEF's air station, where our communication flight of Dakotas and Otters would be based. It would also be the terminus for flights from Naples and other points, bringing in troops on rotation, mail, and stores. Rafah was to be the maintenance area, where UNEF's reserve stocks of food, fuel and lubricants, and other base facilities would be kept. Abu Sueir was currently being used for both purposes, but with the deployment of the force on the demarcation line it was much too far away. The move to the Rafah maintenance area was carried out in the course of the next month, but it was some months more before the air component could move to the El Arish airfield, owing to the need to rebuild the hangar and other facilities destroyed by the Israelis.

After the Israelis evacuated Sharm El Shaikh on March 8, they still had to withdraw part of their transport, some by towing. The road they were going to use ran roughly parallel to the Gulf of Aqaba shoreline, and they retained control of the strip about twenty kilometres wide containing it. The UNEF troops in the Sinai closest to the northern end of the Gulf were a company of the Indonesian battalion. They remained twenty kilometres to the west of Ras El Naqb. Finally, the Israelis were all clear on March 16, and the Indonesians moved up to Ras El Naqb. The Israeli forces were now everywhere behind the October 1956 Armistice Demarcation Line, fulfilling this recommendation of the General Assembly.

The Israelis were greatly angered by the news that an Egyptian Governor was taking over administrative control of the Gaza Strip, and loudly protested that they had been deceived into believing that Egyptian administration of the Strip would not be allowed. The U.S. State Department and the Secretary-General came in for most of their ire, and Dr Bunche was accused of promptly selling the pass to the Egyptians on his arrival in the area. There were scarcely veiled threats that Israel might reoccupy the Strip, and it seems that these were not confined to the blusterings of Israeli editorial writers but had even been heard in diplomatic negotiations.

Almost immediately after UNEF had taken over, while our troops were very thin on the demarcation line and not very certain of what action they should take against infiltrators, there were a number of thefts from several of the *kibbutzim* on the Gaza border. One Israeli vehicle was blown up by a mine, alleged to have been placed by infiltrators. A letter citing these incidents was forwarded by Mr Eban for circulation to the members of the Security Council, and the Israeli newspapers hastened to point out, with support by statements of officials of the Foreign Ministry, that all this proved the uselessness of UNEF for preserving peace on the demarcation line.

All these circumstances obliged me to think of what action UNEF should take if there should be an attempt by sizeable armed forces of one side or the other to cross the demarcation line, in defiance of the Assembly's resolution calling upon them to desist from hostile acts. To what extent ought UNEF to use force in resisting such an aggression ?

Then there was the problem of what powers UNEF had to stop infiltration—individuals or small groups crossing the ADL contrary to the provisions of the GAA which both sides had been called upon to respect. What degree of force could UNEF use ? Infiltration usually took place by night, and if one of our posts or patrols saw the infiltrators they could call upon them to halt ; but it was unlikely that such a command would be obeyed, especially as it would not be given in Arabic (or Hebrew). In the past unauthorized persons moving about in this area in the dark had done so at their peril, and might be fired upon before being challenged. If UNEF could only challenge, and not fire, this would soon become known, and our presence would have little deterrent effect.

I put these problems to the Secretary-General, who in turn discussed them with his Advisory Committee. Following this discussion I was informed that UNEF should not become embroiled in hostilities with the armed forces of either side, and should not fire on infiltrators. The representatives of the contributing nations in the Advisory Committee did not at all like the idea of the force's becoming involved in any serious military action, nor did they like the idea of shooting at infiltrators, doubtless because they thought it would result in an outcry against UNEF similar to that which had followed the firing over the heads of the crowd in Gaza on March 10.

UNEF, however, did have the right to use force in self-defence, and this included the right to fire—that is, the commander of a UNEF post or small body of troops whose command was being attacked by armed groups or individuals had the right and duty to use any degree of force necessary to resist such attack. Also, UNEF posts could not be required to move from their positions, and were entitled to resist if a demand to move were followed by resort to force.

These restrictions on UNEF's liberty of action to use its weapons to ensure that nobody committed acts in contravention of the GAA and the resolutions of the General Assembly were naturally very frustrating to me, as commander. I was in some apprehension that UNEF's inability to use force would become known, and lead to its being ignored as completely ineffective, if nothing worse happened. However, nothing was made public about its powers or lack of them, if one disregarded assertions in the Israeli papers, which may have been made for the purpose of extracting information. No unfortunate incidents occurred, while as time went on we developed a system which made our troops on the demarcation line into a reasonably effective deterrent, as will be described later.

My view that UNEF should have the mandate to resist any attempt of armed forces to cross the demarcation line to the extent of its powers was based on this reasoning. The problem really was whether to resist the Israeli forces if they should try to re-enter the Gaza Strip, or the Sinai, as the Egyptian forces were in no position to invade Israel. I knew, of course, that UNEF, with no heavy weapons of any sort, and scattered over a wide area on public security tasks, could not resist a serious attack by the powerful and effective Israeli Army. On the other hand, the Israelis would never attempt to force the UNEF lines if to do so they had to fire on UNEF and cause casualties, which would bring the anger of the whole of the United Nations and most powerful sanctions down upon them at once. But if they thought that UNEF would make no armed resistance, and they could walk past our posts without interference, they might, in the mood they were in, attempt to do so and re-establish their position in the Gaza Strip, at least. They had been accustomed to pushing UN Military Observers around, and an Emergency Force which couldn't use its weapons would be little more than a corps of observers. However, though this seemed to be a possibility to me at the time, it did not happen. There were a few cases when Israeli patrols crossed the demarcation line and even fired at Arabs after crossing, but they always withdrew when requested by the UNEF troops on the spot to do so, and the IDF authorities usually expressed regret when we drew the incident to their attention, and said it was an error on the part of some very junior leader.

The Secretary-General arrived in Cairo for his conference on March 21. I joined him, having prepared briefs for him on the events since UNEF entered the Strip, and on possible future relations between UNEF and the Egyptian administration. After his first interview with Dr Fawzi, he asked me to prepare a statement of the conditions to which I thought it was necessary the Egyptians should agree if UNEF were to be able to operate on the demarcation line to control infiltration and generally to maintain peaceful conditions. I prepared this paper, and in the next day or so the principles and more important and controversial points were negotiated by the Secretary-General and Dr Bunche with President Nasser, Dr Fawzi, and Mr Ali Sabry. Some of the detail was worked out between Brigadier Gohar, Mr Ali Sabry, and myself. The agreement, or arrangement, as the Egyptians preferred to call it, was not a signed document, or even an initialled memorandum, but definite oral agreement on its terms was established between the Secretary-General and the President. Although there have been some differences of opinion as to meaning and interpretation, the arrangement worked satisfactorily during the period of my command of UNEF. The principal clauses of the agreement were as follows. I shall indicate briefly to what extent the several provisions were implemented.

Egypt was to prevent infiltration by the inhabitants of the Gaza Strip or others across the Armistice Demarcation Line, and give this policy ample publicity among the local population. She was to reinstate the penalties against infiltration which had been in force when she had previously been in control in the Strip. UNEF was to have the right to assist in this work of preventing infiltration, and the population must be fully informed of this right of UNEF by the Egyptian authorities.

The portion of the " arrangement " covering this was published by the Egyptian Government, and fairly adequate measures were taken to inform the Gaza population.

A special unit of the Palestine police was to be set up to control infiltration, and there was to be close co-operation between this unit and UNEF.

No special unit has been set up, but arrangements were made for co-operation between the units of UNEF, and the police detachments of the four districts into which the Gaza Strip is divided—Gaza, Deir el Balah, Khan Yunis, and Rafah. The co-operation has been fairly lukewarm, varying somewhat with the temperament of the governors of these districts, who are Egyptian Army majors or captains. As mentioned in previous chapters, undercover police agents are required to control raiding across the ADL. I hoped that the special police unit would undertake this work. Of course the Gaza administration has plenty of secret-police in the Criminal Investigation Department, as they refer to it, following the British nomenclature. I believe that they are effective, but UNEF has never received direct information of their activities against infiltrators.

UNEF was to have authority to take infiltrators into custody in a zone extending 750 metres back from the ADL. The Governor-General prohibited movement at night in a zone 500 metres deep, and UNEF takes into custody anyone it catches in this zone at night, and turns them over to the police for legal action. We have never been directly informed of the outcome of these cases. The reduction of infiltration in due course, however, led us to believe that effective punishments have been given in a sufficient number of cases.

We asked for authority for UNEF to fire at persons in the prohibited zone, in the hours of darkness, who refused to halt when challenged. The Egyptians did not like this provision, and finally said that they would agree to it if the Israelis would agree to the same provision on their side. Alternatively, they proposed that there should be mixed patrols of UNEF and Palestine police in this zone, who might be given the right to fire. But I refused this proposal after thinking it over, for, if the Israelis, who were patrolling right up to the ADL though only in small groups, had learned that Palestinians were patrolling on the other side, there would certainly have been exchanges of fire across the ADL, casualties among UNEF, and a deteriorating situation.

The Egyptians were from time to time to repeat the announcement of their policy of co-operation with UNEF. This has not been done formally, but the policy seems to be well understood among the population.

It was also to be made known to the people that UNEF had the right to defend itself against any hostile action, firing if necessary. I do not believe there was any formal publication of this either, but after a couple of incidents in which infiltrators had been shot after trying to rush patrols of the Danor battalion, and others after attempting to use force against the Indonesian troops, the word spread around and things became much quieter. There was no agitation about the incidents among the population.

The other provisions related to the rights of UNEF to move freely by road and by air through the Gaza Strip and over the Sinai ; the right to have its air station and terminus at El Arish and its maintenance area at Rafah, and to use Gaza as a port. We asserted the right of UNEF to defend UN property and persons in the event of civil disturbances which the Egyptian authorities could not control. This meant the protection of UNRWA against riotous mobs, which had looted and destroyed UNRWA property in the past. Usually this had followed some Israeli aggression. Fortunately, it has never been necessary for UNEF to act in this way.

This sets out the general understanding under which UNEF

operates in the Gaza Strip and in the Sinai. It took a month or so to arrive at the present working compromise, but though there were disputes and differences of opinion with the Egyptians, no serious difficulties arose. The effectiveness of the system is best shown by the statistics of incidents—thefts, firing, minings, and captures of infiltrators in the prohibited zone.[39] Incidents, while fairly numerous from March until June 1957, declined to a very low figure thereafter.

The Secretary-General made several attempts to get Israel to agree to have UNEF on its side of the demarcation line, in accordance with the recommendations he had made in his report, which had been endorsed by the General Assembly resolution of February 2, 1957. But the Israeli Government was adamant, and never showed the least sign of agreeing.

In April, when infiltrations were frequent, and the Israelis were complaining about the ineffectiveness of UNEF, we revived the proposal to construct an effective obstacle of barbed wire and possibly mines along the ADL. At first Israel advocated this strongly. Egypt seemed to be prepared to have a fence along certain portions of the demarcation line, although they voiced old objections that it seemed to mark off the ADL as an agreed border contrary to the GAA. However, when we asked the Israelis if they would agree to having a fence along their side of the ADL, or along part of it, they suddenly lost interest in the idea, and no answer to the question was ever received in spite of repeated inquiries. So the Israelis by their refusal to have UNEF on their side of the line made it easy for the Egyptians to refuse to grant UNEF the right to erect a fence or to fire at night-travelling infiltrators on their side. Between the two, UNEF's power of preventive action was very restricted, and it is surprising that infiltration has been kept to such low figures.

CHAPTER 19

Conclusion

MY purpose in writing this book has been to describe how the United Nations Truce Supervision Organization, and later the United Nations Emergency Force, operated as a means of controlling the conflict between Israel and her Arab neighbours. A summary of my conclusions as to the effectiveness of these devices for keeping the peace may be useful.

When an armed conflict is in progress it is difficult to tell what is actually happening. Both sides put out their own versions of events, usually censored and sophisticated. If the Security Council or the General Assembly of the United Nations is to take appropriate action in a confused situation of conflict obviously it should have accurate and unbiased information. What is really going on? That is the question which the United Nations first of all wants answered when it sends military observers to Palestine, or anywhere else. Later, if either of the UN organs have made decisions or recommendations, it will want observers to tell it whether the parties are complying with them.

Observers and observation groups are therefore an essential part of any peace-keeping machinery which the United Nations is likely to set up. However, their effectiveness will depend on the co-operation received from the country in which they are observing. If the host country co-operates by giving them reasonably correct and full information, and allows them to go where they must in order to ascertain the true situation, then the task of the observers is relatively easy. Unfortunately, such co-operation on the part of the host countries has seldom been experienced by UNTSO. The narrative has shown how both sides restricted the observers' movements from time to time, especially when they thought that their " military security " would be prejudiced— that is, when they had something to hide, either offensive preparations or some infraction of the terms of the GAA, such as having troops or defensive works in zones where none should have been. In its resolutions the Security Council repeatedly requested the parties to allow the observers full freedom of movement, but these requests were disregarded when the next critical situation arose.

As well as controlling the operation of the observer teams, the

Chief of Staff UNTSO had the quasi-diplomatic function of negotiating with the parties, as the representative of the Security Council, after consultation with, and usually under instructions from the Secretary-General. The purpose of the negotiations was generally either to persuade the parties not to do something contrary to the GAA, or to do something to make compliance with the GAA easier—*e.g.*, set up local commanders' agreements, allow occupation by UN personnel of observation posts in sensitive areas, and so forth.

Diplomatic negotiation is ordinarily a kind of bargaining, wherein each side hopes to get something and is prepared to make some concession to get it. The policies and purposes of the two negotiating parties must be such that at some point their interests coincide, or are parallel, if the negotiation is to be successful. In the negotiations in which the Chief of Staff UNTSO was engaged, the object of his principal, the United Nations, was to preserve peaceful conditions under the terms of the GAA. But the parties were pursuing objects which they esteemed more than the simple maintenance of peace. Israel's ultimate object is to consolidate the Zionist state, to have it accepted by the Arabs in its present form, with its present inhabitants, with no substantial repatriation of the displaced Arab refugees. And, of course, there are many Israelis who dream of expansion far beyond their present limits. The object of the Arabs is to hold Israel to a status in which she could present no threat to her neighbours, and to procure the return of that part of the Arab refugees who want repatriation, and restrict Israel at least to the boundaries set forth for the Jewish part of Palestine in the 1947 partition plan.

These basically opposed objects not only inhibit peace negotiations, as I have several times observed, but they stultified all dealings between the two sides. A point was soon reached where one side or the other reasoned : " If I agree to this proposal which will make conditions more peaceful I shall be limiting the possibility of attaining my ultimate object." So they found some pretext or other for not agreeing, while usually paying lip-service to peace, the sanctity of the GAAs and the Charter of the United Nations. Examples of hopeful negotiations or policies which broke down are the attempt to set up a local commanders' agreement for Gaza, to have a more stable agreement about Mount Scopus, and the efforts of General Glubb and the Jordan Government until March 1956 to stop marauding.

In incidents so serious that the Security Council had to deal with them, it was usually possible for the observers to get sufficiently complete information, even if one side did not co-operate. But when that information was laid before the Security Council, and even if a " strong resolution " was passed, nothing final was achieved. These resolutions never included sanctions to be applied if the parties failed to heed the Council's admonitions, nor even a warning that sanctions would be applied if the resolutions were disregarded. The effectiveness of the Council's resolutions depended mainly on the diplomatic pressure which the permanent members of the Council applied subsequently. This really meant that the United States, Britain, and France would have to either threaten to withhold benefits, or promise to furnish them on condition of good behaviour. The United States could exercise considerable restraint on Israel when it chose to do so ; Britain had influence in Jordan, while the country and the Arab Legion were dependent on British subsidy. Egypt was often willing to make a virtue of necessity, and yield to diplomatic representations, having no desire to push matters to a conclusion with Israel. France generally reinforced any *démarche* of the other powers. The Russians, on the other hand, seemed to encourage the Egyptians and the Syrians to resist any measure or policy which they did not like, and which Russia could veto in the Security Council. And after the autumn of 1955, Russian sales of arms to Egypt and Syria put them in better posture to resist any pressures from the West. Finally, with the increasing interference by Egypt in France's controversies with Tunisia, Morocco, and Algeria, and then the challenge to the West when Nasser nationalized the Suez Canal, the system of control by diplomatic pressures collapsed. After the Sinai campaign French and British power to shape events in the Middle East through diplomatic action practically disappeared. The United States remained, confronted by Russia.

There was also direct diplomatic action by the United Nations— that is, by Mr Hammarskjöld or special envoys delegated by him. Such negotiations proceeded on the assumption of goodwill and desire for peace of all the parties, and their intention to honour their obligations under the UN Charter and the General Armistice Agreements. Mr Hammarskjöld and his envoys could appeal to reason, point out that certain courses of action would probably lead to unfortunate results, and advise that more conciliatory lines should be followed. But it seemed to me that eventually the UN negotiators were reduced to trying to produce a protocol, a form of words to which both sides could agree. However, when the objections of both sides had been circumvented, these protocols usually turned out to be so vague that each side could later adopt the interpretation which suited them, and the interpretations of the two sides would of course be conflicting. There was no provision that either side would accept an independent interpretation (by UN or other arbiters) if they felt it to be to their disadvantage. It appears to have always been impossible to get both sides to sign any agreement or undertaking drawn in such precise form that there could be no escape from its exact meaning.

It is sometimes urged that bringing serious breaches of the GAA before the Security Council served a useful purpose, in that " World Public Opinion " was informed of the facts of the case, and would consequently be a sort of moral sanction against the aggressor. I regret to say that this idea never seemed to work out. The Israelis, who were the party usually condemned, were so convinced of the essential righteousness of their cause that a Security Council reproof had little impact. The only public opinion they were really concerned about was that of the Jews of America, and perhaps other influential Diaspora contributors to the Zionist cause. And they usually managed to defend their actions to the satisfaction of this audience.

How effectively has UNEF served to control the situation between Israel and Egypt ? It would seem to be the judgment of the world that it has worked surprisingly well. Four and a half years have elapsed since it was formed, and during this period all has been quiet along the ADL surrounding Gaza and the International Frontier in the Sinai. The General Assembly of the United Nations each year has voted for its continuation, though some of the poorer nations have complained that its cost is an undue burden on them. Many delegations have spoken with satisfaction of the results achieved, and expressed the view that its continuation is essential, praised the nations that have contributed contingents, and thanked those who have served in the force. (On the other hand, the Soviet bloc countries say UNEF is illegal, and will pay nothing towards its cost ; the Arab countries keep silent, and don't pay either, on the grounds that the " aggressors " should bear the cost.)

Publicists and societies concerned with finding ways and means of strengthening the United Nations' capacity for taking effective measures to maintain peace and security have hailed UNEF as the forerunner of larger, more effective and perhaps permanent " peace forces." The creation of UNEF-type forces could be a substitute for the original provisions of the Charter under which the Security Council would keep the peace, employing when necessary the military measures projected in Chapter 7, which have become inoperative because of the standing quarrel, the cold war, between the U.S.S.R. and the West. These enthusiasts for United Nations peace forces mostly overlook the limitations of UNEF. I have set out the most important of these limitations and the reasons for them in chapters 14 and 18. Those who wish to study a fuller and more authoritative statement should refer to the Secretary-General's " Summary Study of the Experience Derived from the Establishment and Operation of the Force " (UN document A/3943, 9 October 1958). For the convenience of the reader, extracts from Chapter 7 of the report, " Concluding Observations and Principles," are given in Note 40.

A resolution of the General Assembly Special Session had called on the Secretary-General to report on the feasibility of establishing a permanent UN force, which it was hoped could deal with such crises as those of 1958 in Lebanon and Jordan. The United States and other Western nations were in favour of such a force ; the Soviet Union, it need hardly be said, was strongly opposed. Examination of Note 40, or the full text, should convince one that Mr Hammarskjöld could hardly have produced an answer which could be less sanguine as to possibilities of employing UN forces in future disturbed situations, and still leave it a possibility at all. What happened to this *pianissimo* " Summary Study " is instructive.

It became apparent to the Western nations who were trying to devise a resolution which would favour some initiative towards setting up such a force, or laying the groundwork for it, that a debate on the subject would have revealed a great deal of hostility to the project, and not only from the Soviet and its satellites. Many of the Afro-Asian bloc nations were against the idea, seeing in it a possibility of a new form of " colonialist " control of their sovereign actions. India, in spite of her important participation in UNEF, was against the idea of a permanent UN peace force, perhaps thinking of its possible applications in the Kashmir problem. The Soviet bloc representatives naturally took care to intensify the fears of the Afro-Asians by every argument and insinuation. And there were many nations, principally South American, which feared additional expense, objecting as they did to their existing assessment on account of UNEF.

When it became clear that no substantial majority for the intended resolution could be counted upon, it was decided to let the whole thing drop quietly. In the *ad hoc* Political Committee, which has had the subject on its agenda, Mr Hammarskjöld made a brief introductory statement, suggesting that it would not be an appropriate time to discuss the report. The Chairman then said that he presumed that none of the delegations wanted to speak, and with hardly a pause to give anyone a chance to ask for the floor, he declared that the Committee would take note of the report and submit it to the General Assembly.

From these indications it appeared that the United Nations

was not ready for a permanent peace force in 1958, nor even for effective planning or preparation for one.

This chapter was first written in the early months of 1959, and was revised in the spring of 1961. There has been no basic change in the intervening two years. Are the prospects for peace between Israel and her Arab neighbours any better now than at any time during the four and a half years covered by this narrative? I do not believe that they are. To the extent that there have been no serious hostilities since 1956 and consequently no inflammation of passions, there has been opportunity for a calm approach to a negotiated settlement. But if there have been any such approaches, they have been shrouded in diplomatic secrecy, and so far apparent results have been nil. There has been no modification of the positions of Arabs or Israelis which would promise progress towards a negotiated peace. The power of Western nations alone to maintain peace in the Middle East until a peaceful solution is reached has declined. There is a nexus of cold-war hostility between the United States and Russia in this area, with all that implies of danger of a local conflict's getting out of hand, and even setting off a third world war.

An editorial in *The Egyptian Gazette* of March 18, 1961, dealt with the attitude of the new Kennedy administration in Washington to " The Israel Problem." *The Egyptian Gazette* is the only English-language paper published in Cairo, and, like all the Press, is strictly controlled in its presentation of political matters. There is little doubt that this editorial represents the official Egyptian governmental views. It concludes :

> Israel . . . will never of its own free will admit back the expelled Arabs nor will it do anything else to implement the orders which the world, through the UN, has given to it. But if the members of the world body, especially the United States, lived up to their obligations there would be no difficulty at all in placing sufficient pressure on Israel to force it to comply with the UN orders and the dictates of humanity.
> It is obvious that America can never expect full Arab friendship as long as the Zionist support is maintained.

There is no softening of the Arab position, as described in several places in this book. I have heard of no responsible Arab politician or publicist proposing any easier terms of settlement.

What of Israel's position? Israel is well aware that the refugee question is crucial in the attainment of the peace which they profess to desire so ardently. However, their best offer to date, made by Mr Eban during the UNRWA discussion during the General Assembly session of 1958, is that Israel would pay compensation to

Arab property owners. This would presumably be done with the aid of a United States loan, as offered by Mr Dulles in 1955.

The Israel position in 1960 as exposed in the UNRWA debate was no more forthcoming. In the Knesset, Mrs Meir, commenting on this debate, said :

> . . . the situation has changed since Israel offered to accept 100,000 Arab refugees as part of a general peace settlement. That offer had been made immediately after the War of Liberation. Children who were five or ten years old then would now be 18 and 23. To admit them now would be to admit " an army that had been brought up with a single aim : to destroy this State and the people living in it."
>
> (*Jerusalem Post*, March 22, 1961.)

With no coming-together of the positions of the two parties, and consequently no move towards the negotiation of peace, what are the prospects of the present uneasy equilibrium's being maintained? For the present it depends on Israel's superior military strength which makes it too risky for the Arab countries to resort to arms, and to the restraint on Israel exercised by the West since the Sinai adventure.

What factors tend to upset the equilibrium? The Arabs fear that continued immigration into Israel will build up such a population pressure that Israel will burst out beyond her present boundaries, seizing more Arab lands and expelling the inhabitants. Such a policy is definitely part of the programme of the extremist Herut Party, the second largest in the Knesset, and receives occasional encouragement from the speeches of leading members of the leftist labour Ahdut Ha'Avoda and the rightist General Zionist parties. The Israel armed forces, supremely confident of their ability to defeat any and all of the Arab countries surrounding Israel with ease and speed, would take on such a task with alacrity.

What is the forecast of immigration into Israel? Mr Ben-Gurion gives the " ingathering of the exiles," as he likes to call it, the first place in the tasks of Israel during the years to come. Here is an extract from his policy speech to the Knesset when it assembled for its 1957–58 session (*Jerusalem Post* October 22, 1957) : " This country was not meant solely for its inhabitants but for every Jew throughout the world who has been compelled either by circumstances or by an inner urge to return and live in his homeland." He then went on to discuss the development of the Negev, his answer to the question of where room for the many immigrants is to be found. It is presently a desert, essentially an extension of the Sinai, practically waterless, and extremely hot most of the year. Mr Ben-Gurion hopes, however, that Israeli scientists will be able to overcome these handicaps by harnessing of atomic and solar energy and the distillation of sea-water on a large scale.

In April 1958 Mr Ben-Gurion told a correspondent :

> We have yet to complete the integration of the first one million immigrants and we have to provide for perhaps half that amount or even more in the next decade, which together with growth through birthrate should mean another two million increase in our population. . . . There are many Jews throughout the world still waiting to come to Israel. If Russia allowed Jews to leave, we could expect hundreds of thousands. If I had to choose between our economic independence and admitting these peoples I would, of course, unhesitatingly choose mass immigration. (*Newsweek*, April 2, 1958.)

In mid-1958 Israel's central Bureau of Statistics published a forecast of the population of Israel (*Facts and Figures in Israel*, August 1958). At the end of 1957 it was estimated at a total of 2,000,000 approximately, of whom 1,763,000 were Jews, the remainder mainly Arabs. The population increase was estimated under three sets of assumptions as to natural increase of the present inhabitants, and rates of immigration. Immigration was 56,000 during 1956 and 71,000 during 1957, but in the four years from 1952–55 only 90,000 immigrants entered the country, giving a six-year average of about 36,000. The rates of increase and immigration considered most realistic by the statisticians would, with annual immigration of 40,000 Jews, give Israel a total population by 1960 of 2,158,000 of whom 1,928,000 would be Jews, and by 1965 of 2,560,000 of whom 2,292,000 would be Jews.

On the 1958 assumption, the population would increase by 25 per cent. roughly during the next seven years. This, in itself, would not produce irresistible pressure for an adventure to increase Israel's *Lebensraum*. But if, combined with population increase, it were not possible for the present standard of living to be maintained, then a mood for military adventure might develop. What is the present Israeli standard of living, and how is it earned—or provided ?

According to the national population and income shown in *Facts and Figures*, March–June 1958, Israeli national income *per capita* was $700 for 1957. I have converted the national income given in Israeli pounds to dollars by dividing by 1·80, the official rate of exchange. The free rate of exchange at this period was about 2·50, which would indicate that the real *per capita* income, expressed in dollars, should be lower. In any case, comparisons of national income *per capita* when a closed economy such as Israel's is concerned, can have only limited significance. It does show, however, that the *per capita* income of Israel is considerably higher than that of other countries in the Middle East, and of many European countries.

A prime factor in Israel's economic condition and development has been the massive immigration—approximately 910,000 since 1948. These immigrants—greater in number than the Jewish inhabitants of Palestine when the State was established—have had to be transported, housed, and supported until productive work can be found for them. And finding productive work has involved large investment in agriculture and industry.

The second important factor is Israel's need to keep up a relatively very large defence establishment, which is variously estimated to account for a quarter to a half of her public expenditure. Defence costs in any country are hard to establish accurately ; in Israel with its very complicated system of financing, and the high degree of secrecy maintained about all defence matters, it is practically impossible.

In spite of these factors which impose a great strain on Israel's economy, the policy of the successive Israel governments since 1948 has been to maintain full employment, and to provide a rising standard of living—which the figures quoted for national income indicate they have succeeded in doing. These policies have been financed by large deficits in Israel's external balance of payments, involving dependence on foreign grants and loans, reparations payments from Germany, and charitable remittances. They have also resulted in inflation and currency devaluation.

Capital aggregating 2·5 billion dollars was imported into Israel between the founding of the State and March 1957—that is, in nine years. In other words, the average adverse balance of payments was $278 million a year. This sum was made up from the following sources :

	$ million
U.S. grants and surplus foodstuffs	298
German reparation payments	304
Proceeds of United Israel Appeal and philanthropic donations	656
Sterling balances and foreign stocks	150
Import-export loans	107
Independence and development and other loans	258
Personal compensation from Germany	60
Unrequited imports, private foreign transfers, and miscellaneous	718
	$2551 million

Statistics for the years 1959 and 1960 so far available indicate that the adverse balance of payments has remained at the same level—that is, somewhat over $275 million a year. This is a matter of great and understandable concern to Israeli economists, financiers, and some politicians. How to close the gap in the balance of payments is a perennial topic, but as the means of doing this advocated by the financiers and economists runs counter to the established policies of the Government to bring in as many immigrants as possible, and to provide them and the existing population with full employment and a high standard of living, little has been done.

Let us consider the future prospects for the sources of income listed in the table above. U.S. grants have declined of recent years, as Israel, in view of its boasted economic development can no longer qualify as an underdeveloped country. She may still hope for about $40 million a year in agricultural surpluses, which are sold by the U.S. for Israeli pounds, which in turn are put into a fund used for financing economic development in Israel.

The reparations from Germany are paid as a general compensation for economic loss and wrongs of all kinds inflicted on Jews in Germany during the Hitler régime. An agreement in 1952 provided for the payment of $821 million. Almost half had been paid by 1958, and the payments will be completed by 1962. Most of the reparations received are in the form of production goods and transportation equipment, but a quarter of the funds has been used to pay for fuel. The capital goods received have been of great value in Israel's industrial and general development.

In addition to this general reparation from Germany, former citizens of that country, and victims of the Nazis in other countries who are to-day living in Israel, receive compensation on an individual basis for loss of property, professional earnings, and impairment of health. The total of Israel's income in foreign exchange from this source in 1960 was estimated as $105 million (*Jerusalem Post*, February 3, 1961). The recipients are, of course, obliged to exchange their German money for Israeli pounds at the Government-fixed rate. This class of payment is expected to continue for several years, but the annual income cannot be predicted.

In the financial year 1957–58, $48 million in foreign exchange was received from " institutions," the largest contribution coming from the United Israel Appeal, which receives annually about two-thirds of the amount collected through the United Jewish Appeal in the U.S.A., the balance going to local Jewish philanthropic works. The United Jewish Appeal is calling for the collection of $72·7 million in the United States in 1961, which should provide a slightly greater amount to Israel than in 1957–58. A conference of representatives of the Jewish National Fund from all countries called on Jews throughout the world to double their contributions to the JNF-UJA, citing the need to raise $1000 million in the next ten years " to complete the consolidation of the one million immigrants who have already settled, and to ensure the absorption of the third million of Israel's population." (*Jerusalem Post*, December 23, 1960.)

Between 1948 and 1957, an average of $73 million per annum in foreign currency income came from the UJA and other philanthropic donors. About 80 per cent. of this came from Jews in the United States.

In addition to these regular periodical contributions, some $495 million in Israeli bonds have been sold in the United States and Canada, since the bond investment programme began in 1950 in New York during a visit by Mr Ben-Gurion. $18 million of this total was subscribed in advance of the 1960 bond drive, and the target set calls for another $42 million. Of course these sums will some day have to be repaid—in theory, at any rate.

The question Israel economists and others involved in Israel's economic problems ask themselves is, how long can Israel's foreign currency deficit be financed in the present way? Also, how vulnerable would Israel be to pressure applied to make her change any of her policies, including defence and foreign policies, by cutting down or cutting off any of these sources of unearned foreign exchange?

Israelis can count with confidence on the continued philanthropic support of the five million Jews living in the United States (about two and a half times as many as live in Israel). Many of them doubtless grow tired of the constant appeals for money made on behalf of Israel, and they are apt to ask one, " When will there be peace ? " " When will Israel be self-supporting," and questions of a similar nature—as if one could know the answer. The organizations of prominent Jewish citizens who raise the money often seem less than happy with the policies and proceedings of the Israeli authorities who spend it, but if they suggest that they might have a share in determining policies they are told pretty smartly to mind their own business, which is the raising of more money to meet Israel's ever-increasing requirements. But, when all is said, there is little likelihood that the flow of cash from American Jewry to Israel will stop, or even seriously diminish.

Is Israel so dependent financially on the U.S.A. that in a crisis she must accommodate her foreign and defence policies to American wishes? Although loans and grants for 1957–58 only amounted to $64 million out of total foreign currency receipts of $548 million, and have decreased subsequently, loss of this revenue would be serious for Israel, with her chronic financial stringency. We have seen that the U.S.A. suspended payments as a means of pressure after the Sinai invasion in 1956, and what might have resulted had the suspension continued. From time to time there have been discussions as to whether the U.S.A., if sufficiently provoked by Israel recalcitrance, might not take even more severe measures, such as putting impediments in the way of U.S. citizens' raising and transferring money to Israel. The money raised by the UJA is classed as for philanthropic purposes, and carries income-tax exemption, an important consideration to wealthy subscribers. It has been suggested in the U.S. Senate that this privilege might be revoked. Also, any loans for foreign governments are subject to Federal Government control, and those for Israel might be embargoed.

So the goodwill, or at least the tolerance, of the United States is essential to Israel, as the possibility of drastic financial sanctions is always there. But extreme measures such as the above are not likely to be adopted, unless Israel perpetrates some aggression like that of 1956. This assumes that the unquestioning political support of Israel by American Jewry will continue. The United States Jewish community, through its economic power especially as related to many media of mass information, under the leadership of the well-organized Zionist pressure groups, exerts an influence on U.S. policy which goes far beyond what might be calculated from a counting of the so-called "Jewish vote."

Over many years, it is only Israel's side of the Palestine story which has been presented to Americans. The audience was predisposed to be sympathetic to Israel because of the horror the Nazi genocide had inspired, coupled doubtless with guilt feelings of those who have had anti-Semitic impulses. The picture of Israel as a small nation gallantly struggling to rebuild existence in its ancient home, a home guaranteed to it by the prophecies in the Bible, is accepted by the majority of non-Jewish Americans and Canadians, especially those Christians who believe fervently in Biblical inspiration. Thus the Jews of the United States determine the degree of political as well as financial support that Israel receives from the U.S.A. By supporting the policies and actions of Israel they incur a responsibility for them, in spite of having little voice in determining what they will be.

Returning to the balance-of-payments theme, it may be asked whether Israel's considerable efforts to increase productive capacity in industry and agriculture will not enable her one day to balance her imports with exports of agricultural produce and manufactures? The chances for this do not seem very bright. Citrus fruit is the most significant earner of foreign money, and brought in between

$40 million and $50 million in 1957–58. Exports of manufactures brought $33·6 million, the principal item being polished diamonds.

There appears to be no likelihood of such an expansion in Israel's industrial exports in the next few years as will fill the trade gap. Israel manufacture has no advantages over her competitors in the great industrial countries in the West (or in the Communist bloc) ; her nearest markets are closed by the Arab boycott. Her light manufactures enjoy almost a total monopoly of the Israel market, because of high tariffs and subsidies, but their quality and prices are not competitive in the world market.

Israel's natural resources are limited to potash and other minerals from the Dead Sea, some phosphate and copper deposits in the Negev. Oil has been found, but so far only a small percentage of Israel's own needs is produced. Of the exploitation of the Dead Sea minerals and copper, and of the general economic climate in Israel, the London *Economist* of June 14, 1958, had this to say :

> The potash works near the Dead Sea ran a huge deficit and is only now struggling back painfully into normal production. The new copper works in the south calculated on a fairly high copper price during a boom period and must now begin to use up the best ore available in order to keep down the threatening deficit. . . . In many cases the cart was put before the horse ; the trade unions decided what standard of living was due to the worker and did not bother whether the enterprises were able to pay for it. Differences could always be made up in various ways, by subsidies on goods on the domestic market or differential dollar rates for exports. Now that exports have to pay for an increasing part of Israel's dollar needs . . . the problem of profitability looms even larger. At present Israel exports are not cheap enough and the government comes to the help of exporters with a premium added to the official dollar rate.

The status of Israel's agriculture, in which about half a billion dollars have been invested since the foundation of the State, can be given briefly by quoting extracts from a dispatch in the *New York Times* of February 10, 1958, from its Israel correspondent. The area cultivated is 975,000 acres, of which 275,000 is irrigated. The total area of Israeli territory within the Armistice Demarcation Lines is 7993 square miles ; therefore only about 19 per cent. of the area is cultivated. The rest is desert, or rocky, bare hill country. The *Times* dispatch says,

> Today the majority of Israel's farm settlements are still not self-supporting. It will take many more years of expensive aid and subsidies before they will be. Israel has reached the apparent limit of available water sources. The only new source is the Jordan River. Either an agreement on its use must be made in the next few years

with her Arab neighbours or Israel will have to risk a war by going ahead with her part of a development plan.

If and when Jordan water becomes available, it is hoped that an additional 250,000 acres can be tilled. Much of this lies in the zone a few miles south of Beersheba. It will be expensive to farm it and difficult to live in it. Beyond this area are many miles of the Negev, but they are true desert, and all the water in the world would not help.

The last sentence is hyperbolic, but anyway the point is that there *is no more water* in that part of the world.

The statements in the *New York Times* story (and the *New York Times* is surely no detractor of Israel and its prospects) can be backed up by much data from the Israeli Press, and other publications.

So there appears no escape from Israel's economic difficulties by intensive or extensive development of agriculture. The land and the water are simply not there to greatly increase her actual accomplishment, which, in fact, has been remarkable. But it still leaves her producing only 70 per cent. of her needed food supplies, and with no prospect of profitable exports other than citrus.

What has all the above economic discussion to do with the subject of this book, which is keeping the peace in the Middle East, or more exactly on the borders of Palestine ? The relevant fact is that Israel's economic position is likely to deteriorate within the next few years. If it does there will be unemployment, financial stringency, a reduction of the standard of living—a very frustrating state of affairs for a vigorous and highly-strung people, accustomed during the last ten years to a continuous rise in living-conditions, and the appearance of great progress. Israel's leaders have the habit of putting down her economic difficulties to the boycott of all trade and economic relations maintained by the Arab states, and the pressure they exercise on other countries to limit trade with Israel. In such circumstances, there seems to me to be a great temptation to find some excuse to go to war and thus to break out of the blockade and boycott—to force a peace on Israeli terms. Besides this, there is the Jordan water question which might precipitate an outbreak.

The preceding pages will have made clear how important the support, both financial and political, of the Jews of the United States is to Israel. This support both before and after the establishment of the State has been given with the most remarkable generosity and loyalty. Yet there are tensions between the Israelis and the Jews of the Diaspora. The Jewish community in the United States is the most numerous and wealthy of the Jewish communities living in other nations, and contributes some 80 per cent. of all the funds collected for Israel. It also exercises the most important political influence on Israel's behalf, although British and French policies towards Israel are also to some degree similarly influenced by the Jewish communities in those countries.

The common phenomenon of resentment against a wealthy benefactor seems to be present in the relations between Israeli and American Jewry. To this feeling might be ascribed, in part, Mr Ben-Gurion's strictures on present-day Zionism. " The Zionist Organization has lost its soul and its Zionist significance. The longing for the return to Zion no longer lives in the hearts of its members—it is no more than a high-sounding phrase that commits no one and does not lead to any action." On another occasion he said (*Jerusalem Post*, August 13, 1957), " There seemed to be general agreement that a Jew could live in America, speak and read English, and bring up his children in the American culture—and still call himself a Zionist." If that was Zionism he wanted no part of it.

Dr Nahum Goldmann, President of the World Zionist Organization, is reported to have said (*New York Times*, March 19, 1958), " Israel began to regard the Jews of the world purely as helpers. It became indifferent or even contemptuous of Zionism. It began to feel that it could more or less fulfil its destiny without the Jews of the world." He went on to say that both Israel and the Zionist movement had been living beyond their means. The Jewish Agency, which finances immigration and settlement in Israel, was heavily in debt and would soon have to use a large part of its annual budget to repay the loan it had raised. After warning of the eventual drying-up of German reparations payments, and possible reduction of U.S. Government loans and grants, he said that he did not mean that the Jews of the world had the right to determine Israel's foreign policy or mix in her internal affairs. " But I do think that real partnership of the Jewish people will require . . . their right and duty to advise and influence the way their contributions and investments are being used."

The same sort of squabbling between the leaders of World Zionism and the leaders in Israel, with Mr Ben-Gurion usually the spokesman for the latter, has gone on in 1959 and 1960. So far this conflict has not resulted in more than recriminations of the sort quoted above. After the annual conferences in Israel, things are usually smoothed over, and the Zionist organizers go away proclaiming their intention to work for Israel harder than ever. But the tension is there, obviously, and another adventure on the Sinai pattern would possibly cause serious defections. But, if such extreme tests of loyalty are not imposed, there seems little doubt that Israel can count on continuing to enjoy the support of the Jews of the Diaspora. And she certainly will need it.

The conflict of Israel with her Arab neighbours must be related always to the general political conditions in the Middle East. The Middle East is in a process of transition, or upheaval, of which the prime moving force is the ideal of Arab nationalism. Outside influences are the attempts of the Western Powers, of whom only the United States now exercises a potentially decisive influence, to maintain essential economic interests in the area—mainly an assured supply of oil, and protection against confiscation of the capital furnished for the development of this industry. The West is also concerned to ensure that even if strategic bases and staging areas, important from the viewpoint of cold-war strategy, are no longer fully available to it in Arab lands, Western withdrawal will not be followed by Russian effective occupation. And the other outside influence is of course Russia, for the present, working through Arab nationalism, to oust all traces of Western control or influence, to which grand purpose the promotion of native communism has for the present been subordinated in the area. Since 1955, the game has been going the Russian way, enormously assisted by the Suez Canal blunder by Great Britain and France, and the vacillating foreign policy of the U.S. in the area, trying to hunt with the Arab hounds while ensuring that no harm comes to the Israeli hare.

Israelis clearly perceive the danger to their State of the effective union of the Arab states surrounding her. As Nasser is the only visible potential leader of such a union, they have concentrated hostility upon him. However, 1958 saw a number of checks to Egyptian hopes of the union of the " Arab Nation " under Egyptian leadership. The Iraq revolution was not the prelude to union with the United Arab Republic. Brigadier Kassem suppressed those elements of the revolutionary group which wanted union with the U.A.R., and up to the present has kept under control the Iraqi Communists whom for a time he seemed to be using to counterbalance the U.A.R.-oriented nationalists. The acute hostility between Iraq and the U.A.R.—or the leaders of those states—seems in 1961 to have died down.

The 1958 rebellion in Lebanon, which President Chamoun alleged had been fomented by the U.A.R., eventually petered out, after the landing of U.S. forces and the intervention of the United Nations, which placed a large observer group in the country, with the function of watching the borders and ensuring that there was no infiltration of partisans and arms from the Syrian region of the U.A.R. A *modus vivendi* between the contending Lebanese factions was patched up, and political and economic life seems to go on about as it was before 1958. Although no one openly advocates union with the U.A.R., there is basic instability, and anything could happen.

In 1958, also, a revolution in Jordan was threatened by Palestinians opposed to King Hussein and the Samir Rifai Government, when the Lebanese troubles were at their height. After the Iraq revolution, Great Britain, on the Jordanian Government's request, stationed a brigade of paratroops at Amman, and other forces on the Aqaba-Amman line of communications, concurrently with the U.S. landings in Lebanon. They were withdrawn shortly after the American withdrawal. Threats had been made in the Israel Press that if Jordan joined the U.A.R. " Israel would reserve her liberty of action," which, being interpreted, meant that they would seize the Jordan territory of the West Bank, or such part of it they considered strategically and economically advantageous. The reality of this threat, and the obvious inability of Egypt to prevent its execution by military means, seems to have caused Palestinian aspirations for union with the U.A.R. to evaporate for the time being, and there is a certain quiet in Jordan, nourished by American subventions, approximately three times as great as the British used to give. After two years of propaganda warfare, and exchange of insults between the U.A.R. and Jordan, in the spring of 1961 a truce has been declared, with a passing of polite notes between King Hussein and President Nasser. How durable the reconciliation will be is not easy to predict.

From time to time during the past two years, the U.A.R. has obtained increments of modern armaments from the U.S.S.R., and Israel has obtained aircraft from France and lately, some tanks from Great Britain, to the accompaniment of Arab outcries. Great excitement was caused in the Arab states by the discovery that Israel was building an atomic reactor near Bethlehem, keeping this secret from the United States. The Arabs were sure that Israel intended to make herself atomic bombs, and Mr Ben-Gurion's assurances that the reactor will be for peaceful purposes only, have not calmed their fears.

What of the next few years? There is danger that Israel's feeling of being hemmed in by an implacably hostile ring of Arab states, strongly supported by Russia which seems to find it to her interest that the tension in the Middle East should continue, may build up to a state of mind which would induce her to seize any chance of breaking the hostile encirclement. The pre-Sinai mood may be re-created. But before military action could be loosed, there would have to be a recurrence of the pre-Sinai conditions, when Israel could count on the non-interference if not the assistance of the Western Powers.

In mid-1961, who can predict what is going to happen in the Middle East? Whatever it is, it is likely to be unexpected, or undesired by the West. No means of peaceful settlement of the Palestine question is in sight, and there is always the possibility that the smouldering conflict will again burst into the open flame of war.

Notes

1. The words " retaliation " and " reprisals " will be used a good many times in this book, and it seems appropriate at this point to define them, and at the same time apologize if at times they seem to have been used without paying sufficient attention to the difference in their meanings.

   " Retaliate " is defined by *The Oxford English Dictionary* as " To repay (injury, insult, etc., rarely kindness, etc.) in kind ; do as one is done by, esp. return evil, make reprisals." " Retaliate " thus is more general in meaning than reprisals, which it includes. " Retaliation " was the term most commonly used in the day-by-day work of UNTSO, and, indeed, in United Nations documents, such as the Security Council resolution on Qibya of November 24, 1953, which contained the phrase " retaliatory action."

   In Oppenheim's *International Law*, he tells us (page 134, Seventh Edition, 1952) that " retorsion is the technical term for retaliation for discourteous, or unkind or unfair and inequitable acts by acts of the same or a similar kind." He gives the next category of acts of international compulsion as reprisals, which he defines as " Such injurious and otherwise internationally illegal acts of one State against another as are exceptionally permitted for the purpose of compelling the latter to consent to a satisfactory settlement of a difference created by its own international delinquency."

   The justification given by the Israelis for their retaliatory raids would fit them into the definition of reprisals. It is to be noted, however, that the taking of reprisals by the Israelis for alleged delinquencies by certain of the Arab states was specifically condemned by the Security Council as contrary to the cease-fire order of July 15, 1948, the General Armistice Agreements, and the Charter of the United Nations, first in regard to the Qibya incident, and many times thereafter.

   For further discussion of " reprisals " and " retaliation," see Chapter 5.

2. Australia, Canada, Czechoslovakia, Guatemala, India, Iran, Netherlands, Peru, Sweden, Uruguay, and Yugoslavia.

3. The title " Chief of Staff " in military usage denotes a senior officer controlling a more or less extensive staff, and responsible either to a military *commander* or to a Minister of Defence, or to a Government.

   The Chief of Staff UNTSO is not at the head of a staff, but is the administrator of the corps of UN Military Observers and the director of their operations. He is responsible to and receives instructions from the Security Council, usually in the form of its resolutions. He communicates with the Security Council through the Secretary-General, to whom in the first instance he addresses his routine and day-by-day reports.

The title, though not terminologically accurate, has established itself through usage. It would be difficult to change it at the present time, if indeed a title more accurately describing the functions of the appointment could be found. Perhaps the expression used by the Arab Press *Kabir El Muraqibeen*—" Chief of the Observers," or Director-General of UNTSO would be more appropriate.

4. For a fuller account of Count Bernadotte's assassination see Glubb, *A Soldier with the Arabs*.

5. Resolution 194 (III) of the United Nations General Assembly, of December 11, 1948, after setting up the Conciliation Commission for Palestine and outlining what it should do, continued with the following paragraphs :

> II. Resolves that the refugees wishing to return to their homes and live at peace with their neighbours should be permitted to do so at the earliest practicable date, and that compensation should be paid for the property of those choosing not to return, and for loss of or damage to property which, under principles of international law or in equity, should be made good by the Governments or authorities responsible ;
>
> Instructs the Conciliation Commission to facilitate the repatriation, resettlement and economic and social rehabilitation of the refugees and the payment of compensation, and to maintain close relations with the Director of the United Nations Relief for Palestine Refugees and, through him, with the appropriate organs and agencies of the United Nations.

Since 1948 the General Assembly has passed resolutions yearly reaffirming the terms of the above paragraphs. Such resolutions are usually related to the function of the United Nations Relief and Works Agency, the successor of the United Nations Relief for Palestine Refugees referred to in the original resolution.

France, Turkey, and the United States of America comprised the Conciliation Commission.

6. The ensuing narrative will be organized in this way with chapters or parts of chapters dealing with events between Israel and each of her neighbours separately. This has seemed to me to be the most likely way to make a complicated story reasonably easy to follow.

7. See Chapter 6, *Violent Truce* by Commander E. H. Hutchison, USNR, then Chairman of HJKIMAC.

8. " The Spring of the Judge." A collective settlement founded in 1937 by ' pioneers ' from the U.S., and named after Supreme Court Justice Louis D. Brandeis.

9. Moshe Sharett, originally Shertok, was born in Kherson, Russia, in 1894. His father had spent some years in Palestine as a Zionist pioneer, and the family returned there in 1906. They settled in an Arab village north of Jerusalem, where the young Shertok learned the Arab language and to know the Arab peasantry. He went to

high school in Herzlia, and was studying law in Constantinople when the First World War broke out. Returning to Palestine, he taught in various Hebrew schools for a while ; then was conscripted into the Turkish Army and given a commission, serving on various fronts.

After the war he returned to Palestine and became an active member of the Jewish labour and socialist movement. He studied at the London School of Economics, under such teachers as Sydney Webb, Harold Laski, and Hugh Dalton. He also began to work for Dr Chaim Weizmann, leader of the Zionist movement. Returning to Palestine, he was a journalist on the staff of *Davar*, the daily of the Jewish labour movement, and in 1931 was appointed Political Secretary of the Jewish Agency for Palestine, which dealt with the mandatory authority on all questions related to the Jews in Palestine. In this capacity he was involved in the controversies regarding Jewish immigration, Palestine's future constitution, and the place of the Jewish population in it.

During the Second World War he promoted enlistment of Jews in the British forces, and was in charge of efforts by the Jewish Agency to rescue Jews from Hitler's Europe. After the war he participated in the various efforts to find a solution to the Arab-Jewish conflict in Palestine, and on the proclamation of the State of Israel in 1948 was appointed Foreign Minister, which post he held until 1956.

10. From time to time, I shall use the word " border " for convenience and brevity. The proper legal term for the lines separating the territory held by Israel from that held by the neighbouring Arab countries is " Armistice Demarcation Line." The General Armistice Agreements set forth that these lines are of purely military significance, and were " agreed upon by the parties without prejudice to future territorial settlements of boundary lines or to claims of either party relative thereto." The Arabs are very sensitive in regard to the use of the word " border " or " boundary " when the demarcation lines are really meant, and always object if these words appear in official documents. They are, of course, quite within their rights in doing so, and in using the shorter term I imply no meaning contrary to the provisions of the General Armistice Agreements. The attitude of the two sides in respect of boundaries has been indicated in Chapter 2, page 29.

11. " Pasha," a Turkish title, was used, as a complimentary form, after the names of Generals, Prime Ministers, and great landowners in Jordan at this time. The title, formerly extensively granted in Egypt, has been abolished there by the revolution.

12. A good account of this episode, from the Jordan side, is in Lieutenant-Colonel Peter Young's book *Bedouin Command*, Chapter 5.

13. Three Power Declaration, sometimes called the " Tripartite Declaration," or even " Tripartite Agreement." This was a statement that the United States, Great Britain, and France had made jointly in May 1950. It set forth that they would not supply arms to Israel

or any of the neighbouring Arab states in quantities which would upset the balance between the two sides. The Three Powers declared " their unalterable opposition to the use of force or threat of force between any of the states in that area, and that, consistently with their obligations as members of the United Nations, they would immediately take action, within and outside the United Nations, to prevent any attempt by either side to violate frontiers."

14. Article in *Israel and the Middle East* special issue Autumn 1956 : " How the Armistices are Flouted " by Y. Tekoah, Director of Armistice Affairs, Israel Foreign Ministry. The overall figure of 1237 killed and wounded is not broken down between killed and wounded, but taking the proportion established in figures given for several specific periods, in the same article, it may be inferred that about 400 were killed and about 835 wounded. As it is not stated that the casualties were civilian, it is to be assumed that military casualties, including those resulting from Israel's reprisal raids, were included. Naturally, nothing is said of the casualties suffered by the Arabs. Comparative figures for the years 1955 and 1956, collected by UNTSO, are given in Chapter 4, page 47.

15. *Jerusalem Post*, June 16, 1958.

16. " Reprisals in time of war occur when one belligerent retaliates upon another, by means of otherwise illegitimate acts of warfare, in order to compel him and his subjects and members of his forces to abandon illegitimate acts of warfare and to comply in future with the rules of legitimate warfare. Reprisals between belligerents cannot be dispensed with, for the effect of their use and of the fear of their being used cannot be denied. Every belligerent, and every member of his forces, knows for certain that reprisals are to be expected in case they violate the rules for legitimate warfare. But while reprisals are frequently an adequate means for making the enemy comply with these rules, they frequently miss their purpose, and call forth counter-reprisals on the part of the enemy. They have often been used as a convenient cloak for violations of International Law." Oppenheim's *International Law*, Vol. II, " Disputes, War, and Neutrality," Seventh Edition, edited by Lauterpacht, 1952, page 561.
   " The right to exercise reprisals carries with it great danger of arbitrariness, for often the alleged facts which make belligerents resort to them are not sufficiently verified ; sometimes the rules of war which they consider the enemy to have violated are not generally recognized ; often the act of reprisal performed is excessive compared with the precedent act of illegitimate warfare." Page 563.

17. Reported in *Jerusalem Post*, September 4, 1955.

18. Every one who visits or reads about Israel knows the word *kibbutz* (plural *kibbutzim*). It means a communal settlement, in which all property is held in common, and all labour is divided, and the ideal of communism " from each according to his ability, to each according to his needs " is practised. This is not to say that all *kibbutzniks*

necessarily belong to the Communist political party, or sympathize with it. All Israeli political parties are represented in the *kibbutzim*, from Communist to religious, but the general tendency is, naturally enough, left-wing.

The other principal kind of agricultural settlement is the *moshav* (plural *moshavim*). These are co-operative small-holders' settlements, where each family owns its house, and works a particular piece of land.

For a more detailed account of the various forms of agricultural settlement in Israel, and the history of their development, see *Forms of Settlement* by E. Orni, published by the Jewish National Fund, Jerusalem.

19. *Jerusalem Post*, editorial of February 16, 1955.

20. *Sabra*—an Israeli born in the country, or who has come to the country. *Sabra* is the Arabic word for cactus.

21. Lieutenant-Colonel Salah Gohar, as Director of Palestine Affairs in the Ministry of War, had his hands on all the business relating to the functions of the Egypt-Israel Mixed Armistice Commission, the General Armistice Agreements, and Gaza generally, including the United Nations Relief and Works Agency there. The Gaza Strip, placed under Egyptian control by the GAA, but not part of Egyptian territory, was administered through the Ministry of War. Gohar was subsequently promoted to Colonel and then to Brigadier, and transferred to the Ministry of Foreign Affairs. Throughout the period covered by this book, he continued to be a key person in all the transactions between UNTSO, and later UNEF, with the Egyptian Government.

At the Egyptian military college he had been a classmate of President Nasser, who used to call him by his first name. Coming from a family most of whose members were in the learned professions, he was very pleasant to meet socially. However, at first I found him difficult to do business with. He had previously been senior Egyptian delegate to the MAC, and indeed connected with its operation in Gaza since the armistice began. He was, I thought, rigid and doctrinaire with regard to the GAA and the body of precedents which had grown up around it. He was also very suspicious of new proposals, and examined them inside and out at great length, looking for hidden traps. Later, I made allowance for his suspicions when I understood the reasons for them better. In the end we got along very well together.

22. Most Israeli ministries had a Director-General as their highest-ranking civil servant. Mr Eytan's position thus corresponded to that of the Permanent Under-Secretary of the British Foreign Office, or the Under-Secretary of State in the U.S.A. Mr Eytan had been the senior Israeli delegate in the armistice negotiations with Egypt at Rhodes in 1949.

23. See Note 13.

24. Though no one in the Western world except Arabic specialists can have known of this word before 1955, it had an honourable connotation in ancient days.   Edgar William Lane, writing *circa* 1838, in his noted book *Manners and Customs of the Modern Egyptians* gives the meaning at that time.   He was commenting on Egyptian story-telling, in particular on the romance of Sultan El Zahir Beybars, part of which dealt with

> . . . various romantic achievements, and the exploits of the *Fedaweeyeh* or *Fedawees* of his time.   The term *Fedawee*, which is now vulgarly understood to signify any warrior of extraordinary courage and ability, literally and properly means a person who gives, or is ready to give, his life as a ransom for his companions, or for their cause ; and is here applied to a class of warriors who owed no allegiance to any sovereign unless to a chief of their own choice ; the same class who are called, in our histories of the Crusades, " Assassins " : which appellation the very learned orientalist De Sacy had, I think, rightly pronounced to be a corruption of *Hashshasheen*, a name derived from their making frequent use of the intoxicating hemp, called *Hasheesh*.

25. The relevant portions of Articles VII and VIII of the Egypt-Israel General Armistice Agreement, with Annexes, are given below.   These articles will be frequently referred to in the following chapters. Non-compliance with them by both parties greatly weakened the safeguards in the GAA against the resumption of hostilities.

Article VII

2. The areas comprising the western and eastern fronts shall be as defined by the United Nations Chief of Staff of the Truce Supervision Organization, on the basis of the deployment of forces against each other and past military activity or the future possibility thereof in the area.   This definition of the western and eastern fronts is set forth in Annex II of this Agreement.

3. In the area of the western front under Egyptian control, Egyptian defensive forces only may be maintained.   All other Egyptian forces shall be withdrawn from this area to a point or points no further east than El Arish-Abu Aoueigila.

4. In the area of the western front under Israeli control, Israeli defensive forces only, which shall be based on the settlements, may be maintained.   All other Israeli forces shall be withdrawn from this area. . . .

5. The defensive forces referred to in paragraphs 3 and 4 above shall be defined in Annex III to this Agreement.

Article VIII

1. The area comprising the village of El Auja and vicinity, as defined in paragraph 2 of this Article, shall be demilitarized, and both Egyptian and Israeli armed forces shall be totally excluded therefrom.   The Chairman of the Mixed Armistice Commission established in Article X of this Agreement and

United Nations Observers attached to the Commission shall be responsible for ensuring the full implementation of this provision.

2. (verbal definition of El Auja DZ)

3. On the Egyptian side of the frontier, facing the El Auja area, no Egyptian defensive positions shall be closer to El Auja than El Quseima and Abu Aoueigila.

4. The road Taba-Quseima-Auja shall not be employed by any military forces whatsoever for the purpose of entering Palestine.

5. The movement of armed forces of either Party to this Agreement into any part of the area defined in paragraph 2 of this Article, for any purpose, or failure by either Party to respect or fulfil any of the other provisions of this Article, when confirmed by the United Nations representatives, shall constitute a flagrant violation of this Agreement.

Annex II

DEMARCATION OF THE WESTERN AND EASTERN FRONTS IN PALESTINE

On the sole basis of military considerations involving the forces of the two Parties to this Agreement as well as third party forces in the area not covered by this Agreement, the demarcation of the western and eastern fronts in Palestine is to be understood as follows :

a. Western Front :

The area south and west of the line delineated in paragraph 2.A of the Memorandum of 13 November 1948 on the implementation of the resolution of the Security Council of 4 November 1948, from its point of origin on the west to the point at MR 12581196,[1] thence south along the road to Hatta-Al Faluja-RI at MR 12140823-Beersheba and ending north of Bir Asluj at point 402.

b. Eastern Front :

The area east of the line described in paragraph *a* above, and from point 402 down to the southernmost tip of Palestine, by a straight line marking half the distance between the Egypt-Palestine and Transjordan-Palestine frontiers.

Annex III

DEFINITION OF DEFENSIVE FORCES

I. Land Forces

1. Shall not exceed :

    (*a*) 3 inf btns, each bn to consist of not more than 800 officers and ORs composed of not more than

        (i) 4 rifle coys with ordinary inf. S.A. equipment (rifles, LMG's, SMG's, light mortars (e.g. 2″), A/tk rifles or Piat),

---

[1] About ten kilometres due east of Majdal.

    (ii) 1 support coy with not more than 6 MMG's, 6 mortars not heavier than 3″, 4 A/tk guns not heavier than 6 pdrs,

    (iii) 1 HQ coy.

(b) 1 bty of 8 field guns not heavier than 25 pdrs.

(c) 1 bty of 8 A.A. guns not heavier than 40 mm.

2. The following are excluded from the term " Defensive Forces " :

(a) Armour, such as tanks, AC's, Bren-carriers, half-tracks, load carriers or any other AFV's.

(b) All support arms and units other than those specified in paragraph 1(a)(ii), 1(b) and 1(c) above.

26. Lake Tiberias is better known to Bible readers as the Sea of Galilee. The Israelis use the ancient name " Gennesereth."

27. A more specific statement on Israel's position regarding the repatriation of refugees was made by Mr Sharett in the Knesset on January 9, 1956, when he was reported as saying : " Israel was quite unable to take back Palestine Arabs in an effort to help solve the problem. Israel had a policy of permitting the reunion of families under certain circumstances, and no doubt this policy would be continued. But she would not take upon herself the burden of settlement of new Arab families in Israel."

28. The Herut (Freedom) Party takes the extreme Zionist (revisionist) position. It originated as the party perpetuating the Irgun Zvai Leumi (an unofficial Jewish combat organization of Mandatory days) and other extremist groups. Its programme includes the extension of Israel's boundaries to its " historic " frontiers, to include part of Jordan east of the river, as well as Mandatory Palestine. It holds the second largest number of seats in the Knesset. In social and economic affairs, its policies are rightist.

29. Flint, who subsequently became Chairman of HJKIMAC, and was promoted Lieutenant-Colonel, was killed in an incident on Mount Scopus on May 26, 1958.

30. Gamal Abdel Nasser was elected President of the Egyptian Republic in a plebiscite held on June 23, and assumed this title shortly thereafter. Previously his title had been Prime Minister.

31. The " *fedayeen* bases " actually were Egyptian posts a few kilometres back from the border, manned by detachments of the Egyptian Frontier Forces that guarded the Sinai. The post at El Kuntilla had been destroyed in an Israeli retaliatory raid a year previously. It is, of course, not improbable that some of the raiders who were responsible for outrages on the Eilat-Beersheba road started out from these places, and with Egyptian backing.

32. Lieutenant-Colonel R. Bayard, U.S. Army
Lieutenant-Colonel W. M. Brown, New Zealand Army
Lieutenant-Colonel S. Mollersward, Swedish Army

Major A. W. Cooper, New Zealand
Captain R. M. Burrows, New Zealand
Captain J. A. Bor, Netherlands
Mr G. Menendez, Guatemala
Mr R. East, Panamanian

33. Word of the drastic actions taken by the Israeli forces against the inhabitants of the Gaza Strip got to the Arab states, and accusations of massacres and mass deportations were made in the United Nations. The Secretary-General, after some negotiation with the Israeli authorities, sent a representative to inquire into conditions in the Gaza Strip. This was Lieutenant-Colonel K. R. Nelson of the U.S. Army, who had served with the extemporized UNEF staff, but had returned to duty with UNTSO. He was assisted by Captain G. Svedlund (Sweden), who was fluent in Arabic and could interrogate witnesses directly. Lieutenant-Colonel Nelson's report is published as UN Document A/3491, dated December 3, 1956.

He and Captain Svedlund went to Gaza on November 27, 1956, and visited villages and refugee camps. In general, they were afforded adequate facilities for their inquiry by the Israeli authorities in the Strip. Extracts from the report follow :

> I considered that the scope of our investigation should be limited to the conditions as they existed at the time we carried it out. We did not investigate details of any of the alleged incidents which happened prior to our arrival (the Rafah incident and minor riotous conditions subsequent to that time). . . .
>
> The Israel authorities have methodically established a programme to stabilize life in the Gaza area. They are progressively executing that programme. They have established law and order and have dealt with any uprisings or lootings in a strong manner. . . .
>
> Mr Labouisse, who inspected the United Nations Relief and Works Agency . . . operation at the time of our visit, is preparing a separate report on the refugee situation. . . .
>
> Except for some groups of local inhabitants taken out of the Gaza area for questioning, there was no evidence of mass deportation of the inhabitants. . . .

Mr Labouisse's special report, covering the period November–December 1956, was published as UN document A/3212/Add.1. Extracts of the report dealing with the incidents mentioned follow :

> The occupation of the Gaza Strip by the Israel Army resulted in a number of civilian casualties in both the refugee and the local populations, and caused anxiety and fear among the refugees, particularly during the first few weeks.
>
> In other circumstances, it would have been a logical course for the United Nations Truce Supervision Organization to investigate and report upon casualties resulting from armed attack across the demarcation line. In the present emergency, that organization was unable to do so, as the movements of its officers in the Gaza Strip had been restricted by the Israel authorities. The Agency has, therefore, made every effort to ascertain the facts concerning the various incidents affecting the refugees

and it has sought to prevent any repetition of violence against the refugee population. The Agency has been compelled to rely on its own sources of information. These were necessarily limited, but they included eye-witness accounts by UNRWA employees, both refugees and others.

Khan Yunis. The town of Khan Yunis and the Agency's camp adjacent thereto were occupied by Israel troops on the morning of 3 November. A large number of civilians were killed at that time, but there is some conflict in the accounts given as to the causes of the casualties. The Israel authorities state that there was resistance to their occupation and that the Palestinian refugees formed part of the resistance. On the other hand, the refugees state that all resistance had ceased at the time of the incident and that many unarmed civilians were killed as the Israel troops went through the town and camp, seeking men in possession of arms. The exact number of dead and wounded is not known, but the Director has received from sources he considers trustworthy lists of names of persons allegedly killed on 3 November, numbering 275 individuals. . . .

Rafah. On 12 November, a serious incident occurred in the Agency's camp at Rafah. Both the Israel authorities and UNRWA's other sources of information agree that a number of refugees were killed and wounded at that time by the occupying forces.

A difference of opinion exists as to how the incident happened and as to the numbers of killed and wounded. It is agreed, however, that the incident occurred during a screening operation conducted by the Israel forces . . . to find persons who were members of the so-called "Palestine Brigade" or who participated in *fedayeen* operations. . . .

The Israel authorities in Gaza state that the attitude of the refugees in Rafah Camp was hostile and that there was some resistance to the screening operation, during which the casualties occurred. The refugees deny any such resistance. . . . Rafah is a very large camp (more than 32,000 refugees) and the loudspeaker vans which called upon the men to gather at designated screening-points was not heard by some of the refugee population. . . . Sufficient time was not allowed for all men to walk to the screening-points and get there before the designated hour. In the confusion, a large number of refugees ran toward the screening-points for fear of being late, and some Israel soldiers apparently panicked and opened fire on this running crowd.

The Director has received from sources which he considers trustworthy lists of names of persons allegedly killed at Rafah on 12 November, numbering 111.

The incident at Kafr Kasim, an Arab village about 12 kilometres east and slightly north of Tel Aviv, situated almost on the demarcation line, took place on October 29, as the invasion of the Sinai was beginning. In view of the recent tension with Jordan, and the possibility that its forces, as well as those of Syria, might attack Israel in support of Egypt with whom they had a military alliance, Israeli forces naturally had to be disposed defensively against such threats. The Arab population in Israel also had to be controlled, in case of disorders when military operations commenced. There was also the likelihood of Arabs crossing the demarcation line to give information to Jordan. Consequently, the Israel border police was given the task of keeping the Arab villages under control. One of the measures taken was to impose a curfew from 5 P.M. to 6 A.M.

. A platoon of the police was detailed to enforce this curfew at Kafr Kasim. Somewhere, in the process of passing the orders for the execution of the operation on down the chain of command, there had been the unauthorized addition of a provision that any inhabitants found out of doors after 5 P.M. were to be shot. Let us see how the platoon at Kafr Kasim executed this order. The following extract is from the *Jerusalem Post*'s report of the State Attorney's opening address at the trial of the policemen concerned.

> . . . They reached the village about 4:30 P.M. A non-commissioned officer told the mukhtar that a curfew had been imposed from 5 P.M. to 6 A.M. The mukhtar protested, saying that it was impossible to inform all the villagers. Some worked outside the village, and would not return, nor could they be reached and warned before the curfew took effect.
> The first villagers to return after the curfew came into effect were four men riding bicycles. Two were killed. The bodies were left at the side of the road. Then came a wagon driven by a man with his small daughter at his side, followed by two men and a boy. The driver said his daughter had been frightened by the shots. Police sent the boy into the village with the girl. Two of the three men were killed. A flock of goats tended by a man and a twelve-year-old boy approached. Both were killed.

This went on until 47 persons in all had been killed, as well as a number wounded.

> When news of the killings became known at battalion headquarters, an order was issued to the Border Force men in the village to shoot only if anyone tried to escape or forcibly refused to observe the curfew.

These events only became public property some time after the Sinai campaign had ended. Mr Ben-Gurion made a statement in the Knesset, expressing a proper detestation of the crime, and promising that those guilty would be brought to trial. Five months later the trial of eleven defendants began. It went very slowly, dragging out over many months ; but this is a common fault of justice in Israel, and evokes many criticisms. In particular, when the decision of the military court had not been announced for a long time after the trial had concluded (by September 5, 1958) the *Jerusalem Post* published a strong editorial denouncing the dilatory procedure— entitled " Tragedy of Justice."

On October 12, 1958, the verdict was announced. Eight of the accused, including a major and a lieutenant, were found guilty, and three were acquitted. The major was later sentenced to 17 years imprisonment. There is no death penalty in Israel, so the maximum sentence for the crime for which the policemen were being tried was life imprisonment.

Subsequent to the trial, there was a further Government inquiry into the responsibility for the orders which had reached the Kafr Kasim platoon, and as a result the Lieutenant-Colonel in command of the brigade to which it belonged was placed on trial, on December 24, 1958, for murder.

The shocking feature of the whole case is that a group of the border police, who are considered to be a *corps d'élite* selected from men who have served in the armed forces, should have executed such a savage order.   Others who had received similar orders did not carry them out, but allowed obviously innocent villagers to go to their homes.   It is a very sad proof of the fact that the spirit that inspired the notorious Deir Yasin massacre in 1948 is not dead among some of the Israeli armed forces.

34. *Resolution adopted by the General Assembly at its 567th plenary meeting on 7 November 1956* (UN document A/RES/395, dated 8 Nov 56) (UN document A/3308 dated 6 Nov 56 draft resolution submitted by Argentina, Burma, Ceylon, Denmark, Ecuador, Ethiopia and Sweden).

The General Assembly,

Recalling its resolution of 2 November 1956 (A/3256) concerning the cease-fire, withdrawal of troops and other matters related to the military operations in Egyptian territory ; as well as its resolution of 4 November 1956 (A/3276) concerning the request to the Secretary-General to submit a plan for an emergency international United Nations force,

Having established in its resolution of 5 November 1956 (A/3290) a United Nations Command for an emergency international force ; having appointed the Chief of Staff of the United Nations Truce Supervision Organization as Chief of the Command with authorization to him to begin the recruitment of officers for the Command ; and having invited the Secretary-General to take the administrative measures necessary for the prompt execution of that resolution,

Noting with appreciation the second and final Report of the Secretary-General on the plan for an emergency international United Nations Force (A/3302) as requested in the resolution adopted by the General Assembly on 4 November 1956 (A/3276), and having examined that plan,

1. *Expresses its approval* of the guiding principles for the organization of the Force as expounded in paragraphs 6 to 9 of the Secretary-General's report ;

2. *Concurs* in the definition of the functions of the Force as stated in paragraph 12 of the Secretary-General's report ;

3. *Invites* the Secretary-General to continue discussions with Member Governments concerning offers of participation in the Force, toward the objective of its balanced composition ;

4. *Requests* the Chief of Command, in consultation with the Secretary-General as regards size and composition, to proceed with the full organization of the Force ;

5. *Approves, provisionally,* the basic rule concerning the financing of the Force laid down in paragraph 15 of the Secretary-General's report ;

6. *Establishes* an Advisory Committee composed of one representative from each of the following countries : Brazil, Canada, Colombia,

India, Iran, Norway and Pakistan, and requests this Committee, whose Chairman shall be the Secretary-General, to undertake the development of those aspects of the planning for the Force and its operation not already dealt with by the General Assembly and which do not fall within the area of the direct responsibility of the Chief of Command ;

7. *Authorizes* the Secretary-General to issue all regulations and instructions which may be essential to the effective functioning of the Force, following consultation with the Advisory Committee aforementioned ; and to take all other necessary administrative and executive actions ;

8. *Determines* that, following the fulfilment of the immediate responsibilities defined for it in operative paragraphs 6 and 7 above, the Advisory Committee appointed by the General Assembly shall continue to assist the Secretary-General in the responsibilities falling to him under the present and other relevant resolutions ;

9. *Decides* that the Advisory Committee, in the performance of its duties, shall be empowered to request the convening of the General Assembly and to report to it whenever matters which, in its opinion, are of such urgency and importance as to require their consideration by the General Assembly itself ; and

10. *Requests* all Member States to afford assistance as necessary to the United Nations Command in the performance of its functions, including arrangements for passage to and from the area involved.

35. The following were the members of the first improvised staff for UNEF, which was set up in business in Cairo on November 12, 1956 :

Lieutenant-Colonel C. F. Moe (Norway)	Operations Officer
Lieutenant-Colonel K. R. Nelson (U.S.A.)	Organization and Planning
Major K. W. Egerstad (Sweden)	Administration
Captain G. G. Svedlund (Sweden)	Liaison and Intelligence
Captain J. S. Bor (Holland)	Liaison and Intelligence
Miss Marian Warren (Canada)	Secretary and Code Clerk
Mr Vinh Buivan (Vietnam)	Code Clerk

Lieutenant-Colonel Moe acted as commander of the force during my absence in New York. He subsequently became Chief of Operations when the regular UNEF staff was organized.

36. What should be the composition and strength of the headquarters staff for the Force ? What communication, supply, transport, repair, and medical facilities would be needed ? Should the infantry be equipped with the normal scale of weapons ? Were light artillery and engineers required ? What kind of and how much transport should infantry units have ? Should national units be initially self-contained in respect of food, tentage and other supplies, medical facilities, and communications ? What was the condition of airfields and seaports, and were there facilities for unloading heavy equipment ? When would it be feasible to begin air and sea lift of initial units ? How did weather conditions in the area bear on the type of uniform that should be worn, kind of tentage, need for stoves ? What

was there in the proposed base area in the way of water-supply, power, workshops, hospitals, bakeries, supply-depots, and refrigerated storage ? Could logistical needs such as food, transport, tentage, fuel and lubricants, labour, mechanical-transport repairs and replacement parts be provided in Egypt ?

37. The following is an extract from a speech on January 29, 1957, of Fadhil el Jamali, representative of Iraq—a distinguished and relatively moderate Arab politician. (In 1958 he was sentenced to death, in the early days of the Kassem revolution, as a supporter of the Nuri el Said régime.)

> There is no doubt that the permanence of peace in the Middle East depends on the ability of Israel to live with the Arabs and to recognize their rights. If Israel cannot do that it is not entitled to stay in the area. . . . You can never have peace unless you learn to live in peace with the Arabs, and you cannot live in peace with the Arabs until you recognize their fundamental human rights. . . .
> . . . the Suez Canal, the Gulf of Aqaba and that resolution [of the Security Council in 1951] are all tied to the state of war. If there were no state of war the freedom of passage would certainly be guaranteed. But there is a state of war because the rights of the Arabs of Palestine have been denied.
> . . . [Egypt, Iraq, Lebanon and Jordan] all stand as Arab states on behalf of the Arabs of Palestine. If you settle the question of the Arabs of Palestine and respect their right to their own homes there will be no problems. But if you deny them their rights neither Egypt nor Iraq nor Jordan nor Lebanon nor Syria nor Saudi Arabia can have peace with Israel. We cannot recognize an invader who takes away the homes and property of our brethren in Palestine.
> . . . If you want Egypt to observe the Security Council resolution of 1951 with respect to the Suez Canal why do you not observe the General Assembly resolutions of 1947, 1948, 1949 and onward, concerning the refugees and their right to return to their own homes ?
> The issue of Palestine is very clear and very simple, and the settlement of the problems of the Middle East is very simple indeed. There is a question of basic rights and the fundamental principles of the Charter. . . . So long as the Arab people are denied the right to their own country, their own homes and their own property, there can be no peace in the Middle East.

This speech sets forth, simply and cogently, the Arab attitude to the Suez and Tiran Strait questions, and the problem of making peace with Israel.

On January 29, 1957, Mr Kuznetsov, the U.S.S.R. delegate, spoke, citing proposals by representatives of the United Kingdom, Australia, New Zealand, and some other western countries " in favour of United Nations occupation of the Egyptian territory in the Gaza area and in the area around the Gulf of Aqaba," and alleged, " It is apparent that this attempt, in the name of internationalization, to cut off a part of Egyptian territory is being made with a view to putting pressure on the Egyptian government for the settling of problems which vitally affect the interests of that country." Further, " Thus we are faced with a new plan of intervention in the domestic affairs of Egypt, a new attempt to restore in Egypt and in other countries of the Near and Middle East the obsolete and rejected colonial practices, even if this is done under another label. Under this plan Israel apparently is being awarded a definite rôle of instigator and organizer of conflicts with a view to increasing tension in the Near and Middle East."

Mr Kuznetsov also recited the U.S.S.R. argument that the UNEF was created by the General Assembly in violation of the Charter of the UN. Chapter VII of the Charter provides that United Nations troops can only be created by a decision of the Security Council. This stand, of course, stemmed from the Russian objection to the " Uniting for Peace " resolution of November 1950, which was the basis for the General Assembly's action in creating the UNEF.

In a later speech Mr Kuznetsov said :

> It is not difficult to understand that the intentions to use the United Nations Emergency Force in Egypt, including the western parts of Sinai, have far-reaching aims. They are part of the doctrine of President Eisenhower, which includes the flagrant intervention of the United States, including military intervention, in Arab affairs. . . .

He went on to argue,

> After the withdrawal of Israeli forces behind the Armistice Demarcation Line, the United Nations should immediately withdraw its forces from Egyptian territory.

The propaganda appeal of the Soviet line of argument, especially to former colonies or protectorates, is very obvious. It became a favourite theme of Arab newspapers and radio broadcasts in the following months. In the slogans chanted during demonstrations by inhabitants in the Gaza Strip, " Eisenhower " was denounced. It is, of course, not difficult to perceive the reasons why the Russians would wish the UNEF to be out of the Middle East, and the Egyptians probably perceived them very quickly.

The lack of factual basis for the Russian arguments was vividly pointed out by Mr Lester Pearson, the Canadian Secretary of State for External Affairs, in his speech which followed that of the Russian delegate. He said :

> Absurd suspicions have been cast on this force by the representative of the Soviet Union, as an agency for the return of colonialism in a new form to this area. All I can say in this connexion is that the force is under the control not of any one Power, either here in this Assembly or on the spot, but it is under the control of the United Nations, and that it is a force consisting of important elements from those well-known " colonial powers," India, Indonesia, Yugoslavia, and Finland.

38. Gohar had recently been promoted to the rank of *Miralai*—equivalent to Brigadier in the British Army or Brigadier-General in the U.S. Army.

39.

Type of Incident	Occurrences by Month[1]																	
	1957										1958							
	Mar.	Apr.	May	June	July	Aug.	Sept.	Oct.	Nov.	Dec.	Jan.	Feb.	Mar.	Apr.	May	June	July	Aug.
Involving mines	5	1	4	5	0	0	0	0	0	0	1	0	1	0	0	0	0	0
Crossings of ADL involving firing	1	1	2	2	2	0	0	1	1	0	1	1	0	1	0	0	0	4
Firing across ADL	0	3	2	2	2	1	0	3	0	0	0	0	0	0	0	1	1	0
Crossings of ADL involving theft or occasionally kidnapping	10	12	21	39	10	2	3	1	4	1	8	8	5	3	11	4	9	3
Crossings or attempted crossings of ADL *not* involving firing, theft, or kidnapping	6	18	13	6	8	3	2	0	1	7	2	5	7	3	11	4	9	5
Totals	22	35	42	54	22	6	6	0	6	12	3	15	15	10	15	4	13	9

Total incidents for the eighteen months : 288.

[1] Based on figures from UNEF headquarters, which include complaints presented by both parties as well as observations independently made by UNEF. (Type and number of incidents of all kinds other than alleged violations of territorial waters and of air space.)

UN documents A/3694 7 Oct 57 UNITED NATIONS EMERGENCY FORCE Report of the Secretary-General
           A/3899 27 Aug 58 „ „ „ „ „ „ „ „
           A/4210 3 Dec 59 „ „ „ „ „ „ „ „

40. " Concluding Observations and Principles."

> . . . the specific circumstances in which the experience with UNEF has been gained . . . definitely limit any detailed application of that experience to the general problem of United Nations operations of this character . . . UNEF was . . . interposed between regular, national military forces which were subject to a cease-fire agreed to by the opposing parties. UNEF has continued to function along the ' dividing line ' between the national forces. It follows that in UNEF there has never been any need for rights and responsibilities other than those necessary for such an interposed force under cease-fire conditions. The Force was not used in any way to enforce withdrawals but, in the successive stages of the withdrawals, followed the withdrawing troops to the ' dividing line ' of each stage. It is also to be noted that the Force has functioned under a clear-cut mandate which had entirely detached it from involvement in any internal or local problems, and also has enabled it to maintain its neutrality in relation to international political issues. . . .
>
> A further factor of significance is that . . . in Gaza and elsewhere in its area of operations, UNEF has been able to function without any question arising of its presence infringing upon sovereign rights, on the basis that, at the invitation of the Egyptian Government and in accordance with the decision of the General Assembly, the United Nations assists in maintaining quiet on the Armistice Demarcation Line around the Gaza Strip and along the international line to the south. The Government of Egypt has co-operated by taking necessary steps to facilitate the functioning of UNEF in the Gaza area. The same is true of the position of the Egyptian Government in keeping its limited military units in the Sinai Peninsula away from the area in which the UNEF chiefly functions.

The Secretary-General went on to point out the different state of affairs which confronted the UN when the critical situations in Lebanon and the Jordan arose during the summer of 1958, which made it impossible to use a force of UNEF type to control them, and called for other measures. He drew the conclusion that the situations of conflict in which the UN might be required to act would vary greatly, and that any arrangements designed for that end should be very flexible, and specifically that a stand-by peace force would seldom be usable. Few countries would therefore care to take a share in bearing the considerable " sacrifice " involved (*i.e.*, expense).

Among the principles which the Secretary-General thought should apply to the use of a United Nations Force are the following :

As the UNEF or similar forces that may subsequently be organized do not come within the provisions of Chapter VI of the Charter, it follows that " The United Nations cannot station units on the territory of a member state without the consent of the government concerned." As a consequence it would be difficult for the United Nations to engage in such an operation without guarantees against unilateral actions by the host government which might put the United Nations in a difficult position, either administratively or in relation to contributing governments.

The formula intended to guard against such contingencies, worked out with Egypt in the Suez crisis was a bilateral declaration on the one hand by the Government of Egypt that " when exercising its sovereign right with regard to the presence of the force, it would be guided by good faith in the purposes of the force." The Secretary-General, for the United Nations, declared " the maintenance of the force by the United Nations would be determined by similar good faith in the interpretation of the purposes."

Prima facie, it is very difficult to attach any precise meaning to these words. The formula is an example of the vagueness in the written arrangements resulting from United Nations negotiations in the Middle East to which I have referred. The next paragraph in the report, however, clarifies the implicit meaning somewhat, as it says that if Egypt should " refuse continued presence "—*i.e.*, demand withdrawal of the force—or if the United Nations should decide to withdraw the force while Egypt still desired its presence, and the United Nations and Egypt in the respective cases found such action to be " contrary to a good faith interpretation of the purposes of the operation," there would be an exchange of views " towards harmonizing the positions." Another point of principle was the right to determine the composition of the force—what nations should contribute contingents.

> While the United Nations must reserve for itself the authority to decide on the composition . . . it is obvious that the host country . . . cannot be indifferent to [it]. . . . In order to limit the scope of possible difference of opinion, the United Nations in recent operations has followed two principles : not to include units from any of the permanent members of the Security Council ; and not to include units from any country which, because of its geographical position or other reasons, might be considered as having a special interest in the situation which has called for the operation.

Any unresolved dispute between the Secretary-General and the host nation in regard to composition would have to be settled in the end " on a political rather than a legal basis." This presumably means that the question would have to be referred back to the General Assembly—as also presumably would disputes with regard to the withdrawal or non-withdrawal of the force.

Another principle is that the UN force or observers should have freedom of movement in its area of operations (which would have to be defined and agreed to) and facilities for access to the area, including communications necessary for the successful completion of its task. This will generally involve the right to fly over national territory without the restrictions usually imposed by the host country on civil and military flying.

It has proved by the experience of UNEF and UNOGIL that " authority granted to the United Nations group cannot be exercised within a given territory either in competition with representatives of the host government or in co-operation with them on the basis of any joint operation " (*cf.* UNEF co-operation in the Gaza Strip with Palestine police, Chapter 18).

Another of the Secretary-General's suggested rules is that United Nations forces or observation groups could not be employed in " situations of an essentially internal nature." United Nations personnel cannot be permitted to take sides in internal conflicts, and their rôles must be limited to preventing infiltration or other " activities affecting international boundaries." [1]

This rule is apparently a consequence of his judgment of the possibilities of employing a United Nations force, or the observer group in Lebanon, where the conflict was essentially internal, though interference from Syria was alleged ; also in Jordan, where the danger was from internal revolutionary activities, allegedly fomented by the U.A.R. It is obvious that such a rule would greatly reduce the possibilities of employing a UN force in many of the situations of conflict or instability which might lead to breaches of international peace. While the results of the measures taken in Lebanon and Jordan seem to have been satisfactory, experience is perhaps too limited to generalize that no UN armed force could be used in similar situations arising elsewhere.

The Secretary-General also discussed the limitations on the use of arms by such a force as UNEF. He stated that " the decision [of the Assembly] relating to UNEF . . . qualified the operation as being one of a paramilitary [2] nature," while the absence of an explicit authorization for the force to take offensive action excluded the organization by the Secretary-General of units for such action, and consequently the units generally were equipped only with weapons necessary for self-defence.

Finally, the Secretary-General made some observations on the right of self-defence of the force, which I have referred to in Chapter 18. He said :

> I have touched on the extent to which a right of self-defence may be exercised by United Nations units. . . . It should be generally recognized that such a right exists . . . [but it] should be exercised only under strictly defined conditions. . . . A reasonable definition seems to have been established in the case of UNEF, where the rule is applied that men engaged in the operation may never take the initiative in the use of armed force, but are entitled to respond with force to an attack with arms, including attempts to use force to make them withdraw from positions which they occupy under orders from the commander, acting under the authority of the Assembly and within the scope of its resolutions.

[1] This restriction seems to have had a significant relation to the difficulties which the UN force in the Congo has encountered.

[2] I objected to the use of the term " paramilitary " to describe UNEF or its functions. The Oxford English Dictionary defines " paramilitary " as " having a status or function ancillary to that of military forces." Examples are constabularies or gendarmeries organized more or less on military lines and having functions of maintaining order in turbulent areas, with a regular military force behind them. But UNEF was and is unquestionably formed of military units, from the regular forces of the nations contributing. It is not ancillary to any " other " military force.

This inappropriate (in my view) use of the term " paramilitary " perhaps arises from a misapprehension that a military force in all situations invariably and necessarily uses all the arms and means at its disposal to achieve its object. This, of course, is not so, as an army can give " aid to the civil power " under great restrictions as to its use of arms. In my view, UNEF is certainly a military force, but with a strictly limited and defined task and mode of action prescribed for it.

Possibly " paramilitary " in the text was used to allay the doubts of some supporters of the resolution.

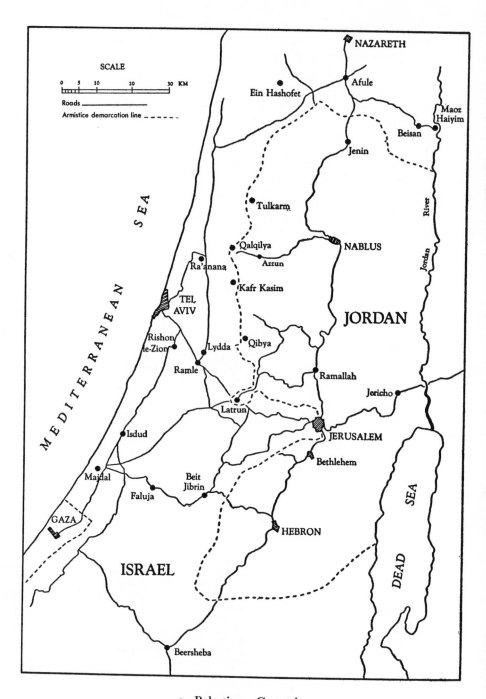

1. Palestine—Central

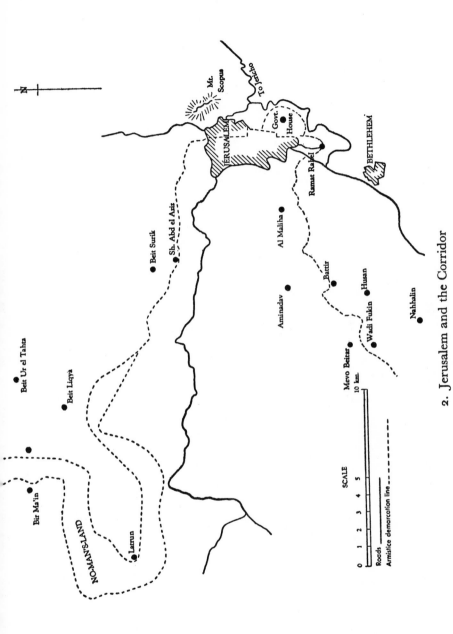

2. Jerusalem and the Corridor

Beit Ur el Taha

Bir Ma'in

Beit Liqya

NO-MAN'S-LAND

Latrun

Beit Surik

Sh. Abd el Aziz

Mt. Scopus

To Jericho

JERUSALEM

Govt. House

Ramat Rahel

BETHLEHEM

Al Maliha

Aminadav

Battir

Husan

Wadi Fukin

Nahhalin

Mevo Beitar

N

SCALE

0 1 2 3 4 5   10 km.

Roads ——————
Armistice demarcation line - - - - -

315

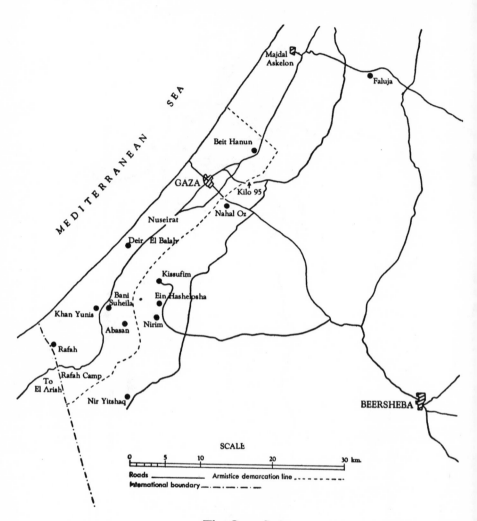

3. The Gaza Strip

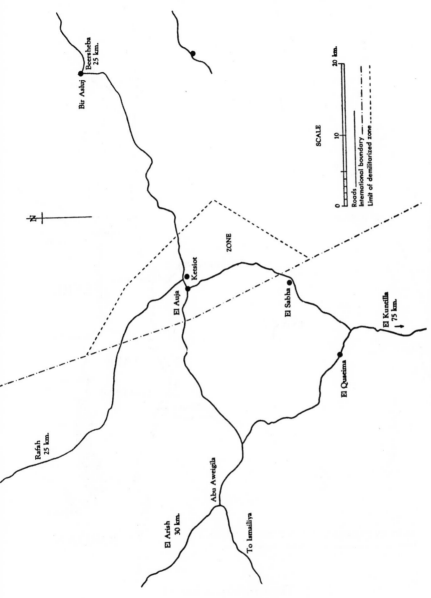

4. The El Auja Demilitarized Zone

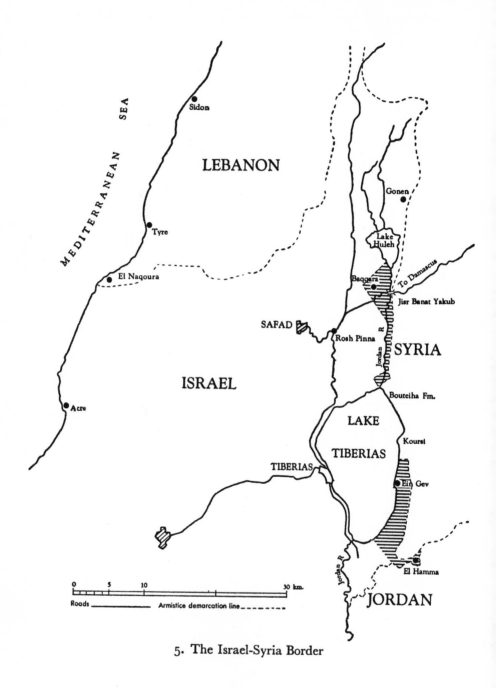

MEDITERRANEAN SEA

● Sidon

LEBANON

● Tyre

El Naqoura

● Gonen

Lake
Huleh

Baqqara ●

To Damascus

Jisr Banat Yakub

SAFAD ▨

Rosh Pinna ●

Jordan R.

SYRIA

ISRAEL

Bouteiha Fm.

LAKE

● Acre

TIBERIAS

Koursi

Ein Gev ●

TIBERIAS

El Hamma ●

Jordan R.

JORDAN

0   5   10   30 km.

Roads _____   Armistice demarcation line _ _ _ _ _

5. The Israel-Syria Border

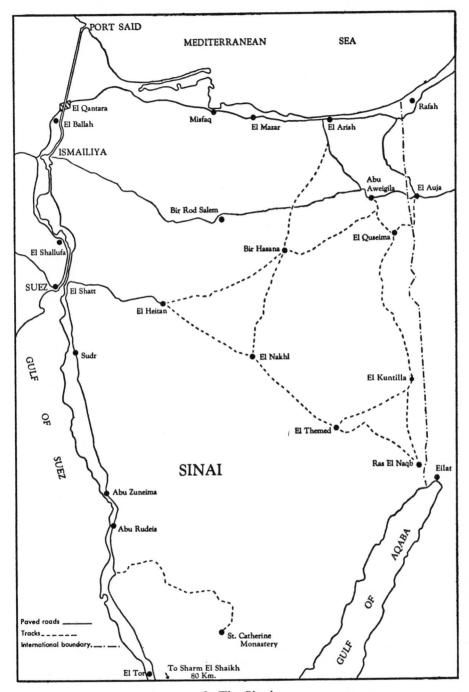

6. The Sinai

Bibliography

History of Middle East and its Peoples

BROCKELMANN, CARL : *History of the Islamic Peoples* (Routledge and Kegan Paul, London, 1949).

HITTI, PHILIP K. (ed.) : *History of the Arabs* (Macmillan, London, 1950).

HULL, WILLIAM E. : *Fall and Rise of Israel* (Zondervan, Grand Rapids, Michigan, 1954).

KIRK, GEORGE (ed.) : *Short History of the Middle East* (Methuen, London, 1957).

MARGOLIS AND MARX : *A History of the Jewish People* (Meridian, New York, 1958).

ROTH, CECIL : *Short History of the Jewish People* (East and West Library, London, 1945).

Middle East : Political and Economic

ANTONIUS, GEORGE : *The Arab Awakening* (Khayat, Beirut, 1938).

BARTH, A. (ed.) : *Israel Economist 1954–55* (Kollek, Jerusalem).

BULLARD, SIR R. (ed.) : *The Middle East—A Political and Economic Survey* (Oxford University Press, 1958).

EUROPA PUBLICATIONS : *The Middle East—Survey and Directory* (London, 1958).

KEDOURIE, ELIE : *England and the Middle East* (Bowes and Bowes, London, 1956).

LAQUEUR, W. Z. : *Communism and Nationalism in the Middle East* (Routledge and Kegan Paul, London, 1956).

LAQUEUR, W. Z. (ed.) : *The Middle East in Transition* (Routledge and Kegan Paul, London, 1958).

LAQUEUR, W. Z. : *The Soviet Union and the Middle East* (Routledge and Kegan Paul, London, 1959).

LITTLE, TOM : *Egypt* (Ernest Benn, Ltd., London, 1958).

NUSEIBEH, HAZEM : *The Ideas of Arab Nationalism* (Cornell University, 1956).

R.I.I.A. STUDY GROUP : *British Interests in the Mediterranean and Middle East* (Oxford University Press, 1958).

U.S. DEPARTMENT OF STATE : *United States Policy in the Middle East (September 1956 to June 1957)*.

WARRINER, DOREEN : *Land Reform and Development in the Middle East* (R.I.I.A., London, 1957).

Palestine Question : General

BERGER, ELMER : *Judaism or Jewish Nationalism* (Bookman Associates of New York, 1957).

GOITEIN, S. D. : *Jews and Arabs* (Schocken Books, New York, 1955).

HEBREW UNIVERSITY STUDY GROUP : *Israel and the United Nations* (Manhattan Publishing Company, 1955).

HUMBARACI, ARSLAN : *Middle East Indictment* (Robert Hale, London, 1958).

IONIDES, MICHAEL : *Divide and Lose (Arab Revolt of 1955–58)* (Geoffrey Bles, London, 1961).

KIMCHE, JON AND DAVID : *Both Sides of the Hill* (Secker and Warburg, London, 1960).

KIMCHE, JON : *Seven Fallen Pillars (Middle East, 1945–52)* (Secker and Warburg, London. 1953).

LILIENTHAL, A. M. : *What Price Israel* (Henry Regnery, Chicago, 1953).

MARLOWE, JOHN : *The Seat of Pilate (Palestine Mandate)* (Cresset Press, London, 1959).

NUROCK, M. (ed.) : *Rebirth and Destiny of Israel (Speeches by D. Ben-Gurion)* (Philosophical Library, 1954).

PERETZ, DON : *Israel and the Palestine Arabs* (M.E. Institute, 1958).

PINNER, WALTER : *How Many Arab Refugees* (Macgibbon and Kee, London, 1960).

TOTAH, KHALIL : *Dynamite in the Middle East* (Philosophical Library, New York, 1955).

UTLEY, FREDA : *There Goes the Middle East* (Devin-Adair, New York, 1957).

Military History

JOSEPH, DOV : *The Faithful City (Siege of Jerusalem)* (Simon and Schuster, New York, 1960).

O'BALLANCE, EDGAR : *The Arab-Israeli War 1948* (Faber and Faber, London, 1956).

WAVELL, A. P. : *The Palestine Campaign* (Constable, 1928).

Suez-Sinai, 1956

BROMBERGER, M. AND S. : *Les Secrets de l'Expédition d'Égypte* (Les Quatre Fils Aymon, Paris, 1957).

FRYE, W. P. : *A United Nations Peace Force* (Oceana Publications, New York, 1957).

HENRIQUES, ROBERT : *100 Hours to Suez* (Collins, London, 1957).

O'BALLANCE, EDGAR : *The Sinai Campaign 1956* (Faber and Faber, London, 1959).

WINT AND CALVOCARESSI : *Middle East Crisis* (Penguin Books, London, 1957).

Biographical

LITVINOFF, BARNET : *Ben-Gurion of Israel* (Praeger, New York, 1954).

MOSLEY, LEONARD : *Gideon Goes to War* (Scribners, New York, 1955).

NASSER, GAMAL ABD-EL : *The Philosophy of the Revolution* (Economica Books, Buffalo, New York, 1959).

ST. JOHN, R. : *Ben-Gurion* (Doubleday, New York, 1959).

SYKES, CHRISTOPHER : *Orde Wingate* (Collins, London, 1959).
WYNN, WILTON : *Nasser of Egypt* (Arlington Books, Cambridge, Mass., 1959).

Memoirs

EYTAN, WALTER : *The First Ten Years* (Simon and Schuster, New York, 1958).
GLUBB, J. B. : *A Soldier with the Arabs* (Hodder and Stoughton, London, 1957).
GLUBB, J. B. : *The Story of the Arab Legion* (Hodder and Stoughton, London, 1948).
GLUBB, J. B. : *War in the Desert* (Hodder and Stoughton, London, 1960).
HUTCHISON, E. H. : *Violent Truce* (Devin-Adair, New York, 1955).
KIRKBRIDE, ALEC : *A Crackle of Thorns* (*Political, Transjordania*) (John Murray, London, 1956).
LAWRENCE, T. E. : *The Seven Pillars of Wisdom* (Jonathan Cape, London, 1935).
MORTON, GEOFFREY J. : *Just the Job* (*Police, Palestine Mandate*) (Hodder and Stoughton, London, 1957).
YOUNG, PETER : *Bedouin Command* (William Kimber, London, 1956).

Index

DATE DUE

GAYLORD			PRINTED IN U.S.A.